CROSSING THE BARRIERS

CROSSING THE BARRIERS

The Autobiography of Allan H. Spear

Allan H. Spear

FOREWORD BY BARNEY FRANK
AFTERWORD BY JOHN MILTON

University of Minnesota Press
Minneapolis
London

The publication of this book was assisted by a bequest from Josiah H. Chase to honor his parents, Ellen Rankin Chase and Josiah Hook Chase, Minnesota territorial pioneers.

Published by the University of Minnesota Press
111 Third Avenue South, Suite 290
Minneapolis, MN 55401-2520
http://www.upress.umn.edu

Library of Congress Cataloging-in-Publication Data

Spear, Allan H.
    Crossing the barriers : the autobiography of Allan H. Spear / Allan H. Spear ; foreword by Barney Frank ; afterword by John Milton.
        p.   cm.
    Includes index.
    ISBN 978-0-8166-7040-6 (hc : acid-free paper)
    ISBN 978-0-8166-7041-3 (pbk : acid-free paper)
    1. Spear, Allan H. 2. Minnesota. Legislature. Senate—Biography.
3. Legislators—Minnesota—Biography. 4. Gay politicians—Minnesota—
Biography. 5. Civil rights workers—United States—Biography. 6. Gay
liberation movement—Minnesota. 7. Minnesota—Politics and
government—1951–   I. Title.
    F610.3.S64.A3   2010
    328.73'092—dc22
    [B]
                                                                                    2010025870

The family and friends of Allan Spear are grateful for their cherished memories of a remarkable person. His accomplishments had a profound impact on the struggle for peace and justice and on individuals from many walks of life.

CONTENTS

FOREWORD

Barney Frank

Allan Spear is one of the great unsung heroes of the LGBT movement in the United States. He is well known in Minnesota, where he served as president of the state Senate, an extraordinary accomplishment for an openly gay man that has only rarely been matched in the years since his tenure. But his very important role in the fight for LGBT rights is far less known throughout the nation than it should be. I believe there are two major reasons for this.

The first is Allan's personality. He was a man of enormous courage and a fierce passion for justice, who at the same time was a model of civility and decency in his personal relations. Nice doesn't always make news. Second, he made his enormous contribution through the political process, which I believe has been both the most important channel by which we have made gains in our fight against anti-LGBT prejudice and also the activity that gets far too little attention compared to more demonstrative, and often less effective, efforts.

For me, Allan was both a hero and a role model. I met him in the seventies, when I was a closeted member of the Massachusetts state legislature. In 1973 I became the first legislator in Massachusetts history to propose a package of gay rights legislation with my own full support (as opposed to simply filing them as a courtesy for a constituent), but I did not feel then that I could survive politically if I were honest about my sexual orientation. Shortly after joining the legislature and beginning my gay rights advocacy, I met Steve Endean, who was a pioneer in working hard to use the political process for the advancement of LGBT rights. Through Steve I met Allan, and his role as a state senator who was open about his sexual orientation was both an example and a goad to me.

What was important about Allan was not simply the fact that he was an openly gay state senator, but the way in which he carried out the enormous responsibilities of that position. The respect his colleagues and others in the political establishment had for him was an enormous asset for us, and his work was extremely important, not just for what he did in Minnesota and the example he set there, but also because of the weight he gave to the argument for using mainstream politics as a primary way to advance our fight for legal equality.

During the time Allan was emerging as a leader of the liberal wing of Democratic politics in Minnesota, and serving as a member of the state Senate, the LGBT community—to apply retroactively a label that we did not use at the time—was debating whether or not political activity was a trap and a device for diverting us from the kind of direct action that would achieve real gains. The case for direct action has always, in my judgment, been much stronger emotionally than intellectually. At first, we had virtually no political gains to which we could point, and that strengthened the argument that marches, demonstrations, and so on were the only way to achieve our rights. But people like Allan Spear understood—correctly, in my view—that availing ourselves of our rights as citizens and of the overpowering logical and emotional appeal of our cause, first to liberals and defenders of minority rights, and then to the broader community, offered us the best way forward.

This approach did not mean opposition to other forms of activity, and Allan was an important figure for all members of the LGBT movement who were aware of what was happening. I remember clearly when he became president of the Minnesota Senate how important that achievement was to all of us working within the political process: it is one of the major historical moments in LGBT history that is too infrequently commemorated.

Sadly, we lost Allan at far too young an age, but his contribution to our movement lives on. I was enormously proud to be selected to give the inaugural lecture named for him at the University of Minnesota, and his enshrinement at one of America's great universities speaks well of the university and is one more contribution Allan makes to our cause. Young LGBT people attending the university will be inspired and strengthened in their own ability to deal with the prejudice that unfortunately remains by knowing that an openly gay man of Allan's stature has been so memorialized for what he accomplished, not simply for who he was.

I close by returning to the personal: fortunately for me, I met Allan Spear early enough in my own political career for him to have had a positive impact on me. He was a role model, a teacher, and a very good friend. I hope the publication of *Crossing the Barriers* will advance the recognition Allan so deserves for his role as a gay hero and leader.

CROSSING THE BARRIERS

1

A DIFFICULT CHILD, 1937–1954

My mother adored me and I doted on her. Yet she told me once later in her life, "Allan, you know you were a very difficult child to raise." It wasn't that I was a troublemaker. To the contrary, I was a little mama's boy who had a hard time cutting the apron strings. I did well in school, was the teacher's pet, and did not have the physical prowess to get into fights with other children. What made me difficult was that I didn't fit the mold. I didn't like the things that small boys in midcentury America were supposed to like. When my mother sent me out to play, I sat instead on my little red wagon and read books. When I went to the Saturday afternoon movies, I refused to go to Westerns and wanted to see historical romances. When we went out to dinner (probably my favorite childhood activity), I wanted the duck à l'orange, not the macaroni and cheese. My mother just didn't know what to make of me. She told me years later that I had started talking at six months, but didn't walk until I was eighteen months old—the reverse of most babies. That pretty well summed it up: my verbal skills always outpaced my physical skills. Some would say that once I started talking, I never stopped.

It was even harder for my father. Unlike many Jewish men of his generation, my father was fully acculturated into the masculine values of mainstream America. He loved boats, guns, and fishing. He knew how to fix his own car and rarely needed an electrician or plumber to make household repairs. He assumed that his sons would be like him. My younger brother, Richard, did fairly well. He never took to shooting or fishing, but he became handy with tools and developed an interest in outdoor sports. But I was hopeless. When my father dragged me with him to the corner service station so that I could watch him and the auto mechanic work on the car, I took refuge inside the station, where I pored over the free road maps, fantasizing about the travel I would do someday. When he took me to the rifle range, I retreated to the clubhouse with my books. And when he asked me to come to his workshop in the basement to learn how to use a lathe, I told him that I wanted to stay in the kitchen to watch my mother cook.

Still, they were good parents. They had lived in Michigan City, Indiana, most of their lives, hadn't traveled much, and never went beyond high school. So their own worlds were limited. But they wanted the best for their children. It was always assumed that we would go to college. And there was an unspoken assumption that we would probably leave Michigan City. My father was a traveling salesman who worked on commission and never had a pension plan. But he faithfully saved money so that he could send his sons to college. The old cliché about Jewish parents insisting that their children become doctors was almost true in my parents' case. They realized early on that neither of us had interests likely to lead us into medical careers. But when we both received PhDs, they were thrilled. Even the insistence of a spoilsport aunt that we weren't "real doctors" couldn't quell their pride.

Later in life, when I became a legislator representing an inner-city district, my colleagues and associates generally assumed that I came from an urban background. I often ran into people in Minnesota who, knowing I was from somewhere else, assumed that I was from New York City. In fact, I grew up in an almost rural setting. Michigan City in the 1930s and 1940s had a population of about twenty-five thousand. Located fifty-five miles from Chicago, around the southern curve of Lake Michigan, it was just far enough away not to be a suburb. A few people commuted into the city, and Chicago was the place to go for culture and entertainment, serious shopping, and big-time sports, but most Michigan Citians worked in the local factories or stores and went to Chicago only on special occasions. Michigan City was basically a working-class town. The two largest ethnic groups were Polish Catholics and German Lutherans, but there was also a sizable population of Lebanese (we called them Syrians) and an African American community that was confined almost exclusively to the rundown "north end" of town. Michigan City did have one attraction that set it apart from most midwestern cities of its size—a magnificent beach that stretched for miles along Lake Michigan and was surrounded by the famous Indiana Dunes, now a national park. As children, my brother and I spent countless happy summer days on that beach.

We lived not on the beach but on the southern edge of town in an area that had not yet been fully developed. My parents bought a house there in 1942, when I was five years old, and I lived in that house until I left home as an adult. It was a comfortable house in an almost idyllic setting. It wasn't large or opulent, just six rooms—three bedrooms upstairs and one bath—but it was big enough and there was a lot of room for outdoor play. The street we lived on, Cleveland Avenue, was four blocks long, and during most of my childhood there were only five or six houses on the street. The rest was undeveloped land—much of it wooded. At the end of the street were the city limits; beyond, the farms began. We had rural mail delivery and had to walk to the end of the street to pick up our mail every day. The woods around the house were full of wild blackberries and dewberries, and it was not unusual in the summer for my brother and me to go out and pick enough berries for my mother to make a pie.

Although my father failed to turn me into a fisherman or a marksman, I loved the outdoors and constructed a rich fantasy life around the woods and fields. One vacant lot I called Dreamland and managed to visualize it as a magical kingdom over which I, of course, ruled. I dubbed a little incline on the street that led to the elementary school Lion Hill and imagined a few cracks in the concrete as the entrances to caves where lions dwelled. Usually my fantasies were solitary, but occasionally I would try to involve my brother and my playmates in my flights of imagination; I suspect that they found it all very strange. We did engage in more conventional play, too. Most of the neighbors were young families, like us, and despite the neighborhood's lack of development, there were enough children my age to keep me company. This was World War II and we often played war games, imagining that every plane that went over was a Japanese Zero that we were ready to shoot down. Later on, many of the neighbor kids went on to play baseball and we constructed a makeshift diamond on one of the vacant lots—but I usually watched or umpired; I was so inept as a player that no one wanted me on their team. It was a real disappointment to all of us in the years after the war when developers moved in and built houses in Dreamland and on the baseball field. Today, the neighborhood is totally built up.

My best friends in early childhood lived in the handful of houses scattered along Cleveland Avenue. Ann and Jean Frehse lived next door and we played together until the age when boys and girls started pursuing separate interests. Kenny Hoerr, who lived two doors away, was my closest friend. He was exactly my age, but he was tall and strong and good at sports and I always regarded him admiringly. I was pleased when he spent time with me and did not seem to be put off by my ineptitude. After the war, when houses were built on the vacant lots on the other side of Cleveland Avenue, more children came into the neighborhood. One, Richard Tomey, whom we called "Tubby," joined our group and became a close friend. "Tubby" was a round-faced, pleasant little boy who, like me, enjoyed sports more as a spectator than a participant. No one would have guessed that he would ultimately become a successful big-time college football coach.

Another group of children lived across the alley from us on the next street, Wrobel Avenue, but our relationship with them was mostly antagonistic. While the Cleveland Avenue kids came from upwardly mobile middle-class families, our Wrobel Avenue neighbors were decidedly working class. Jimmy and Davy Connelly's father ran a service station, and Tom and Freddy Krause's father cleaned furnaces. We regarded the Wrobel kids as out of control and threatening, and they probably saw us as stuck-up "goody-goodies." Jimmy misbehaved regularly in school and at home and when he was angry he threw stones at us, sometimes drawing blood. Freddy Krause beat me up and called me a dirty Jew. My mother clashed continually with Mrs. Connelly, who lived directly across the alley from us, and on one occasion she told her that her children were hoodlums. It was a slur for which Mrs. Connelly never forgave my mother.

My father was the first member of his family to own his own house. He had been born in Philadelphia but was brought to Michigan City in 1909 as a three-year-old. His parents were American-born Jews of German ancestry who saw themselves as distinct from, and clearly superior to, the immigrant Jews from Eastern Europe who came to the United States in large numbers in the late nineteenth and early twentieth centuries. Yet unlike the prominent German Jewish families described in Stephen Birmingham's *Our Crowd*, the Spears had never made any money. Grandpa Nate was a cigar salesman who tried, unsuccessfully, to establish a cigar store in downtown Michigan City. He and Grandma Jen lived in an old-fashioned rented house just off the main street of town. During the Depression they barely eked out a living, and when my father graduated from high school, it was out of the question for him to even consider college. He had dreams of going to medical school, but he had to go right to work to help support the family. To make matters worse, Grandpa Nate became seriously ill in his fifties, suffering from what the family called "premature senility." I assume that today he would be diagnosed with Alzheimer's disease. He died at the age of sixty-two, in the state mental hospital, when I was just six years old.

While I barely remember Grandpa Nate, Grandma Jen played an important role in my childhood. Despite her lack of money, she was a proud, sometimes haughty, woman. She had been one of the founders of the small Reform Jewish temple in Michigan City and saw herself as part of an elite group of old-timers whose manners and values were far more refined than those of the Eastern European Jews who arrived in town later. That latter group included my mother's family, the Liebers. My grandparents Lieber had been born in Eastern Europe, spoke Yiddish, kept kosher, and belonged to the tiny Orthodox shul that struggled for its existence throughout most of my childhood. Grandma Jen acted properly toward the Liebers in public, but privately she could barely conceal her contempt. On one occasion she even said to me, "You know, Allan, your other grandparents are nice people, but basically they are kikes."

Despite that, I loved Grandma Jen. I was her first grandchild and she continually fussed over me. After we moved out of her house, when I was three years old, she visited us often and I spent a lot of time at her house. When Grandpa Nate died, she moved to a small apartment and I was a frequent overnight guest. She thought I was brilliant and taught me how to read before I entered the first grade. She also made me a Democrat. During the Depression, everyone in my family had been Democrats, strong supporters of Franklin Roosevelt and the New Deal. But by the postwar years, my father had begun to make a little money and his loyalty began to waver. He voted for Dewey in 1948 and for Eisenhower twice. Grandma Jen would have none of it. One of the first books she bought me after she taught me to read was a children's book on the American presidents. We started at the end—Franklin Roosevelt. "Look at that strong, honest, handsome face," she said to me as we stared at FDR's picture. Then we flipped back a page. "That's Hoover," she said. "Doesn't he look like some kind of alley dog? He made us all poor." Even though I would later learn that the history of the 1930s was a bit more complicated than that, I never forgot that lesson.

Grandma Jen's attitude toward my mother's family led to some strained relationships. She never fully accepted my mother. My mother realized that and although she tried to be a good daughter-in-law, she could never warm up to her mother-in-law. In fact, according to a story that my mother later related to me, it was this difficult relationship that led to my birth. After they were married in 1935, my parents lived with Grandpa and Grandma Spear. It was very hard on my mother. My father was on the road every week. He would leave on Monday morning and return Friday afternoon. My mother was left in the house with a senile father-in-law and a hostile mother-in-law. One Friday night she told my father that she had had enough. She still loved him, but unless something changed she was going to leave him. He suggested that she go on the road with him the next week, get away from her in-laws for a few days, spend some time with him, and talk it out. They obviously did more than talk. One night that week, so the story goes, in a hotel in Davenport, Iowa, I was conceived. Nine months later, on June 24, 1937, I was born. My mother's difficulties with Grandma Jen didn't end. It was not until after my brother was born in 1940 that my parents moved out on their own. But my mother toughed it out and the marriage lasted until her death almost fifty years later.

By all odds, my parents' marriage should not have been as successful as it was. They were very different from one another. My father, Irving, was something of a loner and a maverick. He had no real friends outside the family and had little interest in socializing. He was quick to criticize other people and could often be rude and abrupt in his relationships. My mother's relatives were favorite targets of his abuse. He refused to accept the conventional wisdom on a variety of issues and was outspoken in his own views. This led to particularly strained relationships with other Jews when he became an ardent opponent of Zionism and the creation of the state of Israel. He was fiercely loyal to his wife and sons, but simply didn't seem to care what anyone else thought of him. He was not a joiner and, with the exception of the Elks, belonged to no men's clubs. He belonged to the Elks, he always said, only because when he was away on business in small towns, the Elks Club was often the best place to have dinner. His major interests were his hobbies—his guns, his cameras, especially his beloved boat, which occupied nearly every leisure hour between April and October. He never enjoyed nights out "with the boys." Even though his job took him on the road for days at a time, he spent his nights away from home eating alone and going to bed early. I suspect that, although he liked to talk about sex, he never had another woman after he married my mother.

My father tried at times to relate to me but was never very good at it. He was disappointed in my obvious lack of interest in the things that engaged him. He often told me that most boys would be grateful to have a father who gave them a gun and took them out on his boat. Why wasn't I? I clearly would have preferred trips to historical sites and natural wonders to day after day on the boat every summer. My father also tried to get me to be less bookish and to participate more in sports and outdoor activities with other boys. He tried to assure me that he was telling me these things for my own good. But his attempts to engage me in serious conversation were awkward and inconclusive. Several times during school vacations, my father invited me to go with him on the road. I loved traveling and welcomed the opportunity, even though our destination was only small towns in Indiana and Illinois. But in those long hours in the car together, conversation was stilted. While he called on customers during the day, I would ferret out the local library and sit and read books—which I am sure exasperated him. My fondest memories of time spent with Dad were when he took my brother and me into Chicago to see the Field Museum, the Shedd Aquarium, and, most of wonderful of all, the Museum of Science and Industry. And these days ended with a visit to Chinatown where I could eat my favorite food—egg roll and chicken subgum chow mein.

My mother, Esther, on the other hand, was a vivacious, outgoing woman with a loud, piercing voice and an easy laugh whom everyone loved. She liked to socialize and to be with people and had many friends. After I was born, she never worked outside the home, but she participated in a wide range of organizations—the PTA, the Temple Sisterhood, various charitable causes, and her weekly mah-jongg club, which was more about socializing than mah-jongg. Her views on issues were wholly conventional and did not go very deep, and she was embarrassed by my father's outspokenness. They had frequent and heated arguments—usually about something my father had said to other people, or how he had treated her family, or why he wouldn't go to some community or family event. Yet within a day or two, the unkind things they had said to each other were forgotten and all was forgiven—until the next time. Their love for and devotion to each other somehow overcame all of their differences. When I grew up and began to develop relationships of my own, it took me awhile to realize that all couples did not relate to each other by arguing and yelling. It had been a natural part of my childhood.

I was much closer to my mother than I was to my father. For one thing, she was always there. In the years following World War II my father was on the road almost every week from Monday to Friday and there were even occasions when he would go to St. Louis or Louisville and be gone for two or three weeks at a time. My mother, on the other hand, was home all day every day—getting us off to school in the morning, cooking lunch for us when we came home at midday, serving cookies and milk after school. She didn't drive until much later in life, when my brother, as a teenager, insisted that he would teach her. Without a car and with my father out of town so much, she was dependent on the bus or the generosity of friends to get around town. I remember her phoning in her grocery orders, which were then delivered to the door. Even when my father was gone, my mother had a full, home-cooked dinner every night. The routine of regular meals served at regular times is one that I still follow—and I continue to believe that families who have abandoned this tradition have given up something very important. But my relationship with my mother was not just a matter of her physical presence. She was more open and easier for me to confide in than my father. I was able to tell her things that troubled me, things I could not talk to anyone else about. I always knew I had her unconditional love.

My mother liked to say that her whole life was devoted to her husband and her sons. I think that was true, but I don't think it was the totally positive thing she thought it was. I don't know whether she ever felt frustrated about having no career or, in some ways, no real identity of her own. For me, it was wonderful as a child to have the security that her warmth and love provided. But as I grew up, it became difficult for her to turn loose and our relationship at times became smothering. Few people believe anymore in the notion that dominant mothers and distant fathers produce homosexual sons. Neither do I.

But I do not think that it is a total coincidence that so many gay men had close relationships with their mothers. I suspect that the causality runs the opposite way from what the Freudians think. Gay boys find it easier to relate to their mothers than to their fathers, and the mothers, in turn, perhaps unconsciously sensing a need and a vulnerability, become especially protective of them.

My brother, Richard, was born when I was less than three years old. Because we were so close in age, we were as children continually together. We shared a bedroom, played together, walked to school together, and sometimes fought with each other. Our personalities were very different. Richard was better coordinated and more athletic than I and made friends more readily. He was more interested in my father's pastimes than I was and generally related to him more easily. I can remember how, when we went out on the boat, it was my brother who handled the lines, while I sat in the cabin with my nose in my book. I also suspect, although he has never told me this, that he was less emotionally bound to my mother than I was and he was never as close to Grandma Jen. Although he did well in school, he was less bookish than I, which is ironic inasmuch as he grew up to become a distinguished scholar of Italian baroque art and the author of many books and articles. He also turned out to be heterosexual. Although our lives took us in different directions, we have remained close over the years.

My parents had no coherent philosophy of child rearing or discipline. Unlike later generations, they did not read books on child care. Since my father was physically absent so much of the time, the major burden fell on my mother. As my brother and I grew up we became harder for her to handle by herself, particularly when we fought with each other. Frustrated, she was often reduced to threats of "Just wait until your father comes home." This was an unfortunate tactic because it reinforced the image of my father as a distant and threatening figure, rather than a warm and loving one. But when Father came home, he was not usually much interested in hearing a long litany of how bad the boys had been in his absence and usually nothing happened. Occasionally my father did beat me. But it did not occur because of some incident reported to him by my mother. It occurred when I directly challenged his authority or said something to him that infuriated him. The beatings were never part of some disciplinary philosophy; they happened simply because he lost his temper. Yet if my parents did things that would be frowned upon today, they left no psychological scars on my brother or me. They succeeded in raising two productive, happy, and reasonably well-adjusted sons.

Other than my parents, my brother, and Grandma Jen, the most important people to me as a child were my father's younger brother, Lester, and his wife, Roz. Lester was the only adult male that my father was really close to, and my mother and Roz were best friends—like sisters, not sisters-in-law, they liked to say. As a result, the two brothers went fishing and boating together and the four of them frequently went out together for nights on the town or trips to Chicago. We spent a lot of time in each others' houses, and Lester and Roz were almost like a second set of parents to me. When their son, Norman, was born, when I was nine years old, I regarded him virtually as my baby brother and as he grew up, I became a mentor to him.

I was not as close to my mother's family. My grandmother Freda Lieber, whom I always called "Mom," was a sweet and loving woman, but she had many grandchildren (my father had only one brother; my mother came from a family of seven) and did not devote the time to me that Grandma Jen did. Moreover, she was an immigrant who, to my ears, talked funny, and she knew little about the things that interested me. Grandpa Jake was an irascible sort of man who was difficult to warm up to. He was always at odds with someone in the family, and when he died he was not even on speaking terms with two of his sons. Grandma and Grandpa Lieber had both been born in Galicia in eastern Poland and had met as teenagers en route to America. They had settled in Scranton, Pennsylvania, and moved to Michigan City to go into the fruit and vegetable business when my mother was thirteen. My fondest Jewish memories are of events at the Liebers' house. Grandpa Jake had done a little better financially than my Spear grandparents, and he and "Mom" owned a cozy little bungalow in a middle-class section of town. We went there for seder every year and for occasional Shabbat dinners. Unlike Grandma Jen, "Mom" cooked wonderful old-fashioned Jewish food, and it was always fun to get together with my many Lieber cousins.

I was particularly close to two cousins who were approximately my age. Frances, or Franny as we called her, was the daughter of my mother's brother Dave. When I was eleven, her family bought a house just a few blocks away from ours, so she became a frequent visitor. She and her younger brother often came to our house to play with Richard and me; I brought Franny into my fantasy world and introduced her to Dreamland and the other enchanted woods and hills of the neighborhood. We remained close through our high school years; then she married and moved to Southern California and I lost touch with her. When we reestablished contact, I discovered a poised, mature woman who had successfully balanced a career and a family. The other cousin had a less stable life. Lenny was the son of another of my mother's brothers, Max. His mother, Pauline, was a totally dysfunctional woman who was constantly whining about everything, and no one in the family could stand her. Pauline and Max were traumatized by the birth of a daughter with profound developmental disabilities, and it was years before they accepted the reality that nothing could be done for her. All of this made Lenny an insecure and neurotic child, but he was smart, funny, and in many ways endearing. When Lenny was eleven, after Max's business had failed, his family moved to California and I saw little of him for many years. When we met again, I found that Lenny had achieved a good deal in his life but had not totally shed the demons of his past. He had earned a master's degree in social work and been a cofounder of Parents Anonymous, a highly successful national organization that worked to prevent child abuse. He had married and divorced three times and still seemed haunted by the memories of his sister.

My memories of Jewish events at the Lieber home are warmer than my memories of the synagogue. There were about 150 Jewish families in Michigan City when I was growing up, and they formed a remarkably self-contained community. A few families had established successful manufacturing businesses—Jack Ruby and his brother-in-law, Jack Gole, produced men's pants at Hoosier Factories; the Winski brothers started a junkyard that ultimately morphed into the Northern Indiana Steel Supply Company; and Irving Salomon, my father's boss, owned the Royal Metal Company, which specialized in chrome-plated office furniture. These businesses provided employment for many of the town's Jews, while other Jewish families created employment opportunities for themselves in small retail shops. Thus the community was remarkably self-contained economically. It also formed a cohesive social unit. Jews rarely socialized with Gentiles and in fact were not admitted to the country clubs or yacht club during my childhood years. In response, they created their own world. I remember on several occasions, when my parents returned from a party I would ask them who was there. "Everybody in town" was the usual reply. What they really meant, of course, was "Every Jew in town." That didn't need to be said.

The center of Jewish life was Sinai Temple. Until I was in high school, Sinai Temple was not really much of a temple—physically. It was a tiny, somewhat rundown former church building on an unattractive block just off the main street. The Jewish community had purchased it many years before and did its best to fix it up and maintain it, but it didn't look like much. Until 1946, a rabbi came in once a week from Chicago; later Sinai Temple had its own resident rabbi. I went there every Sunday morning for Sunday school and often on Friday nights for services. And there were frequent social events in the cramped and dark basement "community room." I had mixed feelings about Sinai Temple. Even as a child, I could sense that the religious instruction was inadequate. The teachers were untrained congregation members who knew little more about Judaism and Jewish history than I did. I sensed too much social climbing within the community—too much catering to the families with money. This became even more pronounced in my later years in Michigan City, when the congregation built an elaborate new temple in an upscale neighborhood— financed largely by the Winskis and the Rubys. And while I enjoyed the companionship of some of the other Jewish children, I resented the notion that I had a common bond with them just because we were all Jewish.

The experiences of my generation of American Jews were strikingly different from that of my parents' generation. My parents' worldview had been deeply influenced by anti-Semitism. They both told me stories of Ku Klux Klan parades down the main street of Michigan City in the 1920s and how their fathers' businesses had been listed by the Klan as "Jewish stores" that good Christians should boycott. My father himself had been denied admittance to the Michigan City Yacht Club despite his avid interest in boating. It was little wonder that their generation had found comfort in a predominantly Jewish world.

But in the World War II and postwar years, overt anti-Semitism was fading. I experienced a little of it—a few playmates would in anger call me a "dirty Jew." But it was not central to my life. The insularity of Sinai Temple and the Michigan City Jewish community gnawed at me. Unlike my parents' friends, most of mine were not Jewish and I assumed that it would always be that way. After I left Michigan City, it would be thirty years until I again attended a synagogue.

Perhaps the deepest flaw in my Jewish upbringing was its failure to provide me with any positive reason for being Jewish. Despite the decline in open anti-Semitism, I always had the sense as a Jewish child in a mostly Christian world that I was missing something. This was particularly true at Christmastime, when my friends were totally involved in the wonders of a celebration that I viewed only from the outside. My parents didn't quite know how to handle it, and their compromises only made things worse. They were insistent that we could not have a Christmas tree, but they permitted me to sing Christmas carols in school—including a totally confusing one about Jesus being the king of Israel, something that I was sure wasn't true. They allowed us to hang up stockings on Christmas Eve but always made it clear that they would fill them, that Santa Claus was a hoax, information I shared too eagerly with my Christian friends much to the consternation of their parents. The Jewish holidays were no substitute for the glories of Christmas. Hanukkah was a pallid affair, halfheartedly celebrated. The High Holy Days held little interest for children. Only Passover had some appeal—and that was primarily because of the good food.

My Jewish upbringing was further complicated by the fact that my parents had very different attitudes toward Jewish life. My mother had grown up in a traditional Jewish household, and while she had rejected the trappings of Orthodox Judaism, she still thought it important that my brother and I attend Sunday school, go to temple, and, she hoped, someday marry Jewish women and raise Jewish families. My father couldn't have cared less and told us frequently that he thought Sunday school was a waste of time, that most rabbis were phonies, and that religion in general was a racket. His own sense of Jewish identity was deeply conflicted. On the one hand, his experiences with overt anti-Semitism made him sensitive to any slight that might be directed at him because he was Jewish. And yet he was himself contemptuous toward other Jews whom he thought acted "too Jewish." He referred to the Chicago Jews who summered at the beach in Michigan City as "yachnas"[1] and mocked their accents and lack of manners. He totally rejected Jewish culture, particularly if it was associated with Eastern European Jews. Yiddish, he insisted, was a jargon, even though he occasionally used Yiddish words himself. He hated most Jewish food and was so adamant on the subject of gefilte fish that he forbade my mother even to have it in the house. He insisted that it smelled so bad that if my mother made it, she would have to burn the house down. One Passover, when half the Sinai Temple congregation got food poisoning from improperly refrigerated gefilte fish at the community seder, he could barely conceal his glee.

Still, I believe that being Jewish deeply influenced the course of my life. Many years later, the historians August Meier and Elliott Rudwick interviewed me while doing research for their book, *Black History and the Historical Profession, 1915–1980*. A disproportionate number of white historians who came to specialize in African American history, they had found, were Jewish. Had my being Jewish, they wanted to know, helped determine my decision to write and teach in this field? I really didn't know how to answer that question. Certainly it was nothing conscious. Yet the more I thought about it, the more I saw connections. Although I rejected what I saw as the self-segregation of my parents' generation of Jews, I understood the outsider status that led to it. And I did not fully escape that status myself. I was spared the overt anti-Semitism of the 1920s that my parents had experienced. But I was always aware of being different from the other kids, of being embarrassed by the Christian prayers and New Testament readings that were integral parts of the school culture of my childhood years, of not sharing in the same religious celebrations. It was neither what Jews experienced in earlier times nor what my African American schoolmates were experiencing at that very time. But it did, I think, make me more sensitive to what it meant to be a minority in American society. And when, as an adult, I came to accept that I was gay, my

---

1. As a child, I never really knew what a "yachna" was, except that it was something bad. Leo Rosten in *The Joys of Yiddish* defines a "yachna" as "a coarse, shallow woman; a malicious, rumor mongering, troublemaking female." My father used the term without regard to gender.

Jewish identity made it easier for me to conceptualize homosexuality not as a mental condition but as membership in a minority group.

My formal education began at Jefferson School. Jefferson was not the proverbial one-room schoolhouse, but it was not a whole lot bigger than that. When I enrolled there in 1942, it had just over a hundred students and four teachers, one of whom doubled as the principal. There were three grades in each room: 1A, 1B, and 2A together, then 2B, 3A, and 3B, and so on. As in a one-room school, the teacher divided her time between each group and told the others to study while her attention was devoted elsewhere. All the teachers were women, and the teaching staff never changed during the six years I attended the school. The building itself dated from the early twentieth century and still had old-fashioned fixed seating with inkwells built into each desktop. The school was about a mile from our house and we walked to school whenever the weather was dry. Our parents saw no need to accompany us; we walked in groups and even at the age of six or seven never had any fear. When it was rainy or snowy, we took the city bus. No one ever thought about school buses in those days except for the farm kids who had to be bused in from outlying communities.

I think my elementary school education was the best I would have in Michigan City—much better than what I would receive in junior high and high school. The teachers were dedicated professionals and the classes were small enough to allow for individual attention. The students were all white and, except for my brother and me and one other Jewish boy, all Christian. There was, however, class diversity. Jefferson School drew from the entire southern edge of Michigan City, which was then only beginning to develop, and the neighborhoods it served included a few rich enclaves, tracts of poor houses along the railroad tracks, and, mostly, areas like ours where young couples were buying small houses and beginning families.

I loved school, was fond of my teachers, and did exceptionally well. Since I already knew how to read, I was well ahead of most of the other children and in the second grade was "skipped" ahead a semester. As a result, I graduated from high school at seventeen— not in retrospect an entirely good thing because as I grew up I was less mature socially than my classmates. My favorite memories of elementary school were the geography lessons. I was fascinated all my life by travel and maps, and I longed to visit the exotic places we studied. Fortunately, I was later able to fulfill many of those dreams. While I made friends at school, I was always something of a loner. I particularly disliked the roughneck games that the boys engaged in during recess on the school playground, and I either jumped rope or played hopscotch with the girls or kept to myself. When I was alone on the playground, I indulged in my fantasies again. I imagined the playground as an island republic that was discovered by the Portuguese, colonized by the British, and then emerged as a republic in a long process that just happened to resemble that of the United States of America. Soon, I had invented political parties, presidents, colleges and universities, and baseball leagues and had drawn elaborate maps of the Republic of Jefferson. This fantasy was so hard to explain that I did not share it with anyone.

I developed several lifelong passions in childhood. One was food. It would be an understatement to say that I was never a picky eater. I loved to eat and I ate almost everything—including foods that children are supposed to hate. Not surprisingly, I was a chubby child and have been overweight all my life. Both of my parents took food seriously and my mother was an excellent cook. She prepared everything from scratch and used only fresh ingredients; having a father in the grocery business helped, especially during the war, when many foods were rationed. Later on, when processed foods and cake mixes came on the market, my mother regarded them with contempt. She was a particularly good baker. Her cakes were the first to go at community bake sales and her caramel-pecan rolls ("schnecken," she called them) were to die for. Most of my mother's dishes were standard American fare— roasts, casseroles, grilled meats—but she did them well. And she never skimped on ingredients. We enjoyed luxury dishes such as beef tenderloins, lamb chops, and lobster tails on a regular basis. When someone asked her how she could afford to buy things like that, she said that if she had to cut her budget, the last thing she would cut would be food. Unlike her own mother, my mother made relatively few traditional Jewish dishes, in part, at least, because my father wouldn't eat them. In fact, her one venture into ethnic cuisine was spaghetti and meatballs, always made with imported pasta and real parmigiano cheese, which my father bought at the tiny local Italian grocery.

Eating out did not mean a quick trip to a fast-food outlet (of which there were very few in those days). My parents took my brother and me with them, even when we were very young, to the kinds of restaurants they liked. We ate in hotel dining rooms, country inns, and steak houses. I always ate "grown-up" food and would protest loudly if the waitress offered a child's menu or suggested something special for the children. My parents were always searching for restaurants with good food and would think nothing of driving forty or fifty miles to try a new place they had heard about. As at home, most of the food was traditional American. But there was one Chinese restaurant in Michigan City and that was probably my favorite place to go—except for those wonderful trips to Chicago's Chinatown. I remember in school one day, my third grade teacher asked the students to name their favorite food. After my classmates had run through the predictable list of hamburgers and hotdogs and macaroni and cheese, I piped in with "Chinese egg rolls." Once again, everyone, including the teacher, thought I was a strange child. But hamburgers were not completely off the menu, if they were made right. On weekdays, during school vacations, when my father was on the road, my mother would often take us on the bus to go shopping in downtown Michigan City. And we would eat lunch at a wonderful place called Harold's Diner. Harold's was the traditional "railroad car" diner, located in the heart of downtown on part of a lot that for some reason had remained otherwise vacant. The burgers were great and, to add to the appeal, Harold himself had only one arm. Watching a one-armed man form and cook those terrific hamburgers was perhaps my first lesson in what people with disabilities can achieve.

I also came early to my interest in politics. The first election I can remember was in 1944, when I was just seven years old. I had only a vague understanding of what was going on, but I learned one important lesson that year. I knew that we were for Roosevelt, that Democrats were good and Republicans were bad. I was shocked, therefore, when I realized that some of my friends' parents were going to vote for Tom Dewey. "Does that mean," I asked my parents, "that Kenny and Larry's parents are bad people?" My parents patiently explained to me that in America people could belong to different political parties and still like and respect each other. Four years later, I was more sophisticated. I knew then that people who were close to each other could disagree politically because my father supported Dewey while my mother was for Harry Truman. Predictably, I was for Truman, but my father convinced me that Dewey was sure to win. I was astounded when I woke up the morning after the election and my mother told me that Truman had been reelected. I had learned another valuable lesson: American politics is never predictable. Throughout the rest of my childhood, I followed politics closely and could never fully understand why my parents were not more deeply involved.

My reading habits also reflected my later interests. I had acquired my own library card at the age of five, to the delight and amusement of the local librarians, and spent many hours in the children's room of the public library. I read every geography book I could find and also worked my way through the library's collection of stereopticon cards, which depicted scenes from far-off places in wondrous three dimensions. I can specifically remember three books that I loved—all of them anticipating interests that would preoccupy me throughout my life. *Timmy Flies the China Clipper* told the story of a little boy who traveled on the first commercial air route from San Francisco to Hong Kong—five days on a Pan American seaplane, stopping every night at one of the Pacific islands. How I dreamed of an adventure like that! *Wiggins for President* was a volume in a series of books about barnyard animals that behaved like people. Wiggins, as I recall, was a cow that ran for president of the barnyard, and the book described how the animals organized themselves into political parties, held conventions, and conducted campaigns. It was sort of *Animal Farm* without the ideological message. When I was a little older, I read all of the books by John Tunis, who wrote mostly about sports, particularly Indiana high school basketball. My favorite was *A City for Lincoln,* which went beyond the usual sports book heroics to tell how a group of Indiana high school students accepted a black classmate and worked to integrate their city. This was one of my first encounters with the issue of race in American society.

My early school years were also the war years, and the war was never far from our consciousness. My father was rejected for military service for medical reasons; he had been diagnosed with osteomyelitis. His job, however, as an office furniture salesman was placed on hold for the duration of the war as Royal Metal converted to military production. He took work instead at nearby war plants, which meant that, for a few years, he was home every night instead of on the road.

Several of my neighborhood friends and schoolmates saw their fathers off to war. As I recall, however, all of them returned safely, so I never experienced closely the tragedy of war. But every week in school, we bought stamps that in time were converted into war bonds. We participated in air raid drills and blackouts. The blackouts were particularly exciting for us kids as we would sit in our darkened living rooms, the only light coming from the dial on our little Philco radios that kept us up to the minute on the war news. There were also drives to collect things that were supposed to be going to the war effort. My mother took leftover kitchen fat to the butcher shop, and we kids saved the tin foil from the back of gum wrappers to be used, we were told, to make airplanes. I learned later that those projects were designed more to give civilians a sense of participation than to bring in anything that was of actual use. And my father and a neighbor tried one year to plant a Victory Garden. That, too, was supposed to help in the war effort by freeing up commercially grown vegetables for the "boys" overseas. It was, however, a fiasco. The tomatoes were invaded by worms, the corn by weevils, and the potatoes by bugs; the only garden vegetables I remember eating were the radishes.

The first historical event I can clearly remember was D-day—June 6, 1944. I was at a friend's birthday party and the adults were talking excitedly, so I knew something important had happened. I asked my mother what it was and she told me we had invaded France and that meant the war would soon be over and we would win. I have even clearer memories of the events of 1945. I was outside playing on April 12 and my mother called me to come home. When I walked in the house, Grandma Jen was crying. My mother told me that President Roosevelt had died. He was the only president I had ever known and I asked who the president was now. Someone named Truman, I was told. A few weeks later, the news was better. Hitler died and the Germans surrendered. And in August, the war with Japan was over. We went downtown to celebrate V-J Day. The sidewalks were packed with people singing and cheering and throwing confetti into the air. It was only much later that I even learned about the atomic bombs.

In retrospect, one of the most surprising aspects of my childhood wartime experience was the absence of any discussion about the fate of the European Jews. In fact, I can recall more discussion about the atrocities being committed by the "Japs" than I can about the behavior of the Germans. I don't know whether my parents were just unaware of what was going on or whether they had decided not to talk about it in front of the children. In later years, however, I did learn that our family had not been wholly unscathed by the Holocaust. In 1939, my father's family had received a letter from Dr. Isidor Spier of Frankfurt, Germany, who identified himself as my father's second cousin. He had been told that if he did not leave Germany within two months, he and his wife and daughter would be put in a concentration camp. He needed help in obtaining a visa for immigration to the United States. My father's brother made some inquiries, but, short of accepting financial responsibility for the German relatives, he was told there was little to be done. My grandparents, my father, and my uncle were at that point barely able to support themselves and did not see how they could support three distant relatives, whom they never previously knew existed and who could speak little English. While they debated what to do, the time for action passed. Dr. Spier and his family were never heard from again. In 1990, when I visited Israel, I registered their names and left their pictures at the Holocaust memorial at Yad Vashem.

After the war, my father, like many Americans, began to prosper. He never became wealthy, but business was good and life became more comfortable. My mother was able to hire a cleaning lady to help with the housework. We took vacations to northern Ontario, where my father could fish and my brother and I could play at the beach. My father's eighteen-foot boat with an outboard motor gave way to a thirty-four-foot cabin cruiser and then to a forty-foot cabin cruiser. As the boats got larger, our summer vacations became cruises on Lake Michigan. We cruised each day, then slept on the boat in a different port each night. As kids, my brother and I got most of the playthings we wanted, but we were not totally indulged. I remember one instance, in particular, regarding our first television set.

It was early 1949; television was just coming in and I desperately wanted one. My father assured me that we would eventually get one, but he thought it was too early. They were not yet perfected, he said, and all we could watch was local programming from Chicago as the coaxial cable to New York had not yet been completed. But I didn't want to wait. Well, he told me, you've saved up money that your grandparents gave you as birthday presents; if you want one so badly, buy it yourself. I had a hundred dollars, not enough to buy a new television set. But I read the want ads and found a used seven-inch television set for sale for a hundred dollars. My father took me to look at it. It was an off-brand, but it worked and I bought it. My father had to put up a giant antenna on the roof of the house, but when he did, I was able to watch *Kukla, Fran and Ollie,* my favorite show from Chicago. A few months later, the cable came through and we could see Milton Berle and Arthur Godfrey. Soon, my father bought a new set and we enjoyed the luxury of a ten-inch screen. We were still the first in the family to have TV and every Friday night all my uncles came over to watch the boxing matches, then one of television's biggest attractions. And I proudly hosted my neighborhood friends, Kenny and Tubby, for the Chicago Cub games, which I eagerly watched all summer.

Our annual vacations on the boat led to one of my most traumatic childhood experiences. When I was seven years old, we had acquired a cocker spaniel puppy named Paleface, who quickly became a beloved member of the family. When we went away each summer, we boarded Paleface at the local kennel. But in 1951, the year I was fourteen, I argued that we should take Paleface with us on our boat trip to northern Wisconsin. The second night, we made port in Sheboygan and left the boat to go out for dinner. We left Paleface in the open aft deck, confident he wouldn't go anywhere. But when we returned he was gone; he had apparently thought we had abandoned him and had tried to find us. We stayed in Sheboygan for several days, unsuccessfully trying to find him. We then went on, but the vacation was ruined. Two weeks later we returned home without him, heartbroken. I believed it was my fault since it had been my idea to take Paleface with us. In a desperate final gesture, I wrote a letter to the Sheboygan newspaper asking anyone who had seen a stray cocker spaniel to please contact the veterinarian in Sheboygan whom we had enlisted as our representative. Amazingly, a week later, the veterinarian called. Paleface had been found—in the suburban town of Sheboygan Falls, along the river near a bridge, in a spot similar to where he had left us, barking at every boat that went by. We drove to Sheboygan for a wonderfully happy reunion. When we went to see the woman who had found Paleface, she refused to take a reward. "Just seeing the happy faces on you boys is all the reward I want," she said. Paleface lived another seven years; he died of heart disease while I was in college.

My father's success led him to become complacent about his job. As a traveling salesman, he was pretty much his own boss. He started spending less time on the road and more time waiting for the orders to roll in. During the postwar boom years, they did. But when the business became more competitive in the mid-1950s, his company began to demand harder work from its salesmen. Irving Salomon sold the company, new bosses took over, and my father lost his job. He never fully recovered from that setback. It was not only a big blow to his self-confidence, it also left him unemployed at the age of fifty-two and he never had a good job again. He began to spend money that had been saved for retirement, and when he did finally retire in the 1970s, there was a lot less to live on than he had anticipated.

As I grew up, I began to lose some of my self-confidence. In 1949, I left the comfortable confines of Jefferson School and entered Michigan City Junior High. Michigan City had just one public junior high school and one public high school, adjoining one another in a central location just south of downtown and about two miles from our house. By this time, klutz though I was, I had learned to ride a bicycle and I now rode my bike to school when the weather permitted and, on inclement days, continued to rely on the public bus system. Junior high was more challenging for me than elementary school—not academically but socially. I continued to do well in class and got good grades. But the social atmosphere was less comfortable. I was a year younger than most of my classmates, short for my age, overweight, poorly coordinated, and, from the time I was eleven years old, wore glasses. In the parlance of later times, I was a nerd—and a perfect target for bullies. I had experienced some bullying even in elementary school, but there the teachers and parents usually brought it quickly to an end. In junior high, the teachers were responsible for many more students and most of the parents didn't know each other. I often came home in tears because someone had beaten me up or said hurtful things to me or damaged my bike. My father urged me to fight back and tried to teach me how to defend myself, an experiment that was, needless to say, entirely unsuccessful. My mother would complain from time to time to the school authorities. I remember once, in seventh grade, a teacher who had spoken to my mother calling me in for a talk. She assumed that I thought I was being picked on because I was Jewish. I had actually never even thought of that and doubt that it had anything to do with it. I was just a very vulnerable little boy.

My problems at school made me withdraw more into myself. I had always had an active inner life, but at the same time I talked a blue streak to whoever would listen—even when my mother told me that "children were to be seen and not heard." And I became excited and enthusiastic about any new adventure. I continued to be that way at home and with people whom I fully trusted—family members, teachers, close friends. But I became more wary of people I didn't know. I was less sure of myself and more self-conscious about my behavior. And this became more apparent as I entered adolescence. Most gay adults are asked from time to time when they first realized that they were gay. This is a very hard question to answer, especially for people of my generation, who grew up at a time when we had only the vaguest awareness of what homosexuality even was. All I can say is that by the time I was twelve or thirteen, it began to dawn on me that I was different from most of my friends. They were beginning to talk about girls; I had no interest. When my parents asked me if I was interested in girls, I shrugged. "Oh, you will be," they assured me. "Boys develop at different ages." But I had already begun to masturbate and my fantasies were definitely not about girls; they were about the boys that I saw naked in the locker room at gym class. I did not tell my parents—or anyone else—about that.

I am not sure when I first become aware of homosexuality as a concept. I remember overhearing a few remarks made by my parents about other people when they thought I was out of earshot. There was, for example, Mattie M.,[2] an unmarried middle-aged woman who owned a greeting card and gift shop in downtown Michigan City. I heard my mother, in a telephone conversation, asking a friend if she thought what people were saying about Mattie was true. "That's a terrible thing to be saying about anyone," she said. When my mother got off the phone, I wanted to know what people were saying about Mattie. "Oh, that she's crazy," she replied. I knew that wasn't it, but I wasn't certain what it was. Later, I heard my parents talking about Roy J., a well-known man-about-town. "When I worked downtown at the men's clothing store,"

2. I have not used the last names of several individuals mentioned in this chapter. All the other names are real.

my father told my mother, "Roy would come in and always pick out the best-looking salesman to measure his inseam." That time I did not ask for further explanation; I could kind of figure it out.

By the time I was an adolescent, in the early 1950s, newspapers and magazines first began to discuss homosexuality—almost always negatively. Senator Joseph McCarthy investigated not only Communists in government but also homosexuals—who were often one and the same. *Confidential* magazine, which I never actually read but certainly heard about, ran stories about homosexuals in Hollywood and in Washington. I did not think of myself as one of them, despite my masturbation fantasies; such an idea was too horrifying to even contemplate. But I was certainly fascinated by the topic. Little bookworm that I was, I did the natural thing. I went to the library and looked it up. I can remember that as I approached the card catalog and opened it to the Hs, I looked over my shoulder to make sure no one was looking. Michigan City's little library had open stacks so, thankfully, I didn't have to ask anyone to get books for me. What I found was not reassuring. First of all, there wasn't much on the shelves. And what the library did have was mostly in the category of "abnormal psychology." There were various sexual perversions, I learned, fetishism, bestiality, and so forth, and among them was homosexuality. It was a devastating psychological illness, dangerous to society, and very difficult to cure. Fortunately, it was rare. Certainly I couldn't have that, I told myself.

There was one exception to this negative literature. Alfred Kinsey's *Sexual Behavior in the Human Male* had been published in 1948. I am not sure when I first discovered the book—probably a few years after that, when I was fifteen or sixteen. Contrary to what I read elsewhere, homosexuality, Kinsey said, was not rare at all. One-third of American males had homosexual experiences at some time in their life and 10 percent were predominantly homosexual. Moreover, Kinsey made no value judgments and saw nothing horrifying about this. Reading Kinsey did not make me come out. But it was certainly a welcome change from the conventional literature of the day. Kinsey has come under fierce attack in recent years for his methodology. But for gay people of my generation, he will always be a hero.

As most of my friends began dating and going to dances and entering into the teenage social life of the 1950s, none of which had any appeal to me, I found a new best friend who shared my outsider status.

Jonathan Feinn was a Jewish boy my age who had recently moved with his family to a small beach community in the dunes, just a few miles west of Michigan City. Jonathan began attending the synagogue and was in many of my classes in junior high—and later in high school. We began hanging out together and found that we had much in common. Like me, Jonathan was overweight, physically awkward, and shy with girls. He, too, had been a frequent target of bullies. He was particularly vulnerable to teasing because his voice was late in changing, and well into his teenage years he spoke with a high-pitched, girlish voice. Together, we established a bulwark against the often-hostile world outside.

Jonathan and I were almost constant companions from the time we met in the ninth grade until we graduated from high school. Since he came to school by bus and couldn't go home for lunch, he often came home with me for one of my mother's hot lunches and my mother came to love him almost as a third son. On weekends, particularly after I learned to drive, I went out to his house and often stayed overnight. Our interests were not exactly the same—Jonathan was not as keen on politics as I was—but we found plenty to talk about. And I brought him into my always rich imaginative life. When we were fifteen, we invented a religion. Our goddess was a black woman named Doodah who had worked as a cleaning woman for Jon's mother when they lived in Chicago. I wrote a holy book for the religion and we came up with an elaborate set of doctrines and teachings. We shared all of this with a few people, but almost everyone else who heard of it simply thought both of us were weird.

Chief among those were our parents. Both my parents and his thought that we spent too much time together and needed other friends. My father in particular was wary of Jonathan because of his voice and asked me once if he were homosexual. I told him no. The truth was that I was no more sure about his sexuality than I was about my own. In fact, Jonathan was gay but we didn't confide in each other until after we had gone away to college and become more certain ourselves about our sexual identities. We never had sex with each other. What gave us a strong common bond was our alienation from the teenage world around us. We didn't date, we didn't go to dances and sock hops, we didn't talk about girls. We were comfortable just being with each other.

The teachers in junior high and high school were a more mixed lot than the dedicated schoolmarms I had had in elementary school. Some were just timeservers whose lack of interest in their work was obvious. I remember one English teacher whose class met in the late morning; five minutes before the bell rang, she had her coat on and was waiting at the door for the bell to ring so she wouldn't miss a minute of her lunch break. A few of the teachers had been hired as coaches and their teaching responsibilities were clearly secondary. Others were simply not prepared. My Spanish teacher could barely speak Spanish. She had taken some courses years before in college, but never kept up with the language; when the school began to get a few native Spanish-speaking students, she had no idea what they were saying. Some of the older teachers had perhaps been competent when they were younger, but they had been there too long and could no longer relate to young people. A few had taught my father—thirty years before—and, to my consternation, called me "Irving."

But I had a few teachers who stand out in my memory. The best were a couple of young teachers, just a few years out of college, who had lasting influence on me. Joanne Morgan taught journalism and public speaking and coached the junior class play. These were all activities I took to eagerly. I loved to write and to talk and Mrs. Morgan honed my skills in both. Public speaking was probably the most useful class I took in high school—other than, perhaps, typing. Curiously, while often unsure of myself when I met a new person one-on-one, I have never been shy in getting up before a roomful of strangers to give a speech. Mrs. Morgan deserves some of the credit for that. Ned Cooling taught government and history and was the faculty sponsor of the Forum Club, which met during the lunch hour once a week and staged informal intramural debates on the topics of the day. Michigan City High School had no debate team, so the Forum Club was our only opportunity to learn debating skills and to keep up with current issues. We discussed everything from capital punishment to McCarthyism to the Rosenberg case to animal rights. Mr. Cooling tried to stay neutral in class and during Forum Club meetings, but I met with him often after school and he freely shared with me his reasons for being a Democrat and a liberal. Grandma Jen had made me an instinctive Democrat, but Mr. Cooling taught me the reasons for being one.

One other teacher deserves special mention. Mr. I. was an English teacher of the old school. He had been teaching for many years and came to class every day wearing a three-piece suit and a watch chain with a Phi Beta Kappa key. He had never married and had lived with his mother until she had died just a few years before. He taught English literature and English grammar, and his grammar class was probably the most feared and hated in the school. He was stickler for precision and his teaching method was as dry as dust—parsing sentences, learning the parts of speech, and so on. But Mr. I. had one curious pastime. He liked to go down to the locker room after football and basketball games and measure the boys for muscular development. He then kept meticulous charts for every boy and told each one how well he was developing. I am not sure why the coaches allowed this. Mr. I. had no legitimate reason to be doing this, and the boys he measured regarded him with a kind of knowing bemusement. He obviously knew how far he could go; there were never any accusations of molestation. But in a vague sense everyone seemed to know what was going on. In my mind, Mr. I. stands as the perfect embodiment of the repressed sexuality of the 1950s, a lonely, celibate closet homosexual whose only opportunity to get his jollies was by measuring the biceps of teenage boys.

Throughout junior high and high school, I found activities to keep me busy after school. I learned to play the clarinet and was a member of the band. I was not particularly fond of marching in parades or playing at the football and basketball games, but I did like preparing for the concerts that we gave once or twice a year, which always included a few pieces of serious classical music. I never became very proficient on the clarinet and when I got to college, I gave it up. But it was a worthwhile experience. I learned to appreciate music and have been an avid concertgoer and record collector all my life. I still particularly love some of the pieces that I was first introduced to in the high school band: the overture of Weber's *Oberon,* Liszt's *Les Préludes,* and the last movement of Tchaikovsky's Fourth Symphony.

Far less successful was my experience with the Boy Scouts. As a young child, I had loved the Cub Scouts. It was a neighborhood affair, my mother was a den mother, and the other members of the den were my friends. But the Boy Scouts were run by men I didn't know and its activities did not appeal to me. I remember the first camping trip we went on. I hated it. I couldn't fall asleep in a sleeping bag, I was bitten by mosquitoes, and the food was awful. My parents urged me to keep trying as they thought the Scouts would be good for me. But they eventually turned against it, too. The troop was sponsored by the First Christian Church. When the church enlisted us to pass out flyers advertising a visiting Christian evangelist, my parents agreed that it was time for me to quit.

I had moved beyond Sinai Temple's weekly Sunday school, but for a few years, while I was in junior high, I went to the temple after school once or twice a week for Hebrew lessons in preparation for bar mitzvah—the traditional coming-of-age ceremony for boys at the age of thirteen. Reform Judaism at this time was in transition. In its early years it had discarded many Jewish traditions that it no longer considered relevant to the modern world. Bar mitzvah had been replaced by confirmation, a ceremony for groups of both boys and girls at the age of fifteen that was a kind of Jewish version of high school commencement. Reformers argued that fifteen was a more logical coming of age than thirteen, that the ceremony should be open to both genders, and that a group ceremony created a greater spirit of community. But in the wake of the Holocaust and the creation of Israel, Reform Judaism had begun to revive some of the old traditions and bar mitzvah was coming back, not in place of confirmation, but in addition to it. My mother, who had grown up as an Orthodox Jew, was eager for me to have a bar mitzvah, but my father, who had always been Reform and who opposed the trend toward traditionalism, was firmly set against it. He and the Reform Jewish men of his generation had not gone through bar mitzvah, and he saw nothing positive in it for me. The age of thirteen, he argued, was not a meaningful transition in modern American life and he could see no sense in it other than as an occasion to get gifts.

I wanted to have a bar mitzvah for two reasons—and getting gifts was not one of them. First, I relished the opportunity to give a speech and be the center of attention for a day. And, second, I had developed a good relationship with the rabbi and liked working with him. Rabbi B. T. Rubinstein was by far the best of the rabbis who served Sinai Temple in my time there. He was then a young man, recently out of rabbinical school, enthusiastic, socially conscious, and thoughtful. His sermons touched on the major social and political issues of the day, and he was not afraid to take stands that might be unpopular in the

congregation. He urged me to study for bar mitzvah and I was prepared to do it. But my father continued to object and my mother finally told me not to fight him about it. So I never had the bar mitzvah.
It was probably just as well, as Grandma Lieber died during the week
I turned thirteen and my mother was devastated. It would have been a
sad occasion. Shortly afterward, Rabbi Rubinstein left Michigan City
for a new pulpit. He was replaced by an older man, a refugee from
Nazi Germany whose wit and homespun wisdom made him a beloved
figure in the community for many years to come. But he lacked Rabbi
Rubinstein's social consciousness and intellectual depth, and I never
really warmed up to him. I was confirmed at the age of fifteen, but I
was just one of seven and my favorite rabbi was gone. Without the
stage to myself, confirmation was not a big event in my life. By the
time I graduated from high school, I had lost interest in the temple.

The final extracurricular activity to occupy my time during my
junior high and high school days was, strangely enough, sports. Certainly not as a participant! I was hopeless at them and gym class was
a nightmare. I remember one day when we were all timed doing the
fifty-yard dash. My time was slower than most of my classmates' time
for the hundred-yard dash! But sports were an important part of life
in Michigan City and I could not avoid them altogether. Indiana high
school basketball is legendary and from the time I was in seventh
grade, I never missed a home game. During the state tournament, I followed the Michigan City Red Devils as far as they went, which during
my high school days never went beyond the regional round in Ham-
mond. I also became an avid baseball fan at an early age, and by the
time I was nine was an avid Chicago Cubs fan. I spent many summer
days listening to Cub games on the radio and, later, watching them on
television. Occasionally, my parents would take me to Wrigley Field to
see a game in person. The most contentious issue between me and my
uncle Lester was baseball. He was the unthinkable: a White Sox fan.

In high school, I contributed to the sports culture in a more formal
way by covering the games for the school newspaper and editing the
sports section of the yearbook. And I became the student manager of
the baseball team. "Student manager" was really a fancy name for
a batboy and all-around flunky. But there were certain parts of it I
liked. I loved keeping scores of games; that centered on what I liked
best about baseball: its intricate system of statistics and its meticulous

record keeping. Taking care of the equipment and shagging fly balls was not as much fun. The coach had clearly chosen me for the job because he thought it would make me a more "regular guy." He urged me to talk more with the boys and become part of the group. But I had little in common with most of the boys on the baseball team. What I liked most about them was watching them undress in the locker room.

By this time, my parents were becoming increasingly concerned about my unwillingness to date girls. When I was thirteen or fourteen, they could attribute it to "late development." But when I was sixteen and seventeen, they began to worry. Even my little brother had started to date. I just wanted to spend weekends with Jonathan. Dating in the 1950s was highly ritualized—much more formal than the casual "hooking up" that teenagers engage in today. If a boy wanted a date for the weekend, he was expected to call the girl by Wednesday at the latest to ask her out. On the night of the date, he called at her home, spent a few minutes chatting with her parents, then went off to a movie or a dance or, perhaps in the summer in Michigan City, the small amusement park adjacent to the beach. At the end of the evening, there would be a soft drink at the Sugar Bowl or an ice cream sundae at Scholl's dairy and then home. A successful evening would be rewarded with a good-night kiss. By the third or fourth date, the girl might be willing to go "parking," usually at Fedder's Alley, a short road parallel to the beach named after Michigan City's most notoriously corrupt mayor, which was dark enough to permit necking and petting. There was nothing in this entire routine that appealed to me at all.

Nevertheless, by the time I was sixteen, my mother would pester me every week about getting a date. She would even suggest nice girls whom I could call and who, she was sure, would love to go out with me. While my mother assumed that I would eventually marry a Jewish girl, she didn't expect me to date Jewish girls. The Jewish community in Michigan City was just too small for that. Any girl was fine—better in her mind than another weekend with Jonathan. Occasionally, I succumbed. I dated a few times, usually double-dating with Jonathan, whose parents were similarly pressuring him, and did what was expected of me—except for the necking and petting. That was just too gross. Until my last months in high school, I rarely dated the same girl twice.

Senior year presented a special challenge. There was a series of big events for which having a date was absolutely necessary—the senior class dinner; the Demolay formal, sponsored by a local Masonic group; the senior prom; the commencement parties; and so on. Finally, I found a girl whom I liked who was willing to go with me to these galas. Margaret Larson had been, prior to that year, the steady girlfriend of my neighborhood buddy, Kenny Hoerr. After our junior year in high school, Kenny's father took a new job in another town and Kenny moved away. That left Margaret without a boyfriend. I had known Margaret through Kenny and liked her, so I started asking her out. She was not an especially pretty girl, but she was smart and lively and when I failed to make any moves toward her, she initiated the kissing and some light necking. We never went beyond that, but I was more comfortable with her than any other girl I knew in high school and we went to the various senior class activities together. My parents were glad I was dating someone, although they weren't quite sure what I saw in Margaret. She came from a Lutheran family and her mother was not pleased that she was going out with a Jewish boy. After graduation, we stopped seeing each other and I completely lost track of her.

A bigger decision than whom to take to the senior prom was where to go to college. College admission in 1954 was not the highly competitive business it is today. Far fewer young people went to college— in my high school it was only about 30 percent—and I probably could have gotten into almost any place I wanted to go. There was no SAT then, and admission was based mostly on grades and perhaps an informal interview. I graduated second in a class of 235—a position that was sometimes called salutatorian, although we did not use that term at that time in Michigan City. I was chosen for the National Honor Society and had a long string of extracurricular activities. But it never even occurred to me to apply to one of the elite eastern schools. No one from Michigan City ever went there, no teacher ever suggested them to me, and those schools were far beyond my parents' world. Most Michigan City high school graduates went to Indiana University, Purdue, Valparaiso University, or, if they were Catholic, Notre Dame. Some of the better students went to Michigan or Wisconsin or one of the schools in the Chicago area—Northwestern or the University of Chicago. I narrowed my choice down to Northwestern and the University of Chicago.

The University of Chicago would have been the better fit. It was the more intellectually oriented of the two schools and had a reputation for welcoming offbeat and somewhat eccentric students and faculty. I was admitted and offered a scholarship. But my parents were dead set against my going there. They believed Chicago would nurture all of the traits in me that worried them—my bookishness, my weird imagination, my resistance to being a "regular guy." Northwestern, they believed, was a more normal place and would make me a more normal person. Since Northwestern was a good school, too, and since it also offered me financial aid, I didn't fight my parents on this one and agreed to go to Northwestern. Ironically, three years later, when my brother graduated from high school, he went to the University of Chicago without any resistance from our parents. They apparently thought he was such a "regular guy" that Chicago couldn't spoil him. In fact, it did. It turned him, not into a weirdo, but into a more disciplined intellectual and scholar than I would ever become.

I was just seventeen years old when I graduated from high school, but I was ready to leave Michigan City. My intellectual interests were already growing beyond what Michigan City could offer. I was uncomfortable with most of the people my age. I had made halfhearted efforts to adjust to the small town high school culture, but I was never really part of it. And I was beginning to chafe under my mother's constant pressure to behave like a more normal teenager. As I look at my high school yearbook, with its handwritten notes from my classmates, I find a lot of polite but not particularly heartfelt wishes for good luck in the years ahead. I was respected by many of my classmates for my "brains," as they would have put it, but most of them did not feel especially close to me. The bullying had stopped as we all matured, but there was no doubt that I was still regarded as a nerd. Among all of those messages, two stand out: a full-page, very sweet note from Margaret Larson and a six-page note from Jonathan recounting many of the things we had done together over the past several years. The major theme of Jonathan's message was that both of us were crazy— and it was fun to be crazy together. That pretty well summed it up. Our friendship, our mutual willingness to reject the norms, to be crazy if you will, had kept us both sane. I left Michigan City a little battered psychologically, but still fairly self-confident about my ability to succeed in a larger world.

2

BRIGHT COLLEGE YEARS, 1954–1958

Northwestern University is situated on one of the loveliest college campuses in the United States. It stretches for more than a mile along Lake Michigan, with the lake as its front yard and the elegant suburb of Evanston behind it. Northwestern occupies a unique position as the only private university in the Big Ten. It has many of the features of large midwestern state universities—big-time college football, an active fraternity-sorority system, and a reputation for good times and parties. But it also has a selective student body, a strong faculty, and highly regarded professional and graduate programs. It was a perfectly good place for me to have received my higher education, and had I stayed there for four years I think I would have left well educated. But my first year at Northwestern was in many ways a stormy one—a time when I was first beginning to think of myself as an adult, developing an identity of my own, and breaking away from my parents. It was all of those things—rather than any real defects in Northwestern—that led me to leave after just one year.

The most important aspect of my freshman year in college was that I was away from home. Evanston was just seventy miles from Michigan City and I could have easily gone home on weekends, but I did so only rarely. I went home for holidays, I talked to my parents frequently on the phone, and they sometimes came in to see me. But I relished being on my own. I lived in a dormitory on campus and within a short period of time had found a group of friends who shared many of my interests and enthusiasms. Among them, two were particularly important in my development. Joel Samaha came from a small town in Ohio; his father was Lebanese and his mother old-stock American, and he had even thornier problems in relating to his parents than I did. We talked a lot about our families, how we wanted to create lives for ourselves different from the way we had been brought up, and how, in general, we viewed the world. Leon Waldoff was a Jewish boy from Mississippi, two years older than I and far more sophisticated. He had already dealt with the "parent issue" and encouraged me to be less dependent on my parents and to develop my own value system.

The three of us, sometimes joined by other friends, had endless "bull sessions" about family, philosophy, religion, life, and death—all the topics that engage bright young people in their early stages of intellectual development.

My courses were less important than what I learned from my friends. First-year students at Northwestern took mostly large lecture courses taught by senior faculty with a small discussion section once a week conducted by a junior faculty member or teaching assistant. My only memorable course was a wide-ranging introduction to world literature taught by an array of professors from different departments who led us through literary works that started with Plato and the Bible and went on to *Huckleberry Finn* and *The Brothers Karamazov.* That course, together with strong encouragement from my friend Leon, who had become something of a mentor to me, led me to discover serious literature. I had always been an enthusiastic reader, but what I had read before had not been very well focused. Now I started reading all of the classics—not just those assigned for class. My favorites, unsurprisingly, were the bildungsromans, the novels of development that told of sensitive young men searching for their purpose in life.

I was particularly fond of D. H. Lawrence's *Sons and Lovers,* W. Somerset Maugham's *Of Human Bondage,* and Samuel Butler's *The Way of All Flesh.* I identified with the heroes of those novels and, in the spirit of adolescent angst, saw myself as a kind of tragic figure, misunderstood by my family but determined to fulfill my destiny in life. I remember something one of the professors in the world literature course said to the class when he assigned a play by Molière: "Most of you probably won't like this; you are too young for comedy. At eighteen, tragedy is far more appealing than comedy." That was certainly true of me. I was a less avid reader of poetry, but I discovered one poet who I thought spoke directly to me. A. E. Housman was out of fashion in literary circles and I doubt if I ever would have read him in an English poetry class, but someone, probably Leon, led me to him. I not only read all of his poems—which were relatively few—I also memorized many of them. Again, particularly in *A Shropshire Lad* I could read of misunderstood, sensitive youth and of hopeless, unrequited love. Only many years later did I learn that Housman was a closeted homosexual. But I think I always sensed it.

In addition to literature, my other big discovery during my first year in college was classical music. I had experienced a few classical works in high school band and liked them, and toward the end of my senior year in high school I bought, in the still relatively new LP format, the Beethoven symphonies conducted by Toscanini. I took a small record player with me to college for my dorm room and gradually started buying LPs of some of the other basic classical works. But what really whetted my enthusiasm was my access to live performances by the Chicago Symphony Orchestra. The CSO was in the 1950s in one of the most glorious periods of its long and distinguished history. Its conductor was Fritz Reiner and the orchestra attracted top-flight soloists. On Friday afternoons, I could take the El to the Loop, buy a ticket for a gallery seat for two dollars, walk up five flights of stairs, and hear the performance. I went almost every week and, in addition to Reiner's wonderful orchestra, I heard some of the best pianists, violinists, and singers in the world—many of them in the twilight of their careers. Among them were Walter Gieseking, Wilhelm Backhaus, Robert Casadesus, Zino Francescatti, Nathan Milstein, and such guest conductors as Bruno Walter and Hans Rosbaud. It was an exhilarating experience.

Young people related to music differently in that prerock era than they do today. There was no special popular music aimed at youth and the standard Tin Pan Alley music was trite and simplistic. No one with any musical sophistication had much interest in "How Much Is That Doggie in the Window?" or "Shrimp Boats Is A-Comin'." Bright young people with an interest in music generally went in one of two directions: to jazz or to classical music. I never developed much affinity for jazz, although I always respected it. My true love was classical and my circle of budding young intellectuals at Northwestern sat around our little low-fi record players and listened to it and then spent hours discussing the relative merits of Beethoven and Mozart, whether the nineteenth-century romantics were too sentimental, and what Bartók was really trying to say. Later on, as the rock culture emerged, I tried to give popular music another chance. But it never took. I liked the Beatles, but even they did not seem to me to be a match for Mozart.

Beyond the symphony, there was much else in Chicago to engage me. I had been to some of the museums as a child and now had the opportunity to revisit them whenever I wanted. I went for the first time to the Art Institute, which had not been on my father's itinerary of

Chicago museums. I enjoyed its great collection of impressionist and postimpressionist works, particularly Seurat's *A Sunday Afternoon on the Island of La Grande Jatte*. But I never developed the passion for the visual arts that I did for literature and music. My very favorite exhibit at the Art Institute was a relatively lowbrow attraction—the wonderful Thorn Miniature Rooms, which, in a series of tiny, intricately detailed dollhouse-like rooms, display the development of the decorative arts over the past four centuries.

It soon became clear to my parents that Northwestern was not shaping me in the way they had hoped. Without their constant pressure, I never dated. Instead of hearing about Jonathan all the time, they heard about Joel and Leon. "Why no girls?" they asked me when we spoke on the phone. "Why are you spending so much time in 'bull sessions' with other guys? Why don't you start socializing more?" The solution, they soon decided, was that I should join a fraternity. I had absolutely no interest, but to appease them I signed up for freshman rush. Fraternities at Northwestern at that time were segregated by race and religion. There were two Jewish fraternities, and if I were to pledge, I was expected to pledge one of them. So I visited their houses. That was enough. Living and spending my time in a Jewish fraternity where the major interest seemed to be finding a nice Jewish girl to marry was the last thing I wanted to do.

My growing differences with my parents led to a series of long arguments that year—sometimes on the phone, sometimes during visits home. They often ended with yelling and tears. It began on Thanksgiving weekend, my first extended visit home after leaving for college. I had asked my parents if I could bring Leon with me; he lived too far away to go home for the weekend. They readily agreed, but when they met him, they instantly disliked him. Admittedly, he did not behave very well. He was outspoken, critical of many things that were dear to my parents' hearts, and open in telling them that their son was no longer a child and shouldn't be treated like one. They decided that he was a bad influence on me. Later in the year, Joel came to visit, too. They liked him better but still couldn't understand why I bonded only with other young men.

My attitude toward my parents did not help matters. My new interests in literature and music and philosophy convinced me that I had become much smarter than they were and I did not hesitate to let them know that. How could they dare tell me what to do when they had never even listened to Beethoven's Ninth or read a novel by Dostoyevsky? When I went home to visit I made clear to everyone who would listen that I no longer accepted or valued the world in which I had been raised. Over the winter holiday break, Sinai Temple held a special homecoming Sabbath service that featured short talks by all of the young people in the congregation who had gone away to college. I let the congregants know without hesitation that I no longer believed in God and didn't have much respect for anyone who did. My mother was deeply embarrassed. I further exasperated her by telling her that her relatives were all stupid and I didn't really care to visit them. That was a view my father shared, but my mother didn't need to hear it from me, too. And I didn't spare my father's family. I got into a long argument with Uncle Lester—the first I had ever had on a subject other than baseball—when he suggested that musical preferences were just a matter of taste. I angrily rejected that notion: how could preferring Perry Como to Beethoven be anything other than a deep moral and intellectual failing? Everyone soon came to the conclusion that I had become insufferable. Even Grandma Jen, in whose eyes I usually could do no wrong, warned me that I was becoming an intellectual snob.

My conflict with my parents came to a head in the spring when I announced that I wanted to leave Northwestern. As I look back on that decision from a perspective of fifty years, it is hard for me to make sense of it. I had thrived at Northwestern. My grades were good, I had developed a circle of close friends, I enjoyed the attractions of Chicago, and I had certainly matured intellectually. I think three things entered into the decision. First, while I had found much that appealed to me at Northwestern, I had come to resent those aspects of the university that had initially made it attractive to my parents. My friends and I spent hours railing about the idiocy of fraternities and of big-time football and of the superficial values of many of our classmates. Second, I was disappointed in my big lecture classes and the lack of opportunity to get to know my professors. When I raised this issue with my faculty adviser, he pointed out that after my first year I would find myself in smaller classes and that I should suspend judgment for a while. But I wasn't willing to wait. Third, I had become aware of an entire category of colleges of which I had known nothing the previous year when I was applying for admission. No one in Michigan City had suggested that I look into the small liberal arts colleges—places like Oberlin, Carleton, Swarthmore, Reed, and Antioch. Now I was coming to believe that a college like that would be a perfect fit for me—small classes, no fraternities, no big-time athletics, a student body that seriously pursued intellectual interests. During spring break, I went with Joel to his home in Ohio and visited the campus at Oberlin, which was just a few miles away. I decided at once that Oberlin was where I belonged.

I applied to the college as a transfer student and was immediately admitted. I started telling everyone I was going. Leon and Joel encouraged it. They told me they would miss me, but I would be much better off at Oberlin. Ironically, they both stayed at Northwestern; Joel, in fact, got not only his BA at Northwestern but went on to earn a JD and a PhD there. But the real issue was what my parents would say. Despite getting some financial aid from Oberlin, I would still need financial support from my parents and couldn't transfer unless they agreed. So I went home to tell them what I wanted to do.

They were simply baffled. Even though they were not pleased with how Northwestern seemed to be shaping me, they had been led to believe I was very happy there. I had talked enthusiastically about my friends—and they had met some of them—and of the marvelous new world I was discovering. Why did I want to leave? And why Oberlin? They knew very little about Oberlin, but my father had a customer whose son had gone there. "It's an absolutely crazy place," my father told me. "The students all have long hair and sit around on the floor singing folk songs." "Yes," I said. "That's one of the reasons I want to go there." I then proceeded to tell my parents that I was not going to be the son they wanted me to be. I was different and I liked being different. And I wanted to go to a college where my differences would be understood and appreciated.

That night when I went upstairs to bed, I saw the light on in my parents' bedroom and could hear them talking. They heard my footsteps and asked me to come in and sit down. "We need to talk seriously," my mother said. "Your father wants to ask you a question." Then my father took over. "What did you mean when you said you were different? What were you trying to tell us? Are you a homosexual? Is that what this is all about?" I swallowed hard. Then I answered. "No," I said. "That's not it at all. That's not what I was trying to tell you. What I meant was that I am interested in different things than you are. I don't fit into your mold. I don't want to join a fraternity and date Jewish girls. I want you to let me be myself and stop trying to make me be what you want me to be."

My answer was not a total lie. I was, of course, being less than candid on the homosexual issue. In my own mind, I was coming to realize that my sexual interests were primarily in other men. But I had not yet acted on this; I was still a virgin. And I had not yet told anyone about it. My friends at Northwestern and I had occasionally discussed homosexuality in the abstract. We knew of a group of young men in the dormitory who were homosexual and formed a little clique. But I was not one of them. And none of my friends identified as homosexual. Moreover, this was not what I was trying to tell my parents. I was trying to tell them that I wanted to make my own decisions about my life, that they could no longer make them for me, and that transferring to Oberlin was one of those decisions that I should be allowed to make.

Reluctantly, my parents agreed to the transfer. I told Oberlin I was coming, finished my year at Northwestern, and went home to Michigan City for the summer. I worked that summer as a Fuller brush man. I wasn't much good at it, but it did give me some experience in door knocking that would be useful later on when I became a politician. At the end of the summer, I went to Mississippi to visit Leon. Seeing the Deep South for the first time in 1955 was a fascinating and troubling experience. I had been vaguely aware of Jim Crow but had not seen it firsthand. I had taken for granted the kind of spatial and social segregation that had existed in Michigan City, but it was something else again to see the "Whites Only" signs and the legally segregated railroad cars and restrooms. The year before, the U.S. Supreme Court had ruled school segregation unconstitutional, but the South—and especially Mississippi—was preparing to resist. More immediately, during the very time I was in Mississippi, a young black teenager from Chicago named Emmett Till, who was visiting relatives in Mississippi, was kidnapped and killed for allegedly whistling at a white woman. The newspapers were full of this story and we talked of little else.

Leon and his friends were convinced that the South had to change. They knew that the segregation system was wrong and that the murder of Emmett Till was a moral outrage. But they also tried to persuade me that change would be difficult and would come slowly. They predicted accurately that the murderers of Emmett Till would not be convicted. They hinted darkly that we were going to see blood run on the streets of Mississippi before this issue was resolved. All of this was an unsettling experience for me. And when I went to Oberlin that fall, I began to look more deeply into the issue of race in America. And the more I did, the more passionately I became committed to the cause of African American rights.

While I was in the South, Leon and I drove from his home in Hattiesburg for an overnight trip to New Orleans. We stayed in a hotel in the French Quarter, ate at Antoine's (the food there was still good then), and went drinking at Patrick O'Brien's. It was a heady experience as I had just turned eighteen and never before traveled without my parents. I felt very grown up eating with a friend in a fancy restaurant and drinking legally in a bar for the first time in my life. At the end of the evening, Leon suggested that we hire prostitutes. He told me that it was easy to do and perfectly safe in New Orleans and that he would even pay for me. I panicked. I had been ready and eager for everything else we had done that evening, but not for that. I made excuses and told him I would meet him back at the hotel. He went without me and came back with a full and glowing report of what I had missed. He had trouble understanding why I wouldn't go.

The next month, September 1955, I went to Oberlin to begin my sophomore year of college. At first, Oberlin was a bit of a disappointment. Because I had been admitted so late in the year, there was no room for me in the dorms and I was assigned a room at the home of a professor of German and his wife. While my roommate and I soon became good friends, I missed the camaraderie of dorm life that I had enjoyed at Northwestern. I also missed Chicago; Oberlin was a small, isolated place and students were not allowed to have cars so it was difficult to get out. And I particularly disliked the eating arrangements. Instead of the informal meals I had taken at Northwestern, Oberlin required students to be at an assigned dining hall at a set time for lunch and dinner. At dinner, men were expected to wear coats and ties and we all marched into the dining room in unison and said grace before we could eat. On Sunday, grace was an explicitly Christian prayer called the Doxology. It was a lot of trouble for food that was invariably bad. Finally, while my classes were smaller than they had been at Northwestern, most of them were still taught by the lecture method and it was not easy to get close to the professors.

Gradually I came to appreciate what Oberlin had to offer. It was more competitive than Northwestern and I had to work harder for grades. Most of the students were serious about their studies, and when there was opportunity for discussion in class, they asked probing questions and made intelligent comments. No one went to Oberlin for its social life and even dating often centered on a peculiarly Oberlin tradition called the "libe date"—the romantic young couple went to the library together to study. While most of the professors conducted their classes in a traditional manner, they were committed teachers and I found my courses more challenging and interesting than those I had taken at Northwestern. Once again, the course I liked best was in literature. In Andy Hoover's course on the modern novel, we read British novels the first semester and American novels the second. Half of the first semester was devoted to just one novel—but what a novel it was! While I had been reading a lot on my own, I don't think I ever would have read James Joyce's *Ulysses* had Professor Hoover not assigned it and skillfully guided us through it. It was a difficult and challenging novel to read but immensely rewarding, and despite the revisionist criticism of recent years I continue to think it is the greatest novel ever written in English.

Although I loved literature, I decided during my sophomore year to major instead in history. Since I had been a child, I had been fascinated by history and what it could tell us about the society in which we lived. The history courses I took in high school had mostly been badly taught—except for those with Mr. Cooling—but I had read quite a bit of history on my own. And my parents were now assuming that after college I would go to law school. History, I was advised, for reasons that I never fully understood, was a good background for law school. I took two history courses during my sophomore year; both were primarily lecture courses, but they were taught by thoughtful and provocative historians.

Frederick Binkerd Artz—known on campus as Freddy—was the most eminent historian on the Oberlin faculty and by the 1950s was nearing the end of his career. He had long been one of the real characters on campus—a short, plump man who even at sixty had the face of a small child and who was always formally dressed in a suit and bowtie. Freddy was full of himself and never let us forget how lucky we were to be sharing in his wisdom. But he did know his stuff and his introduction to European history was a marvelous distillation of a thousand years of history. I had his course at eight in the morning and was often late. He hated that and when I walked in he would stop talking and say, "Mr. Spear, how nice to see you this morning." I soon started getting up earlier. Freddy had no formal office but instead held office hours at his house, which was located two doors off campus. There, amidst his beautiful antiques and artwork, acquired during his annual trips to Europe, the student would literally sit at his feet—on a little footstool—while the great man sat on his throne. It was an arrangement that would certainly not be allowed on a college campus today. Everyone on campus knew that Freddy was homosexual. He had been involved for many years in an affair with the college secretary, and his mannerisms and style were those of the classic "queen." But even though this was the repressive fifties, no one seemed to care much. Freddy's homosexuality was simply part of his eccentricity.

Barry McGill was a much younger man who had come to Oberlin just a few years before I did, but already he was developing some of the same traits as Freddy Artz—except for his physical appearance and his sexuality. He was a tall thin man who even on the coldest winter day wore only a scarf, no overcoat. And so far as I knew, he was entirely heterosexual. But like Freddy, he had a high opinion of himself and his lectures tended toward the theatrical. And he also could be terrifying. Sometimes he would suddenly stop talking, look at the class, point his long bony arm at a student he had picked out arbitrarily, and ask a question. If the student hadn't been paying attention or was unprepared, he took no pity. "Why are you even taking this course, if that's the best you can do?" he would say. Yet I learned a lot from him. I took his courses in English history and modern European history and still remember many of his interpretations. He also, in his somewhat awkward way, did attempt to relate to students. At the end of each semester, he would invite the class to his house for a party and he would serve beer, a bold thing to do in those days. The parties were not exactly hilarious—even in a social setting, Barry tended to lecture—but he was at least trying.

I also found that the disadvantages of Oberlin could be mitigated. The best way to get out of the stifling dining hall environment was to join a co-op. I started taking my meals at Grey Gables, a big old house on the edge of campus, which served as a dormitory for women and a dining facility for both women and men. At the co-op, students helped with the cooking and did all of the serving and cleaning up. This made the meals cheaper, but what was more important to me was the informal atmosphere. There was no dress code, no prayers before meals, no housemother supervising table manners. The students drawn to Grey Gables tended to be what in those days were called bohemians; a decade later they would have been called hippies. They were the people my father had warned me of. Boys had long hair, girls wore denim work clothes, and almost everyone listened to folk music and sometimes performed it. The highlights of the year were visits by Pete Seeger and Odetta. I never fully got into that culture, but I liked Grey Gables a lot better than the formal dining halls, and I learned a little bit about cooking. When my parents came to campus, I wisely made certain never to take them there.

My living arrangements became more tolerable as I developed a close friendship with my roommate. Roommates were arbitrarily assigned, and I was particularly lucky in this case to have been placed with someone I liked. In a dormitory setting, an incompatible roommate matters less as there are plenty of other people in the building to bond with. But at the German professor's house, there were just the two of us and we necessarily saw a lot of each other. So it was fortunate that Michael A.[1] and I became good friends. Michael was a tall, heavy-set young man—two years older than I—from a northern New Jersey suburb. His father had started a manufacturing business on a shoestring just before the war and it had prospered. By 1955, the company had a worldwide market for its industrial temperature-measuring equipment and had major defense contracts. As the only son, Michael knew that he would eventually take over the business

---

1. Michael A. is a pseudonym.

regardless of how well he did in college. He had come to Oberlin two years earlier and promptly flunked out. Now he was back for another try, but he was still not exactly a serious student. He was far more interested in learning how to lead the good life—something his self-made father had never managed to do. He wore expensive clothes, liked good food, and had already begun to travel abroad. Eventually, he would become an important art collector.

Michael was far different from the friends I had made at Northwestern. He read a lot but didn't pretend to be a serious intellectual. He had a cheerful, upbeat disposition with none of the angst of my Northwestern friends. He was charming and could often be very funny. When he came to Michigan City to visit, my parents liked him at once and were glad I had a friend who was so "down to earth." Michael and I argued often as he thought I took myself too seriously and I thought he did not care enough about the weighty problems of the world. But our differences never spoiled our friendship. We laughed a lot—particularly about our stuffy, overbearing landlords. And even when we were not in our room, we spent a lot of time with each other, going to movies, eating out, attending concerts. Later when we moved to the dormitory, we continued to room together and we remained friends for many years after. In retrospect, I think Michael was what I needed after the Sturm und Drang of my freshman year. He helped me lighten up and be less pretentious.

Nothing much could be done to alleviate Oberlin's isolation. Cleveland was just thirty miles away, but without a car it was hard to reach; there was a bus, but service was infrequent. There were, however, a lot of cultural events on campus. The weekly convocations at Finney Chapel, which were supposed to be compulsory, often featured major national figures. Oberlin was one of the first northern colleges to bring in Martin Luther King Jr. after he assumed the leadership of the Montgomery bus boycott. Cultural and literary luminaries also came to give lectures. The college sponsored a film series, which gave me a chance to see many of the classic films that had never before been accessible to me. And the little commercial theater in downtown Oberlin, the Apollo, catering to the student body, showed all the European art films that were then making such a splash among film cognoscenti. It was there that I first saw the films of Ingmar Bergman, Federico Fellini, Vittorio De Sica, François Truffaut, and the other great directors of the day.

Most important, Oberlin provided me with a full menu of classical music. The college at that time consisted of three separate units: the liberal arts college, the Conservatory of Music, and the Graduate School of Theology. The Theolog, as it was called, was about to be phased out. But the conservatory was thriving, and even for those of us who were not there to study music it provided many opportunities to listen to and learn about music. I took my only course in music appreciation that first year at Oberlin, but I learned more about the world of classical music from the conservatory students I met. And while nothing quite replaced those weekly visits to Orchestra Hall in Chicago, I heard plenty of good music. Three times a year, the Artist Recital Series brought in the Cleveland Orchestra—like the Chicago Symphony, then one of the best in the world—under its distinguished conductor, George Szell. On other occasions, it featured top performers in recital; I heard Dame Myra Hess, Claudio Arrau, Jerome Hines, Glenn Gould, Victoria de los Angeles, and many others. On one memorable occasion, the audience gathered in Finney Chapel to hear a young American pianist named Leon Fleischer. To our disappointment, an announcement was made that Fleischer was suffering from a pain in his right hand and could not perform. (We didn't know it then, but this was the beginning of a disability that would plague Fleischer for decades.) As a substitute, we heard another young American pianist who at the time was virtually unknown. But he was extraordinary. His name was Van Cliburn.

I also became involved in political and social issues. I joined the Young Democrats and a student branch of the liberal action group, Americans for Democratic Action, called logically Students for Democratic Action. I continued to identify with the emerging civil rights movement by joining and soon becoming an officer in the campus branch of the NAACP. Oberlin had a long tradition of commitment to racial equality. It had been a center of antislavery activism in the pre–Civil War era and was one of the first colleges to admit African American students. But even Oberlin was not free of the racism endemic in American society. Our NAACP chapter took on a local barbershop that refused to cut the hair of black men and a local restaurant that was reluctant to serve blacks.

The highlight of my political activity during that first year at Oberlin was the mock political convention. Legend had it that the first

Oberlin mock convention had been held in 1860 and had nominated
Abraham Lincoln. Since then a convention had been held in the spring
of each presidential election year. Usually they had been Republican.
But the student body voted to hold a Democratic convention in 1956.
This reflected in part changes in the political inclination of Oberlin
students, but the students also realized that a Republican convention would be cut-and-dried—Eisenhower and Nixon were sure to
be nominated—while the Democratic field was wide open. Michael
and I were both eager to participate. In the fall, the organizing committee held interviews for delegation chairs. Most students asked to
chair the delegation from their home state; Michael went for New
Jersey. But I was new to campus and sensed that Indiana would be
very competitive. I looked through a list of the home states of Oberlin
students and looked for a state no one at Oberlin hailed from. That, I
thought, would be my best chance. I applied for the chairmanship of
the Montana delegation and got it. Michael ended up as vice-chairman of New Jersey.

I had never been to Montana and knew nothing about its politics.
But I sent away for information, which the Montana Democratic Party
was happy to provide, and read everything I could. I recruited people
to join my delegation and we began to meet to plan our strategy. Montana in the 1950s had one prominent nationally known Democratic
leader: Senator Mike Mansfield. He was not running for president,
but we decided to nominate him as our favorite son. This would get
us noticed (and give me a chance to make a speech) and then allow
us to be courted by the major candidates—Adlai Stevenson, Averell
Harriman, Estes Kefauver, and Stuart Symington. We also had to build
a float. The convention was preceded by a parade through the streets
of Oberlin in which each state delegation was represented. Oil had recently been found in Montana, and we decided to feature on our float
an oil derrick that would actually have some kind of liquid gushing
out of it. Constructing mechanical things had never been my strength,
but somehow we found people who knew how to build such a thing
and miraculously it worked.

The convention was great fun. It was held on a weekend in May
in the field house and had the kind of excitement that on most campuses was reserved for the Big Game. My parents and brother drove
in to see it, and Michael's parents were there, too. He was particularly

pleased that the keynote speaker was the governor of New Jersey, Robert Meyner. After the introductions, we placed the candidates in nomination, I gave my speech for Mansfield, and we began the balloting. At two in the morning, on the fourth ballot, after hours of political jockeying, we nominated Adlai Stevenson, who did, of course, ultimately become the Democratic nominee that year. More prescient, I think, was our choice for vice president: a little-known senator from Massachusetts named John F. Kennedy. His appeal to a group of eager college students was a harbinger of his future career. The Oberlin mock convention was abandoned in the 1960s when college students started participating in real politics and no longer wanted make-believe. But in its day it was a wonderful experience for young people just developing an interest in politics. And the 1956 convention had one unintended consequence. Governor Meyner, the keynote speaker, was the houseguest that weekend of the president of the college, and he met the president's daughter. A year later they were married, and Helen Stevenson Meyner became a leading figure in New Jersey politics.

That summer I returned once again to Michigan City and worked at a series of temporary jobs. My relationship with my parents was improving and I even accompanied them on a boat trip; my father had bought a new cabin cruiser and we went to St. Louis to pick it up and then bring it back on a week's voyage up the Illinois River and into Lake Michigan. Back home, I eagerly followed the political conventions and told everyone who would listen that they needed to vote for Adlai Stevenson. My parents were not convinced, but Grandma Jen was certainly pleased; I went to her apartment to watch the Democratic convention and together we cheered Stevenson on. It was the last chance I would have to be with her as she died just six months later. Toward the end of the summer I went to New Jersey to visit Michael, and we spent time together in New York City. I was excited by New York. We went to the theater, ate in good restaurants, and saw the sights. I thought for many years that I wanted to live in New York—an idea I ultimately got out of my system.

It was also that summer that I first openly discussed my sexuality with another person. Jonathan Feinn had graduated from high school a year later than I did and had gone on to the University of

Chicago. He was back in Michigan City after his first year of college and we saw each other frequently. I can't remember for sure who first broached the forbidden subject, but I think it was Jon. He told me that he had started picking up men on the streets of Chicago, mostly hustlers, and that his homosexuality was not just in his head, that he really enjoyed gay male sex. I told him that I was gay, too, which did not exactly surprise him, and that I had not yet actually done anything but was ready to try. It was tacitly understood that neither of us was interested in sex with the other, but we agreed that sometime we would go together to Chicago to pick up hustlers. We also spent hours talking about whom we were attracted to—running through the names of our mutual high school friends and discussing them in terms that we would never have dared do before. On one level, it was liberating to finally get this all out and be able to discuss it with someone. But throughout these discussions ran the assumption that there was something wrong with us. Jonathan wanted to be cured and had already begun seeing a psychiatrist. Neither of us could imagine living our lives as gay men. Other than the pay-for-sex encounters Jon had had in Chicago, we knew nothing about the varieties or possibilities of gay life.

When I returned to Oberlin, I hoped that I might be able to open the subject with Michael. I was pretty sure he was gay, too. He rarely dated and never talked about women. That semester we roomed together in the dormitory and I began to hear rumors about him. Someone who lived on our floor told me that Michael and another young man had gone into the student lounge and locked the door from the inside. Others had tried to get in to use the lounge, but Michael and his companion wouldn't open the door. "They must have been having sex," I was told. I didn't confront Michael with this, but I did gingerly try to raise the issue of homosexuality with him. Whenever I did, he changed the subject. Many years later, when Michael and I finally did discuss our sexuality, he remembered that incident in the dorm and my efforts to raise the subject, but he said he was just not yet prepared to deal with it in an open way.

Michael and I continued, however, to be best friends. We were both eager to follow the political campaign and decided to buy a television set for our room. From the perspective of the twenty-first century, this may seem totally unremarkable. But it was virtually unheard of in

1956 for a college student to have his own TV; there was one provided for the entire dorm in the student lounge and that was expected to suffice. When I told the housemother of our intention, she said she was sure it was against the rules. But then she backtracked and said that apparently there was no rule, it was just that no one had ever done it. We bought the TV and watched the nightly coverage of the campaign. In October we joined several other Oberlin Young Democrats and went to Columbus to hear Eleanor Roosevelt, who had come to the state to campaign for Stevenson. She was particularly forceful on the need to end nuclear testing, an issue Stevenson had made a centerpiece of his campaign. But nothing seemed to work as he lagged far behind Eisenhower. Just weeks before the election, two major international crises erupted—the Suez War and the Hungarian Revolution. We followed those events too on our little television set. I even went into Cleveland to join the Hungarian American community in a protest over the Soviet invasion of Hungary. But in terms of domestic politics, these crises seemed only to cement Eisenhower's popularity.

On Election Day, I joined a busload of Young Democrats who went to Cleveland to work on door-to-door get-out-the-vote efforts in a heavily Democratic working-class neighborhood. This was my first experience with grassroots political campaigning and I enjoyed it. One incident, however, was unsettling. When the campaign worker at Democratic headquarters gave me the list of Democratic candidates to promote, he told me not to mention Judge White. "Why is that?" I asked. "Because," he replied, "when you vote White you vote black." I urged the people I met to vote for Judge White. By the time we got back to Oberlin, the results of the election in the eastern states were already in. It was an Eisenhower landslide. Michael and I had friends over to watch the results with us on our television set, but it was a long, disappointing evening.

Oberlin offered two programs away from campus for juniors in their second semester. One, called the Washington Semester, provided an opportunity to intern in a congressional office. The other was an exchange program with a group of African American colleges in the South; an Oberlin student would go there for a semester while a southern black student came to Oberlin. The summer before I had casually mentioned these programs to my parents. They thought the

Washington Semester would be good for me, but they certainly did not like the idea of the exchange program. Nevertheless, with my growing interest in the racial issue, I decided to apply. I wrote on my application:

> I have a sincere desire to observe racial relations in the South and to obtain first-hand information about the segregation problem. . . . I believe that only by spending some time in the South can I gain a real insight into the problem and an understanding of the factors that make segregation one of the most difficult and complicated problems in contemporary America. . . . Youth, I believe should be a time for gaining as many different and varied experiences as possible. . . . The experience of being in a racial minority in a race-conscious society is one in which, in all probability, I will never again have an opportunity to participate.

I was chosen for the program and prepared to go to Nashville in January to spend a semester at Fisk University.

When I went home that year for winter vacation, my parents were not pleased with me. They thought I had begun to settle down and now I had come up with a crazy idea again. I had never really asked my parents for permission to go to Fisk. After all, it was an authorized program of the college I was already attending and it cost no extra money. But my mother was worried sick. She knew that I was not going to be content simply to observe the Jim Crow system, that I was likely to try to challenge it. And she had visions of my becoming the next Emmett Till. Years later, when she was in the advanced stages of an autoimmune disease called scleroderma—the disease that ultimately killed her—she told me that the symptoms of her disease first appeared the day I told her I was going to Fisk. My medical friends have told me that any connection is highly unlikely, but my mother clearly remembered this venture of mine as a cause of great stress. Other family members reacted not so much with concerns about my safety as revulsion against my crossing the color line. One aunt asked me where I would live. "In a dormitory," I told her. "Oh my God," she said. "It will be full of bugs." Even at Oberlin, not everyone approved. Freddy Artz saw me one day in the library, came up, put his hand on my shoulder, and said, "Well, I hear you're going steady with the blacks."

Fisk University is one of the oldest and most distinguished black colleges in America. It had been founded just after the Civil War by the American Missionary Association, an arm of the Congregational Church, as part of its educational outreach to the newly freed slaves. It was rescued from bankruptcy in the 1870s by the Fisk Jubilee Singers, who toured the United States and Europe introducing the world to what came to be called the "Negro spiritual." Its most famous alumnus was the great scholar and civil rights activist W. E. B. Du Bois. For most of its history, its administration and faculty had been all white, but when I arrived in 1957, Fisk's faculty was split down the middle racially, and the administration of its first black president had just ended with the untimely death of Charles S. Johnson. The student body of about seven hundred—less than half the size of Oberlin—was still all black except for nine exchange students, of whom I was one.

My first impression after arriving at Fisk was exactly what I had written about in my application for the program: I was "in a racial minority in a race-conscious society." I looked around me and then looked into the mirror—I was the one who was different. When I later shared this reaction with black friends at Fisk, they smiled and said, "You experienced color shock; we experience that all the time." My second impression was that despite its distinguished history, Fisk was still a struggling institution. Compared to Oberlin, or to its local white counterpart Vanderbilt University, it was a shabby place, reflecting the inequalities of a segregated society. The dormitory where I lived, Livingstone Hall, was a big, solid nineteenth-century building, but it had not been modernized in years. The rooms and the bath facilities were shockingly rundown. There were a few new buildings on campus, but most were old and in need of repair. The faculty couldn't compare to what I had experienced at Oberlin or Northwestern. Among the whites, there were a few who had made the conscious choice to contribute to black education, but many were people who simply hadn't made it in predominantly white colleges. The black faculty included some genuinely distinguished scholars, but many were of an older generation. Two—the writer Arna Bontemps and the artist Aaron Douglas—had been members of the Harlem Renaissance of the 1920s.

Of the professors with whom I studied at Fisk, the biggest disappointment was Theodore Currier, who taught American history. I had heard of Currier as the beloved mentor of John Hope Franklin. Franklin was not yet in 1957 the towering figure he would become, but he was already well known among historians and he never failed to credit Currier for starting him on his highly successful career. But something had happened to Ted Currier between the 1930s, when Franklin had been at Fisk, and the 1950s, when I was there. A white man who never completed his PhD, Currier seemed to feel trapped at Fisk and his attitude in class was bitter and petty. He spent much of the class time talking not about history but about the defects of Fisk, and he attacked colleagues and even students by name. When I told him near the end of the semester that I had not learned what I had expected to learn in his class, he responded by saying that if his teaching was good enough for John Hope Franklin it should be good enough for me. And he then proceeded to give me a B, even though I had received As on all the exams.

The one exception to the general mediocrity of my teachers at Fisk was the only black professor with whom I studied—the poet Robert Hayden. I enrolled in Professor Hayden's class in creative writing, which met once a week in his home just off campus. There were only nine students in the class and we were expected to bring examples of our writing each week to share with the group. I never wrote very much, but I learned a lot from Professor Hayden. He shared with us his writing in progress, gave us a sense of how the creative process worked, and offered incisive critiques of some of the leading literary figures of the day. He was a wonderfully sensitive and caring person. I felt ashamed that I didn't contribute more to his class, but I learned one important thing about myself. I was reasonably adept at expository writing, but I had no talent whatsoever for writing fiction or poetry and I never attempted it again.

Whatever the deficiencies of Fisk's physical plant and its faculty, my semester there was an exhilarating experience and one of the important turning points of my life. I met fascinating people, learned more about African American life than I could have ever found in books, and had a chance to observe the Jim Crow system just at the dawn of the civil rights era. Because my classes were undemanding—and I had not really come to Fisk for class work anyway—I spent much of my time meeting and talking with my fellow students. I found a perfect hangout in the International Student Center, which, despite its rather grandiose name, was really just an informal lounge in the basement of a dormitory where students could get together. It tended to attract the more serious-minded and socially conscious students. There I got to know two senior history majors—Ed Harper and Harry Stephens—who shared my frustrations with Professor Currier and told me that I had unfortunately just missed a really interesting history professor who had left Fisk the year before I came. He was August Meier, who would later have an important influence on my own career. Harry and his roommate, Elliott Troup, became two of my best friends and later in the semester I visited both of their homes in Georgia. We were occasionally joined in the International Student Center by a freshman named Julius Lester. Julius later gained fame as the author of *Look Out, Whitey! Black Power's Gon' Get Your Mama,* and then when other black militants were becoming Muslims, Julius turned to Judaism.

Our conversations included all of the usual college bull session topics, but for me they were also a crash course in African American life. I had a smattering of knowledge about the Jim Crow system, but I knew nothing about the internal dynamics of the African American community. For example, I couldn't understand why northern black students, who could have gone to integrated colleges in their home states, chose instead to come south and go to Fisk. I put the question to Ed Harper, who came from New York, and Roma Jones, a bright young woman whose father was a lawyer in Chicago. They explained to me that black students who went to predominantly white colleges often felt isolated and marginalized. Fisk gave them the opportunity to relate to their own community, to develop a far fuller social life than they would have had in the North, and to establish contacts that would be useful to them throughout their lives. I came to understand that one way in which African Americans survived in a racist society was to develop and nurture their own community institutions. This concept would be at the center of my own work on the history of the Chicago black community a decade later.

The time I was at Fisk—early 1957—was a kind of brief respite in the development of the civil rights movement. The Montgomery bus boycott had just ended successfully and Martin Luther King was exploring ways to expand on this victory through his new organization, the Southern Christian Leadership Conference. The big lunch counter sit-ins were still several years in the future. King came to Fisk to give a speech while I was there and he was quite properly greeted as a hero. But some of us who heard him were disappointed in his message. He spoke at a high level of abstraction, explaining how the rise of the civil rights movement fit into the Hegelian dialectic. There was, however, no specific plan for action in the years ahead. King's biographer, David Garrow, writes that King was at that time being considered for the presidency of Fisk—a position that was vacant. This might explain why he chose to emphasize his credentials as an intellectual rather than as an activist. It would have been an unlikely appointment and nothing ever came of it. King had just turned twenty-eight and had no administrative experience, and a position as a college president would have removed him from the kind of movement work at which he just proved himself so adept.

Nashville was still officially segregated, and there were not yet any direct challenges to the system. Fisk was located in a black neighborhood that provided the kind of basic services that college students needed—informal restaurants, convenience stores, barbershops and beauty salons, and a few bars and nightclubs. I went to these places with my friends and never had any problem getting served. But we didn't go downtown, where the movie theaters, hotels, and restaurants were open to white people only.

One day several of us were sitting around the International Student Center and noted in the newspaper that a new movie we all wanted to see was playing at a theater in downtown Nashville. To me it was simply absurd that a group of college friends could not go together to do something as innocent and natural as watching a movie. "There's got to be a way," I said. Someone had an idea. There had recently been a series of widely reported incidents in other parts of the country in which diplomats from African countries had been refused service in restaurants and at lunch counters. The federal government had been embarrassed and was forced to issue apologies. Perhaps if the black students wore African clothes to the movies the management would be afraid to bar them. We found a couple of the African students who were attending Fisk and asked to borrow their tribal robes. Two of my friends put them on, and they and I, as well as another white exchange student, headed downtown.

It was a remarkable evening. As we walked from the bus stop to the movie theater, every head turned to stare at us. When we arrived at the box office, I bought four tickets and we walked into the lobby. The manager immediately ran up to me. "These people with you," he said, "they're not Negroes, are they?" "They are Africans," I said. "OK," he replied. "As long as they're foreign." When we bought popcorn, the woman at the refreshment stand asked me where my friends were from. When I said "Africa," she was incredulous. "Gee," she said. "I never seen no Africans before." This was all working so well that after the movie, we decided to go to a restaurant. It was filled with rural Tennessee bankers in town for a state convention. We ordered pizza and our orders were taken without question. But as the food arrived, we noticed that conversation at the other tables had stopped, that everyone was listening to us. At this point, without any planning, we went into a "shtick." "What do you eat in Africa?" I asked my friends. "Oh, the usual things—beef, pork, chicken, monkey, sometimes people." As we could hear the forks dropping, I went on. "What does your father do in Africa?" "Oh, he hunts heads."

When we told others on campus the next day what we had done, the reaction was mixed. Some thought we had been irresponsible in dealing with the system by subterfuge rather than directly. One friend told me it was a bad idea to encourage white people to make a distinction between African Americans and foreigners in applying the segregation laws. And of course the ridiculous things we had said about Africa did not exactly contribute to better international understanding. But to me the incident had sharply exposed the irrationality of the system. To see a movie and eat a pizza in a city in the United States, American citizens had to pretend to be foreigners. Just a few years later, students braver than we were would do what we had done without wearing costumes. They would go to jail for it—and in the process change the course of American history.

Several weeks later, our little group in the International Student Center read another interesting item in the newspaper. The Ku Klux Klan would be holding a regional rally in Cleveland, Tennessee, 150 miles away. Wouldn't that be something to see? Of course, it was out of the question for any black person to try to attend, but the white exchange students could go and report back. Four of us arranged for a car and made the trip. Years later I became good friends with a man who had grown up in Cleveland, Tennessee. He remembered that rally and told me that the local people had opposed it and that it was entirely the work of organizers from the outside. It did seem that way as we drove into Cleveland that evening; cars, vans, and pickup trucks were coming in from outlying areas and converging on a hill on the out-skirts of town. There a fiery cross was already burning, and many in the crowd were wearing white robes and hoods. We got as close as we could and listened. The speeches were the pathetic ramblings of losers. It was not just the "niggers" who were threats to American society but the Jews and the Catholics and the liberals. Even Vice President Nixon was not exempt. "I saw that Nixon was visiting Africa last month," noted one speaker. "One of the big chiefs over there offered him a nigger wife. I didn't see that he refused either." I still remember one bit of doggerel: "I'd rather be a Klansman dressed in white / Loyal to America my home / Than a priest in a robe as black as night / Loyal to that dago pope in Rome." During the rally, we noticed a man standing with a clipboard taking notes. He turned out to be a reporter from the *New York Times*. When a Klansman spotted him, he rushed over, grabbed the clipboard, and unceremoniously escorted the reporter off the premises. We were glad that we had not tried to take notes. Fortunately, we had good memories and when we returned to Fisk we regaled our fellow students with our observations. Our presenta-tion, which attracted a large crowd, was titled "We Peeked Behind the White Curtain."

At spring break, Harry and Elliott invited me and another white ex-change student, Fred Lipp from the College of Wooster in Ohio, to come with them to Georgia. Our plan was to get a ride to Atlanta and spend a couple of days there meeting Harry and Elliott's friends. Then we would take the train to Macon, where Elliott's parents would pick us up and take us to their home in nearby Fort Valley. Harry would go on to his family in Columbus, and Fred and I would come to visit him there later. We eagerly accepted the invitation. And as we made our plans, the four of us vowed that we would not at any point in our travels split up. We were four friends traveling together—two white and two black—and we were not going to abide by the rules of Jim Crow.

In Atlanta, we stayed in a dormitory at Morehouse College, the college for black men that Martin Luther King had attended a few years earlier. That presented no problems, but we soon came to realize that segregation in Atlanta was far more strictly enforced than segregation in Nashville. We could not, for example, get a taxi. White drivers would not take black passengers, and black drivers told us apologetically that their licenses would be jeopardized if they took white passengers. We went out for dinner at a black restaurant near Morehouse. In Nashville, although white restaurants would not serve black customers, black restaurants had not shown any hesitation in serving whites. The restaurant in Atlanta served us, but the manager called Elliott over and asked him not to come again with white people; by serving us, he said, he could get in trouble with the authorities.

The most illuminating experience for me, however, came when we tried to go out socially. Elliott told Fred and me that we needed to see the Walla-hajji, a black nightclub that, he said, was the hottest spot in Atlanta. He promised to get dates for all four of us. Elliott was a good-looking and self-assured young man with lots of connections in Atlanta, and after just a few minutes on the telephone he had arranged for the dates.

"Do the girls know that Fred and I are white?" I asked. "I told them that you are exchange students," he replied. "I assume they know what that means." The next night we arrived at a beautiful home in an elegant section of black Atlanta; it was the first time I had ever met wealthy black people. When we walked in the door, four nicely dressed young women were waiting for us. It was clear from the expressions on their faces that they had not understood what Elliott meant when he said we were exchange students. As we sat in the living room making small talk with the girls, one of the mothers started frantically calling the other girls' mothers to tell them that there was a crisis. After a few minutes, she came back to inform us that we could not possibly go to the Walla-hajji. Instead there would be a party for the eight of us right there in their finished basement. Elliott explained later that the mothers believed that if their daughters were seen at a nightclub with white men, their daughters' reputations would be ruined. It was assumed in upper-class black society in Atlanta that white men would be interested in black women only for sex. We never left the house that evening.

The next day we took the train to Macon. The Supreme Court had recently ruled against segregation in interstate transportation, so the Atlanta train station had three waiting rooms: an integrated waiting room for interstate passengers only and segregated waiting rooms for intrastate passengers. Since we were not leaving Georgia, we headed for the waiting room marked "Colored Intrastate." On our way in, a station employee—a black man—stopped Fred and me and informed us that we were going the wrong way, that the white waiting room was across the hall. "No," we said. "We're going here." He shrugged and muttered that we must be Yankees. In Macon, we were met by Elliott's parents, who drove us to Fort Valley. Elliott's father was the president of Fort Valley College, a state school for "colored" students. Fred and I spent the weekend with them at their comfortable home on the Fort Valley campus.

President and Mrs. Troup were gracious hosts and seemed genuinely pleased to have Elliott's friends visit. But one incident that weekend illustrated the precarious position of an African American professional working for a state institution in the Jim Crow South. Just after breakfast on Sunday, a white man drove up to the Troups' house and asked for a tour of the campus. President Troup obliged. The man did not ask who Fred and I were, but after he left, Mrs. Troup wondered aloud what he might have thought about their having white houseguests. Any perceived deviation from the etiquette of Jim Crow was clearly cause for concern. Later something else occurred to me about this visit. The white man, who was totally unknown to the Troups, thought it was perfectly acceptable to call at the home of a black college president without an appointment on a Sunday and receive a personal tour of the campus. This would never have happened at the University of Georgia. That afternoon we went to Columbus to meet Harry's family. Harry's background was more working class than Elliott's, but again his family greeted us warmly. Then we returned to Atlanta and back to Nashville. We had had a few close calls, but we had kept our promise never to split up.

As the semester came to an end, I was genuinely sad to leave Fisk. On my last night, I never went to bed; I stayed up all night in the International Student Center talking to friends. I knew that I would never see most of them again and I would miss them. I did see Harry some years later when he came to Minneapolis for a conference; he had become a school administrator in Benton Harbor, Michigan. Elliott ended up settling in Minneapolis at about the same time I did. He did a residency at the University of Minnesota Medical School and then established a successful practice in ophthalmology. I lost track of the others. But the experience had been a transforming one. It had immeasurably broadened my horizons and cemented my commitment to the cause of African American equality.

Back in Oberlin in September, I wanted to build on what I had learned at Fisk. The focus of the country was now on Little Rock and the attempt by Governor Orval Faubus to prevent the desegregation of Central High School. The heroics of Martin Luther King and the black community of Montgomery were now followed by the courage of the nine black teenagers who walked through taunting and threatening mobs every day just to enter school. The civil rights struggle was regaining momentum. Meanwhile, I enrolled in a course in Negro history, as it was then called. It was the first time a course in this subject had been offered at Oberlin, and one of the first at any predominantly white college. It turned out to be the best course I ever took at Oberlin, and ironically it was taught by a man who was not even a regular faculty member. Leslie Fishel had a PhD in history and had written his dissertation on African Americans in the late nineteenth century, but in the tough job market of the 1950s, he had been unable to land a college teaching job. He had come to Oberlin, his alma mater, to take the position of alumni secretary—essentially administering the affairs of the Alumni Association. He taught just one history course and it met in the evening, after he had finished his day job. There were fewer than a dozen students and Mr. Fishel did not lecture. We discussed the assigned reading, Mr. Fishel shared his insights, and then he listened to what we had to say. There was no intimidation as there had been in some of my other history courses; the atmosphere was one of mutual respect. It was the only course in African American history I ever took, and when I taught the subject some years later, it provided me with an excellent model.

African American history was just being recognized as a legitimate field of study in the late 1950s. Before then, mainstream white historians dealt with black people only as backdrops to issues such as slavery and the sectional crisis. They were factors and causes but not active players in the development of the American nation. There was a body of scholarship that took African Americans seriously, but it was written either by black scholars or by white radicals and was virtually ignored by the academic establishment. Works such as W. E. B. Du Bois's *Black Reconstruction in America, 1860–1880* and Herbert Aptheker's *American Negro Slave Revolts* received little attention in the historical journals and were rarely assigned in American history courses. But this was beginning to change. Younger scholars—both black and white—were challenging the old interpretations. Kenneth Stampp's *The Peculiar Institution,* published in 1956, viewed slavery not as a benign institution but as a system of economic exploitation; John Hope Franklin's work on free blacks during the slavery era focused on an important segment of the African American population that had been previously neglected; and August Meier had begun his study of black leadership in the post-Reconstruction era. Moreover, scholars like Du Bois and Aptheker were being rediscovered and reevaluated. Mr. Fishel tied all of this together and provided a really exciting introduction to the field.

I took one other course that year that would have a lasting influence on me. Clyde Holbrook's Modern Religious Thought should really have been called Modern Christian Thought as it was basically a survey of Christian theologians from Søren Kierkegaard to Karl Barth and Paul Tillich. But it was eye-opening to me, who had previously been exposed only to traditional concepts of God. I was particularly taken by the work of a contemporary Christian theologian named Henry Nelson Wieman. Wieman provided me with the best answer I have ever encountered to the question Dostoyevsky raises in *The Brothers Karamazov:* if there is no God, are not all things permissible? As a moralist, I could not accept the proposition that all things are permissible, yet I no longer believed in the traditional transcendent God. Wieman turned the question on its head. He argued that it is the very quality in humans that insists on moral standards, demands decency in human behavior, and refuses to accept all things as permissible that constitutes God. God is not something beyond us, but something within us. I have continued to hold this belief throughout my life. The irony is that I could have found it in Jewish tradition. Jewish thinkers from Baruch Spinoza to Martin Buber have posited similar views. But my Jewish education was far inferior to the Christian education I received at Oberlin and later at Yale. To this day, I know more about Christianity than I do about Jewish theology.

Michael had flunked out of Oberlin again and returned to New Jersey to begin working with his father's company. He soon got an apartment in Manhattan and invited me to come to visit whenever I wanted. I went there when I could during school vacations and continued to appreciate the attractions of New York. At Oberlin during my senior year I roomed with a rail-thin, somewhat ascetic music student named Don Anthony. Don could not have been more different from Michael. He was serious-minded and usually quiet with no taste for the high living that Michael so enjoyed. But he had a wry sense of humor and was a political liberal and we got along well. I learned a lot from him about music. Unlike most music students at Oberlin, he was not training to be a performer but was studying musicology. We often listened to music together and he explained things to me that I would never have heard on my own. I had traded my little record player for my first stereo system—a pretty modest affair but still a step up. And I was now eagerly buying stereo records. I started hanging around the local record shop and got to know its owner, a woman named Susan Arnold. After seeing me so often, Mrs. Arnold asked me if I wanted to work there, so I took a part-time job. I don't think I was much of a salesperson, but I had a lot of opinions about what Mrs. Arnold should buy and occasionally she let me accompany her on trips to the wholesale house in Cleveland. The best part of the job was that I could buy records at a discount.

My musical tastes were evolving at this point beyond the symphonies of Beethoven and Brahms. I was beginning to listen to chamber and piano music. One of Don Anthony's friends—a talented pianist—taught me what to listen for in evaluating piano performances, and although I have never played the piano, I have been a devotee of it ever since. I also began to appreciate some of the more accessible twentieth–century music—Béla Bartók, Sergei Prokofiev, Igor Stravinsky—although I never developed much of a taste for the twelve-tone composers. It is interesting how musical fashions change. Two composers who are much revered today were scorned by all of my musical friends in the 1950s—Gustav Mahler and Anton Bruckner. There was a small student group on campus called the Mahler-Bruckner Society, which we constantly ridiculed. They were considered total weirdoes, as were the composers they idolized. It has taken me a long time to develop any taste for Mahler, and I still have trouble with Bruckner.

My romantic and sexual life remained nonexistent. I would occasionally ask a woman out for a date, we might go to a movie and have something to eat, but that was it. It would be no different from spending an evening with a male friend. I realized that there were people around me who were gay, but I was still not prepared to reach out to them. It was not that I was asexual. I thought about sex a lot and saw many men who sexually attracted me. But even liberal Oberlin did not provide a climate that encouraged gay students to deal honestly with their sexuality. Homosexuality was a subject for jest and ridicule. My roommate, Don Anthony, was straight, but there were many music students who were not and we frequently joked about them. Twenty-five years later, Oberlin asked members of the class of 1958 to submit a brief statement for inclusion in a reunion booklet and in that statement I came out for the first time to my classmates. I had not been in touch with Don since we left Oberlin, but I received a letter from him apologizing for thoughtless things he remembered saying when we roomed together. Don had not been especially homophobic and whatever jokes or comments he may have made I had long forgotten. But I deeply appreciated his concern that he may have said things twenty-five years earlier that would have hurt my feelings. We have remained in contact since then.

By the winter of my senior year, I had to start thinking about what I would do next. As early as my high school years, I had assumed that I would ultimately go to law school. I am not sure how this assumption developed as I knew very little about the practice of law, but among the learned professions it seemed best suited to my interests in politics, history, and the social sciences. My parents strongly encouraged it as becoming a lawyer was a thoroughly suitable and potentially lucrative career goal for a bright Jewish boy. As I became committed to the African American movement, law developed even more appeal. Among the heroes of the early civil rights movement were the lawyers who had won landmark victories at the Supreme Court and in the lower federal courts. I could readily see myself becoming a civil rights lawyer. At the same time, Mr. Fishel's course had given me a strong interest in pursuing graduate work in African American history. I spoke to him about this and he pointed out to me that no university at the time had a specific program in African American history, but that I could go to a graduate school with strong offerings in American social history, find a sympathetic adviser, and essentially create my own program. My parents did not find the prospect of their son becoming a college professor nearly as attractive as his becoming a lawyer, and they urged me to at least give law school a try.

It was not certain in my mind whether I would be admitted to a first-rate law school. My college grades were not nearly as strong as my high school grades had been. I had allowed myself too many distractions and had often preferred a movie or a concert or an all-night bull session to studying for an exam. In my senior year, in particular, I had cut classes frequently. And I had attended three different colleges in four years, which may have raised questions about my stability. I had as many Bs as I did As, and I did not make Phi Beta Kappa. But I aced the LSAT, finishing somewhere in the upper part of the ninety-ninth percentile. With that, I was offered the Erwin Griswold Scholarship, an award open only to Oberlin graduates who wished to attend Harvard Law School. Griswold was then the dean of Harvard Law School and was himself an Oberlin alumnus. That was hard to turn down. Harvard was considered the top law school in the country and I was being offered full financial aid. I accepted the offer. I never even applied to graduate school.

My parents were very proud. They came to commencement, along with my aunt Roz, and felt satisfied with how things had turned out. Despite the conflicts and the anxieties, I had graduated with flying colors and now I was off to the best university in the country to become a lawyer. After a brief visit with Michael in New York, I went back to Michigan City for the summer. By this time, I had acquired a regular summer job, one that was available to me each year. It involved mail room and office work and was not very exciting, but it was not physically difficult and the people I worked with were pleasant and friendly. And it gave me a small measure of financial independence. I spent the summer working, dealing with my family, and visiting with my old friend Jonathan, who was also back home.

Now it was my brother Richard's turn to be the rebellious son. He had just completed his first year at the University of Chicago and was eager to assert his independence, much as I had after my year at Northwestern. But the action he chose was more radical than what I had done. He dropped out of Chicago and booked passage on a ship sailing for Europe at the end of the summer, and he planned to tell our parents what he had done only after he arrived. He had no specific plans as to what he was going to do in Europe, but he had discovered art during his year at Chicago and would immerse himself in European art and culture. He told me all of this and now I played the role of sensible older brother. I told him that he would have plenty of time later to go to Europe and that to do it this way would needlessly hurt our parents. Moreover, he had cut himself off from Chicago and had no guarantee that he could return. Jonathan Feinn, whom Richard respected, also became involved and helped convince Richard that he was making a mistake. As a result, Richard told our parents what he was going to do; they talked him out of it and promised him that if he returned to school they would make sure he got to Europe the following summer. I think he was relieved that it all ended the way it did and that Chicago readmitted him and reinstated his scholarship. Richard went on to graduate from Chicago, pursue graduate work in art history at Princeton, and spend a good portion of his life in Europe—traveling, doing research, and spending summers with his Greek wife at their country house in Greece.

I saw a lot of Jonathan that summer. He was still the only person to whom I had come out, and we decided to finally do what we had talked about a couple of years earlier. We went to Chicago to pick up hustlers. It was my first sexual encounter with another human being—and it was not a success. Jon knew where to go and we drove around the Near North Side until he spotted a young man with whom he had previously tricked. We picked him up and Jon told him that we needed someone else for me. He saw another young man standing on a street corner and told us to stop. "If you want to make some money," he said, "hop in." The other man did, but he looked dubious. To make sure that there was no mistake, I put my hand on his leg. He yelled at my angrily, "Get your filthy hand off me, I'm not into that." We let him out of the car and eventually found a good-looking guy who *was* into it. But by that time, I was nervous and scared and ashamed of myself. We went to a cheap hotel; the four of us got into one big bed and took off our clothes. I looked at the attractive man next to me—the first time I had ever been in bed with anyone—and I couldn't do a thing. Jon and I paid the hustlers and went home. All I could think of after that experience was that maybe it was all in my head; maybe I wasn't homosexual after all. Jonathan doubted that.

At the end of the summer, my brother drove me to Cambridge to begin Harvard Law School and a new chapter in my life.

3

DISCOVERING THE AFRICAN AMERICAN PAST—AND PRESENT, 1958-1964

My year at Harvard Law School was the most frustrating of my life. Within the first two months, I had lost interest in my classes and decided that I did not want to be a lawyer. At the time, I thought legal studies just did not appeal to me and that I had made a mistake in going to law school. But years later, as a legislator in Minnesota, I served on the Judiciary Committee and ultimately became the first nonlawyer ever to chair that committee. I found legal issues fascinating. In retrospect, I think that I could have become interested in legal studies and might very well have finished law school if I had been introduced to the law in a different way. The problem may have had more to do with Harvard and its approach to legal education than with the law itself.

Harvard may have been the top law school in the country, but it was essentially a trade school. Its goal was not to present the law as an intellectual discipline but to train young men (and a very few women) to be high-powered and highly paid lawyers. Its first-year curriculum reflected that objective: there were no electives and everyone took the same mandatory course of study. The emphasis was on the meat-and-potatoes subjects that form the core of a legal practice: property law, torts, contracts, agency, and civil procedure. The one abbreviated course in criminal law seemed to be regarded as an afterthought. Constitutional law did not appear in the curriculum until the second year, when electives were allowed. The professors were among the best legal scholars in the country, but the material they presented was as dry as dust and totally unrelated to the kinds of issues that concerned me. Even Archibald Cox, who would later gain fame as the Watergate prosecutor fired by Richard Nixon in the notorious Saturday night massacre, could arouse no interest in me when he was teaching a subject as tedious as agency.

My attitude toward Harvard Law School was further soured by the general atmosphere of the place—which was conveyed with great accuracy in the 1973 film *The Paper Chase*. My classmates were highly ambitious and fiercely competitive young men who were determined to succeed. A story was told that a passerby looked up at the windows of a law school dormitory late one night and saw all the lights out; then one light came on—and within a few minutes all the other lights came on. If your classmates were studying, you needed to be studying too. It would not do to let anyone else get ahead of you. When I mentioned to friends that I might like to be a civil rights lawyer, this was greeted with derision. Where was the money in that? Many of my classmates had their careers all mapped out: the firm they would start with, where they would be at thirty, where they would be at forty, and so on. No one was studying the law because it was the basis of civilized society, or because they might want to teach it, or because it was good training for a life of public service. There obviously were young people at the time who were going to law school for those reasons, but I did not meet them at Harvard.

By the end of the fall, I started sitting in on Oscar Handlin's course in American social history, which he taught at Harvard College, just a few blocks away. What a contrast this was to the courses I was taking in law school! Handlin was not a flashy lecturer, but he had put together a synthesis of social history that was wholly original and enormously stimulating. It illuminated all the areas of American society that most fascinated me—race, ethnicity, class divisions, migration patterns. When I went home for winter break, I told my parents that I was not going to finish law school and that I wanted to go to graduate school in history. They were disappointed but did not argue the point. I had given law school a try, it hadn't worked out, and I needed to do what I wanted to do. Meanwhile, I called Les Fishel at Oberlin and sought advice from him about applying to graduate school. He had just accepted a position as the director of the Wisconsin Historical Society in Madison, and although he would have no formal connection with the history department at the University of Wisconsin, he did point out to me its merits as one of the top programs in the country. He also strongly recommended Yale, where his friend and former classmate John Morton Blum was teaching, and told me that he would recommend me to Blum. And my experience in Handlin's course made the Harvard history department attractive to me as well. So I decided to apply to those three departments and see what would happen.

I did not think it would be wise to simply drop out of law school in the middle of the year. I didn't want my academic record to look any spottier than it already was—and I couldn't begin graduate school until the next September anyway. So I toughed out the rest of the year, attending classes sporadically and doing enough studying so that, I hoped, I could pass the final exams in June and not have my record marred with the stigma of having flunked out. I found a few things that interested me in civil procedure and criminal law and occasionally in torts, but to this day I find it hard to understand why anyone would choose to practice property law. When I chaired the Judiciary Committee years later and property law issues came before us, I had all I could do to stay awake.

My unhappiness that year at Harvard extended to my social life. I lived in a dormitory and made a few friends—mostly people who were also frustrated with the place. But for the first time since high school, I felt pressured to date and to conform to a heterosexual lifestyle. At Oberlin, dating was so casual that if you didn't do it, no one really noticed. But Harvard law students were as hard driving in their social lives as they were in their professional lives. If the dormitory conversation was not about class work, it was about women and everyone's latest conquests. When I had little to say on that subject, my friends did me the favor of finding women for me, women who they assured me would be "easy marks." I usually found excuses to get out of these dates, but it was all very unpleasant.

Finally, I decided I needed some help. I went to the Student Health Service and asked to see a psychiatrist. My shrink initially assumed I was there because of my dissatisfaction with law school, but I soon made it clear that I thought I could handle that. I had confidence in myself intellectually, and if I didn't like law school I was sure I could succeed in graduate school. What I needed help with was my sex life. I told him that I was a homosexual and that I needed to change. He was sympathetic and not judgmental, but he told me that curing homosexuality was a long-term and difficult process and could not be done in the few sessions that the student health program would provide. He urged me to seek help from a private psychiatrist. I didn't have the money for that, so I decided that any attempt to change my sexuality would have to wait.

The only thing I liked about Harvard Law School was its location. It was good being back in a city again and both Cambridge and Boston had many attractions. The Boston Symphony Orchestra, like its counterpart in Chicago, offered student tickets for remarkably low prices at its Friday afternoon concerts, and once again I had the opportunity to hear top performers in music that I loved. Harvard brought in world-famous lecturers on every conceivable subject. The most memorable speech I heard that year was by Fidel Castro. Castro came to power in January 1959, and before his relations with the United States had totally deteriorated he went on a tour to present his case to the American people. Harvard was one of his stops. Interest was so high that the event had to be held in the football stadium, and there Fidel gave us all one of those long harangues for which he would later become famous in his own country.

There were also lots of good places to eat in the Boston area. I was pleased that Harvard did not force dormitory residents to buy a contract for meals, so I ate out every day. I couldn't afford fancy restaurants, but Cambridge offered a wonderful range of casual, affordable places—from the overstuffed sandwiches at Elsie's to the Jewish deli food at the Midget, where Oliver and Jenny went on their first date in Erich Segal's famous potboiler *Love Story*. Across the river in Boston there were plenty of cheap ethnic restaurants—Italian, Greek, Chinese—and for special occasions, terrific seafood at the Union Oyster House and thick slabs of roast beef at Durgin-Park.

The frustrations of the year were also relieved by occasional trips to New York to visit Michael A., and he came to Cambridge once or twice to see me. In the spring, I went with him to Florida for a week to stay at his family's vacation home in Vero Beach. By that time, I had received responses from my applications for graduate school and could begin to make plans for the following year. I was not admitted to Harvard. Wisconsin admitted me, but with limited financial aid. Yale admitted me and provided me with generous financial assistance. Les Fishel's personal recommendation to John Blum had obviously been very helpful. Without hesitation, I accepted Yale's offer. At the end of the term, I took my final exams at law school, on which the entire year's grades depended. Predictably, I flunked property. But I did well enough on my other exams to receive a notice saying "Admitted to the second year at Harvard Law School." I happily ignored that and prepared to move to New Haven.

When I enrolled at Yale in September 1959, it was the fifth college or university I had attended in five years—two Ivy League universities, a Big Ten university, a private liberal arts college, and a historically black college. It was a virtual Cook's Tour of American higher education. But now it was time for me to settle down—and I did. I was a student at Yale for the next five years, four of them in residence. I never developed a deep affection for the place, but I received a first-rate graduate education, and when I left I was well prepared for an academic career in history. I also made cherished friendships, some of which would last a lifetime.

Yale in 1959 was a university in transition. Yale College, its undergraduate arm, was still pretty much the rich boys' club that it had always been. There were a smattering of blacks and a few more Jews than there had been in earlier years, but there were no women and more than half the students were still the products of prep schools. An applicant whose father had been an "old blue" was likely to be admitted regardless of his own qualifications. When I arrived at Yale, I immediately noticed several strange windowless buildings scattered around campus that resembled mausoleums. These, I was told, were the secret societies, the most famous of which was Skull and Bones, whose members were selected in a bizarre ritual known as "Tapping Day." Fortunately, I had little to do with Yale College as graduate and undergraduate courses were completely separate. But it seemed to me like something from another era. The college would change radically a decade later, but by then I was gone.

The graduate and professional schools, however, had already begun to change. The law school included on its faculty several left-wing professors who had been targets of red-baiters earlier in the decade, and unlike Harvard it had developed a curriculum that approached the law as a social science and not just as a trade. The graduate school had admitted women for a number of years and was putting together an outstanding faculty. In several fields, it was already the best in the country. The history department would be the best in the country by the 1970s; it was not quite there yet in 1959, but it was well on

its way. The department had hired several outstanding young scholars in the decade before I arrived: my mentor, John Morton Blum,
in twentieth-century American history; Edmund Morgan in American
colonial history; Leonard Krieger in European intellectual history;
Robin Winks in the history of the British Commonwealth. It had just
hired the husband-and-wife team of Arthur Wright and Mary Wright,
which in one fell swoop put Yale on the map in Chinese history. But
there were still signs of an older ethos. Yale had just started hiring
Jews. Mary Wright was the first woman in a tenured position, and
although she was a scholar equal to her husband, she had the rank of
associate professor rather than full professor. Other than the Wrights,
there was no one in Asian or African history whereas there were too
many professors of English history. And there was still dead wood on
the faculty—men who had been hired at a time when gentility had
been more prized than productivity.

The courses I took my first year in graduate school reflected this
range in the Yale faculty. Blum's seminar in twentieth-century American history was everything I expected it to be. Although not yet forty,
Blum had already published significant books on Woodrow Wilson
and Theodore Roosevelt and was then deeply involved in New Deal
history as the editor of the Henry Morganthau diaries. He was sharp,
articulate, full of ideas, and somewhat brash. He had a wealth of
wonderful stories about both Teddy and Franklin Roosevelt and
their associates. Although his primary focus was political history, he
had a lively interest in social history as well. I developed much of
my conceptualization of twentieth-century American history in that
seminar—and from listening to Blum's undergraduate lectures when I
graded papers for him. Although I would later come up with ideas of
my own, I continued throughout my career to share many of Blum's
likes and dislikes, for example, his admiration for both Roosevelts and
his distaste for the self-righteousness of Woodrow Wilson.

I got a glimpse of the older Yale in Lewis Curtis's seminar in eigh-
teenth- and nineteenth-century English history. Curtis was certainly
well read in his subject and his course was a good introduction to the
literature of English history. But he had not published anything new
for many years and his interpretations were hardly cutting-edge. He
was the very epitome of Yale's genteel tradition. He lived in a facsimile
of an English manor house, complete with well-groomed grounds, just

on the edge of grimy New Haven. Probably the highlight of his seminar was the afternoon when he invited us all to his remarkable house for a proper English tea.

Both sides of Yale were on display in the third course I took that year—the Literature of American History, a course required of all first-year graduate students in American history that was taught by four members of the senior faculty. Each week there would be a lecture and then, later in the week, a discussion of the historiography of a particular topic in American history. It was an invaluable introduction to the various schools of historical interpretation and, later at Minnesota, several of us who had been students at Yale tried, without complete success, to replicate it. Three of the four teachers for the course were superb: Morgan in colonial history, Blum in the twentieth century, and David Potter, a distinguished historian of the South and the nineteenth-century sectional crisis; I would take Potter's seminar in my second year. The fourth was Samuel Flagg Bemis, who gave the lectures in the history of American foreign policy. A generation earlier, Bemis been a leading scholar in this field, but his ideas and approach were long out of date. Moreover, unlike Curtis, who was an amiable anachronism, Bemis held to his views belligerently and would tolerate no disagreement. He believed that the foreign policy of the United States had always been generous and altruistic and that every war the country had ever fought was totally justified—an approach that earned him the sobriquet "American Flagg Bemis." To make matters worse, Bemis refused to let any other faculty member venture into his field. Blum, for example, whose work on Teddy Roosevelt and Wilson gave him considerable expertise in American foreign policy, had to limit his courses to domestic history only. As graduate students, we had to work around Bemis and learn our own foreign policy history.

When I went to Yale and Blum agreed to be my adviser, I told him that I wanted to concentrate on African American history. He already knew that from Les Fishel, but he teased me a little by suggesting that all Oberlin students seemed to have that in their genes. He did suggest, however, that in my first year I try to write my papers in other areas of American social history in order to develop a broader perspective. Both his seminar and the Literature of American History course required major research papers. For Blum's seminar, I wrote a paper on the development of suburban life in the early twentieth century, linking the attraction of suburbia to ideas about the city held by Americans of the Progressive Era. And for the historiography course I did a study of Marcus Lee Hansen, the first major historian of immigration, showing how Hansen's approach to immigration was an outgrowth of Frederick Jackson Turner's famous frontier thesis. The following summer, when I visited Les Fishel in Madison, he suggested that I submit the Hansen paper to the *Wisconsin Magazine of History* for possible publication, since both Turner and Hansen had Wisconsin connections. I did so and it eventually became my first published article.

At every college I ever attended, I learned as much from my fellow students as I did from my professors. That was particularly true at Yale, where most, although not all, of my friends were also studying to be historians. While our conversations ran the usual gamut of topics, they were more focused than they had been when I was an undergraduate. We talked about books we had read, new historical interpretations, and, sometimes obsessively, what our dissertation topics would be. I made four particularly close friends in my first two years at Yale—and I am not using pseudonyms when I identify three of them as Smith and one as Jones. I first met Al Jones and Kent Smith in John Blum's seminar. Al was from Oregon; he had the fresh-faced looks of an all-American boy and was planning a career in American history. He and I became sounding boards for each other, testing out our developing ideas about the American past. Kent Smith had come to Yale to study Chinese history with the Wrights. He came from a middle-class family in New Jersey and had gone to Princeton as an undergraduate, where he had become temporarily infatuated with the Tory ideas of the Eastern elite. He soon got over that and by the time we roomed together during our third year at Yale, we had become political soul mates. He was also deeply religious in a way that I wasn't, but that proved to be a source not of conflict but of learning and exchanging ideas. Kent ultimately became an Episcopal priest. I met Don Smith later in my first year over lunch. He hailed from Tennessee and had just arrived at Yale from Oxford, where he had been a Rhodes scholar and was studying English history. Don and I shared two interests that soon cemented our friendship. We both loved politics, particularly the minutiae of state and local politics. And we were both devotees of classical music, although his tastes ran more toward opera than mine. I met Larry

Smith in my second year when he returned to Yale after a stint in the military. Larry was another American historian and like me was from Indiana—but he was much more of a small-town Hoosier than I was. He too was fascinated by politics and ultimately pursued a career as a high-level Washington aide rather than an academic.

I lived for two years in the Hall of Graduate Studies, a massive Gothic building with architecture as pretentious as its name. One wing of HGS housed classrooms and faculty offices; the other wing was a dormitory and dining hall for graduate students. The rooms were large, but sparsely furnished, and I got my first experience in interior decorating when I went downtown and bought chairs, lamps, and plants for my room—mostly at the Salvation Army. For the first time in my life, I had a private room and a private telephone line. Unlike the situation at Harvard, HGS residents were required to buy a meal contract, so I had to eat the generally unpalatable food served cafeteria-style in the dining hall. When I did eat out in New Haven, however, I realized that I wasn't missing much. Other than a few legendary pizzerias, the culinary scene was pretty grim.

New Haven was, in general, the worse thing about Yale. It was often referred to at the time as a fading industrial city, but even that description understated its bleakness. Other than the central Green, with its three traditional New England churches, and a few eighteenth-century houses, there was little left to suggest its colonial past. It was located on Long Island Sound, but to get any sense of a waterfront it was necessary to go outside the city itself. It had a large population of working-class Italian Americans, who were beginning to drift into the suburbs and were being replaced by African Americans and Hispanics. An impoverished black ghetto stretched out from the edge of the Yale campus. New Haven, at the time I lived there, was in the midst of an ambitious urban renewal program that ultimately failed. What it billed as "slum clearance" merely destroyed affordable housing and pushed poor people, mostly black, into even worse neighborhoods; and the housing was replaced with stores, hotels, and high-rise apartment buildings for which there was no market.

Downtown New Haven was adjacent to the Yale campus, but it held few attractions. The only place there that I frequented was the Shubert Theater, a venue for pre-Broadway tryouts of new plays and musicals. It was fun to see shows before the New York critics had their say and to guess which would be hits and which would be flops. I was almost invariably wrong. The New Haven Symphony allowed me to continue to hear live classical music; it played on campus and brought in distinguished soloists, but the orchestra itself was no match for the three great orchestras I had heard in previous years. The Lincoln Theatre, in a residential neighborhood not far from campus, showed the latest European art films, and I went there often to indulge in the cinema habit I had acquired at Oberlin. New York was a long seventy miles away on the rundown and unreliable New Haven Railroad— too far for casual visits. But Michael A. still welcomed me as a guest, and on holidays and long weekends, I visited him, went to the theater, ate good food, and enjoyed the city.

During five years in graduate school, I never went out with a woman, and I never felt the pressure to date that I had at Harvard Law School. A few of my friends, including Larry Smith, were married. Don Smith so resolutely suppressed his homosexuality that I didn't learn of it until years later. Al Jones and Kent Smith were straight and later married, but they rarely dated while in graduate school. There was something about the place that seemed to discourage romance and repress sexuality. I'm not sure what it was—perhaps the scarcity of eligible women or the continual pressure to write papers and study for oral exams—but sex was not even a frequent topic of general conversation. The only exception to this that I can recall was so bizarre as to help prove the general rule. A young woman who lived in New Haven went through the phone directory and started calling all the names she could find whose address was "Hall of Graduate Studies." Whoever answered she asked for a date, and those who agreed to meet her (I was not one of them) found her eager to hop in bed. One graduate student became so enamored of her (or of the sex) that he asked her to marry him; it took intervention by the Yale chaplain to prevent what would have been a real misalliance.

Still, I continued to be troubled by what I perceived to be my abnormal sexual desires and I was determined to follow up on the therapy I had begun the year before. I learned that the Yale Student Health Services, unlike its Harvard counterpart, would provide long-term mental health treatment for just a small co-pay. So, shortly after arriving at Yale I entered into therapy and continued it for over a year. I did not experience any of the horrors that some gay men of my generation have described; no one tried to give me shock treatments or aversive therapy or to institutionalize me. My therapist was kind and well meaning. But it was a big waste of time. I had read a lot of the traditional literature about the etiology of homosexuality and started telling my therapist stories about my childhood and my relationship with my mother. He steered me away from that and tried to get me to talk about what I felt at the present time. But what was there to say? I was attracted to men. He thought it was more complicated than that. After all, he pointed out, I was in my midtwenties and other than an unfulfilled incident with a hustler had not had sex with a man. He told me he doubted I was a homosexual. My problem, he said, was that I couldn't relate to other people emotionally, that I related to people on too intellectual a plane. If I could loosen up with people and let my barriers down, I would be able to relate to women and no longer think of myself as a homosexual. I did not find any of this particularly helpful and gradually started canceling appointments. Finally, we decided by mutual agreement to end the therapy. I never went to a psychiatrist again.

In February 1960, midway through my first year at Yale, the civil rights struggle entered a new phase with the first lunch counter sit-in at Woolworth's in Greensboro, North Carolina. For me and many of my friends at Yale, this was a galvanizing event. Up to this point, the civil rights effort had been dominated by NAACP lawyers, who won landmark court cases, and churchgoing Southern blacks, who were the core of the Montgomery bus boycott. Now the central figures were college students, young people like us, who were taking the fight for their future into their own hands. We wanted somehow to be involved, but we were miles away from the front lines and, furthermore, had committed ourselves, at least for the time being, to our studies rather than to social activism. Within a few weeks after Greensboro, a support group emerged on predominantly white campuses in the North called the Northern Student Movement. I immediately joined its Yale chapter and our first activity was to picket the Woolworth store in downtown New Haven. The New Haven Woolworth did not discriminate against black people, but the logic of our action was to put pressure on the Woolworth Company to insist that lunch counters in all its stores, south as well as north, be integrated.

By the late spring, the sit-ins had spread throughout the South and a new organization, the Student Nonviolent Coordinating Committee, emerged to coordinate the efforts. The Northern Student Movement continued to provide support and the following year a group of us from New Haven went to Cambridge, Maryland, to join local people in the picket lines. The eastern shore of Maryland was as close as the southern struggle got to New Haven and the only place that we could reach in a day, so it provided an opportunity to become directly involved. But gradually many of us began to realize that racial discrimination was not just a southern problem. There were issues for us at home to deal with and we needn't make forays into the South. In my second year at Yale, I joined the New Haven chapter of CORE— the Congress of Racial Equality—which confronted racism not in the South but in New Haven itself.

My involvement with New Haven CORE was the first time since I had been at Fisk that I worked closely with African American people. Its membership included a number of Yale students, but its leadership came mostly from the New Haven black community. The chair was a charismatic and slightly raffish young man named Blyden Jackson. Among its most active members was an African American law student from Washington, D.C., named Eleanor Holmes; later, as Eleanor Holmes Norton, she would become congressional representative for the District of Columbia. CORE took on several businesses that either did not hire or did not routinely promote black employees—most notably the local electric utility company. More controversially, we took on New Haven's city government and its much-vaunted urban renewal program, which we saw instead as a "Negro removal" program. Urban renewal at that time was generally seen as a liberal initiative, and New Haven's liberal white mayor, Richard Lee, was genuinely stung to see black people and their allies picketing city hall to protest his policies. It was the beginning of a breach between African Americans and white liberals that was to have profound consequences for the subsequent history of the civil rights movement.

As I entered my second year of course work at Yale, I was ready to plunge back into African American history. I had taken John Blum's advice and focused on urban and immigration history in the papers I wrote the first year. That approach had proved rewarding and later I would teach in both of those fields. But my renewed commitments to civil rights led me back to what had been my original interest when I entered graduate school. I took seminars in late-nineteenth-century American history and in southern history, and in both of those courses I wrote papers that would bear directly upon what ultimately became my doctoral dissertation.

The seminar in the Gilded Age was taught by William Miller, a man who was not a regular member of the Yale faculty or even an academic. He was a freelance historical writer who lived in the New Haven area and had written several well-reviewed books in late-nineteenth-century American history. Yale brought him in for a year as a visiting lecturer. His course was not especially memorable, but the paper I wrote for it brought me as close as I would ever come as a scholar to a eureka moment. I had begun to think that I would write my dissertation on black urban history, perhaps a study of a particular black urban community, and I decided to test out this idea for Mr. Miller's course with a paper on a black community during the period that we were studying. I picked Baltimore, primarily because it already had a well-developed black community by 1870 and because I could find material in the Yale library. When I submitted my first draft, Mr. Miller returned it with one brief, devastating question: "So what?" He was right. I had plenty of data, but the paper had no thesis. What was important about the activities of the Baltimore black community?

I was sitting despondently in the library one day shortly after that and came across a book review by August Meier, the young historian whom I had first heard of at Fisk. Meier took issue with the generally accepted view that the late nineteenth century had been the "nadir" of African American history. It was the "nadir," perhaps, in how white people treated blacks, but it was, he argued, a period of ferment and creativity within the black community. Suddenly, I had the thesis for my paper. The organizational ferment and leadership struggles within the Baltimore black community were important because they demonstrated the vitality of the African American community even in the wake of the devastating setbacks it had experienced with the collapse of Reconstruction and the rise of ideological racism. This in a sense reaffirmed what I had learned from my black classmates at Fisk. African American life was not just a series of passive reactions to white oppression. It was an ongoing effort to create a community in which black people could survive and even flourish. I rewrote my paper and Mr. Miller gave me an A. More important, I had found the context for my future work in African American history.

My seminar in southern history was taught by David Potter, one of the most respected members of the Yale faculty. Potter was as different from John Blum as two scholars could be. He worked slowly and deliberately. Although a decade older than Blum, he had not published as much, but what he had done was of exceptionally high quality. His seminar reflected this approach. He answered questions only after pausing to think them through, and everything he said was carefully considered. His political and social views defied categorization. He was a southerner who clearly dissented from southern racial orthodoxy, but he was also highly critical of the consumerism and glitz that had been brought on by northern capitalism—the America that had become, in the words of his best-known book, a "people of plenty." He was a beloved figure among the graduate students, many of whom found him a more thoughtful alternative to the more overtly brilliant Blum, and when we learned at the end of the year that he was about to leave Yale to take a position at Stanford, there was genuine sorrow. The paper I wrote for Professor Potter was a study of black migration out of the South in the World War I era. It introduced me to a wealth of material about the migration that I would later incorporate into my study of black Chicago. Its thesis complemented the theme of the Baltimore paper. Black migration was not just a response to changing economic conditions—to the coming of the boll weevil and the decline of cotton culture—as many contemporary observers supposed. It was a deliberate and positive strategy to escape the ever more oppressive system of Jim Crow, segregation, and lynching in the South—an instance of black people voting with their feet.

When I first spoke to Les Fishel at Oberlin about the possibility of doing graduate work in African American history, he told me that I would have to create my own curriculum. That was essentially what I did at Yale. Talented teachers like Blum and Potter were helpful in criticizing my work and training me in the rudiments of historical research. But no one at Yale claimed to be an expert in African American history, and I had to master the subject on my own. It would have been no different at any other graduate school at the time; African

American history as a recognized field of study was still just over the horizon. There were scholars working in the field, but they were not yet at major universities with graduate programs. So in addition to writing papers in African American history for my seminars at Yale, I set out on my own to meet African American historians at other institutions.

The best-known scholar of African American history in the early 1960s was John Hope Franklin, who a few years earlier had made nationwide news by becoming the first black department head at a predominantly white college, Brooklyn College. Franklin has always considered himself a historian of the American South rather than an African American historian, and his wide-ranging work has indeed gone well beyond the history of black Americans. But his best-known book, *From Slavery to Freedom,* was, and still is, the leading general survey of African American history, and his first book was a pioneering community study of free blacks in pre–Civil War North Carolina. Al Jones and I were discussing Franklin one day and we concluded that we should try to meet him. Al was not planning a dissertation in African American history, but he decided to take a year off from his studies to teach at a black college and he wanted Franklin's advice on where to go. I wrote to him and he graciously invited Al and me to come to Brooklyn. When we did, he spent several hours with us, took us to lunch, and discussed what he saw as the many opportunities for research in African American history. He also had suggestions for Al regarding his teaching plans. Professor Franklin would generously continue to give me advice and support as I proceeded with my career, even though we never had any formal institutional connection.

The other historian I wanted to meet was August Meier, who had not yet published a major book but whose articles and reviews had already begun to influence me. Meier was then teaching at Morgan State in Maryland, but he was doing much of his research on black leadership in the late nineteenth century at the Schomburg Library in Harlem. I arranged to meet him at the Schomburg and he, too, became a kind of long-distance mentor to me as my career developed. Over the next several years, I continued to arrange as many meetings of this sort as I could. When I was in Michigan City visiting my parents, I took a side trip to Butler University in Indianapolis to meet Emma Lou Thornbrough, who had just published a book on blacks in nineteenth-century

Indiana. When I learned of a graduate student at Columbia named Gilbert Osofsky, who was doing a community study of black Harlem, I arranged to meet with him. By taking these initiatives, I not only discovered what was happening in the field of African American history, I also made sure that the major players in the field knew who I was.

The final course I took at Yale in 1960–61 had nothing to do with African Americans, but it was nonetheless memorable. Roland Bainton's seminar on the Reformation was open to students in both the history department and the Yale Divinity School. Bainton was at that time nearing retirement; he had had a long and eminent career and had written dozens of books about the leading figures of the Reformation. His biography of Martin Luther was generally considered to be the best study of Luther in the English language. His approach to the Reformation was straightforward: the Reformation was about religion. He rejected the ideas that had been prevalent earlier in the century, namely, that the Reformation was really about the rise of the nation-state or the emergence of the middle class and that religious reform was really a cover for some political or economic agenda. The Reformers, he insisted, meant what they said. Religion in the sixteenth century was quite literally a life-and-death issue, and people were willing to die and go to war for their religious beliefs. Bainton worked us hard; we read not only the major works about the Reformers but the source material as well. We were even required to read at least one of Luther's sermons in the original German. I learned a great deal, and most important I learned to take religion seriously as a force in history. Bainton himself was a model of the serious religious thinker. An ordained minister, he had worked his way through several Protestant denominations and had ended up a member of the Society of Friends, a pacifist, and a vegetarian. He was a genuinely saintly man—but without even a whiff of self-righteousness. It was a great opportunity to have been able to study with him.

In 1960 I was old enough to vote for the first time in a presidential election. Early in the year I watched with some reservation the rise of John F. Kennedy's political fortunes. Like many liberals, I was disturbed by the influence of Kennedy's family, particularly his father, by his failure to firmly oppose Joseph McCarthy in the early 1950s, and by what I saw as his inadequate commitment to the cause of civil rights. My heart was really with Stevenson, but I realized that he was a two-time loser and probably couldn't win. When Kennedy was nominated, I became an enthusiastic supporter. The alternative, after all, was the most loathsome figure in American politics, Richard Nixon. While I followed the election closely and wrote a few letters to the editor, I was not actively involved. Whatever time I had beyond my studies I was devoting to civil rights work. And very few students in those days became involved in politics in university towns. It never occurred to me to even register to vote in New Haven; I voted by absentee ballot in Indiana. That would all change in the late 1960s with the rise of political activism among students, and when I became a politician in Minneapolis I urged students at the University of Minnesota to become involved in the politics of the community in which they lived—something I had never done myself.

I was excited by Kennedy's victory and by the idealistic rhetoric of his inaugural address, but I quickly became disillusioned with him. I remember sitting down for breakfast with Kent Smith the day of the Bay of Pigs invasion. I think that was when Kent finally realized that he was no longer a conservative. We looked at each other and quickly agreed that this was the most idiotic thing Kennedy could have done. Moreover, my litmus test was civil rights and in that area Kennedy was failing miserably. He had proposed no new civil rights legislation, had not issued the executive orders that he had promised to end discrimination in federal programs, and refused to identify personally with the movement. When the sit-ins were succeeded in the spring of 1961 by the freedom rides, the administration acted belatedly to protect the protesters and Attorney General Robert Kennedy called for a "cooling-off period." Many years later, when I taught the history of this period, I had difficulty persuading my students that the president most of them regarded as a hero had not looked particularly heroic at the time.

I was fortunate to have fellowships throughout my graduate school years and never had to resort to student loans that would need to be repaid after I began to work. The fellowships covered my tuition and left me with enough to live on, but there wasn't a lot to spare. I never had a car while I was a student and, more frustratingly, could not travel much. I looked on enviously when my brother, who was willing to take on more physically demanding and, hence, better-paying summer jobs than I was, went to Europe in the summer of 1959 with my friend Michael, while I stayed home. But I did begin to explore Mexico in 1960 and 1961. At the end of the summer of 1960, my brother and I borrowed the family car and drove through Mexico for a month. We traveled on a tight budget, stayed in some less than savory rooms and ate street food that inevitably made us sick. But we saw a lot of the country—from Mexico City and Acapulco to Oaxaca and the Tehauntepec Peninsula—and visited not only the usual tourist attractions but also small-town fiestas and markets where our passable Spanish served us well.

My parents had also been fascinated by Mexico after taking a tour a few years earlier, and my father had begun to talk about retiring there. He was particularly interested in a small fishing town on the west coast that was yet undeveloped but, he was told, had great natural beauty and was incredibly cheap. It was called Puerto Vallarta and was getting its first wave of publicity as the setting of a new film called *The Night of the Iguana*. He proposed that all four of us go there over Christmas in 1960. It was not yet possible to drive into Puerto Vallarta, so we drove to Guadalajara and flew the rest of the way. Those familiar with Vallarta as the glamorous Mexican resort it later became would not have recognized the Vallarta of 1960. There were four small, basic hotels along the harbor front and miles of totally undeveloped beach. It was possible, for a few pesos, to charter boats for fishing or exploring the unspoiled coastline, or to rent horses to ride up into the mountains behind the town. We all loved it so much that we returned the following year. And ten years later, after my father retired, my parents moved to Vallarta and lived there for five years.

Until this time, I had continued returning each summer to Michigan City and working at my dull but undemanding office job. But by 1961 I was ready to go somewhere else for the summer. I had preliminary exams coming up in the fall and did not want a job; I needed the time for studying. And I wanted an alternative to either New Haven or Michigan City. Michael A. told me that he was going to Europe for the summer and that I could stay in his apartment for free. I asked him if Al Jones could come with me and he readily agreed. So Al and I spent the summer in Michael's apartment at 112th and Riverside in Manhattan, near Columbia University. It was the only opportunity I ever had to live in New York.

I did get some studying done, but Al and I also managed to see parts of New York that we had never been able to get to during short visits. Our interests in African American life drew us to Harlem, where we spent one full day walking the streets, listening to the nationalist orators who held forth on the street corners, exploring the bookshops, and having lunch at a restaurant operated by Elijah Muhammad's Nation of Islam. We went to the Bronx Zoo and the United Nations and the Statue of Liberty—the kind of tourist spots we had previously avoided. And we walked for long distances to absorb the diversity of the city's neighborhoods. A few weeks after we arrived, Al heard from a friend whom he had met as an undergraduate at the University of Oregon—Greg Calvert. Greg was now a graduate student in European history at Cornell and would be sailing for France at the end of the summer to begin research for his dissertation. His wife had just left him and he was in no mood to remain in Ithaca alone for the summer. Could he stay with us in New York if he were willing to sleep on the couch? We agreed and Greg joined us in Michael's apartment.

Greg Calvert was an interesting addition to our household. First, he taught me how to cook. I knew how to make a few basic dishes, but I had up until that time lived in dormitories and never had a kitchen of my own. Now, in Michael's well-equipped kitchen, Greg and I began to experiment. He was far ahead of me, and with his guidance I began to cook the simpler French and Italian dishes that were to become the staples of my repertoire. Second, Greg forced me to think about what kind of balance I wanted to strike in my life between academics and activism. With the sit-ins, the freedom rides, and black voter registration drives throughout the South, the civil rights movement was escalating. I had dabbled in it at the edges, but was I doing enough? One day, a friend of Greg's from Cornell named Mendy Samstein came over to visit. Mendy was spending the summer in Harlem, teaching black children to swim, and he told us that he had decided to drop out of graduate school and go south for full-time civil rights work. Greg tried to discourage him; we could all be more helpful in the long run, Greg argued, if we finished our degrees and established ourselves and used our scholarship and teaching to advance the causes we believed in. Greg didn't persuade Mendy, but he did persuade me—at least for the time being.

In the end, both Greg and Mendy chose the activist life. Mendy went south and devoted the rest of his life to civil rights and black education. Greg went to Europe, as he had planned, and I saw him in Paris the following summer. He returned and taught for two years at Iowa State. But he never finished his PhD and in 1966 he left his job and went to work full-time for Students for a Democratic Society, soon becoming its national secretary. Greg led SDS through its fateful transition from a predominantly student group steeped in the idea of participatory democracy to what he hoped would be "the first serious American revolutionary organization in 175 years." I saw Greg some years later, long after the SDS dream was in shambles, in Austin, Texas, where he ultimately settled. My career had taken a different path from his—to a tenured academic job and into liberal, but not radical, politics. We did not question each other's decisions but talked fondly about that summer in New York. Not only had we both been troubled over how we would integrate activism into our lives, we had also been troubled over our sexuality. With the collapse of his marriage, Greg was first coming to terms with his homosexuality. In Paris, he became actively gay and when I met him in Austin he was in a long-term relationship with another man.

Al Jones chose yet a different way to act out his commitment to the civil rights movement. At the end of the summer, when Greg went to France and I returned to New Haven, Al went to Alabama to take a one-year teaching position at Tuskegee Institute, the school that had been made famous years before by Booker T. Washington. Later in the year, I visited Al at Tuskegee and admired the way he had settled into southern black life. He had made many friends on the faculty and had become directly involved in the successful campaign to end white efforts to gerrymander the black majority out of the town of Tuskegee so they could not participate in municipal affairs. Unlike Greg, Al returned to Yale, finished his PhD, and later became my colleague in the history department at Minnesota.

The major item on my agenda in the fall of 1961 was to take my PhD preliminary examinations. Yale had a more streamlined doctoral program than many universities. After two years of course work, students took an oral preliminary exam and then wrote a dissertation. There was no written preliminary exam, nor was there an oral "defense" of the dissertation. This made it possible to get a PhD in four or five years, rather than the long-drawn-out process often found elsewhere. The oral prelim was a two-hour exam, and I was responsible for the whole of American history plus two outside fields of my choice—in my case eighteenth- and nineteenth-century English history and Reformation history. I was most worried about early American history, as I had taken no courses in this area, and I had spent much of my time over the summer reading in colonial and early-nineteenth-century history. My examiners were Professors Blum, Morgan, Curtis, and Bainton, and inevitably during the exam I thought I was doing very poorly. But when it was over and after they had deliberated, Blum told me that I had passed with distinction. I was now ready to proceed with my doctoral dissertation.

I have never been a model of self-discipline and after the prelims I spent several months not doing much of anything before I seriously got to work on the dissertation. I was living that year in a rather cramped basement apartment in an Italian neighborhood some distance from campus, which I shared with Kent Smith. The kitchen had virtually no work space, but it had the basics and I used it to hone the cooking skills that I had begun to acquire the previous summer. Kent had little interest in cooking, so he left it up to me and was glad to eat whatever I whipped up. I had my share of disasters: soufflés that didn't rise, casseroles that I dropped on the floor, desserts that didn't gel. But by the end of the year, I was turning out some decent meals and we had begun to invite people over for small dinner parties. I came to realize that I really enjoyed cooking, and I especially liked the compliments I got when I served guests something they thought was delicious. It would become a lifetime hobby.

With my exams over, I also made more frequent trips to New York. My brother had now graduated from the University of Chicago and had begun graduate work in art history at Princeton. So we met in New York from time to time, where Michael was happy to host both of us. One occasion was particularly memorable. My mother had gone to Pennsylvania on a business trip with my father. Richard and I suggested that she come to New York for a couple of days, while my father was tied up, and we would show her the town. She had never been to New York before and was excited by the prospect. We picked her up at Pennsylvania Station, took her to her hotel, and then, joined by Michael, we all went to have drinks at the Rainbow Room at Rockefeller Center with its spectacular views over the city. This was followed by dinner at a nice French restaurant and a Broadway musical. My mother was thrilled; she told my father that she had felt like a "queen for a day." She concluded, I think, that despite whatever tribulations she had had in raising her boys, it had come out pretty well. Both of her sons were now pursuing advanced degrees at prestigious Ivy League schools and they were still thoughtful enough to care about her. She would still have a few rough days ahead, but the worst was over.

By the middle of the academic year, I had narrowed down my choice of dissertation topics. I decided to focus on the development of a black community in a northern city in the years immediately before and after the World War I migration, looking at how the migration affected white attitudes toward blacks and the internal structure of the black community itself. This was a topic that flowed directly out of the two papers I had written in my second-year seminars. What remained was to choose a city. Although I had done some work on Baltimore, I did not want to study an older eastern city. I wanted to look at a city that came of age in the late nineteenth century and had no roots in the slavery era. I finally got it down to Chicago and Detroit. When I went back to Michigan City for winter break, I went to both cities to look for material. Chicago had more complete files of black newspapers, while Detroit had some remarkable collections of black organizational records. Either city could be done. But my heart was in Chicago. I knew the city better and had more affection for it. I went back to New Haven and wrote my dissertation proposal. The original plan was to study the black community in Chicago from 1900 to the eve of World War II. That chronology would ultimately be modified when I got into the material and found out how much there was. I submitted my proposal to Professor Blum, who readily accepted it. At his suggestion, I applied for a research grant from the Social Science Research Council for the following year to do my research in Chicago. By spring, I learned that I had received the grant.

During the 1961–62 academic year, I also worked as an assistant for John Blum's undergraduate lecture course on twentieth-century American history. Grading papers—either then or later on in my career—has never been one of my favorite activities. But sitting in on Professor Blum's lectures was eye-opening. He was a marvelous lecturer, and although I never became as skilled as he was, he was always a kind of model for me when I developed my own lectures at Minnesota. He was never afraid to ham it up; his impersonation of Teddy Roosevelt was legendary on campus. At the same time, he didn't just pander. His lectures were in the end analytical and always had a serious purpose.

By June I was ready to begin my research for the dissertation. With the stipend provided by the SSRC, I could have gotten a small apartment in Chicago. But instead, I decided to live with my parents for the year in Michigan City and commute into Chicago every day on the train. Other than summers, I had not lived with my parents for eight years, and I knew that it would not be a perfect arrangement. But I would live in a comfortable house, eat my mother's meals, sleep in my old room, and, most important, save a lot of money. With the money I saved, I could do what I had been dreaming of for years—go to Europe. So I went back to Michigan City, established myself at my parents' house, located the major research sources in Chicago, and then, in August, took off to Europe for six weeks.

I started out in the Netherlands and Germany and then met my brother in Venice. He was traveling with a friend from Princeton who had bought a Volkswagen in Europe and the three of us then drove through Yugoslavia for a week, which was perhaps the highlight of the trip. Yugoslavia had not yet developed much of a tourist infrastructure and accommodations and roads were relatively primitive. But we really saw a slice of Eastern European life in a country that was Communist but not Soviet dominated. Then we came back to Italy and drove through France to Paris. French food was a revelation. We were traveling on a student budget and didn't eat in the kinds of restaurants I would frequent in later years, but even in the more modest places I realized that the French approached food more seriously than I had ever thought possible. In Paris, I saw Greg Calvert, who seemed far different than he had been the year before in New York; no longer a working-class kid from the Northwest, he had taken on the affectations of a French intellectual. I also saw Larry Smith and his wife, who were vacationing in Paris; Larry was still the Hoosier boy who would eat nothing but steak and fries, which were fortunately available at any Parisian bistro. Finally, I went on to London before returning home. It was the first of many trips to Europe, and while others would be far more luxurious it was perhaps the most memorable.

Back in the States by mid-September, I began seriously researching the dissertation. Every morning I took the South Shore railroad, the little electric line that runs from downtown Michigan City into Chicago in just a little over an hour. My basic materials were in a number of different places: the Chicago Public Library in the Loop, the Chicago Historical Society on the Near North Side, the offices of the *Chicago Defender* just south of the Loop, and the University of Chicago Library on the South Side. I also found a remarkable collection of notes for a study never written that had been compiled by employees of the Works Progress Administration in the 1930s and deposited in a branch of the Chicago Public Library in the heart of the South Side black community. I supplemented the written record with interviews of my own with old-timers who could remember events in early-twentieth-century Chicago. I spent several days at the apartment of Alfreda Barnett Duster, whose mother, Ida Wells-Barnett, was the legendary antilynching crusader who had been driven out of Memphis in the 1890s and settled in Chicago. Mrs. Duster shared with me diaries and family papers that had been left to her by her mother—and each day I was in her home she even served me lunch. This kind of hospitality was typical. Later in the decade, as the Black Power and Black Nationalist movements developed, I did experience distrust from people who questioned my ability as a white person to understand African American life. But this never happened at the time I was doing my research in 1962 and 1963.

Research techniques were pretty basic in those days before computers and copying machines. I made notes on index cards and stored them in file boxes. As the stacks of file boxes grew, certain themes began to emerge. For one thing, the time frame began to shift backward. I had originally thought I would start with a brief introduction on the small premigration community, discuss the great World War I migration, and then devote the bulk of the study to the development of the community in the wake of the migration. But I soon found that there already was a fully developed, complex black community in Chicago before World War I, and I decided to focus on its development, ending rather than beginning with the impact of the migration.

Second, the theme of community building, which I had looked at in my earlier papers, became central to the dissertation. Racial segregation was tightening in the North as well as the South at the turn of the twentieth century, and African Americans reacted by turning to their own resources; developing their own religious, economic, and civic institutions; and trying to become more self-sufficient. And finally, borrowing again from August Meier, I found that the famous division between the more accommodating followers of Booker T. Washington and the militants who looked for leadership to W. E. B. Du Bois had social as well as ideological roots. The Washingtonians represented a new middle class with a base primarily in the emerging black community; Du Bois's followers came from an older, better-educated professional class who still clung to the integrationist dream of the Reconstruction era.

The work kept me busy every day in Chicago, but evenings in Michigan City were dull. I had no friends there anymore, my brother was in Princeton, and my parents and I began to get on each other's nerves. Finally I found something useful to do. Michigan City had a substantial black community. When I was growing up, I had very little to do with it. Black people were residentially segregated, confined to mostly unskilled jobs, and had their own social world. In junior high and high school, I had black classmates but no close black friends. One day, on the train going into Chicago, I sat next to one of my black high school classmates. He asked me what I was doing and when I told him he was flabbergasted. At first he thought he had misunderstood me; he could barely conceive of a white man working full time studying the black community. I asked him about black organizations in Michigan City and he told me where and when the local chapter of the NAACP met. I started attending and was soon appointed the chair of the education committee. My job was to monitor the Michigan City school board to look out for the interests of the black community. The board met in the evening, so I was able to attend the meetings and I began raising embarrassing questions about de facto segregation. Michigan City had only one junior high and one high school, so they were necessarily integrated, but the elementary schools were neighborhood based and virtually all African American children went to the same school. I wanted to know if there was any plan to integrate the elementary schools. There wasn't; nor was this something the board wanted to discuss. Later in the year, the president of the NAACP, the minister of a local African Methodist Episcopal church, ran for the city council, raising some of these same questions about segregation in the city. I worked actively on his campaign, which, not surprisingly, was unsuccessful.

When my name started appearing in the *Michigan City News Dispatch* as a "white leader of the NAACP," my parents were not pleased. Once more they had to explain to their friends what their crazy son was up to. One episode I found particularly revealing of the gap between white and black in a place like Michigan City. My mother's closest friend was a woman named Devera, and for years I had heard my mother speak of Devera's beloved black maid—a woman whom she always referred to as Devera's Geneva. Devera was one of the people who gave my mother a hard time over my activities with the NAACP. Then one day I started talking to my mother about an NAACP leader whom I knew only as Mrs. Watson; after a few minutes something dawned on my mother. "Oh my God," she said. "That's Devera's Geneva. She should only know!"

Another episode that year was far more hurtful to my mother, and it is one I have always regretted. The fall of 1962 ushered in yet another phase in the civil rights struggle with the confrontation at Ole Miss over James Meredith's attempt to enroll and the clash between President John F. Kennedy and Governor Ross Barnett. Kennedy was still not acting decisively enough on this issue to satisfy me, but at least his hand had finally been forced and he had come down on the side of justice. Shortly after that, my mother had her family over to the house for Thanksgiving dinner. The Meredith affair was the center of conversation. My mother's only sister, Cele, and her husband, George, lived in Gary, twenty-five miles away, which was at that time changing from a predominantly white, working-class ethnic city to a predominantly black city. Cele and George lived in what was still a middle-class white neighborhood, but they saw themselves as threatened and had nothing kind to say about black people. I found my ire rising and then Cele finally set me off when she said, "Why does Meredith have to go where he isn't wanted? Why can't those people stay in their own place?" I blew up and wrecked the dinner party. I called Cele a racist and told her I never wanted to see her again. My mother was humiliated. Cele of course *was* a racist, but I should have had better self-control in dealing with my mother's sister in my mother's house, and the next day I was ashamed of myself. I called Cele and apologized, but she refused to accept my apology. I did not see her again until my mother's funeral almost twenty years later.

One of the perils of historical research is to become hopelessly bogged down in the sheer quantity of the material. At some point, the researcher has to say, "OK, I have enough now; there is probably more, but I can never find everything. It is time to stop, make sense of what I have, and start writing." By the spring of 1963, I had reached that point. I had decided that I would focus on the pre–World War I period and the Great Migration and end in 1920, leaving the 1920s and 1930s for another project or, more likely, another historian. I would return east, tie up a few loose ends at the Library of Congress, and then begin writing. I moved back to New Haven in June. My friend Don Smith alerted me to an apartment just off campus that he was leaving. I lived there for the next year, sharing the apartment with two other graduate students, one in math and one in American studies. It was the upper floor of an old house—somewhat shabby but much roomier and better located than the apartment I had shared with Kent Smith. And its big kitchen gave me the opportunity to improve my cooking skills.

The last remaining piece of research I needed to do was in the Booker T. Washington papers at the Library of Congress. Al Jones, who had now returned to New Haven and had just passed his preliminary exams, also had some work to do in the D.C. area and he had a friend in Baltimore with a vacant apartment we could live in for several weeks. The apartment was spectacularly located in the historic heart of Baltimore, but it was infested with cockroaches. Still, I was able to make the short drive into Washington every day to work on the Booker T. Washington papers, which were the treasure I expected them to be. A vast collection that touched on every aspect of African American life in the late nineteenth and early twentieth centuries, the papers helped answer questions I still had about leadership struggles in Chicago. I also took some time out for contemporary history. After the confrontation in Birmingham in May 1963, in which the police used dogs and high-pressure fire hoses on peaceful demonstrators, many of them teenagers, President Kennedy had finally identified himself fully with the civil rights movement. He had proposed a civil rights bill that, among other things, would ban discrimination in all facilities engaged in interstate commerce. Hearings had begun before the Senate Commerce Committee, and on several mornings I headed to Capitol Hill instead of the Library of Congress to sit in on the hearings.

During the summer of 1963, the major civil rights groups began making plans for a massive March on Washington at the end of the summer to mobilize support for Kennedy's civil rights bill. There was serious doubt as to whether the bill could pass the Senate, where it took a two-thirds vote to forestall a filibuster. And Kennedy, for his part, doubted that a march would help—particularly if it was predominantly black and had a militant edge to it. Bayard Rustin, the brilliant organizer who put the march together, was determined that it would be broad-based and interracial and that nothing would be said or done to undermine Kennedy's agenda. I was back in New Haven by that time, but I knew I would return to Washington to participate in the march. My cousin, Norman, Roz and Lester's son, now sixteen, had come to New Haven to visit me ,and when he arrived I asked him if he wanted to go on the march. He was thrilled by the prospect (although I doubt his parents were). He has told me many times since that attending that march was one of the highlights of his life. Don Smith had a friend who was driving to Washington, and the four of us went down the day before the march.

When we arrived on the Mall on the morning of August 28, 1963, it did not at first appear that the crowd would be large. Then they started coming. What was most impressive was not just the numbers but the diversity. The crowd was truly interracial, about half white and half black, with contingencies from churches and labor unions and civic groups—all ages, representing all parts of the country. The mood was serious and determined, but not bitter or angry. After we had marched to the Lincoln Memorial and the speeches began, they too were passionate but self-controlled. We later found out that only after delicate negotiations were some of the speakers persuaded to drop some of their more incendiary lines. I have only one regret about that memorable occasion. It was a very hot August day in Washington and after several hours standing in the blazing sun, I suggested to Norman that we take a break and go to an air-conditioned snack bar just off the Mall for a cold drink. When we returned, we asked someone what we had missed. "Oh," we were told, "you missed Martin Luther King's speech. It was about his dream. It was a good speech."

Writing the dissertation went more slowly than I thought it would. I remember one day when one of my roommates walked into my room near the end of the day and looked over my shoulder at the typewriter to see what I had done that day. There, exposed to the world, were three words: "Chicago was a . . ." "Is that it?" he asked. "That's it," I said. It was harder to put it all together than it was to collect the data. Besides, I was easily distracted. During the summer, there were excursions to the beach. In the fall and winter, there were trips to New York, or people to invite over for dinner. But gradually, I began to grind out a few chapters. My adviser, John Blum, was not in residence that year. He had gone to England to take the prestigious position of Pitt Professor of American History at Cambridge University. I had two choices for an adviser to fill in for Blum. When David Potter had left Yale, he was replaced in southern history by C. Vann Woodward, the preeminent historian in the field and the leading authority on the rise of the Jim Crow system. But Woodward did not approach African American history in the way that I did; he looked at it from the outside in rather than from the inside out. So instead I chose Robin Winks. On first glance, Professor Winks was a strange choice, as he was not even an American historian, but a historian of the British Common-wealth. He had, however, recently published a book titled *The Blacks in Canada,* which I very much admired and which was much closer in spirit to what I was doing than Woodward's work. Winks proved to be an excellent adviser; he was a man of enormously broad tastes and knowledge who could converse intelligently about almost anything.

On the afternoon of November 22, 1963, I had just walked into the Yale Library when I noticed a group of students clustered around the main circulation desk listening to a small radio. I walked over and asked someone what was going on. "President Kennedy has been shot," I was told. I rushed back to the apartment, where my roommates and a few other friends were already gathered around the television set and one of them said as I walked in, "He's dead." We hardly moved away from that television the rest of the weekend. I was never a full-fledged Kennedy admirer. I had come to like him better in the last six months of his administration after Birmingham and his support for the civil rights movement. But I thought it was too little too late and I always thought he was too much of a cold warrior (Vietnam was already beginning to worry me). Still the assassination was a shock—and it was compounded late Sunday morning when the entire nation watched Jack Ruby murder Lee Harvey Oswald live on network television. When Don Smith came over to join us, the discussion turned political. What was the implication of all of this for the Democrats? It was not clear in November 1963 how Lyndon Johnson would handle the succession or that he would become an unbeatable presidential candidate in 1964 or that he would become a more committed civil rights leader than Kennedy had ever been.

Sometime that winter, Professor Winks told me that beginning with the 1964–65 academic year, I could stay on at Yale as a member of the junior faculty. The term "junior faculty" had a different meaning at Yale than it did at most universities. Elsewhere, it meant faculty members who had not yet received tenure; at Yale it meant faculty members who would never receive tenure. Yale made a sharp division between its junior and senior faculty. Junior faculty taught undergraduate classes only and did not participate in the governance of the department. It was assumed that after a few years at Yale, junior faculty members would move on and get a job at another institution. In my experience at Yale, only one junior faculty member was ever promoted to a tenured position—Jonathan Spence, who eventually became a leading scholar in Chinese history. Senior faculty members were established scholars brought in at substantial salaries from other universities: John Blum from MIT, Edmund Morgan from Brown, C. Vann Woodward from Johns Hopkins, Arthur Wright and Mary Wright from Stanford. Yale, in a sense, used the rest of academia as its farm system; it waited to see who proved himself elsewhere, then bought whomever it wanted. The only other university with the prestige and resources to get by with that approach was Harvard.

To be offered a junior faculty position at Yale, therefore, was a mixed blessing. It provided a few extra years to look for a job and a chance to get some teaching experience. But it was like a way station between being a graduate student and being a full-fledged faculty member, akin perhaps to a residency in medical education. And it meant staying in New Haven. For some of my Yale colleagues that was a plus. During my time living in Cambridge and New Haven, I became convinced that the Northeast was the most provincial part of the United States. Many of my fellow graduate students absolutely shuddered at the prospect of living anywhere west of the Alleghenies, and they competed fiercely for jobs at second-rate colleges in rundown New England mill towns while refusing even to consider positions in Madison or Ann Arbor. As far as I was concerned, I would be perfectly happy to leave the East and particularly New Haven. The Yale position was a welcome backup, and since my dissertation was not completed I did not actively pursue a job in the academic marketplace. But if something attractive came along, I would certainly consider it.

My generation of academics was unusually fortunate. In the 1950s the job market had been tight. When I first asked one of my history professors at Oberlin about pursuing a PhD in history, he warned me that college jobs were scarce and that I might end up teaching high school at least for a while. My mentor, Les Fishel, had been forced to take an administrative position at Oberlin. Later, the job market would be tight again. Beginning with the 1970s, when I was teaching at the University of Minnesota, we struggled each year to find academic jobs for our PhD students and there were always some who had to take other kinds of work. By then, most graduate programs had begun to cut the number of students they would admit because it seemed unfair to train more students than they could place. The image of the PhD driving a taxi may have been a stereotype, but it did have a basis in reality. But for a brief time in the 1960s, as I was finishing my PhD, jobs were abundant. The first wave of baby boomers was just turning eighteen and colleges and universities were preparing for them by expanding their facilities. New campuses were going up, particularly in underserved urban areas, and existing campuses were growing. And all of these new facilities had to be staffed, mostly with newly minted PhDs.

In late February, Professor Winks asked me to come to see him. When I arrived at his office, he showed me a letter that the department had received from Professor Harold Deutsch, chairman of the history department at the University of Minnesota. Professor Deutsch said that his department had been authorized to hire an American historian and would consider someone about to complete the PhD in any field of American history that complemented the department's current strengths. He would welcome a recommendation from Yale. Professor Winks said that Yale was prepared to recommend me if I were interested. He then started to persuade me that I should consider it, that Minnesota was one of the best schools in the Big Ten, that the Big Ten was really a strong group of institutions, and so on. Apparently he assumed that any Yale graduate student would need to be convinced to give up a junior faculty position in cultivated New Haven for the arctic wilds of Minnesota. I told him that I needed no persuasion, that I would be honored if Yale recommended me, and that I would carefully consider an offer from Minnesota if I received one.

John Blum soon weighed in from England with a long letter outlining the pluses and minuses of leaving Yale for Minnesota. He advised me to take the Minnesota job only if "(a) you will be teaching in the areas of your interest; (b) you will have time—in terms of teaching load and of leave schedules—for your continuing scholarship during the coming five years; and (c) there is a clear future ahead if you earn it." Those considerations, he said, "weigh more than do rank and salary." He also pointed out the advantages of staying at Yale, but recognized that "Yale cannot point to an open road ahead, as Minnesota may be able to." "Remaining at Yale," he concluded, "involves large benefits for a period that will probably be terminal." When I spoke to Professor Blum later on the telephone, he had one further remark about Minnesota: "It's damn cold out there."

A few days later, I received a call from Harold Deutsch inviting me to come to Minnesota for a job interview. In early March 1964, I went for the first time to the state that would be my home for the rest of my life.

4

BECOMING A MINNESOTAN, 1964–1967

John Blum was right. When I stepped off the plane at Minneapolis–
St. Paul International Airport on March 5, 1964, it was "damn cold."
But the welcome was warm. I was met at the airport by a young
faculty couple, Bob and Gene Berkhofer, who took me to their house
for wine and cheese and conversation. I was immediately struck by
the difference in Bob Berkhofer's position as a junior faculty member
at Minnesota and the junior faculty I knew at Yale. Bob was thirty-
two years old, still a year or two away from tenure, but he advised
and taught graduate students, was fully involved in the affairs of the
department, and, with the security that came with the almost certain
prospect of tenure, had bought a beautiful house overlooking the Mississippi River. His wife, Gene, was a graduate student whom he had
met at Minnesota. They were both very chatty and they gave me a
rundown on the faculty and what they would be looking for in the
interview sessions the next day. One theme came through everything
they said: the department considered itself on trial as much as I did. In
the seller's market of the 1960s, Minnesota had been having trouble
landing the job candidates it really wanted and it didn't want to lose
me. While we talked mostly about my upcoming interview, the conversation also wandered into politics. I remember one thing they told me
that night: "If you come to Minnesota, within a few months you will
know Hubert Humphrey and Gene McCarthy. Politics are very casual
here; everyone knows everyone else." That, too, was very different
from New Haven, where I had never even met my alderman.

The next day I made my way to the history department's new quarters on the West Bank campus. The department had, quite unwillingly,
been forced to leave the comfortable offices that it had occupied for
many years in Ford Hall on the old East Bank campus to be among
the first occupants of the new campus the university was building on
the west bank of the Mississippi River. The West Bank campus was
at this point little more than a construction site. Only three buildings
were occupied—two office towers and one classroom building—and
they were of no architectural merit. Most classes were still held across

the river, which involved a long and, in the winter, cold walk. All of the support services—library, bookstore, food facilities—were still on the East Bank. The administration promised that within a few years a new library would be built on the West Bank, there would be a heated, covered bridge linking the two campuses, and services on the new campus would be comparable to those existing on the old. Most of those things did happen, although the heating on the covered bridge never worked, but it took time. I remember being somewhat taken aback on the day of my interview by the primitive conditions. There was no place to even take me to lunch. Faculty members who wanted to meet me brought brown bags to a bleak conference room, and I was provided with a box lunch.

Otherwise, the interview went well. I was introduced to the chairman and the other faculty members, taken across the river to meet the dean of the College of Liberal Arts, and given a library tour, and in the late afternoon I gave a talk on my research to interested faculty and graduate students. Since the vacant position was broadly defined, there was considerable discussion after my talk about what I might teach. It was understood that I would help with the basic lower-division survey courses, but I would also offer one upper-division course in a specialized area of American history. I suggested African American history (or Negro history as it was then called), but that was still seen as a little narrow. I then mentioned that I had also done some work and had, in fact, published an article in immigration history. There was great interest in that as Minnesota had just launched an immigration history archive (which I had visited during my library tour), but did not yet have a specialist in the field. We then talked about the possibility of combining African American and immigration history into a single course, which is what I ultimately did. It was also made clear to me that John Blum's other two conditions would be met. I was being considered for a tenure-track position, and assuming I published within a few years, I would receive tenure. The Berkhofers described department policy to me less reverently: there is a one book/two book rule, they said—one book for associate professor with tenure, two books for full professor. That turned out to be generally accurate. And finally, the department would do everything possible to provide me with the time I needed to ready my dissertation for publication and begin a second project.

In the evening, I was taken for dinner at the home of Clarke Chambers and his wife, Florence. In later years, when it finally became clear that faculty wives had lives of their own, we took job candidates to restaurants for dinner. But in 1964, it was still assumed that it was the job of a faculty wife to prepare dinner for a visiting candidate whom she had never met as well as four or five of her husband's colleagues. Florence Chambers graciously hosted us and served a delicious shrimp Creole. One episode that night signaled to me how the interview had gone. The conversation had turned to academic novels and Clarke asked me if I had read C. P. Snow's *The Masters*. I said that I had not. "Oh, you must," he said. "It is the best academic novel ever written. I'll loan you my copy." "Fine," I replied. "When I finish it, I will mail it back to you." "That won't be necessary," he said. "You can just give it to me when you arrive in September."

I was prepared to accept an offer, although two incidents gave me pause. The first occurred at lunch. A prim little man in a three-piece suit introduced himself to me as David Harris Willson, professor of English history. I later learned that Professor Willson was a specialist in the Tudor-Stuart period and had written a biography of King James I that in the course of five or six hundred pages never even mentioned the rather salient fact that the king was a homosexual. I was also to learn that Professor Willson came from a prominent Pennsylvania family—the Harris in his name was that of the family that had founded Harrisburg. Professor Willson asked me the day of my interview what kind of research I did. I told him that I was writing a dissertation in "Negro history." "Oh, the Negroes," he replied. "Well, they certainly have ruined Philadelphia." At that point, I caught a glimpse out of the corner of my eye of Professor David Noble, the department's American intellectual historian. Professor Noble had a bad back and was forced to lie flat on the floor. At Willson's remark, Noble started visibly writhing in embarrassment. It was as though he was saying to himself, "Oh my God, we've probably lost another one."

The second incident occurred on my final morning, before I returned to New Haven. Professor Hyman Berman and his wife, Betty, had invited me to their house for breakfast. In the course of the conversation, I sensed from things that they said that Hy and Betty did not realize that I was Jewish. So I said that I was, and indeed they hadn't known—my name is not as recognizably Jewish as theirs. What

Hy said next, however, disturbed me: "Don't tell anybody else until after you get the job." I asked him why; would it actually make a difference? He said that he wasn't sure, that it probably wouldn't, but that it was better to be safe. He then gave me a little history lesson. When Hy had been a graduate student at Columbia in the mid-1950s, his adviser had told him that he should forget about getting a job at Minnesota because the history department, under the influence of a man named A. L. Burt, did not hire Jews. Burt retired and things began to change. When Hy came to Minnesota in 1961, he was the third Jewish member of the department. But he said that there were still people around who didn't want too many Jews to be hired, who wanted to maintain an informal quota. If that was true—and I never saw any evidence of it after I joined the department—that group certainly failed to achieve its goals. Following me, at least half of the next dozen or so appointments were Jews.

A week or two after returning to New Haven, Professor Deutsch called to tell me that I would be receiving a formal offer in the mail. I would be appointed as a lecturer until I completed my Ph.D. and then my rank would automatically become assistant professor. My annual salary would be seven thousand dollars, the going rate at the time. Given the difficulty Minnesota had been having in hiring that year, I probably could have bargained the salary up, but that was not my style and I didn't do it. I accepted the offer. Soon I began receiving letters from the people I had met during the job interview welcoming me as a new colleague. I particularly appreciated hearing from the Berkhofers, who put me on the trail of an apartment. Their friend, Frank Sorauf, a political scientist who had a sabbatical coming up, wanted to sublet his apartment for a year. They told me that it was well located, nicely furnished, and fully equipped, so I could move right in without any hassle and have a year to look around for my own place. I took it without hesitation. Now all I had to do was finish my dissertation. There was no possibility of completing it in time to get my degree at Yale's commencement in June of 1964. But if I could finish it before going to Minnesota in September and drop it off before leaving New Haven, I could start my new job without it weighing on my mind. Yale had commencement only once a year and I would have to wait until June of 1965 to get the degree, but that would be just a formality. So I determined to buckle down over the spring and summer and get it done.

I did some work in New Haven during the spring, but I came to realize that if I was going to meet my goal, I would need a quieter setting with fewer distractions. After five years at Yale, I knew a lot of people and there was always someone coming by the apartment to visit or to invite me to go somewhere. And I did not have enough self-discipline to say no. Meanwhile, Larry Smith had accepted a position at Dartmouth; it was ironic that the most midwestern of my friends got the Ivy League job that the easterners had most coveted. The job didn't begin until September, but Larry, who by this time was divorced, told me that he was going to New Hampshire for the summer to get oriented and that he had sublet a house from a history faculty member who was on sabbatical. If I wanted to share it with him, there would be plenty of room. I decided that I was likely to get more work done in Hanover, New Hampshire, where I knew nobody, than I would in New Haven. Besides, northern New England is a lovely place to spend a summer.

Before leaving for New Hampshire, I bought a car. I had never owned a car before; my father had always taught me not to buy anything unless I knew exactly how I was going to pay for it and I generally took that advice. But now that I had a job, I could afford a car. My father recommended a Rambler as the best of the economy cars and he arranged for me to buy it from the dealer in Michigan City where he could get a good price. My brother drove it out to New Haven; I loaded in my books and notes, and headed to New Hampshire. The car added to my enjoyment of the summer. While I did work every day on the dissertation, I was able to take breaks and enjoy the beautiful countryside. On many afternoons, I went for a swim at a little pond just outside Hanover. I drove across the river into Vermont to see some of the postcard-pretty New England villages. And when my work was almost done, I took a few days off and went across the border to Montreal and Quebec City. I found Montreal an exciting and vibrant city, but Quebec City struck me as a Disney version of a French town—and I was disappointed that rural Quebec looked nothing like France.

Larry Smith proved to be a perfect companion. He respected my need for work time and didn't interrupt me when I needed to be left alone. Since I knew no one else in Hanover, that forced me to stick to my writing. Larry probably should have been as disciplined with his own work. He was not nearly as far along with his dissertation as I was and, ultimately, he never finished it and had to leave Dartmouth. But he had made good political contacts while he was there and went to Washington to become chief of staff for New Hampshire senator Tom McIntyre. Politics was not far from our consciousness that summer of 1964 in Hanover either. I had my usual pangs of guilt over the decisions I had made about my life as I watched the tragedy of the three civil rights workers unfold in Philadelphia, Mississippi. And as Larry and I watched the Democratic National Convention in Atlantic City, I realized for the first time that the civil rights movement was beginning to evolve in directions that I could no longer follow. The drama of that convention was not the inevitable nomination of Lyndon Johnson but rather the controversy over the seating of the Mississippi delegation. The predominantly black Freedom Democrats challenged the regular Democrats who had come to Atlantic City with an all-white delegation. When a compromise was offered that had been brokered by people like Bayard Rustin, Hubert Humphrey, and Joe Rauh of Americans for Democratic Action, I was sure the Freedom Democrats would accept it. It would have given them two delegates and, more important, promised that there could be no more segregated white delegations from Mississippi in the future. They turned it down, insisting that their entire delegation be seated and taking the movement down a path of ultramilitancy and irreconcilability that eventually led to its decline. I was still a mainstream liberal Democrat—although within the next year, I would be put to the test, too.

By August, the manuscript was finished and I hired a typist to put it in its final form. Then I drove to New Haven and dropped the dissertation off at the history department office. I rented a trailer, loaded it with my stuff (mostly books and records), and headed west. My first stop was in Princeton, where my brother was breaking up his apartment and had some things to give me. He had completed the PhD program in a phenomenal three years and, at the age of twenty-four, had accepted a teaching position at Oberlin. He would be at Oberlin for the next thirty-five years, which led me to visit my alma mater far more often than I otherwise would have. From Princeton, I drove to Michigan City, where I attended my tenth high school reunion. I received the prize for the baldest member of the class of 1954—a Beatles wig. Then it was on to Minneapolis. When I arrived, just after Labor Day, I was pleased to find Professor Sorauf's apartment exactly as it had been described. It was small, just one bedroom, and located in one of the many two-and-a-half-story walk-up buildings that were sprinkled throughout the neighborhoods around the campus. But Professor Sorauf's taste was impeccable; the place was attractively furnished and it had all the bedding and kitchenware I needed. It was the first nice apartment I ever had—far different from my rundown graduate student digs. And with it came another luxury I never had before: a cleaning lady who came in every two weeks to tidy up.

The first year of teaching inevitably entails an enormous amount of work. Every class meeting requires all-new preparation; there are no old lecture notes to fall back on. My first year, 1964–65, was no exception. The department gave me two classes to teach in the fall and winter quarters, with a third class added in the spring. The theory was that I would need some extra time earlier in the year to complete my dissertation. In fact, the dissertation was no issue. I learned early in the fall that my advisers had accepted it, and since Yale had no final oral defense, I had nothing left to do except collect the degree. But the preparation even of two courses kept me incredibly busy. My upper-division course, which combined African American and immigration history, was called Race and Nationality in American History. Since it was entirely my creation, there were no models to follow, no syllabi to look at. I had to put it all together from scratch. The lower-division course I was given to teach was not a history course at all. It was called Introduction to Social Science and it was divided into three parts: Personality, Work, and Community. The course had originally been a product of the general education movement of the 1940s and was on its last legs. It might have made sense if it was team-taught by people from different disciplines, but it was instead given to young instructors who were usually unprepared to handle a course of such scope. I certainly fit into that category. I had no background in psychology, but ended up teaching the Personality segment of the course three times during my first year at Minnesota.

My teaching burden was compounded by the fact that before I came to Minnesota I had never before been in front of a classroom or received even five minutes of training in how to teach. The American educational system somehow assumes that it takes years of instruction and months of practice to train a high school teacher, but that it takes none at all to prepare a university teacher. In many graduate schools, including Minnesota, most graduate students gain teaching experience as teaching assistants while they are studying for their doctorates. But I had had no teaching experience at Yale. And while I believe mastery of a subject is by far the most important asset for a successful university teacher, I could have used a little instruction in teaching methods. When I walked into my Race and Nationality course my first day, I found forty students waiting for me. Some of them were graduate students—exactly what I had been just a few weeks earlier. I said to myself, So now what do I do? I somehow got through it. But it took a real effort.

I developed a steady routine in preparing for classes that year. My classes met on Mondays, Wednesdays, and Fridays, so I had Tuesdays, Thursdays, and weekends to read and put my notes together. On nights before class, I was often up late and then I got up at 6:00 a.m. to put the finishing touches on my notes. Race and Nationality was a lot of work, but I enjoyed it. It was, after all, my field and the course was my idea. In some areas, I already knew enough so that I didn't have to do a lot of additional reading; it was more a matter of organizing my thoughts. In other areas, such as Chinese and Japanese immigration, I knew very little and had to start from scratch. But I knew what to read and had a good enough grasp of the overall field to be able to conceptualize it.

The greater problem I had was organizational. The idea of combining African American and immigration history had pretty much come off the top of my head and in the end it didn't work very well. The problem was that I viewed the two experiences as having more differences than similarities. While white immigrants gradually assimilated into American society, blacks did not; among the oldest of immigrant groups, they remained the most separate. They faced barriers, such as legal segregation, that set their experience apart from that of Europeans. The Asian immigrants proved the rule. As nonwhites, they too were legally segregated and, in the case of the Japanese, forcibly removed to camps during World War II. As I taught the course, then, I had wholly different stories to tell about each group. And in organizing the material, I simply went back and forth between African Americans, white immigrants, and Asian Americans; I never found any coherent organizing principle. Nevertheless, the students seemed to like the course. The material was fresh and most of them had never been exposed to it before. In the spring quarter, representatives from the campus radio station, KUOM, approached me; they said that each quarter they broadcast one university course live from the classroom and would like to do mine. I agreed and for ten weeks my lectures were broadcast—live and unrehearsed—each day.

The social science course was a less happy experience. It was a lot of work, too, but for no apparent end. I knew that I would never teach the course again—no one with any choice in the matter ever did. And the course was dropped just a few years later. Here I did have some models to follow as the course had been taught for years. The Personality segment was generally conceived as a kind of general introduction to Freudian psychology. So I bought a book, came up with a few ideas to throw out every day, and hoped that I could spark some discussion. Sometimes I did, sometimes I didn't. Unlike the Race and Nationality course, most of the social science students were taking the course to meet a requirement and the interest level was not high. After a cursory introduction to Freud, I tried to steer the course toward subjects I knew something about. We spent a couple of weeks on national character, using David Potter's *People of Plenty*, and then I focused on the impact of culture on the personality of African Americans. In the spring, I had a third course preparation—the American history survey. I was still fairly fresh from my prelim preparations and could put together a synthesis of American history since the Civil War without too much trouble. And in that course, I had only to give the lectures. I had teaching assistants to handle the discussion and grade the papers.

If my introduction to teaching was abrupt, so too was my introduction to the responsibilities of being a university faculty member. Within a few weeks, I was deeply involved in the affairs of the history department. It was expanding, and since I was the only new hire that year, there were several vacancies still to be filled. We began to search for specialists in the history of American foreign policy, American economic history, and eighteenth-century American history. As someone who had just recently been a graduate student, I felt almost giddy when I was asked to call senior scholars in those fields and ask them for recommendations. In December, I went to the American Historical Association meeting in Washington and participated in interviewing job candidates. We hired three new American historians that year, and in one case I think my participation made a difference. I promoted the candidacy of John Howe in eighteenth-century American history; I had known John as a graduate student at Yale and knew that his current position at Princeton was only temporary. John turned out to be a strong candidate, got the job, and spent the rest of a distinguished career at Minnesota.

Helping to shape the future of the department was heady stuff for a twenty-seven-year old with no previous teaching experience. But not all aspects of the academic life were equally edifying. I was shocked to discover how much of the faculty's time was spent on issues that seemed self-serving and trivial. The department met once a month—more often if there was an urgent issue to consider—and meetings sometimes lasted three or four hours. One ongoing issue in my first year at Minnesota was the role of television in the classroom. The university had installed television sets in several rooms and had asked faculty members with large introductory courses to consider giving their lectures over closed-circuit TV. This allowed students to hear the lectures at different places on campus and even at different times. Harold Deutsch, the chairman of the history department, thought this was a great idea and was participating in the program. Other members were horrified and regarded it as a major threat to our careers; soon, they argued, the university would just buy standardized lectures and dispense with our services altogether. Hours were spent debating this issue. It was all foolishness, as few professors wanted to teach via television, most students didn't like the idea, and the entire experiment collapsed within a few years.

Even sillier was the amount of time spent in department meetings discussing the Ford Room. When the department was forced to move across the river, it had to abandon a cozy department library named after former university president and historian Guy Stanton Ford. The administration would not pay to re-create the library on the West Bank, so Professor Deutsch spent a year soliciting contributions from alumni to build and furnish a new Ford Room. The room had just opened when I arrived in the fall of 1964 and Professor Deutsch was very proud of it. It looked like a corporate boardroom, with paneled walls, built-in bookshelves, and Danish modern tables and chairs. We held our department meetings there and used it for oral examinations.

Professor Deutsch always had some proposal to enhance it. So forty men with doctorates in history sat around every month discussing whether to buy dishes or plants or whatever for the Ford Room.

I soon began to make friends within the department, particularly among the younger members. Bob and Gene Berkhofer were my first good friends in the department and through them I came to know Kim and Anne Munholland. Kim was a specialist in modern French history, and he and Anne soon invited me to dinner. Within a few months, the Berkhofers and Munhollands and I had started an informal cooking club, inviting each other back and forth for dinners that sometimes included other people as well. Bob Berkhofer would also customarily invite me to come home with him for dinner after department meetings, where Gene would be eagerly waiting to hear what had gone on. The Berkhofers soon gave me their interpretation of department politics. Harold Deutsch, they told me, was a timeserver who would soon be gone as chairman. The department, they thought, was divided into two factions, which they named the Hoytentots and the Wolverines. The Hoytentots were followers of medieval historian R. Stuart Hoyt while the Wolverines were the acolytes of French historian John B. Wolf. It was not easy to see the differences between the two factions. Ideological lines in the department would harden later in the decade when, like much of academia, the department became embroiled over issues such as affirmative action hiring, democratization of decision making, and student participation in departmental affairs. But the all-white, all-male department of 1964 and 1965 was still a fairly clubby operation and alliances shifted depending upon the particular issue. The Berkhofers' analysis, however, was not totally wrong. Within two years, Deutsch was gone as chairman and replaced by Stuart Hoyt. And John Wolf, for whatever reason, then left the university for a new position at the University of Illinois at Chicago.

My new friends in the department also helped me adjust to life in Minnesota. The Berkhofers told me shortly after I arrived that to lead the good life in Minneapolis I must immediately become acquainted with Dayton's, Lunds, and Haskell's. This was good advice. Dayton's was still a great department store in 1964. It sold almost everything, provided excellent service, and would exchange merchandise without question. I soon acquired a Dayton's credit card and began shopping there for everything from clothing to kitchenware to travel service. When someone said Dayton's in those days it meant the downtown store at Seventh and Nicollet. There was a Dayton's store at Southdale and a few Target stores had just opened. But they were decidedly secondary and no one anticipated a day when Target would overshadow and ultimately discard Dayton's itself. The name Lunds also meant one store—the Lunds on Lake Street in Uptown. I did not immediately start doing all my grocery shopping there as there were stores more conveniently located for me. But I soon realized that if I wanted quality products or items that were out of the ordinary, Lunds was the place to go. Haskell's, located downtown next to the Radisson Hotel, was the only serious wine store in the Twin Cities. It was presided over by its ebullient and highly opinionated owner, Fritzi Haskell, who believed that the only wines worth drinking came from France. When I asked her one day about California wine, she dismissed all of it, with a wave of her hand, as "reconstituted dreck." A few months later, I read that Fritzi's husband, who had been ailing for years, had died. When I next visited the store I offered her condolences and she responded with a long, detailed account of his agonizing final days. Then, without skipping a beat, she tried to sell me a wine that she assured me was the only thing that had brought her comfort while she witnessed her husband's terrible ordeal. Of these three institutions, only Lund's survives today in anything like its original form.

The restaurant scene in Minneapolis in 1964 was far less promising. The big downtown establishment restaurants—with such uninspiring names as Charlie's, Harry's, and Murray's—catered to the region's tastes for steak, chicken, and the only fish most Minnesotans would eat, walleye pike. I later discovered that it was possible to get a good meal at Charlie's—but only if you went with a regular customer and ordered items that were not on the menu. Otherwise the food was highly unimaginative. Restaurants that offered "foreign" food never even thought of authenticity. The most popular Chinese restaurant in downtown Minneapolis, the Nanking, specialized in a kind of celery mush it called chow mein, while the leading Italian place, the Cafe di Napoli, served everything swimming in oversweetened tomato sauce. There were a couple of Jewish delis in the increasingly Jewish suburb of St. Louis Park; they were open on Yom Kippur and closed on Christmas and their sandwiches were pale imitations of what I had found on the East Coast. The one French restaurant, the Château de Paris, featured waiters wearing berets and smocks and food that no one in the real Paris would have recognized. The Berkhofers and Munhollands alerted me to some offbeat restaurants with a bit more authenticity and together we tried them. There was a Chinese restaurant in the northern suburb of Fridley, with the improbable name of the Fireside Rice Bowl; it served food that had at least some resemblance to the cooking of China. And an even more remote suburban restaurant called the Cedars of Lebanon offered Middle Eastern food that could not be found elsewhere in the Twin Cities. But for the most part, with the help of Lunds, we could cook better food at home than what was available in restaurants.

The restaurant scene would not notably improve for another decade, but the Twin Cities was already beginning to experience a cultural revolution. The Guthrie Theater had just opened in the Loring Park area, a few blocks from downtown Minneapolis, and was offering some of the best repertory fare in the country. The Minneapolis Symphony Orchestra, not yet the Minnesota Orchestra, was perhaps not quite up to the standards of Chicago or Boston, but it was not far behind. Its major drawback was its venue, Northrop Auditorium, a barn of a hall on the university campus. When it acquired its new home in downtown Minneapolis in the early 1970s, it came into its own as a major orchestra. Minneapolis was also beginning to develop a lively community theater scene. I saw several productions at the Firehouse Theater, in a rundown neighborhood off Lake Street, that were superb. And in 1970, the Walker Art Center opened a handsome new building and immediately became a major venue for contemporary art. My brother was then director of the museum at Oberlin and came to Minneapolis for opening day, so through him I was able to attend the gala festivities.

While a few of the younger faculty members became good friends, I had relatively little in common with most of my older colleagues. They dutifully invited me to dinner, but we did not develop deep friendships. In terms of age and lifestyle, I had more in common with the history graduate students. At twenty-seven, I was still younger than some of them and not much older than the rest. I soon started socializing at a popular graduate school hangout just off campus called the Mixers. When the university expanded across the river, its new campus was adjacent to an old, working-class neighborhood called Cedar-Riverside, which had historically been home to first-generation European immigrants. The main thoroughfares of the neighborhood, logically called Cedar Avenue and Riverside Avenue, were lined with bars, and while some of them maintained their working-class orientation, a few changed with the times and welcomed the newly arrived university community. The Mixers was one of those. It retained the grunginess of its blue-collar origins, but it was now packed almost every night with graduate students taking a break from their studies. It was there that I began some long-lasting friendships. Don Koenig, a graduate student in German history, whom I met at the Mixers, remained a friend until his death almost forty years later. Joan Campbell, whose husband, Gregg, was a graduate student in American history, became a friend and later a political ally when I began my political life. Elizabeth Katz, another American history graduate student, was to play an important part in my decision to come out as gay a few years later. And Mike Kopp and Norman Zimmerman, who went on to academic careers, were friends with whom I kept in touch throughout my life.

Don Koenig and Joan Campbell steered me to my initial involvement in Minnesota politics. When I arrived in Minnesota in September 1964, I was deeply committed to the reelection of Lyndon B. Johnson. Johnson had embraced the civil rights movement to a degree that I had never anticipated. He had made the passage of Kennedy's civil rights bill his top priority and had used his remarkable political skills to get the bill through Congress despite a Senate filibuster rule that basically required a two-thirds majority for any important legislation to pass. The War on Poverty and a wide-ranging series of domestic programs that Johnson called the Great Society promised to complete the unfinished agenda of the New Deal. Barry Goldwater, his Republican opponent, the first unabashed conservative to win the Republican nomination for president in a generation, had voted against the civil rights bill and opposed all aspects of the Great Society. The only issue that gave me pause was Vietnam. Johnson was committed to increasing American involvement in a war that to my mind made little sense. Still, even on this issue, he was far preferable to Goldwater, who promised victory in Vietnam at any cost. So shortly after I settled into my new apartment, I found my way to the headquarters of the Democratic-Farmer-Labor Party, Minnesota's version of the Democratic Party, and volunteered to pass out literature for the Johnson reelection campaign.

I found the DFL Party highly compatible with my political values. Its other candidates in 1964 included Senator Gene McCarthy and Congressman Don Fraser, both attractive liberals whom I was pleased to support. And Don and Joan told me about a local race in the university area in which they were involved. Alpha Smaby was a woman in her midfifties who had been involved in liberal causes for years; her husband was an official in the farmers co-op movement and both of them had roots in the Farmer-Labor Party, which had merged with the Democrats in the 1940s. Alpha was now making her first run for public office as a candidate for the state House of Representatives. I called Alpha and she invited me to her house for a campaign meeting. She was a tall, thin woman with a striking voice and I was immediately impressed with her. I did what I could for her campaign in the few weeks that were left. On election night I was excited by Johnson's sweeping victory and by Alpha's election to the state legislature. Alpha was to be one of my mentors when I launched my own political career a few years later.

While I was making friends at the university and through politics, I developed one of my most cherished Minnesota friendships in an unlikely way. When young people move to a new part of the country, they often carry with them a parental admonition to be sure to look up some long-lost friend or distant relative who lives nearby. And just as often, they never do it. My mother told me that when I got to Minneapolis I had to call the Goldsteins. I had known Rosalie Goldstein, then Rosalie Benowitz, in Michigan City. She was about fifteen years older than I and had grown up next door to my Lieber grandparents. She was too old to have been my friend when I was a child and a little too young to have been a close friend of my mother's, but of course the families knew each other well, as did all Michigan City Jews, and Rosalie's sister-in-law was in my mother's mah-jongg club. Milt Goldstein had come to Michigan City to work for the Rubys' pants company and met Rosalie there. A few years after they were married, Milt had been transferred to Minnesota as a sales representative for Jaymar-Ruby pants, as they were now called, and they had moved to

Minneapolis with their two young children. I couldn't imagine that I would have anything in common with them other than our Michigan City origins, so I promptly forgot my mother's wishes. But Rosalie called me and invited me to dinner. And to be polite, I accepted. I fully anticipated a boring evening. When I arrived at their house in suburban St. Louis Park, I realized that I had been too hasty in my judgment. Their front lawn was covered with DFL campaign signs. The Goldsteins were both deeply involved in DFL politics and liberal causes, especially the civil rights movement. And a few years later, Rosalie would become a committed feminist and abortion rights activist. More important, they were delightful people with wide-ranging interests. They soon were among my best friends.

I had been warned by many people about the Minnesota weather, but I was still not completely prepared for what I encountered during the winter of 1964–65. My first winter in Minnesota turned out to be one of the coldest and snowiest in history. By late November, when I returned from Michigan City after spending Thanksgiving weekend with my parents, the temperature had dropped to –18°F. I had been used to zero temperatures when I was growing up, and I blithely thought that twenty or so degrees colder couldn't be all that different. I could not have been more mistaken. I tried one day in December to walk across the bridge that connected the two parts of the university campus; the temperature was –20°F and I thought I was going to die before I got to the other side. As the winter went on, it didn't get any better. We broke the record for consecutive below-zero days. The cold was accompanied by one snowstorm after another. By February there were more than thirty inches of snow on the ground and my car often sat useless for days. Either it wouldn't start or, if it did, it couldn't gain enough traction to move. Finally, I equipped it with snow tires and an engine heater, which I dutifully plugged in every night. But I was certainly relieved when spring arrived.

The spring of 1965 might have brought better weather but it also brought troubling political developments. First, there was the last great surge of the civil rights movement and once again I experienced an internal conflict between activism and my career. The brutal repression of Martin Luther King's march in Selma, Alabama, occurred just before spring break at the university. Supporters from all over the country, including a contingent of historians, mobilized to go to Selma to march with Dr. King when he tried again to lead his forces out of Selma to the state capitol in Montgomery. Students and staff at the University of Minnesota chartered a bus to go to Selma. With the university on break, I clearly could have gone and I seriously considered it. But I had also planned to use that week for class preparation, which I urgently needed given my three-course load in the upcoming quarter. So I didn't go—and I always regretted it. I often thought back on that decision later in my life, and my regret made me more willing to turn my back on academic responsibilities in order to take on political causes.

More troubling was President Johnson's escalation of the war in Vietnam. My support for Johnson's reelection had seemed amply justified by the remarkable legislative program that he pushed through Congress in the winter and spring of 1965. I told my students that spring, when I was lecturing on Wilson's New Freedom and Franklin Roosevelt's New Deal, that they were witnessing in Johnson's Great Society the third great outpouring of reform legislation in the twentieth century. Medicare, federal aid to education, the landmark Voting Rights Act, the various antipoverty programs and immigration reform achieved what liberals had been hoping for since the 1930s. Yet in late February, Johnson also announced the unlimited bombing of North Vietnam. And by summer, he had committed more than a hundred thousand American troops to Vietnam and had managed to internationalize what had previously been a civil war. One day in early spring, I went to lunch at the Campus Club, the faculty club on the top floor of Coffman Union. A philosophy professor, whom I knew to be an active Democrat, came up to me and asked, "Have you sent back your Johnson buttons yet?" I was shocked and replied that I certainly hadn't and that I was proud of what Johnson was doing domestically. But as the spring wore on, it became harder for me to maintain this position. By May, I was one of the organizers of the first antiwar "teach-in" at the University of Minnesota.

Opposition to the war in Vietnam built slowly. As late as January of 1968, the majority of Americans supported Johnson's position on the war. Antiwar activism began on college campuses and only gradually spread to other segments of the population. It has often been said that the early and intense opposition to the war in college communities was the result of the draft and represented a selfish unwillingness on the part of male college students to serve in the military. I think this explanation is vastly oversimplified. Certainly draft resistance became an important part of the antiwar movement, but that in itself was a courageous act that risked imprisonment. And most college students—and younger faculty like me—had educational deferments that kept them out of the military. Opposition to the war went deeper than self-interest and was multifaceted. At the beginning, most of us who questioned Johnson's policies were liberals who had supported the basic thrust of American foreign policy during the cold war. I had been appalled by the Bay of Pigs but thought Kennedy had behaved admirably in the Cuban missile crisis. Vietnam, however, seemed the wrong place to confront communism. The conflict in Vietnam was essentially a local crisis, it represented no crucial American interests, and it required the support of a repressive and unstable regime in South Vietnam that had little popular appeal. As the war went on, it had a radicalizing impact on many of us who opposed it, and later on I became more critical of American cold war policy in general. But initially, my opposition was that of a liberal who felt betrayed by a liberal president whom I had admired.

The teach-ins exemplified this early stage of the antiwar movement. The first teach-in was held at the University of Michigan in late March 1965 and the idea spread rapidly to other campuses. It was a uniquely academic approach to the issue. While the term "teach-in," with its echo of "sit-in," was clearly intended to evoke the civil rights movement, the events did not involve any kind of civil disobedience. A "teach-in" was merely a marathon session of lectures and seminars and roundtable discussions designed to raise awareness of the war issue among college students. The logic was that the more one knew about the circumstances of the war, the more one would oppose it. At Minnesota, we were even careful to make certain that supporters of the war were fairly represented. The student leader on the steering committee, Jim Johnson, who would later become a key aide to Walter Mondale and after that served as the chair and chief executive officer of Fannie Mae, commented that "our teach-in was really much less a protest of America's Vietnam policy than some others have been." On the evening of May 24, four speakers debated the war before a packed house at Northrop Auditorium—two on each side of the issue. One of the antiwar speakers was Norman Thomas, the venerable leader of the Socialist Party of America, then in his eighties. I picked up Thomas at the airport and was thrilled to have had a chance to meet and talk with him personally. He had always been one of my heroes. While I never voted socialist, I found his brand of principled democratic socialism highly attractive. After the forum at Northrop, the teach-in moved to Coffman Union and broke up into a series of small seminars and workshops that went on until 4:00 a.m. Most of the small-group sessions were led by faculty members and most had an antiwar thrust, but we still made sure that all views were represented. Speakers ranged from political science professor Mulford Q. Sibley, a committed pacifist, who urged young men to resist the draft, to a visiting professor in my department who said that the effect of protest movements on foreign policy was "negative and even disastrous."

Shortly after the teach-in, the academic year ended and I made one last trip back to Yale to get my PhD. I would have been glad to have skipped the ceremony and received the degree in absentia, but my mother insisted that she wanted to go. My father said, sensibly I thought, that he had attended enough commencements and would let us go without him. So I drove to Michigan City, picked up my mother, and then drove on to New Haven. The best part of it was the opportunity to see my Yale friends again, most of whom my mother had never met. But the ceremony was totally forgettable and I never participated in a graduation exercise again until I was awarded an honorary degree many years later at Oberlin.

I also participated in ceremonies of a different kind that summer. The previous fall, my parents had visited me in Minneapolis and told me that my brother was planning to marry. Shortly after arriving in Oberlin, he had started to date a curator in the art museum, Athena Tacha. Athena was Greek, a sculptor who had received an MA in art history at Oberlin, gone to Paris to earn her PhD at the Sorbonne, and returned to Oberlin to work in the museum. When my parents first gave me the news, my mother was visibly upset. She had always retained the hope that her sons would marry Jewish women, even when neither son showed any great interest in Jewish life and one son showed no interest in marrying any woman. Now one of her sons wanted to marry a woman who was not Jewish, who was a foreigner, and who was several years older than he. I told my mother that she would be making a big mistake if she demonstrated her unhappiness to my brother. She was not going to change his mind and she would simply strain her relationship with one of her sons—a relationship that was central to her life. My father, who had no interest in the Jewish issue, agreed with me, and we persuaded her to accept her prospective daughter-in-law warmly. Athena came to Michigan City to visit during the 1964 Christmas vacation. She was an attractive and vivacious woman who charmed everyone who met her. Both of my parents came to love her. Richard and Athena were married the next summer in Oberlin in an ecumenical service that incorporated bits of both Jewish and Greek liturgy. I was the best man and my parents were as proud as they could be. Shortly thereafter, they went to Greece to meet Athena's family; when I asked my mother how they communicated without a mutual language, she said, "We just hugged and kissed a lot."

I was also best man that summer at Larry Smith's wedding. After his first marriage failed, he started dating one of the few eligible female graduate students at Yale and soon they became engaged. It was one of the very few successful romances that I witnessed during my time at Yale Graduate School. Louise was from Oklahoma and so I flew to Norman, Oklahoma, for the wedding. It was a lovely ceremony, but I think Larry and Louise were both happy they would not be living there. It was beastly hot and the wedding reception was "dry," which was completely incomprehensible to someone like me who had grown up casually accepting alcoholic beverages as a natural part of life. And I got a little sample of the political climate of the place when a faculty couple at the University of Oklahoma invited me over to their house for a "real drink" and then carefully looked around to make sure we were alone before putting a Pete Seeger record on the turntable.

Back in Minnesota, I taught two classes during summer session. When I had interviewed for the job at the university, I had been told that despite relatively low salaries, which were characteristic of academic life everywhere at that time, Minnesota offered many opportunities for faculty members to supplement their income. Summer school was one of those. Summer session was divided into two five-week terms, so it was possible to work for just over a month, earn some extra money, and still have most of the summer free. I taught during the summer for most of my career at Minnesota. In the fall of 1965, I also taught an extension course at night—another opportunity for extra income. That, however, I did for only two years and then gave it up. I enjoyed some of the older students who enrolled for the evening classes, but I found it too tiring to teach at the end of what had already often been a long day.

One of the most interesting older students I met was actually enrolled in a regular daytime class, the American history survey that I had taught spring quarter. Even though it had been a large lecture class, I could not help but notice Leo Giovannini's gray hair and weathered face. He asked one of my teaching assistants whether it would be proper to invite me to his house for dinner and was assured that I would not object. When I went, his wife, Vi, served a multicourse Italian dinner and Leo told me his story. He and Vi were both from the Iron Range in northern Minnesota; their fathers had been miners—his an Italian immigrant, Vi's an immigrant from Finland. Leo was so appalled by the conditions he saw in the iron mining towns in the 1930s that after graduating from high school he joined the Communist Party, the only organization that seemed to have a real program for economic change. He came to the Twin Cities and enrolled at the University of Minnesota with the goal of becoming a lawyer. But the party told him that it didn't need any more lawyers and that he should drop out of school and go to work in a factory where he could help organize the workers. He dutifully did what he was told. When he married Vi he warned her that she was marrying a Communist and that the party would always come first. For thirty years, it did. Leo did factory work, organized for the Communists, and became active in left-wing labor unions. Vi, who was never a party member, got a job as secretary for the United Electrical union, which was expelled from the CIO in the 1940s for its refusal to purge union officials who were Communists. In the 1950s, Leo became a victim of the Red Scare. He never lost his job, but when the House Un-American Activities Committee held hearings in the Twin Cities, he was cited as a known Communist and even Vi was mentioned in the committee report as having served sandwiches at Communist cell meetings. Finally, by the early 1960s, with the revelation of Stalin's crimes, Leo had had enough. He quit the party and decided to pick up where he had left off thirty years before—at the University of Minnesota. He hoped at first that he could still study law, but soon realized that it would take more years than he had to spare to become a lawyer. But he completed his BA degree and took a job as a vocational counselor in state government.

Leo soon became a good friend. He invited me frequently to his house for dinner and in the summer I spent weekends with him and Vi at their cabin near Pequot Lakes in north-central Minnesota. Lake cabins, I soon learned, were central to Minnesota culture. Minnesotans of every class had them, although they varied widely from the elaborate second homes of the rich to simple one-room cabins without indoor plumbing. Leo and Vi's place was at the low end of the scale; it took me awhile to get used to the outhouse. I also came to realize that when you are a Communist you never totally get away from the party. Leo's cabin was located next door to that of Clarence Hathaway, one of the most prominent Minnesotans in the CP, a former editor of the *Daily Worker,* and for a time the American representative to the Comintern. Leo told me how he and Clarence had spent hours out on the lake fishing and discussing the class struggle. Once another boatload of fishermen had passed them and yelled out, "Hey, Commies. Fishing is an American sport." Clarence had died a year or two before I met Leo; Clarence's widow, Vera, was living in the cabin. But during my first visit to the lake, Vera died, and the next year, Leo took over the considerably more comfortable Hathaway cabin. When I visited there, I particularly enjoyed looking through the book collection. Leo told me to take what I wanted and I ended up with some interesting items, such as an autographed copy of Paul Robeson's autobiography.

Minnesota's left-wing political tradition was fascinating to me. I saw another aspect of it when my graduate student friend, Don Koenig, took me to the Iron Range for a weekend to meet his family and friends and to visit some of the local institutions. Those institutions included a lot of bars and ethnic halls, which prominently featured bars. But there was also a political edge to some of the places we visited. We went to a picnic at a Finnish park that Don told me would be dominated by Finnish Communists. The left-wing Finnish community in northern Minnesota and Wisconsin was still large enough in the 1960s to support a Communist Finnish language newspaper. This was the community that had produced Gus Hall, the perennial Communist Party candidate for president. The day we went to the picnic, however, the speaker was a far more moderate political figure, DFL state senator Rudy Perpich, who would later become the longest-serving governor in Minnesota history. That was the first time I had met Perpich, and I thought he could have appealed to the crowd more effectively than he did. When we talked to him afterward, he referred to the audience as "liberals." I don't know whether that was just a euphemism or whether he didn't know the actual politics of the group he had been addressing.

I became more immersed in left-wing politics as I became involved in the antiwar movement. After the teach-in, antiwar activities in Minnesota developed a harder edge. I began to attend meetings of a group that called itself the Minnesota Committee to End the War in Vietnam. The committee brought together people with a wide range of ideologies. Some were liberal Democrats, like myself, who were becoming increasingly disillusioned with the Democratic Party under the leadership of Lyndon Johnson. Others were pacifists, like Mulford Sibley, who opposed all wars. And still others came from the Marxist left and saw the war primarily as an organizing tool to bring people to understand the basic nature of American imperialism. The Marxists were divided into two hostile camps—the Communists and the Trotskyites. Many histories of the 1930s and 1940s emphasize the destructive role the Communists played in coalitions with liberals and how they used popular causes for their own purposes. But I had no trouble in working with Communists in the Minnesota antiwar movement; they were generally reasonable and seemed genuinely committed to our common goal of ending the war. My real problem was with the Trotskyites who organized under the banner of the Socialist Workers Party. They were a tightly disciplined cadre of people who met as a caucus prior to every meeting of the Committee to End the War to plot their strategy. They insisted on certain slogans, on certain themes for every demonstration, and above all on no cooperation with anyone inside the government, even those who wanted to work with us to end the war. I finally came to the conclusion that the "Trots," as we called them, didn't really care about the war, that if prolonging it would help their movement, so much the better. But it took too much energy to fight them—energy that could better be used to help end the war—and after a while I stopped attending committee meetings and looked for other ways to work against the war.

Meanwhile, I had more mundane issues to attend to. Frank Sorauf had returned from his sabbatical in Italy. He was a great addition to our cooking club and shared some of the wonderful recipes that he had picked up in Bologna. But he also reclaimed his apartment and I had to find another place to live. I located a similar one-bedroom apartment, just two blocks from Frank's, and set to furnishing it. Gene Berkhofer was eager to help, as was my mother, who came to Minneapolis full of ideas about what her "bachelor" son needed to set up housekeeping. I particularly enjoyed buying for the kitchen. I started out with the basics, but within a year or two, I had acquired sets of fine German china, Swedish crystal, and Danish stainless tableware. I loved things like that and did not expect to marry and receive them as wedding gifts. Many years later, when gay marriage became a political issue, I liked to joke that the major reason I wanted the right to marry was so that I could register my china and silver patterns at Dayton's.

I also, unexpectedly, had to acquire a new car. Just before fall quarter began, I went to Michigan City for a few days to see my parents. On my way home, driving on I-94 through Wisconsin, I fell asleep at the wheel and plowed into the back of a milk truck at seventy miles per hour. My car flipped over. As the car was turning over, I could feel my seat belt holding me in. I am convinced that had I not been using it, I would have gone through the windshield and been seriously injured. As it was, the car was totaled, but I walked away unscathed. After that experience, I never doubted the value of seat belts. But the accident was nevertheless a big inconvenience—and of course I had no one to blame but myself. I had to take the bus back to Minneapolis with whatever I could salvage from the wreck. And I had not planned to buy a new car so soon and had no money saved up. So with the insurance money I collected I bought a used car, which got me around for the next three years.

Now that I had my PhD in hand, I was able to teach a graduate-level seminar. I put together a two-quarter seminar that I called The Negro in American History. I later boasted that it was the first course of its kind in the Big Ten; it was probably one of the first at any major research university. But the time was certainly ripe. The class attracted twenty-three students—an unusually large number for a graduate seminar and too many, in my mind, for the kind of informal discussion I envisaged. So I voluntarily increased my teaching load by dividing the seminar into two sections, one meeting in the afternoon in a regular classroom and the other meeting in the evening at my apartment. I taught this seminar until 1974 and it was probably the most rewarding class I ever taught, especially in the first few years. We started with the slave trade and went all the way up to Malcolm X. The reading was heavy, but the students were committed and some of them were truly outstanding, as good as any I had met at Yale. Several went on to distinguished careers both within and outside academia. I was young enough so that the atmosphere was collegial; the students were not afraid to challenge my judgments and I often had to rethink my opinions as a result of discussions in the seminar.

My undergraduate lecture course, Race and Nationality in American History, attracted eighty students in its second year. The large enrollment in both of my courses probably had less to do with my teaching ability than it did with a mounting interest throughout the country in African American history. The civil rights movement was evolving into a search for black identity, and part of that search was the quest for a usable African American past. I think this trend was a mixed blessing. It attracted its share of charlatans who constructed a semimythical African American past that was in many ways a mirror image of the racist white history it was attempting to replace. But it also created a strong interest in the serious study of African American history. It was during the mid- and late sixties that universities began offering courses in the subject, publishers started looking for manuscripts, and bright students, both black and white, became interested in the field.

In addition, the focus of the black movement began to shift from the South to the North. Race riots in Rochester, New York, and Harlem in 1964 and particularly the Watts riot in Los Angeles in 1965, presaged the wave of urban racial violence that would sweep the country in 1967 and 1968. Martin Luther King moved from Atlanta to Chicago and civil rights leaders began focusing on the spatial segregation of the northern ghettoes rather than the legal segregation of the Jim Crow South. That was what I had been studying since the late fifties, and not surprisingly I began receiving more invitations to speak than I could handle. I spoke throughout the Twin Cities metropolitan area to human relations councils, chambers of commerce, and African American groups, and I was frequently interviewed on local television.

I also began attracting attention in the historical profession. I regularly attended the annual meetings of the American Historical Association, the professional organization for historians of all regions and eras, and the Organization of American Historians, which limited itself to historians of the United States. At those meetings, I met my counterparts at other universities and soon discovered that everywhere there was growing interest in African American history. In the spring of 1966, I presented a paper, based on my dissertation, at the OAH in Cincinnati as part of a session titled "The Northern Negro Ghetto." As a result of all of this exposure, I began getting feelers from a number of universities asking if I were interested in moving. These included some rather distinguished institutions: Cornell, the University of Virginia, Rutgers, the State University of New York at Stony Brook, the University of Texas, the University of Connecticut, Boston University, and the University of California at Santa Barbara. At one meeting, John Blum even arranged for me to be interviewed by Oscar Handlin for a possible position at Harvard. Nothing ever came of any of the overtures. In some cases, I didn't pursue the leads; in others, such as Harvard, the institution didn't pursue me. In one case, however, which I will discuss later, I almost took the offer.

My major academic goal now was to prepare my dissertation, "Black Chicago: The Making of a Negro Ghetto, 1890–1920," for publication. There was no lack of interested publishers. I had met Herb Cohen a few years earlier when I was still at Yale and he was working for a New York publishing company called the Free Press. He expressed interest in the dissertation before it was even written and urged me to keep in touch. About the time I finished the dissertation, he wrote again to tell me he had left the Free Press and was now working for the University of Chicago Press and was eager to see the manuscript. I thought the University of Chicago Press was a better fit than the Free Press would have been; after all, this was to be a book about Chicago. Moreover, the University of Chicago Press had a strong list in history and was beginning to expand its offerings in African American topics. Herb Cohen liked the manuscript and I signed a contract. The target was to complete the revisions by September 1966 and publish the book in the spring of 1967. The revisions were not extensive. The people at the press made some suggestions, my mentors at Yale made some, and my colleagues at Minnesota weighed in with some more. Many were stylistic; others involved establishing a broader context for my analysis. I also pushed the starting date back from 1900 to

1890; I had originally seen the 1890s as a kind of prelude to the main story, but as the manuscript had evolved that decade had become an integral part of what I had to say.

I also continued my involvement in departmental affairs. The department was still expanding, although most of the new hires in 1965–66 were in European history. But Clarke Chambers, who handled twentieth-century American history, persuaded his colleagues that large enrollments in his undergraduate courses required assistance at the junior level, freeing him to spend more time directing graduate students and supervising his newly created Social Welfare History Archives. I had the training to teach those courses—and later on I did—but I was busy with my Race and Nationality and African American courses and had all that I could do. In the meantime, my friend from Yale, Al Jones, had just taken a temporary position at Michigan State. I saw him over Thanksgiving when he came to Michigan City for a visit, and I told him about the opening at Minnesota. He immediately applied.

I was, of course, eager to have Al join me at Minnesota. But it was not all clear sailing. When he came for his interview there was some hesitation about hiring him. For one thing, he looked very young; he was actually a year older than I was, but he looked five years younger. Second, he had a kind of "gee whiz" quality about him that I found charming, but others found off-putting. And finally, some of my colleagues thought that his dissertation topic, about the use of Lincoln imagery by New Deal intellectuals, would be more suitable for American studies than for history. The Berkhofers in particular were not impressed, and although they knew Al was my friend and tried not to hurt my feelings, I could tell that they had misgivings. The other serious candidate for the job was a much older historian who already had a record of publication. I thought he would get it. But there were even more misgivings about him—about the quality of his work and why he did not yet have a permanent job elsewhere. In the end, Al was hired. I was delighted to have one of my best friends become my newest colleague.

My work on "Black Chicago," together with a heavy teaching schedule, kept me from doing much traveling, but I was regularly attending academic conventions that provided me with some travel opportunities. The American Historical Association meeting in December

1965 was held in San Francisco and since I had never been west of the Rockies I made a trip out of it. I flew to Phoenix, rented a car, and drove to the Grand Canyon. It had snowed the day before and there was some question as to whether I could even get through to the canyon, but I bought chains for the car and had no trouble. When I arrived, the sun had come out and I was greeted by an absolutely magnificent sight—the trees on the rim of the canyon were covered with snow while the sun illuminated the oranges and reds of the canyon itself. To make it even better, I had the place virtually to myself. I then drove on to Utah for a few days and visited Zion and Bryce national parks, both of which I also found extraordinary. I came to believe that foreigners who come to the United States should first visit the natural wonders of the Southwest rather than New York and Washington, D.C. I have found many great cities elsewhere in the world but nothing like the scenery of the Desert Southwest. After all of this Las Vegas was a sad anticlimax. What Rudyard Kipling had said about Chicago pretty well summarized my feelings about Las Vegas: "In order to understand my century, it is necessary to see it, but having seen it once, I urgently desire never to see it again." I got out of Vegas as quickly as I could, drove to Los Angeles, and then up the scenic coastal highway to San Francisco, with a stop at the Hearst estate at San Simeon. I instantly disliked Los Angeles and loved San Francisco and would come back to San Francisco many times in the future. I was not yet aware of it as a "gay Mecca."

There was a much-discussed election for governor in Minnesota in 1966. The incumbent DFL governor, Karl Rolvaag, was challenged by his own lieutenant governor, Sandy Keith, and at the party convention in June, Keith was endorsed over Rolvaag after twenty contentious ballots. It was almost unprecedented for a political party to try to dump its own governor, and I was particularly puzzled because I could see few ideological differences between Rolvaag and Keith. They both seemed like standard mainstream DFL liberals. It was all explained to me one night by David Graven, a law school professor, who belonged to the same faculty eating club that I did. The faculty eating clubs were informal organizations that met once a month at a restaurant for dinner usually followed by a talk given by one of the members. I found the whole experience a little too much like an old-fashioned men's club, but I went to the dinners because it was an opportunity to meet interesting people from other departments. Graven had been one of the organizers of a secret meeting held in the summer of 1965 at a ski resort in northern Minnesota called Sugar Hills, where a group of prominent DFL leaders decided that Rolvaag could not be reelected and that Keith should be urged to run against him. Rolvaag, Graven explained, had been a journeyman within the party who had served for years, first as party chair, then as lieutenant governor. His major asset was his name: his father was the famous Norwegian American writer Ole Rolvaag. But Karl had no particular talents, was out of his depth as governor, was inarticulate and gaffe-prone, and worst of all was an alcoholic. Keith, on the other hand, was a bright and talented young lawyer who had distinguished himself as a state senator from Rochester before becoming lieutenant governor. He could keep the office of governor in DFL hands.

Rolvaag had promised to abide by the party endorsement and drop out if Keith were endorsed. He broke his promise and entered the September primary. That summer Minnesotans witnessed a bitter, nasty internal fight within the DFL, while the Republicans just watched and waited. For the first time in my adult life, I sat out an election. The Vietnam War had driven me to the left and the Rolvaag-Keith contest seemed to confirm my disdain for Democratic Party politics. Here we were in the midst of what I considered a great national crisis and one of the most liberal state parties in the country was expending its energy on a dispute that centered on personalities and lifestyles rather than on issues. To make matters worse, neither Rolvaag nor Keith would even comment on the war, which they said was not a state issue. And Walter Mondale, who was running for reelection to the United States Senate, was following his mentor, Vice President Hubert Humphrey, in supporting the war policies of Lyndon Johnson. I attended only one political meeting that summer. A group of us active in the antiwar movement tried to persuade Mulford Q. Sibley to run against Mondale as an independent peace candidate. But Mulford's wife, who I learned later was a levelheaded and practical woman, thought it was a terrible idea and Mulford declined. In September, Rolvaag won in a landslide, running particularly well among older and less affluent voters who resented the Keith candidacy as the work of an arrogant elite. But the party was so deeply divided that the Republicans regained the governorship and most of the other statewide offices in November. Only Mondale was comfortably reelected.

The antiwar movement demonstrated its indifference to the 1966 election by holding the university's second teach-in on Monday, November 7, the evening before Election Day when more conventional political activists were rounding up last-minute votes. Once again, I was one of the principal organizers and I invited the speakers to my apartment for drinks. The movement now had moved well beyond the polite, gentle teach-in of 1965. No attempt was made to provide a balanced presentation of the issues involving the war. The speakers were all passionate opponents of the war; they included Edward Keating from *Ramparts* magazine, Lincoln Lynch from CORE, and Clark Kissinger from SDS. Once again we followed the main speeches with smaller group sessions that went on until the wee hours of the morning.

Al Jones arrived in the fall of 1966 and I had promised to try to find a suitable apartment for him. During the summer months, I followed up on a few leads and finally found a place near the campus that I thought he would like. I told the landlord that I was interested but that it would not be for me but for a friend who was moving to Minneapolis in September. "What is your friend's name?" he asked. "Alfred Jones," I replied. He hesitated for a moment, then asked, "Is he one of the white Joneses or one of the black Joneses?" It had never before occurred to me that "Alfred Jones" would be identified by many people as a black name, but I was furious. "What difference does that make?" I asked. "Well," he said, "I'm not sure if the apartment will be available in September." Then I lashed into him. I told him that Al Jones was white but that he would not want to rent from a landlord with such blatant racial prejudices. I further told him that the questions he had asked violated state law and that I fully intended to report him to the state authorities. He begged me not to do that as I walked out. I called Al that night, and he agreed that he would not have wanted the apartment under the circumstances. The next day, I filed a complaint with the Minnesota State Commission Against Discrimination. I was told that the case was an unusual one as no minority person was involved, but that the questions the landlord asked were improper and that they would investigate. In October, the commission advised me that they had made a determination of "probable cause to credit the allegation of discrimination." The landlord was required to sign a statement that he would not discriminate in the future. In the meantime, I had found another apartment for Al that, when he saw it, he didn't like at all. He finally found his own place to live.

Al and I saw each other frequently that fall as I helped acclimate him to the department and to Minneapolis. A few months later, he met the woman who would become his first wife at a party in my apartment. I also made a new friend during the 1966–67 academic year who would come to play an important role in my life. Marcia Greenfield enrolled in my graduate seminar in African American history. She was a graduate student in American studies who had come to Minnesota from New York City and still spoke with a heavy Queens accent. A small, dark-haired woman, she always had a lot to say and, in the New York Jewish tradition, was not hesitant in expressing her opinion about any subject. The first thing she said to me when we met was, "A lot of people have told me that you look like my husband." When I met her husband, Leon, or Lee as he preferred to be called, I could kind of see it but not exactly: we were both short, balding, and overweight, but otherwise there wasn't that much of a resemblance. Nevertheless, throughout our parallel political careers, people continued to confuse us with each other. Lee was also from New York, but he had met Marcia in Minnesota, where he had come to do graduate work in the philosophy of science. Lee and Marcia held political views similar to mine and also shared my passion for food. Marcia was an excellent cook, and we learned from each other as we shared recipes and cooking tips and hosted dinner parties for mutual friends. Marcia ultimately became my aide in a variety of capacities: she graded papers for me at the university and then became my administrative assistant at the state Senate. Lee was to serve as my campaign manager (and I as his), and we were political allies for many years. Both Lee and Marcia have been close personal friends for forty years.

In late November 1966, I received a "feeler" from another university that I could not ignore. The University of Wisconsin at Madison had for many years offered one of the two or three strongest history programs in the country. Moreover, unlike the somewhat encrusted Ivy League schools, Wisconsin had welcomed innovative and even radical scholars such as the left-wing historian of American foreign policy William Appleman Williams, who was considered a pariah in much of the profession. And Madison was, to me, an exceedingly attractive place—not as big or as cosmopolitan as the Twin Cities, but lively and beautifully situated. When I was invited for an interview, I went. I was hosted by the chairman of the department, E. David Cronon, who had himself written an important book in African American history, a pioneering biography of the black nationalist leader Marcus Garvey. Cronon was on to other things and was not teaching in the field, which was why they wanted me, but he clearly would be a compatible colleague. I also had dinner, while I was in Madison, with Les Fishel, my mentor from Oberlin, who was still running the Wisconsin Historical Society. He was not a member of the history department, but he had connections to it and he urged me to come. The campus itself seemed very different from Minnesota. Minnesota was primarily a commuter campus; most of the students dispersed and went home every night, which made it difficult to sustain a sense of community life. The Wisconsin campus was teeming at all hours with activities spilling over into the nearby streets of downtown Madison. And it was clearly a political hotbed. One of the first signs I saw sprayed on the side of a building on campus read: "Lee Harvey Oswald—Where Are You Now That We Need You?"

Shortly after I returned, I received a letter from Professor Cronon. I was offered an associate professorship with tenure, contingent upon the publication of my book, at a salary of eleven thousand dollars. I would teach the Race and Nationality course at the upper-division undergraduate level, a graduate research seminar, and eventually a third course. In addition, I was promised a semester research leave with full pay within my first two years at Wisconsin. A few days later I received a letter from Les Fishel, cogently outlining the reasons why I should come to Wisconsin, centering particularly on its strong reputation in history and its ability to attract first-rate graduate students and faculty. I was tempted, but in accordance with academic custom, I first gave Minnesota a chance to respond. I took the offer to Stuart Hoyt, who was in his first year as chair of the department, and asked if Minnesota would match the salary, which was the only real difference between the Wisconsin offer and my situation at Minnesota. Within a few days, after consultation with the dean, Professor Hoyt reported back that the salary would be matched.

I spent the winter holidays agonizing over what I should do. My

Minnesota colleagues wanted me to stay, but there was one exception. The Berkhofers, who were becoming disillusioned with Minnesota, thought I should go to Wisconsin. They thought the Wisconsin history department was more promising than Minnesota's and would offer me better opportunities. Two years later, they themselves went to Wisconsin and within a short time became disillusioned there, too. I went to Michigan City for the holidays and my parents were enormously excited as the phone rang constantly with deans and professors from Minneapolis and Madison calling to make their arguments. Their son, they decided, had become an important person.

Finally, I had to decide. I returned to Minneapolis and on January 2, 1967, wrote a letter to Professor Cronon telling him that I was reluctantly declining his offer. My decision, I assured him, "in no way reflects on the quality of the Wisconsin department or on the terms of the offer itself. I was, in fact, very favorably impressed, when I visited Madison in November, by the vitality and congeniality of the department, and I considered the offer most attractive indeed." Instead, I continued, "the determining factor in my decision was my reluctance to leave Minnesota. I have been treated well here, have many friends, and enjoy life in the Twin Cities. Moreover, Minnesota's response to the offer from Wisconsin assured me that my future here is a bright one and that the department has the will and the strength to become one of the best in the country. I consider my decision, then, to be an expression of confidence in Minnesota rather than a rejection of Wisconsin." That pretty well summed it up. I had in two and a half years become a Minnesotan. Never again would I contemplate leaving.

5

LOVE, WAR, AND POLITICS, 1967-1969

I spent the winter and spring of 1967 putting the final touches on my dissertation. In the process, I learned a great deal about how to prepare a manuscript for publication as I did it all myself. I decided that in the time it would take to get the manuscript in shape for a professional typist, I could do my own typing. I was a pretty fast typist; my parents had insisted that I take typing in high school and, even though I was one of the very few boys in the class, I never regretted it. When the page proofs came, I also decided to do my own index. I have found the indexes to most books unsatisfactory, and I think that is because they are often put together by someone other than the author; only the author understands the contents well enough to know what should be indexed and under what category. The University of Chicago Press had originally announced a spring publication date. We didn't quite make that, but we weren't far behind. *Black Chicago: The Making of a Negro Ghetto, 1890–1920* was finally slated for publication on August 8, 1967.

The publication of my book was something I had long anticipated. But something else happened to me in the late winter of 1967 that I never anticipated: I fell in love with a woman. In later years, after I became well known in Minnesota as a gay man, many people, hearing this story, assumed that my affair with Sally B.[1] was a cover, that I was looking for a relationship with a woman to hide my homosexuality. That is not true. I was not looking for this kind of a relationship at all; I stumbled into it. And it was absolutely genuine. Sally B. was the only person of either gender who, I believe, I truly loved until I met my partner, Jun, fifteen years later. If this makes me less of a homosexual, then so be it.

Sally B. was a married woman of about my age who lived with her husband and two children in a Minneapolis suburb. She was very attractive with dark hair ("black Irish," she later explained to me) and a good figure. She enrolled in the fall of 1966 in the section of my Race

---

1. Sally B. is a pseudonym.

and Nationality course that I taught in the evening in the extension division. Most of the students in the evening class were, like Sally, older students who worked or cared for children during the day. We met once a week for three hours and in the middle of each session took a half-hour break and retreated to the snack bar. Sally always sat next to me during the break and gradually I heard her story. She had married and had children while still very young and had not finished her university degree. Now she was bored staying home every day with the kids and had returned to school with the hope of finishing her degree, then going on for a master's degree in social work. It also soon became clear that she had lost interest in her husband. He was a good-looking guy and, she conceded, a good father, but she was smarter than he and her interests were beginning to range far beyond his. All in all, it was not an unusual story. Had I been so inclined, I could certainly have made a move on her as she was clearly ripe for an affair.

One evening, while we were in the snack bar, a graduate student friend, Bruce Z.,[2] walked by. Sally and Bruce locked eyes, and the next thing I knew they were exchanging telephone numbers. Bruce later told me that he was smitten by Sally. "She's married," I said. "Well," he replied, "so am I. But we both need a little change." Soon, they were seeing each other whenever they could—sometimes in my apartment when I wasn't home. But eventually their spouses found out and it got nasty. One night, at about eleven o'clock, as I got ready to go to bed, the phone rang. It was Sally and she was obviously distraught. "I need to talk to you right away," she said. "Can I come over?" I told her she could. When she arrived, she told me that she and Bruce couldn't see each other anymore and that it was becoming increasingly difficult for her to live with her husband. She didn't want to go home to him that night and asked if she could stay with me. Then she told me that I was the one she had always really wanted, that she started up with Bruce only because I had seemed so indifferent to her. I told her that I had not meant to reject her personally, but that I was afraid of a relationship with a woman. I also told her that I had never had sex with a woman and wasn't sure I could even do it. She told me she thought I could with her help. She was right.

---

2. Bruce Z. is a pseudonym.

I never told Sally that I was gay. In fact, when I was with her, and particularly when I was having sex with her, I didn't think I was. I thoroughly enjoyed the physical contact with a beautiful woman who responded to me and genuinely cared about me. I began to believe what the psychiatrist at Yale had told me, that my problem was not homosexuality but my inability to relate emotionally to other people. Sally and I continued to see each other throughout the spring and into the summer. She separated from her husband and he moved out of the house; the children stayed there with her. I sometimes went to the house but we never had sex there; she was not comfortable acting out her affair while her children slept in the next room. More often we went out together for dinner or some event and then went to my place. When I was invited out, I was usually asked to bring her and soon my friends had begun to regard us as a couple.

Sally was sometimes brutally direct in the way she related to people. One night in the Mixers bar, a drunk patron made a pass at her. She responded by putting her lit cigarette out on the top of his head. But what was appropriate in the Mixers did not always work at the chic little dinner parties that Sally attended with me. Her behavior did not always meet the expectations of my academic friends. For one thing, she was under a lot of stress, trying to decide whether to divorce her husband and how that would affect her children, and this sometimes came out in her behavior with other people. She also told me how different my friends were from the people she and her husband had socialized with. Our parties centered on food and conversation; theirs had mostly been about drinking. She was at times shockingly frank in the opinions she expressed and the questions she asked of other people. But she could also be charming and endearing. My friends were of two minds about her. Some liked her high spirits and thought a relationship with a woman like Sally was just what I needed. Others thought she lacked self-control and that I was heading into a disastrous relationship. When we were alone, we began to talk about her divorcing her husband and marrying me, but she was not ready to commit herself to that idea yet. I had long planned a trip to Europe for the summer of 1967, and it seemed to both of us a good idea to take a break from each other for a while.

My work on *Black Chicago* was finished by the end of the academic year; I now had only to wait for the press to get it out. So this seemed to be the ideal time to take a second trip to Europe. Moreover, with the salary increase that the Wisconsin offer had provided, I could afford to travel in a little better style than I had five years earlier. In those days of a strong dollar, getting to Europe was more expensive than lodging there, so it made more sense to stay overseas for a long period of time than it does today. And I was still into the mind-set of trying to see as many different countries as I could—something I have since gotten over. So I put together a six-week itinerary that included the Netherlands, Belgium, Denmark, Germany, Italy, Turkey, Greece, Bulgaria, the Soviet Union, and Finland. In most of these countries, I arranged to meet someone or travel with someone. I traveled with my brother and sister-in-law in the Low Countries. A Danish historian who had been a visiting professor at Minnesota the previous year hosted me in Copenhagen. And for the last three weeks of the trip, I traveled with my old friend, Michael A., to Istanbul and Athens, then via Sofia, to Kiev, Moscow, and Leningrad and home through Helsinki.

It was an exhilarating, if exhausting, trip. This was the height of the Vietnam War and opposition to American policy was widespread in Europe. Yet I encountered no personal hostility. In Amsterdam, I came across an anti–Vietnam War demonstration in the Rembrandtplein and picked up a microphone to remind the crowd that not all Americans supported Johnson's war policy. But if I had found common ground with Communists in the antiwar movement at home, I certainly saw nothing in Europe to attract me to the Communist model. In Berlin, I went through Checkpoint Charlie and was shocked by the contrast between lively West Berlin and drab East Berlin. And the Soviet Union became another candidate for the Rudyard Kipling line that I used in regard to Las Vegas. I am glad that I went, but I never wanted to return. Some of the historical sites were spectacular—Red Square, the Kremlin, the Hermitage, the Summer Palace—but the cities were unattractive, the service rude and inefficient, and the food inedible. In Moscow, when we complained that we had no hot water in our room, we were casually told that the hot water had been shut off for nine days and would not be available during our entire stay. That was in a first-class hotel. There was nothing we could do, as we were assigned hotels and could not change. But I saw some of the great sights of

Europe that summer—the Colosseum, the Parthenon, Mycenae, Hagia Sofia, the Golden Horn at sunset—and nothing disappointed.

Black Chicago was published while I was in Europe. The timing could not have been better for the promotion of the book, and the University of Chicago Press took full advantage of it. The northern urban violence of the 1960s had begun in 1964, but 1967 was the bloodiest summer yet, with riots in Detroit and Newark that claimed scores of lives and caused millions of dollars in property damage. Although my book dealt with a period that ended in 1920, the press launched an advertising campaign that attempted to link the book to current events. Most spectacularly, it ran an ad that featured a news photograph of a white police officer with his billy club in the air poised to strike a crowd of cowering black people. Next to the picture was a quotation from Santayana: "Those who cannot remember the past are condemned to repeat it." The ad was placed in a number of national magazines with highly literate but nonspecialist readerships, such as *Harper's,* the *Atlantic,* and the *New Republic.* A representative of the Chicago Police Department soon called the press to protest that the picture was not that of a Chicago policeman. The hat was of a type that had never been used in Chicago. A columnist for the *Chicago Daily News* then searched the newspaper's files and found that the picture was not of an American police officer at all, but of a racial confrontation in Durban, South Africa, in 1960. This caused a big stir: the press was accused of dishonesty and was forced to withdraw the ad. The controversy was reported widely in Chicago and in the national press. I was flying from Rome to Istanbul and picked up a copy of *Time* magazine and there came across an article about it. This was the first I knew of it.

When I returned from Europe, I found a letter from Dorothy Sutherland, the publicity manager of the University of Chicago Press, expressing regret that my "book should have become the center of this storm." But, she added, "no adverse criticism of your work was made by anyone at any time," and "sales were *not* at all harmed by the fact that a very large number of people heard of your book who might not otherwise have done so." When I replied that I was not alarmed by the controversy, Ms. Sutherland expressed relief but reminded me "to drive very carefully if you're in Chicago soon because you'd never be able to talk yourself out of a ticket." Meanwhile, the press found new and less incendiary ways to advertise the book and began arranging promotional interviews for me. I flew to Chicago to appear on *The Irv Kupcinet Show*—the city's most popular local television talk show. And I did many radio interviews over the telephone. Soon, the reviews started coming in and they were almost universally favorable. In addition to the predictable reviews in Chicago and Minnesota newspapers, others appeared in newspapers around the country and even in Britain. By the end of the year, the scholarly journals had begun to weigh in. Again, the book was well received. The *Journal of American History*, the leader in its field, called it "a distinguished addition" to the literature; the prominent historian Eugene Genovese said "it stands out as one of the best such books yet written"; and August Meier, one of the real pioneers in the field, concluded, "Impeccably researched, unusually well written, this volume is certainly the best monograph in American Negro history to have appeared this year."

Black Chicago turned out to be a best seller as academic books go. The controversy over the ad, and the link, made by many reviewers, to current urban racial unrest, boosted its sales in the first year. Good reviews in the scholarly journals led to classroom adoptions in history and sociology and, later, African American studies courses, which assured a steady stream of sales in years to come. In 1969, the book came out in paperback, with the same enigmatic cover photograph of a black hand holding an oddly shaped picture of a little black boy. The University of Chicago Press approached me in the late seventies about preparing a second edition. But my life had moved on to other things by that time and I never did it. Forty years after its publication, *Black Chicago* is still in print and has sold more than sixty thousand copies.

In the fall of 1967, I was clearly on the verge of a highly successful academic career. At the age of thirty, I had a tenured position at a major university, I had just published a successful book, I was in a hot field, and I was getting frequent offers for speaking engagements and "feelers" from other universities. The big question that I was asked wherever I moved in academic circles was what I was going to do next, because it was assumed that a serious scholar who had completed one project then moved quickly into another. And while I was now a tenured associate professor, if I wanted to become a full professor with the appropriate salary increase, I would be expected to complete a second body of major scholarly work. I spent a good deal of time thinking about this second project. The easiest thing would have been to have written the sequel to *Black Chicago*. I had already done some of the research for the 1920s. One of the reviewers had in fact suggested that "Allan Spear [should follow] Jane Addams's example and give us soon *Black Chicago's Second Thirty Years*." But this idea seemed to me rather unimaginative. I wanted a new subject and I wanted something ambitious enough to make another major contribution to the field of African American history.

Although I was trained as a twentieth-century American historian, I found my interests leading me back into the nineteenth century. As I had probed the first generation of black people to come to Chicago, I had begun to wonder about the transitions they had made in the years since Emancipation. There was no shortage of historical scholarship on the politics of the Civil War and Reconstruction and the tragic events that led to the collapse of Reconstruction. But there was very little on how the lives of ordinary African American people had developed as they struggled not just with the gift of freedom but also with the burden of new responsibilities in the midst of a hostile white world. I put together a grant proposal to do research on the topic "The Transition to Freedom: Southern Negroes, 1861–1877." I would explore "the attitudes of the freedmen toward their old masters and their new Yankee mentors, their behavior in regard to work, the kind of leadership that they developed and the extent to which it was independent of white control, and the differences in behavior among various classes of ex-slaves." I submitted the proposal to the National Endowment for the Humanities and learned a few months later that I had been awarded a grant. I would receive the equivalent of my salary from January 1 to August 31, 1968. In the 1967–68 academic year, I taught only fall quarter, then had the rest of the year off to pursue my new project.

I had found an excellent topic, a study that definitely needed to be done. It eventually was. But not by me. In 1979, Leon Litwack, a prominent historian at the University of California, Berkeley, published *Been in the Storm So Long*. It covered the very topic that I had outlined in my proposal to the NEH and did it very well. I've never met Professor Litwack, so we never discussed the transition to freedom in the

Civil War and postwar South. Had I gotten much further along with the research, I am sure we would have met and compared notes. But I ran out of steam after *Black Chicago* and within the next year was spending most of my time in the antiwar movement and in politics. I continued for a few years to believe that I would eventually get back into historical research, but I never did. I gradually lost interest in an academic career altogether. How this happened is a long and complicated story and will be touched on over the next few chapters. I am not sure that I fully understand all of it myself.

Meanwhile, my romantic life had its ups and downs. Sally and I had corresponded frequently while I was in Europe and started seeing each other again after I returned. But she seemed more troubled now about the relationship. She was devoted to her children and increasingly anxious about the strains that her separation and her affair with me were putting on them. She worried that she was putting her own personal pleasure ahead of their well-being. There wasn't much I could say in response to her concerns. First, it was really her decision. And second, I had so little personal experience with the kinds of issues she faced that I had few insights to offer. I still cared deeply about Sally and wanted to continue to see her. But more and more often now, when I called she didn't want to see me. There was no dramatic break in the relationship; we just saw each other less. But it was not yet over. We were to resume the relationship with even greater intensity the next year.

In the late summer of 1967, I began to look for a larger apartment, preferably in a duplex. I liked to entertain and wanted more space, and since my relationship with Sally had begun, I was also having overnight company. I was eager to move out of the kind of faceless apartment buildings in which I had been living. Minneapolis was cursed with too many 1950s-style jerry-built walk-up apartments, but it was also blessed with a large stock of single-family houses and duplexes from the prewar era, many of them with hardwood floors and paneling, built-in cabinets and bookshelves, and wood-burning fireplaces. I found an upper duplex that fit this description on the west bank of the Mississippi, overlooking the river and just a few blocks from my office on campus. An older woman lived downstairs; her family owned the house. She proved to be an agreeable neighbor and I stayed there for six years until I bought a house of my own. I now had a large living room, a sunroom, a full dining room, and two bedrooms, so I had the pleasant chore of going out and buying more furniture to fill it up.

It was at one of my first parties in the new apartment that Al Jones met the woman who would soon become his wife. Bonnie Marvy was a young Jewish woman from St. Paul who was going to art school. She was pretty, lively, and, while not an intellectual, a good and interesting conversationalist. I liked her a lot. When their relationship had its predictable ups and downs over the next year, I become something of a confidant to both Al and Bonnie. By the time they married, in the summer of 1968, I considered them both good friends. We later saw a lot of each other, even after they left Minnesota in 1972.

I also developed another close friendship in the fall of 1967. Stuart Schwartz had been hired by the history department the year before to teach Latin American history. The department, like most around the country, was only now gradually moving out of its traditional emphasis on American and European history. There had been a Chinese and an Indian historian for several years, and in 1966, the department hired a Japanese historian. Now it was bringing in a second Chinese historian and a full-time Latin American specialist. Latin American history up to this point had been handled by an older colleague who also taught American diplomatic history and who approached Latin America primarily as an object of U.S. foreign policy. I was still struggling to get my colleagues to hire an African historian. We had finally hired someone to teach one course in African history on a part-time basis. But there was great resistance to fully embracing a field that many historians still saw as "prehistory" because it did not have written records.

Stuart Schwartz was a Brazilian specialist, trained at Columbia and fresh out of graduate school. We immediately hit it off and found that we had many interests in common. He was working on sugar production in colonial Brazil and was necessarily drawn to topics involving slavery and race relations. Soon we were giving guest lectures in each other's courses and planning a team-taught course. We came up with one joint performance, which we did in Stuart's Latin American survey course, that soon became a campus legend. It was a reenactment of a famous debate that occurred in 1550 in Spain between the Dominican friar Bartolomé de las Casas and the humanist scholar Juan de Sepúlveda over the treatment of Indians in the New World. Stuart played Sepúlveda and dressed in full academic regalia; I played de las Casas and wore a monk's habit that I had borrowed from a friend who was a Roman Catholic priest. We got serious points across but also hammed it up and the students loved it.

Stuart and I also saw a lot of each other outside of the classroom. We frequently met for dinner and a few years later traveled together. One dinner was particularly memorable. Stuart had invited Charles Boxer, a British historian who was perhaps the leading authority in the world on the history of the Portuguese colonial empire, to come to Minnesota to give a series of lectures. He asked me to join him in taking Boxer to dinner; I invited Sally, and Stuart invited the woman he was dating. We went to the Rosewood Room, then one of the poshest restaurants in downtown Minneapolis. Charles Boxer had been an officer in the British army, was full of stories about his military escapades, and was soon in his cups. He began leading us in verses of bawdy British military barracks songs. The maître d' finally came over and asked us to cease and desist. After dinner, Sally told me that during all of this, she was struggling to keep Boxer's hand out of her inner thigh. I was relieved that she hadn't crushed a lighted cigarette on top of his head.

Another new addition to the department that year would influence my career in a different way. Rudy Vecoli came to Minnesota to become director of the Immigrant Archives, a major scholarly project housed in the university library that collected material relating to immigration to America from eastern and southern Europe. It was also assumed that Professor Vecoli would teach a course in immigration history and direct graduate students in that field. That meant the days were numbered for my Race and Nationality course as it made little sense for me to continue to teach the immigration component of it when the department had a full-time specialist in the field. The idea of combining African American history with the history of European immigration had been problematic anyway, so I agreed that within a few years I would drop the course and instead teach an undergraduate course that mirrored my graduate seminar—in African American history.

What I did not yet foresee was the growing resistance among some young African Americans to the presence of white academics in the field of African American history. I was, of course, aware of the enormous shift that had occurred since the midsixties from the interracial, integrationist spirit of the civil rights movement to the nationalism of the Black Power movement. SNCC and CORE had expelled their white members and become Black Power organizations, generally destroying their effectiveness and leaving hurt and bewildered white supporters in the wreckage. While Martin Luther King and the NAACP still proclaimed the goal of an integrated society, younger leaders like Stokely Carmichael and H. Rap Brown said that the aim of the black movement was now black economic and political self-sufficiency and black cultural pride. I had duly noted all of this in my courses and in the talks I gave to various civic groups. But I tended to see it in a historical context. Whenever black aspirations had been raised and then thwarted—after the collapse of Reconstruction, again after the northern migrations of the World War I era—there had been an upsurge in black nationalism. The pattern was repeating itself once again. And my message was that if white people found black power threatening, the best solution was to end racism and discrimination in American society.

Yet I did not see these developments as affecting me personally. I had been fully accepted by my fellow students at Fisk. I had always been received cordially when I went into the black community to do research. My book was well reviewed by black newspapers and periodicals. My students were mostly white, reflecting the racial composition of the university and of the state, but the black students who did take my classes seemed to be satisfied with them. There were, however, premonitions of things to come. Shortly after the release of *Black Chicago,* the publicist at the University of Chicago Press asked me if I would come to Chicago to speak about my work to a community group that was interested in meeting me. I readily agreed and when I arrived at a community center on the West Side of Chicago, I found a large hall packed with black people from the local community. I don't think they were expecting a white man. I had barely started speaking when the hostile questions began. "Why do you think you have the credentials to write about black people?" "Why are you trying to make money off black people?" "How can you possibly know what it is like to be black?" None of the questions related to any of the specific points I had raised in the book. The hostility was centered entirely on the color of my skin. As a white man, it was assumed, I could not possibly understand the life of African Americans.

I was not easily intimidated by this argument—on that day or in the future. I had spent too many years and worked too diligently to be told that I didn't understand African American history because I wasn't black. I pointed out that many people who read *Black Chicago*, including, I suspect, many who were in the room that day in Chicago, could not identify me racially from the content of the book. There was no picture of me on the cover and it was not until they saw me that they knew that I was white. That illustrated my major point: it was impossible to distinguish good work done by a white scholar from good work done by a black scholar. I conceded that there were some aspects of the African American experience that I could never comprehend as fully or as deeply as someone who had grown up black. But none of us have lived through historical events that occurred prior to our lifetimes. The art of history is to make the imaginative leap to another time and another mind-set. The people who confronted me on the West Side of Chicago in 1967 had never been slaves in the antebellum South—or, for that matter, migrants to Chicago in 1900. They, as much as I, would have to make an imaginative leap if they were to write a history of their ancestors. These arguments, predictably, did not resonate with people who were angry and in no mood for rational discourse.

A much better-known event in Chicago in the late summer of 1967 further illustrated how race relations were evolving and, although I wasn't there, influenced the political decisions I would make over the next year. The convention of the National Conference for New Politics was held at the Palmer House over Labor Day weekend in an effort to bring the antiwar movement and the black movement together around a possible independent presidential candidacy to oppose Lyndon Johnson in 1968. Martin Luther King, who had by this time become a sharp critic of the Vietnam War, had agreed to keynote the convention and many of the participants foresaw a "dream ticket" of King for president and the legendary baby-care expert and now antiwar leader Benjamin Spock for vice president. I was in Europe at the time of the convention and might have attended had I been in the country. I had become alienated from the Democratic Party and was certainly looking for a political alternative. But the convention tore itself apart along racial lines. The black delegates constituted about a quarter of the convention but insisted on equal voting rights as a bloc, arguing that they represented in essence a separate nation. The majority of white delegates, willing to concede anything to prevent a threatened black walkout, agreed and then accepted a far left platform written by black radicals. More moderate antiwar activists went home in disappointment. Martin Luther King took one look and turned to other things. The idea of an independent ticket in 1968 was left in the wreckage.

I had become convinced, however, that the only hope for ending the war in Vietnam lay in political action. Since the teach-in of 1965, I had attended scores of meetings, participated in dozens of demonstrations and vigils, and even gone to Washington for national protests. None of it seemed to have any effect on the Johnson administration as American involvement in the war deepened. Peace in Vietnam, it seemed obvious, would require a new president. The Republicans were unlikely to nominate an antiwar candidate, and the New Politics convention killed the idea of an independent candidate. That left the Democratic Party. It would be necessary to dump Lyndon Johnson from within the Democratic Party, a political task that would be very difficult to achieve. Antiwar Democrats throughout the country were coming to the same conclusion and a young activist named Allard Lowenstein had begun to search for a plausible Democratic alternative to Johnson.

In Minnesota, three activist law students, who were establishing a political base in the countercultural Cedar-Riverside community, adjacent to the West Bank campus, led the Dump Johnson effort. Vance Opperman, Howard Kaibel, and Bob Metcalf had all been active in the radical group Students for a Democratic Society, but in 1966 they entered the DFL and managed to take over the largely moribund Sixth Ward organization. Under their leadership, the Sixth Ward DFL was the first party organization in the state to pass an antiwar resolution, a development that was troubling to Vice President Hubert Humphrey, who watched as a state party he once totally controlled became deeply divided. In the summer of 1967, Howie Kaibel attended a national meeting with Al Lowenstein, who had advised the attendees to go back to their states and find party leaders who might be willing to unseat the president. Kaibel found two: State Representative Alpha Smaby, who represented the university district, and Forrest Harris, a university professor, who was also a vice-chairman of the state DFL. In September, they met with a small group of academics and party activists to form Minnesota Dissenting Democrats, later given a more conciliatory name, the Conference of Concerned Democrats.

I can't remember when I first became involved with Concerned Democrats. I no longer trusted the Democratic Party as an instrument of social change. But the other forms of political activism that I had tried had proved to be dead ends, and with the collapse of the New Politics convention there was really no alternative. The problem in the fall of 1967 was that Lowenstein had not found a candidate to oppose Johnson. Robert Kennedy, his first choice, had turned him down, as did several other prominent antiwar senators. Then, on November 30, Minnesota's own Senator Eugene McCarthy announced that he would run against Johnson for the Democratic presidential nomination. McCarthy was an unlikely candidate to take on such a crusade. He was highly intelligent and thoughtful, but low-key, given to understatement, and, rumor had it, a little lazy. He would be going not only against Johnson but against his Minnesota colleague, Hubert Humphrey, one of the most dynamic and ebullient figures in American politics. The race was sure to divide the DFL party even more deeply than the Rolvaag-Keith contest of the year before. But this time, I would not be watching from the sidelines. I knew immediately where I stood: I became a committed partisan for McCarthy.

The Second and Sixth wards, which bordered the university campus, were at the center of the effort to organize for McCarthy. Students and faculty members had been the first to oppose the war and had played a major role in organizing Concerned Democrats. Antiwar sentiment had spread now to other parts of the Twin Cities, to the suburbs, and to a few outstate communities. But in much of Minnesota, loyalty to Humphrey remained strong, and a good showing for McCarthy would depend upon a massive turnout in the university area and in middle-class neighborhoods in Minneapolis and St. Paul. The precinct caucuses were scheduled for March 6, 1968. Minnesota did not have a presidential primary. It chose its national delegates through a complicated process of precinct caucuses, which were open to everyone, and a series of delegate conventions on the ward, county, congressional district, and state level. Before the so-called McGovern-Fraser reforms, which were adopted by the national Democratic Party after the 1968 elections, delegates were chosen at each level on a winner-take-all basis. This put a premium on bringing out massive numbers of people to the precinct caucuses.

In January, the McCarthy campaign, which had looked like a real long shot when it began (former governor Orville Freeman had called it a "footnote in history"), became a serious effort. The Tet offensive in Vietnam had turned the majority of Americans against the war for the first time and made McCarthy a serious candidate. We intensified our efforts in Minnesota. I worked with a neighbor, an antiwar activist named Charlie Christiansen, to organize my precinct, but we had no idea until we walked into our local school on caucus night how well we had done. Hundreds of people had come to an event that in the past had attracted forty or fifty. I didn't know who most of the people were and my first impression was that the "machine" had out-organized us. My cynical view of establishment politics told me that there was no way we could win, that it would all somehow be greased for the other side. Then the voting began. I was on the McCarthy slate and to my total amazement not only did our slate win all of the delegate slots, but I came in first. Even the two elected officials who lived in the precinct, Representative Martin Sabo and State Senator Jack Davies, both Humphrey supporters, failed to be elected delegates. Later that night we found out that the results were similar throughout Minneapolis and St. Paul and in many of the middle-class suburbs. The McCarthy campaign had taken off.

When I moved in 1967 from the east bank of the river (southeast Minneapolis) to the west bank, I had moved to a different legislative district, but I was still in the same ward. I was no longer represented by Alpha Smaby, but I was in the Second Ward even though the West Bank campus itself was in the Sixth Ward. This bit of arcane political geography was to have a major impact on my career in 1968. As an elected precinct delegate, it meant that my next stop was the Second Ward convention, where delegates to the state convention would be chosen. The Second Ward spanned the river, but its heart was a faculty neighborhood called Prospect Park in southeast Minneapolis, a major hotbed of antiwar politics. I soon discovered, as I met with delegates from Prospect Park, that the enemy was not just the Humphrey Democrats, of whom there were not many in the Second Ward, but antiwar Democrats who might put the party above the cause. Internal conflict in the Second Ward DFL reminded me of the strife that had torn apart the Minnesota Committee to End the War in Vietnam, and I didn't like it any better. I'm not sure who was at fault. Representative Smaby, together with Maurice Visscher, a distinguished physician at the University Medical School, put together a slate that included people with long experience in the DFL party. The newcomers thought they were being excluded, that the Smaby slate was elitist, and that Smaby and Visscher and their allies could not be trusted to continue to oppose Humphrey. So, led by my friend Charlie Christiansen and his southeast Minneapolis ally, Jim Beck, the newcomers put together their own slate. Alpha's slate was soon dubbed the "Doves," the rival slate the "Superdoves."

I ultimately went with the Superdoves, the first of a number of foolish decisions I was to make in 1968. I was still an outsider to the party and felt more loyal to the antiwar movement than I did to the DFL. I was close to Charlie Christiansen and soon Jim Beck became a friend. Moreover, Marcia and Lee Greenfield, whom I had met the year before when Marcia took my seminar, were also with the Superdoves. And I simply didn't see the most valid reason for electing Alpha's slate. At the state convention, where the national delegates would be chosen, Humphrey would likely have a majority of the delegates. To maximize McCarthy's strength, it would be useful to have as delegates experienced and respected party people who understood how the process worked. But for many of us in 1968, the party was not important; it was just a vehicle for our antiwar passions. At the Second Ward convention, the Superdoves prevailed, except that Alpha and her closest friend, an experienced liberal Democrat named Esther Wattenberg, were elected delegates.

In the days after the Minnesota caucuses and ward conventions, the political landscape changed with almost breathtaking speed. On March 12, McCarthy polled 42 percent in the New Hampshire primary and seemed almost certain to win the next major primary contest in Wisconsin. Four days later, Robert Kennedy, long considered the most viable antiwar candidate, entered the race. Kennedy's decision caused great consternation in Minnesota. Had he chosen to run six months earlier, he probably would have had the united support of antiwar Democrats. But now he looked like an opportunist. McCarthy had made the tough decision to oppose Johnson when the president looked unbeatable and had laid the groundwork for an anti-war campaign. Kennedy was stepping in only after McCarthy had demonstrated Johnson's vulnerability. Moreover, McCarthy was a native son and, despite his sometimes erratic behavior, commanded our loyalty. Kennedy drew very little support in Minnesota.

The Minnesota DFL put its delegates through an almost endless series of caucuses and conventions in the 1960s. The process was somewhat streamlined a few years later and the functions of the ward and county conventions were shifted to the state senate district conventions in order to eliminate a few steps. But in 1968, after the caucuses chose precinct delegates and the ward conventions chose state delegates, there were then state senate district and county conventions to endorse candidates, elect party officers, and draw up platforms. The Minnesota endorsement system was unlike anything else in the country. The parties endorsed candidates for a wide range of offices, even those that were officially nonpartisan, such as the state legislature, which ran without party designation until 1974. The endorsements, however, had no official legal status. Anyone, endorsed or not, could still run in a primary and the primary ballot did not indicate who had party endorsement. The endorsement was nevertheless important for two reasons. First, it carried a kind of moral weight; candidates who lost the endorsement were under considerable pressure to unite the party and rally behind the endorsed candidate. Second, the endorsement brought with it whatever political support the party could provide—volunteers, contributions, and, perhaps most important, inclusion on the party's sample ballot, which was widely distributed just before the election. Over the years, the endorsement has lost its force in parts of the state; many candidates no longer abide by it and the party has limited resources to offer its endorsed candidates. But in 1968, particularly in the Twin Cities, it was still considered a major political prize.

Since my move to the West Bank, I lived in the Forty-second Legislative District. It included just a sliver of the Second Ward, where I lived, most of the predominantly working-class Ninth Ward, and the sprawling Sixth Ward, which brought together the student- and hippie-dominated Cedar-Riverside area, depressed neighborhoods bordering the downtown business district, and the bulk of the city's low-income senior high-rise buildings. Its senator, Jack Davies, was

not up for reelection in 1968. But both of its members of the House
of Representatives were running. Today, Senate districts are divided
geographically into two House districts. At that time, however, the
two House candidates ran at large in the Senate district. One of the
incumbent House members was Martin Olav Sabo, considered one of
the most promising young Democrats in the state. He had first been
elected to the legislature just out of college, quickly won the respect of
his colleagues, and now, at the age of thirty, was on track for a major
leadership position within the DFL caucus in the next legislative session. Although not a particularly good speaker, Sabo had a thorough
grasp of the issues, a strong commitment to traditional DFL liberalism, and superb political instincts. The other incumbent, Jim Adams,
on the other hand, was barely known outside the district. An electrician at City Hall, Adams had been chosen by organized labor, still a
considerable force in the DFL, and had been in the legislature since
1958 without leaving much of a mark. He was a well-intentioned but
bumbling man, whose answers to even basic questions about legislative policy could sometimes be embarrassing.

The Forty-second District endorsing convention was scheduled for
March 30, and after the antiwar delegates recovered from the excitement of the ward convention we began talking about whether we
should run our own legislative candidates. Although Sabo and even
Adams had expressed reservations about the war, both supported the
reelection of Johnson and Humphrey, which made them anathema to
the zealots. But nearly everyone, even Charlie Christiansen, agreed
that it made no sense to take on Sabo. We decided that we should
support the endorsement of Sabo but try to find a candidate to run
against Adams. We held a number of meetings that included Christiansen and myself from the Second Ward, the three student leaders—
Opperman, Kaibel, and Metcalf—from the Sixth Ward, and a group
of young Democrats, led by Jeff Spartz and Harvey Olson, who had
taken on the pro-Humphrey, labor-oriented leadership in the Ninth
Ward. Opperman and Kaibel were cautious and thought we had our
hands full just working for McCarthy. But Christiansen, Metcalf, and
an older peace activist named Audrey Carney were eager to go after
Adams. The problem was to find a plausible candidate.

As I was sitting down to dinner on March 29, the evening before
the convention, the phone rang. It was Bob Metcalf. He told me that

he was looking through a delegate list and realized for the first time that I lived in the Forty-second District. "Bob," I said, "I've been attending these meetings. Of course, I live in the district." Well, he replied, a lot of people had been coming from outside the district to offer advice and he thought I was one of those. Then he got to the point: "You'd be the perfect candidate against Jim Adams. You ought to run." I had honestly never thought of myself as a candidate before that moment. A few weeks earlier, I hadn't even thought I could get elected a precinct delegate. Bob went on to argue that I was a professor, that people respected me, that I had a strong base at the university, that I was articulate, that I could nail Adams on the issues, and that I would be a great legislator. We decided to call a meeting for later that evening. There was so much political excitement in the air that year that it was possible to call a meeting on two hours' notice and bring out dozens of people. Sure enough, at ten o'clock, more than twenty people gathered at a neighbor's house to discuss my candidacy. By the time we adjourned, sometime after midnight, I had decided to run for the endorsement at the convention the next morning.

The convention was held at Dania Hall, a ramshackle building on the corner of Cedar Avenue and Fifth Street that had been built in the late nineteenth century as a social center for Danish immigrants and was now a venue for hippie dances and light shows and a magnet for teenagers from the suburbs who wanted to buy drugs. The building's mixed past made it an appropriate site for a convention that included long-haired radical young people with tie-dyed shirts, soberly dressed labor union officials and retirees, and a few antiwar professors from the university. Since I had no literature or campaign paraphernalia, I just started walking around and talking to people about my candidacy. My supporters did the same thing. Jim Adams, who walked into the hall thinking he was unopposed, soon realized that something was going on. When the speeches began, I talked, of course, about the war. But I realized the state legislature did not make foreign policy, so I also talked about education and human rights, which I knew something about, and taxation and natural resources, which I knew very little about. Endorsement required a 60 percent vote. The convention was split right down the middle. After two ballots, we each had 49 percent of the vote. I had the support of the antiwar McCarthy delegates; Adams retained the loyalty of the Humphrey delegates, particularly in the Ninth Ward. Today, a deadlocked convention simply ends the endorsement process and creates an open primary. But the complex rules of 1968 allowed for an appeal to the next level; the endorsement would be decided a week later at the Hennepin County convention, where the McCarthy delegates would have a big majority. I had not won endorsement that day, but by fighting Adams to a deadlock I had kept the process alive. And I had done so as a last-minute candidate whose only campaign occurred on the convention floor.

I was exhilarated. After celebrating with my political friends, I wanted to go tell everyone I knew what had happened. Al Jones and Bonnie Marvy weren't home and I couldn't find Leo Giovannini, so I ended up at the Berkhofers' house. While they listened politely to my excited account of the convention, it was clear that they were not pleased. They realized, I think, what I did not. By agreeing so readily and casually to run for the legislature, without really thinking through the implications, I had taken a major step away from a serious academic career. I had already used up three of the nine months of my grant from the National Endowment for the Humanities without having done much. I had been too busy organizing for the caucuses. Now, assuming I won the endorsement and ran for the legislature, I would be spending the rest of the time on the campaign. And if I were elected, the focus of my life would shift to my legislative career. To be sure, the Minnesota legislature did not meet full time. In the 1960s, it met only every two years for five months. But there was already talk of changing the constitution and going to annual sessions, which would actually happen in 1972. And even if I kept my teaching job at the university, when would I get the time to complete an ambitious project like the one I had proposed to the NEH?

Why did I do it? A year before, I had been enormously excited by the publication of *Black Chicago* and the good reviews it had received. I liked teaching and I liked my position at the university. I had excellent prospects for the future. Why did I commit myself to a life of ward club meetings, door-to-door campaigning, fund-raising, and, if I was successful, long, mind-numbing legislative sessions? I am not sure, but I can venture a few guesses. First, I had been fascinated by politics since I was a little boy and the chance to be a candidate had great appeal to me. Politics seemed real, an opportunity to influence society in a concrete way. Teaching and scholarship were several steps removed from real life. Second, I had throughout the 1960s always made responsible, career-oriented decisions. I did not interrupt my graduate education to work in the civil rights movement, even though I was tempted. I did not even go to Selma when I had courses to prepare. Now I had tenure and I could put my career on hold for a few years and do what I really wanted to do. Third, I had never really gotten into the "second book" project. The topic was a great one, but it was massive and probably too ambitious, at least for me at that time. The prospect of spending the next ten years of my life on this project was daunting. Finally, tenure gave me security. I say this with hesitation as I support the principle of tenure for university and college faculty. But in my case, it removed the sense of urgency that I apparently needed to discipline myself and get work done on a schedule. I told myself in 1968 and again in 1972, when I ran for the legislature the second time, that I would eventually return to the university full time and resume my scholarly career. Since I had tenure, there was no hurry. I had plenty of time. But it never happened.

There was just one week between the Forty-second District convention and the Hennepin County convention, but it turned out to be a momentous and tragic week. On Sunday, March 31, the day after the district convention, I attended a history department party at the home of the chairman, Stuart Hoyt, and his wife. Once more, I regaled everyone with accounts of the convention and again my colleagues were not overimpressed. In the background, I could hear a television set from the next room. President Johnson was droning on with a speech justifying his policies in Vietnam. I paid no attention until I thought I heard him say, "I will not be a candidate for reelection to the presidency in 1968." Surely, I didn't hear that right. But conversation stopped throughout the house. Everyone had heard it as I did. The movement that had begun with Allard Lowenstein had achieved its goal; Johnson had been forced out of the race.

Johnson's withdrawal had a special impact on Minnesota. Within days Hubert Humphrey became a candidate for president and immediately garnered the support of the party regulars who had previously been loyal to Johnson. In much of the country, McCarthy and Kennedy fought each other to win the antiwar Democrats. In Minnesota, where Kennedy was not a major factor, this assured a direct confrontation between two Minnesotans for control of the party in their home state. When Johnson had been in the race, Humphrey had been a surrogate. Now he himself became a presidential candidate. This intensified the bitterness within the DFL Party. Humphrey's supporters thought him the ablest political leader the state had ever produced; they were incensed that another, less experienced, Minnesotan would try to deprive him of his chance to become president. The McCarthy Democrats believed that regardless of what Humphrey had achieved in the past, he had destroyed his credibility by supporting an immoral and seemingly endless war in Vietnam and remaining unconditionally loyal to Lyndon Johnson. In the coming months, as the campaign unfolded in Minnesota, Humphrey himself would become as much the issue as the war. Humphrey's reputation as an icon of liberalism made his position on the war seem, to many of us, even more odious than it would have been had he been a person of lesser stature.

I spent the rest of the week trying to win delegate support for the Hennepin County convention. There would be more than six thousand delegates—some said, probably inaccurately, that it was the largest delegate assembly in the English-speaking world. I couldn't call them all, but I contacted those whom I was told had been key McCarthy organizers. In the process, I met people who would become friends and political allies for years to come. Carol and Dick Flynn were a young couple in the solidly middle-class Eleventh Ward who had come out for McCarthy and stayed involved in DFL politics for the rest of their lives. Ken Enkel had been a left-winger as a young man back in the 1940s; now a lawyer, he had returned to politics to oppose once again the great bête noire of his life, Hubert Humphrey. Fred and Millie Ptashne were also old lefties; now comfortably ensconced in a western suburb, they promised to help me win support among suburban McCarthy supporters.

I had setbacks, too. On Tuesday evening, I appeared before the endorsing committee, which would make recommendations on endorsements to the full convention. Although McCarthy delegates dominated the convention, the committees tended to be made up of more established party people who were reluctant to dump incumbents without compelling reason. The committee members questioned me sharply as to why I wanted to replace a loyal DFL legislator with a good liberal voting record who had done nothing particularly wrong.

When I started talking about the war in Vietnam, Jim Rice, a crusty longtime party leader from north Minneapolis, interrupted me and said, "Fine, when you're elected to the legislature, you can serve on the foreign policy committee." The endorsement committee recommended that the convention endorse Jim Adams.

On Thursday evening, just as I was about to leave for a ward club meeting, a friend called with terrible news: Martin Luther King had been assassinated in Memphis. That evening and the next, racial violence shattered the calm in scores of American cities as African Americans struck out in rage to protest the murder of the man who had done so much to give shape to the civil rights movement. King's influence had been waning since 1965, and the advocates of Black Power had sharply deviated from his message of integration and nonviolence. But his death was deeply troubling not only to African Americans but to all Americans who were committed to racial equality. Within hours, I was helping to plan an interracial march through the black community in north Minneapolis on Sunday to demonstrate that peaceful solidarity and rededication to King's vision rather than violence was the appropriate response to his assassination.

King's death and the outbreak of racial violence increased the level of intensity at the county convention on Saturday. For the antiwar delegates, the nation was in crisis and the times called for new leadership. I was now better prepared than I had been the previous week. I had a simple brochure to distribute that clearly laid out the choices as I saw them: "politics as usual—old, safe, unimaginative" or "vigorous and enthusiastic leadership that will help point the state toward more creative solutions to its problems." But my endorsement was a sideshow. The big battle, especially for my new friends from Cedar-Riverside, was the campaign to elect Vance Opperman as chair of the Hennepin County DFL. It would be a major coup for the new politics to elect a twenty-five-year old law student, with just two years' experience in the party, as chair in the largest county in the state. Vance, however, was no ordinary law student. His father, Dwight Opperman, was the CEO of West Publishing, the largest legal publisher in the country, and although Vance lived in a grubby student apartment in Cedar-Riverside, he had grown up in an affluent household and, in time, would come into great wealth. Moreover, he was good looking, articulate, and had sure political instincts; despite a background in

SDS, he was already beginning to position himself as a reasonable person who would listen to everyone. Some of the more zealous antiwar people distrusted him, more so after he was quoted in the *Minneapolis Tribune* the previous Sunday as preferring Jim Adams to me. Vance assured me that he was misquoted, and his people did everything they could at the convention to help me. They came equipped with walkie-talkies and thoroughly controlled the proceedings. Vance was easily elected. When it came time for the state house endorsement, I asked Esther Wattenberg, Alpha Smaby's friend, to speak on my behalf. Esther had forgiven me for supporting the Superdoves and she gave a forceful speech that perfectly captured the mood of the day. "I have just returned from Washington, D.C.," she began, "and saw the city on fire. This is not the time for politics as usual." I picked up on the same theme in my own speech and emphasized my background in African American history and my familiarity with issues of urban conflict. When Jim Adams got up, he could only mutter helplessly, "I wish I could talk like those people." Despite the recommendation of the endorsement committee, I was easily endorsed by the full convention on a voice vote.

Jim Adams had made it clear that he was running as the DFL incumbent regardless of who was endorsed. It was hard for me to make the usual argument about uniting the party, since I was the one who had initiated the intraparty challenge. Moreover, I could not raise the specter of a bitter primary opening the seat to a Republican. The district was solidly DFL, and although there would probably be a token Republican candidate, the outline was already clear: the contest would go all the way to November, Sabo would win one of the seats, and Adams and I would vie for the other. The real question was what Sabo would do. He had personal loyalty to Adams and was close to labor, which strongly supported Adams. On the other hand, he believed in the DFL endorsement system and he was aware of Adams's limitations. He was not happy with the outcome of the Hennepin County convention, and he called Esther Wattenberg and scolded her for speaking on my behalf. But he told me, the day after the convention, that he would run his own race and remain neutral between Adams and me.

A few days later, the Second Ward club met, and as was usual that spring hundreds of people attended. Before the meeting, Charlie

Christiansen and Jim Beck told me that they were offering some important resolutions and that they would be watching to see how I voted. The implication was that, as an endorsed candidate for public office, even a candidate whom they had encouraged to run, I was now vulnerable to selling out. Their principal resolution went beyond the usual pledge never to support Hubert Humphrey. Now, they resolved, no Second Ward Democrat should ever support anyone who supports Hubert Humphrey. This was clearly aimed at Congressman Don Fraser, a staunch liberal who lived in the Second Ward and opposed the war, but favored Humphrey. Even for many Second Warders this resolution went too far. Debate was spirited and the vote, taken on a show of hands, was close. I voted for the resolution and it passed. The next day, Martin Sabo came to visit me. He told me that he had watched my vote the night before with dismay and had decided that he would run a joint campaign with Jim Adams. As he left the house, his last words to me were, "This fanaticism has got to stop."

Martin Sabo might simply have been looking for an excuse to rethink his original decision and run jointly with Adams. He might have done it no matter what I had done. But it was extraordinarily foolish of me to have given him any reason to move in that direction. The resolution was meaningless, and it was a gratuitous slap at one of the best liberal congressmen in the country. The price I paid for supporting it was enormous. Once Sabo decided to run with Adams, I had no chance of winning the election. With Adams on his own, I might have pulled it off. Adams had never before had a contested election, and especially in the highly charged atmosphere of 1968, he might not have known what to do. His labor friends were also out of touch with the changing political scene. But Sabo knew how to play it down the middle and he carried Adams with him. They ran as a team, campaigned door-to-door together, and had joint lawn signs, joint literature, and joint fund-raisers. They solidified their base in the Ninth Ward and worked hard to demonstrate their liberal credentials among the seniors in the Sixth Ward and the middle-class families in the Second Ward. I was left with solid support only among the students and radicals in Cedar-Riverside.

Despite the odds, we ran an energetic campaign, even if we didn't always know what we were doing. Bob Metcalf, who had been most responsible for recruiting me, appropriately agreed to be my campaign manager. Bob was twenty-four years old, with boyish good looks and, like Kaibel and Opperman, a law student at the university. Of the three Sixth Ward organizers, he was the most radical politically. Bob and Vance had both been active in SDS before moving into the DFL, but Bob retained more of his SDS outlook and, I gradually learned, was also close to the Communist Party. He was as new to electoral politics as I was, but he was wholly committed to my campaign, worked diligently, and was constantly coming up with ideas to get my name across in the district. He told me years later that he felt chagrined that he managed the only losing campaign I ever ran; I replied truthfully that no one could have pulled a victory out of that campaign. Bob soon found a location for our campaign headquarters—a rundown storefront on Cedar Avenue that we were given rent-free by the developers who were planning to tear it down in the next few years. Ironically, all of us opposed their development, but it didn't stop us from accepting their largesse.

The campaign headquarters were constantly abuzz; there was always someone there. Volunteers sat at desks in the front compiling lists, collating literature, and making phone calls. In the back, husky young men assembled lawn signs. Even at night, there were usually a few hippies who would ask if they could lay out their bedrolls and sleep on the floor; we didn't turn them down. For some, the campaign was more of a social occasion than a political cause. Every few weeks, we would hold fund-raising parties at Dania Hall that we called "Spear Beers." There would be live music, a light show, and cheap beer. What other chemical stimulants were available I didn't want to know. The Spear Beers didn't bring in much money, but they made certain that everyone in Cedar-Riverside knew who I was. At the same time, some of the volunteers took it all seriously and gained valuable political experience. Lee and Marcia Greenfield lived across the river, but they decided to adopt my race as their own, and they were a constant presence at headquarters. Marcia wrote most of the campaign literature and Lee organized precincts—both skills that they would use when Lee ran for the legislature a decade later. Jeff Spartz and Harvey Olson, from the Ninth Ward, tried to inject some realism into the campaign; their experience in a working-class ward taught them that we couldn't win solely with light shows and psychedelic literature.

I tried to learn how to be a candidate. I was told to leave the day-to-day operations to others and spend my time meeting people. As soon as we had campaign literature, I started knocking on doors every day between 5:00 p.m. and sundown. It didn't come easily to me. I didn't like interrupting people's private lives, and some folks let me know that they didn't like it either. Others were cordial and listened politely but were usually noncommittal. Some wanted to talk and took up too much of my time. In the poorest parts of the district, near downtown, many of the buildings were divided into so many units that I had difficulty even finding the individual doors. When I did find people home, most of them were unregistered and uninterested, so overwhelmed with their own personal problems that they had no time or patience for anything else. I came to realize how difficult it was to use politics as a tool to change the lives of the people who needed change the most.

I also met with leaders in the district, asking for support, and gamely wrote to the labor unions seeking their endorsements. I knew that the unions were a long shot. They had produced Adams and were not about to abandon him. But they met with me and I told them how committed I was to union issues: minimum wage, unemployment compensation, workers' compensation, collective bargaining, and so on. In the end, they always asked me whom I supported for president. When I replied "McCarthy," that was the end of it.

There was one exception. United Electrical Local 1139 had once been the largest union local in Minneapolis. In 1947, along with its international affiliate, it had been ousted from the CIO because of the refusal of its leaders to take an anti-Communist pledge. Most of its members went to the IUE, which was newly organized as an anti-Communist alternative to UE. Local 1139 struggled on, much diminished, and blamed Hubert Humphrey for luring its workers to the IUE. When I wrote to UE, I put my McCarthy identification upfront. At the interview, its chairman, Tony De Maio, told me that Local 1139 hadn't endorsed a candidate for any political office since it endorsed Hubert Humphrey for mayor of Minneapolis in 1945. "He was a professor like you, " he said, "and he screwed us. What will you do?" I pledged undying loyalty and they endorsed me. It was my only union endorsement and it allowed me to put the words "Labor Endorsed" on my literature. Thirty years later, when I was a veteran state senator, UE asked me to vote against an important environmental measure that they thought would lead to job losses at one of their shops. I remembered that exchange with Tony De Maio, and to the consternation of my environmentalist colleagues, I voted against the bill.

The UE endorsement is illustrative of one of the more interesting features of politics in Minnesota in 1968. The McCarthy movement brought out a lot of new people, but it also brought back some old people. Twenty years earlier, shortly after the Democratic Party and the Farmer-Labor Party had merged to form the DFL, there had been a bitter split between the anti-Communist liberals, led by Hubert Humphrey and Orville Freeman, and the old Farmer-Labor left wing, most of whom opposed the foreign policy of the Truman administration and the emerging cold war and supported Henry Wallace for president. Some, but not all, of the leftists had been Communists. Humphrey and Freeman won in the caucuses and at the state convention, and the left wing walked out, never to return—until 1968. Now many came back to support McCarthy, even though he had been a Humphrey Democrat in 1948.

I met many of these people and tended to identify with them. Some, like Leo Giovannini, I had known before. Others I met at the conventions—Ken Enkel, the Ptashnes, and an interesting man named Jim Youngdale. Youngdale, who now lived in the Second Ward and was pursuing graduate work at the university, had been a farmer in western Minnesota for much of his life. As a young left-wing activist in the 1950s, he had been a DFL candidate for Congress who was repudiated by the state party leadership, including Hubert Humphrey, for his opposition to the war in Korea. Youngdale set up a forum, held in late June, at which I appeared along with former governor Elmer Benson, Minnesota's last Farmer-Labor governor. Benson had served from 1936 to 1938, had been the titular head of the left-wing forces in 1948, and continued as an old man to nurture a hatred for the Humphrey-Freeman Democrats. The title of the forum was "Radicalism in Minnesota Politics—Yesterday and Today." Governor Benson represented yesterday; I represented today. I was thrilled to share a platform with a man who embodied Minnesota's radical political tradition.

In retrospect, I think I overromanticized the old left. All of the old leftists I met were decent and honorable. I never knew which ones had been Communists and which ones had not unless they told me, and it probably didn't matter as there had not been much difference in the 1930s and 1940s between actual party members and the so-called fellow travelers. My experience with the old left has led me to doubt the more extreme conclusions of historians like John Haynes and others who have worked in recently released Soviet archives, who see the Communist Party USA as merely a rubber stamp for Moscow. Whatever went on at the top, many Communists and fellow travelers at the grassroots level were conscientious and well-meaning idealists dedicated to improving the human condition. But what I don't think I adequately considered in 1968 when, for example, I shared the podium with Governor Benson, was that the old left had often been on the wrong side of major turning points in history. I was so convinced that Humphrey was wrong about Vietnam that I extrapolated from that and decided that the entire cold war policy of the United States had been wrong. I still think Humphrey was wrong about Vietnam, but I now believe he was right in 1948, that Truman's policy of containing Soviet expansion in Europe made sense and that a Wallace presidency would have been a disaster. It was at least in part the influence of the old left that led me to develop an intense hatred of Humphrey, which made it impossible for me to vote for him that fall even when the alternative was Richard Nixon.

Some of my friends went even further than I did in their rigid opposition to Humphrey. In the spirit of the Second Ward resolution demanding that antiwar Democrats refuse to support anyone who supported Humphrey, a small group of people met to discuss a primary challenge to Don Fraser. Wisely, I did not attend. Fraser, unlike Sabo, had told me that he supported all DFL-endorsed candidates, including me, and that I could use a statement from him on my literature. But my friends Lee Greenfield and Dick Flynn attended the meeting, at which it was decided to back the candidacy of a university philosophy professor named Grover Maxwell. Lee and Dick had urged Maxwell not to run, but when they were outvoted, they went along with the majority and ended up managing the campaign. When I asked Maxwell why he was running he said, "Humphrey equals death, and Fraser supports Humphrey, therefore Fraser supports death." I hope he wasn't teaching that syllogism in his classes on logic. He had no issues to use against Fraser other than the presidential race. Lee and Dick told me to stay away from the Maxwell campaign, which I tried to do. But I was so close to the people who were behind it that I ended up saying some positive things about Maxwell's candidacy that got back to Fraser. He called me and pointed out that he had taken some risks to support me. I apologized and felt deeply ashamed, as I rightly should have. In the primary, Fraser beat Maxwell by a margin of about 7 to 1.

The national political scene was once again taking some strange and tragic twists. McCarthy and Bobby Kennedy battled each other in primary states throughout the country while Humphrey picked up the largest bloc of delegates by concentrating on convention states, many of which were controlled by party bosses. Kennedy won most of the primaries. The last and most delegate-rich was held in California on June 4. That evening I went to a bachelor party for Al Jones, who was engaged in marry Bonnie Marvy later in the summer. When I returned home I turned on the television just in time to hear Kennedy making his victory speech; he had won a close election in California. It looked like it would come down to Kennedy versus Humphrey, and I was prepared to switch to Kennedy. Just as I was getting into bed, a news bulletin came in from Los Angeles. Bobby Kennedy had been shot in the head after he left the podium at the Ambassador Hotel. He was taken to the hospital in critical condition and died one day later.

Bobby Kennedy's assassination, coming just two months after the murder of Martin Luther King, was an enormous shock to the country, and it took everyone time to recover. But Gene McCarthy's reaction was inexplicable. I expected that after a reasonable length of time for mourning, he would resume his campaign and try to rally the antiwar wing of the Democratic Party behind him to present a united front against Humphrey. Instead, he basically withdrew, stopped campaigning, and even spent part of the summer in a monastery. By the time of the Democratic National Convention in Chicago in August, despite efforts by Senator George McGovern of South Dakota to rally the Kennedy delegates, the antiwar Democrats were in disarray. Many historians think that Humphrey had the nomination wrapped up even before California. I think that if Kennedy had lived it might have been very close. As it was, the Chicago convention was stained by violence and bloodshed and left Humphrey with a tainted nomination.

I didn't go to Chicago, but I remember gathering in the old Milwaukee Road depot in downtown Minneapolis to welcome home our Minnesota McCarthy delegates after the convention. We heard from them what most of us had already seen on television: Chicago police officers, acting under orders from Mayor Richard Daley, beating up demonstrators and even bystanders on the streets outside the Hilton Hotel; Daley shouting down Senator Abraham Ribicoff of Connecticut when he criticized the police on the convention floor; Humphrey blithely accepting the nomination without even an acknowledgment of what was going on around him. It was on that occasion that I decided I would never vote for Humphrey. I voted for a third-party candidate in November. It was one last foolish decision that I made that year. Humphrey was a flawed candidate and a flawed human being. But the history of the past forty years would have been far better had Humphrey and not Nixon been elected president in 1968.

The September primary was simply a blip in my campaign. There was no doubt that Sabo, Adams, and I would all survive; the primary was simply a trial run. I came in third, behind Jim Adams; I would need a stronger showing to win in November. I continued to knock on doors and distribute campaign literature. My mother came to Minneapolis and worked the senior high-rises for me; she thought my candidacy was a crazy idea, but she nevertheless was willing to do what she could to help her son. But I was in a bind. I had become a hero to the hard-core antiwar Democrats throughout the city, and if I tried to move to the center I would antagonize that base without picking up much support from moderates who would never trust me. A few of the more extreme antiwar activists even criticized me for putting Don Fraser's picture in my literature. On the other hand, my refusal to endorse Humphrey and my strong identification with the black movement made it difficult for me to penetrate the white working-class sections of the district. In the end, I ran eleven hundred votes behind Jim Adams in the general election and lost the race. I carried Cedar-Riverside and one precinct in the Ninth Ward; I lost everywhere else, even my own precinct. The results throughout the city that night demonstrated that while the McCarthy insurgents could successfully organize precinct caucuses, we could not yet win elections. Every candidate who came out of the antiwar wing of the party was defeated. Even Alpha Smaby, a two-term incumbent, one of a handful of incumbent legislators to support McCarthy, lost her bid for reelection. She had tried to replace the other representative in her district, a conservative Democrat, with an antiwar candidate, and both of them had gone down in defeat. Either Minneapolis was not ready for our brand of "new politics," or we had not yet developed the skills to get our message across. Most likely, both were true.

Meanwhile, my romantic life had taken another curious turn. During the course of the campaign I frequently saw Sally B. at meetings of antiwar delegates. She had been an organizer for McCarthy in her suburban community. Gradually, we started seeing each other again. She had finally decided that her marriage was irreparable and she was heading for a divorce. We began to talk about what she would do after the divorce had come through and whether marriage between us would work. We acknowledged the differences in our personalities and recognized that any long-term relationship would not be all smooth sailing. Sally was far more mercurial than I, more inclined to moodiness, and her outbursts still often embarrassed me. And she found me too judgmental and feared that I would try to boss her around, which she assured me she would never tolerate from anyone. But we did express our love for each other and liked being together. On election night, after seeing the disappointing results at campaign headquarters, I found solace by spending the rest of the night with Sally.

When I went to Michigan City for the winter holidays, I told my parents that I thought I was going to get married. A few years earlier, they would have disapproved. My mother in particular would have resisted the idea of my marrying a non-Jewish woman with two children who was just leaving a difficult marriage. But by this time, I was thirty-one years old and had never previously had a girlfriend. The deep dark thought that had surfaced years before when I wanted to transfer to Oberlin had begun to trouble them again. What was wrong with their son? Could he be a homosexual? Within this context, they welcomed the news that I was seriously involved with a woman and was thinking of marriage. They fussed over the pictures of Sally's children and told me how much they wanted to meet Sally when they next visited Minneapolis.

But it never happened. Sally had begun a course of study at one of the local private colleges to fulfill her long-standing ambition to become a social worker. When I returned to Minneapolis after New Year, I began hearing about one of her professors of social work and it soon became clear that she was seeing him outside the classroom. When I called her, she became more and more reluctant to spend time with me. Finally she told me that she thought she was falling in love with her professor. Our relationship ended, not bitterly, but with the realization by both of us that it probably would never have worked. Sally eventually married Professor C.[3] and they have been together ever since. I was disappointed but not heartbroken. I still think I was genuinely in love with Sally, but I don't think a marriage between us would have lasted very long. Not only were our personalities very different, but my homosexuality was not something that I could simply turn off. Sooner or later, it would have resurfaced and caused us both great pain.

By early 1969, then, I had been through an election campaign and a love affair that had ended unsuccessfully. But both had in different ways been extraordinary learning experiences. The outcome of the election had been deeply disappointing, of course. Not only had I failed despite seven months of hard work, but Richard Nixon had been elected president. The antiwar Democrats had succeeded in dumping Johnson, but our hopes of ending the war through electoral politics, so bright in April, now seemed as distant as ever. But I was not disillusioned with the political process, as I had been a few years earlier. I had found Minnesota politics far more open than I had anticipated. I believed that those of us who came into the DFL in 1968 had made real inroads and permanently established ourselves within the party. We hadn't yet learned how to win elections, but we believed we would learn from our mistakes and do better next time. A few days after the election, I had a brief conversation on campus with Doug Pratt, the antiwar candidate recruited by Alpha Smaby to run with her in the legislative district across the river. Doug, also a university professor, had been totally demoralized by the experience. "Wasn't that awful?" he asked me, commiserating with me on my loss. "I'll certainly never do that again." "Well, Doug," I replied, "I just hope that someday I'll get another shot at it."

The lessons from my love affair are more complex and harder for

3. Professor C. is a pseudonym.

me to fully comprehend. It certainly did not demonstrate that I was not truly a homosexual. While I was very happy when I was with Sally, I never stopped noticing men or thinking about them. But what I do think it demonstrated was how much I needed someone whom I loved and who loved me. That need transcended gender. While I had been influenced by the new politics of the 1960s, I never came under the spell of the counterculture. Notions about free love and sexual experimentation had little appeal to me. I was resolutely traditional in my need for a relationship with one caring person. I had always had lots of friends and, especially since I came to Minnesota, was well respected in the community. But that could not replace the emptiness that I felt when I came home at night. When things were going well with Sally, I felt a kind of security and inner peace that I had never experienced before. Sex was part of it. That was new to me, too, and I liked it. But it was far more than that. And it would be another thirteen years before I would find it again.

6

CAMPUS AND COMMUNITY, 1969–1972

My National Endowment for the Humanities grant to begin the research for a second book had ended in September 1969, so even before the election I was back teaching at the university. With my defeat, I now had to reconcile myself to being a full-time professor for the foreseeable future, certainly not a dire prospect. The real question was whether I could continue as a productive scholar, with the commitment of time and energy that entailed, or whether I would now be constantly distracted by politics. I wrote to the NEH at the conclusion of my grant, fulfilling the endowment's requirement that I sum up what I had done on my project: the development of community life among the freedmen in the Civil War and Reconstruction period. I did not tell any outright lies in my statement, but I certainly embellished the facts. I admitted that "I had not accomplished as much as I had hoped" and that "I was not able to get into the manuscript material." But I claimed to have done wide reading in secondary sources and printed primary sources, including newspapers, manuscripts, and government documents. I had done a little of this, but "wide reading" vastly overstated the case. I also reported truthfully on some minor projects I had completed: introductions to reprints of several classic works in African American history, which were subsequently published, and a readings book on slavery, which I ultimately abandoned when the publisher asked for changes that I was unwilling to make. As for the main project, I concluded my report by assuring the NEH that although my original plan to ferret out the views of "the inarticulate black masses" was perhaps too ambitious, I was nevertheless optimistic that the study would eventually be completed.

Over the next three years, however, until my next try for elective office, I never got back to the freedmen project. My energies were diverted in several different directions. First, I continued to be an ardent advocate for African American history, speaking in a wide variety of venues and working to expand the field at the university. Second, I became deeply involved in the internal politics of the university faculty at both the departmental and the campuswide level. This was a time in which universities throughout the country were becoming sharply divided over issues such as the handling of student demonstrations, the inclusion of students in decision making, the expansion of the curriculum to make it more "relevant," and affirmative action in faculty hiring. The University of Minnesota was no exception, and I had strong views on all of these subjects. Finally, I continued to be active in DFL politics. My experience with the McCarthy campaign and as a legislative candidate in 1968 had made me one of the leaders of the antiwar faction within the party, and I was drawn into every conflict and issue involving party politics. And I was soon to learn that my role at the university and my activities within the DFL could not be kept completely separate.

As soon as the election was over, I undertook an ambitious extracurricular educational project in African American history. I presented a twenty-week series on Twin Cities Educational Television that covered the full range of African American history, from ancient African civilization to Malcolm X. The program was televised every Tuesday night for an hour; this was live television, so there was no margin for error. It required serious preparation and intense concentration. I also had to do more than just stand in front of a camera and talk—if I expected anyone to watch. So I needed to gather a wide range of visual material. Fortunately the station, KTCA, provided me with an assistant who hunted down the visuals and reproduced them in a format suitable for television. But I had to work closely with her to decide what I wanted to use and how to coordinate the visual material with my lecture. I also brought in visitors to interview on a variety of topics. Mahmoud El-Kati, still known then as Milt Williams, a local community-based historian, discussed misconceptions about the African American past. Several of my colleagues—Stuart Schwartz in Latin American history, Hy Berman in labor history, and Vicki Coifman, who had begun to teach African history on a part-time basis—discussed their specialties. It was all a lot of work and some programs were more successful than others, but overall the station told me that the public response was highly positive.

Concurrently, I hosted a lecture series for the university on African American history. I invited six of the outstanding scholars in the field to come in and give a public lecture. The visitors included Eugene Genovese, who was emerging as a preeminent scholar of slavery; Willie

Lee Rose, an authority on Reconstruction; Louis Harlan, the biographer of Booker T. Washington; and Paul Puryear, a political scientist whom I had met when I visited Al Jones a few years earlier at Tuskegee. I introduced each speaker and shepherded all of them around the Twin Cities. In several instances, I was also able to use the visiting lecturers as guests on my television program. And all of them appeared as guests on a local radio interview show hosted by a rather idiosyncratic media personality named Henry Wolf. Wolf was an Alsatian who spoke with a heavy French accent and had none of the casual glibness of the usual radio host. His show was broadcast every night from the cocktail lounge of a downtown hotel, which gave him a built-in studio audience. He did his homework and had appropriate questions for his guests. His style was far different from the kind of confrontational talk radio that was just beginning to make an appearance in the Twin Cities at the time and would soon make shows like Wolf's quaint relics of the past.

In both the TV show and the lecture series, I opened myself to criticism by failing to achieve anything approaching racial balance. Other than Mahmoud El-Kati and Paul Puryear, all of my guests were white. I was aware of this and wanted to include more black scholars. But I invited people whom I knew, who were available, and whose work I respected. Most of these people happened to be white. The demands of a significant segment of the African American community were moving in a different direction. The assassination of Martin Luther King had not ushered in a return to interracial cooperation or the renewed white commitment to the black struggle for which many of us had hoped. Instead, it had led to increased demands for recognition of black autonomy and an ever-sharper white resistance to those demands, which the popular press dubbed "the white backlash." On university campuses, this had taken the form of demands for black studies programs with curricula determined by black students and faculty, black student centers, and, on some campuses, separate black dormitories. When these demands were not fully met, black students were prepared to do what predominantly white student protesters had done earlier in the decade—to take over administration buildings by force if necessary. The most dramatic confrontation occurred at Cornell University in December 1968, when black students emerged from the administration building armed with semiautomatic rifles. To many white Americans, the widely reproduced photograph of this incident reflected their worse fears of black violence and rebellion.

The University of Minnesota had been relatively peaceful throughout the 1960s. There were antiwar demonstrations, to be sure, but there were no major confrontations comparable to those at Berkeley or Columbia or San Francisco State. But there were signs now of black student restiveness. Shortly after the King assassination, two black student groups, the African American Action Committee and Freedom Now, had written to the administration deploring the lack of course offerings in African American studies and demanding a "curriculum and faculty needed to bring a full reflection of the experience of black people in America." The letter had acknowledged the existence of my Race and Nationality course, but called it "inadequate since this sequence is not offered on a regular basis, and as an upper division course it fails to meet the needs of an academic community of this size and reputation." The course was, in fact, offered regularly, except when I was on leave, but I wrote a letter to the campus newspaper, the *Minnesota Daily*, agreeing that more needed to be done. The unspoken assumption in the black student demands, which I could not acknowledge, was that courses taught by white people didn't count. The university appointed a committee to look into the issue, but nine months later, no further action had been taken.

The Cornell confrontation emboldened the students at Minnesota. Less than a month later, on January 14, 1969, black students entered and took over the office of university president Malcolm Moos in Morrill Hall. The occupation ended the next day and there was no violence. There was, however, some vandalism; one estimate put the damage to office equipment and furniture at seven thousand dollars. President Moos chose conciliation rather than confrontation. He negotiated an agreement with the students, promising the establishment of an African American studies department, although rejecting the demand that the department be controlled exclusively by black students and faculty. He also agreed to an augmented scholarship program for minority students, but not to the demand that the program be administered by black community leaders outside the university. He promised to assist financially with a black student conference and to give black people a larger voice in running programs that directly affected them. In my judgment, he handled the situation well. Moos had come to the university in 1967 after a career that had included a stint as speechwriter for President Dwight Eisenhower. This was his first major crisis as president. He had seen that the hard-line approaches taken by administrators at Berkeley, Columbia, and Cornell had been counterproductive, that they had succeeded primarily in uniting the student body behind the protesters. Not incidentally, he must also have noted that most of the uncompromising presidents had ultimately been forced to resign. Moos would be tested again with more widespread student protests in 1970 and 1972. While he would continue a generally conciliatory approach, his leadership became less sure-handed as time went on.

I was asked by the administration to visit the students in Morrill Hall during the takeover. They let me in and we had a cordial conversation. But I played no decisive role in the settlement that was reached. After the incident ended, I was invited to serve on the committee to establish the African American studies department, which began meeting immediately and issued its report later in the spring. I also wrote an article for the *Minnesota Daily,* arguing for the importance of African American studies in a university curriculum and justifying the student action at Morrill Hall. I did, however, insist that the African American studies program that was soon to be developed must be "wholly sound from a scholarly and educational point of view" and "interracial in the best sense of that word." I concluded that it must "recognize the need for both black and white student participation and . . . provide training for students of both races in a field that has for too many years now been disgracefully ignored." As a member of the committee establishing the program, I would have my work cut out for me.

It soon became clear that the Morrill Hall takeover and President Moos's response to it were contributing to the much-discussed white backlash. Even among my colleagues at the university, I heard comments about how the administration needed to learn how to say no. But in the general community, the backlash was far sharper and more explicitly racist than that. The Twin Cities in 1969 were far different from what they are today. Both cities were overwhelmingly white and the suburbs were almost exclusively so. There were three small, mostly segregated black communities: in north Minneapolis along Plymouth Avenue, near Central High School in south Minneapolis, and in the University-Dale section of St. Paul. The St. Paul black community was being dispersed by the construction of the I-94 freeway. There was also a Mexican American community on the west side of St. Paul, across the river from downtown. Otherwise, Minneapolis was heavily Scandinavian and German Lutheran, and St. Paul had a large Irish Catholic population. No one had ever heard of the Hmong or Somalis. There had been racial violence on Plymouth Avenue in 1967—minor by national standards but alarming enough to drive out the few remaining Jewish families from what had once been a predominantly Jewish neighborhood. The mayor, Arthur Naftalin, had been heavily criticized for not taking a tougher stand, just as Malcolm Moos was now a target of criticism. Assertive black people were extremely threatening to white Minnesotans, and despite the small nonwhite population, fear of black crime and violence loomed large in the popular consciousness. A *Minneapolis Tribune* editorial on January 28 commented on the large number of letters the newspaper had received criticizing Moos, calling for stern measures against the demonstrators, and scoffing at the students' demand for an African American studies program. Nonetheless, the *Tribune* defended Moos and reprinted my article from the *Minnesota Daily.*

President Moos appointed a university-community committee to investigate the takeover and make recommendations for possible disciplinary action against the students who had participated in the takeover and caused the vandalism in Morrill Hall. But before the committee could report, Hennepin County Attorney George Scott presented the case to a grand jury, and on March 5 the jury indicted three of the student leaders, Horace Huntley, Rose Mary Freeman, and Warren Tucker. I had just begun teaching my Race and Nationality class that morning when one of the students entered the room and told us of the indictments. This was my last year to teach Race and Nationality and enrollment had mushroomed to two hundred students, most of them there for the African American segment. Once they learned of the indictments, they insisted that I stop lecturing and that we discuss what we could do. There was particular consternation that three students had been picked out for punishment even though there was no specific evidence as to who had caused the property damage. After about thirty minutes of discussion, one of the students suggested that we march on City Hall in protest. I agreed to join them. Several students visited nearby classrooms and, much to the displeasure of some of the professors, interrupted the classes and invited students to join us on the march. About three hundred of us, including approximately 80 percent of my class, walked the mile and a half to city hall, where we met briefly with George Scott. Joe Kroll, the president of the Minnesota Student Association, who was one of my students, presented a protest statement to Scott and also took responsibility for keeping the demonstration peaceful and orderly.

Among a number of things I learned from this episode was the power of the sound bite. Later on, as an elected official, I learned to be cautious with the use of short pithy statements that could be lifted, sometimes out of context, for use on television newscasts. But I was still naive about media relations in 1969. As soon as our march reached city hall, I was asked by reporters if I had initiated it. I answered: "I'm no Pied Piper. The whole thing was completely spontaneous." The quotation "I'm no Pied Piper" was used on every television station and newspaper in the Twin Cities over the next twenty-four hours. It was not a terribly damaging sound bite, but probably not something I would have said if I had thought about it carefully. To those who were hostile to the protest, my denial convinced them that I was indeed a "Pied Piper." In any case, the publicity that the march engendered elicited perhaps the vilest hate mail of my entire career. Even after I became a well-known gay rights leader, I don't think I ever received letters as full of insults and taunts as what I received over this incident. The very idea of a white professor at the university teaching "mumbo-jumbo" called black studies "(whatever that is)" and marching with mostly white students in support of black protesters obviously struck some raw nerves in a city trying to cope with new racial and social tensions. One letter writer concluded, "And to think, you are a professor. Excuse me, I wish to vomit."

The most important lesson I learned, though, was that as I became a more public figure, it would become increasingly difficult to compartmentalize my life. My notoriety as the "Pied Piper" of student protest at the university soon spilled over into my political life within the DFL Party. I was deeply involved that spring in the Minneapolis mayoral election. Arthur Naftalin, a close associate of Hubert Humphrey's and Orville Freeman's, who had served eight years as mayor, had announced that he would not seek reelection. The race for his successor was wide open, with the DFL endorsing convention scheduled on March 1, the primary on April 29, and the general election on June 10. The Minneapolis DFL had, for a number of years, been divided into two factions. One, commonly known as the "goo-goos" (good government) faction, was made up largely of middle- and upper-middle-class professional people and academics and had its strength in the university community and in the more affluent wards of south Minneapolis. The other, the labor faction, was, as its name implies, mostly blue collar and was centered in north Minneapolis and in the working-class Ninth and Twelfth wards in the southeastern quadrant of the city. The differences had more to do with lifestyle and approach to politics than with specific issues. In fact, the environmental and social issues that would split middle-class and working-class Democrats in coming decades were just beginning to emerge in the 1960s. But the conflict was nevertheless a bitter one. In 1966, the goo-goos had supported Sandy Keith, the labor Democrats had remained loyal to Karl Rolvaag, and the wounds were fresh.

Each faction had a candidate for mayor in 1969. The goo-goos supported Alderman Bob McGregor of the Second Ward, a Presbyterian minister with good liberal credentials but an aura of self-righteousness. McGregor had the backing of Mayor Naftalin and Congressman Don Fraser, but labor loathed him. The labor Democrats supported State Representative John Salchert, a north Minneapolis physician who was a close associate of north side DFL leader Jim Rice, once an aide to Rolvaag. The real question was what the McCarthy wing of the party would do. Alpha Smaby, Forrest Harris, and some of the more party-oriented antiwar Democrats were supporting McGregor, but those of us who had come into the DFL for the first time in 1968 for McCarthy now held the balance of power at the city convention, and we didn't like either McGregor or Salchert. It didn't take us long to get back into a mode of almost constant meetings to plot our strategy. There was no one in our group who would be a credible candidate for mayor of Minneapolis. But we wanted our own candidate, someone who would represent the values that we thought we had brought to the party. We had already established an organization, the New Democratic Coalition, to keep the spirit of the McCarthy campaign alive. Now we needed a mayoral candidate who would run on its principles. We were soon approached by a young Minneapolis alderman named Gerard Hegstrom, who represented the mostly poor, inner-city Eighth Ward.

Hegstrom had not been with us in 1968, any more than McGregor or Salchert had been. Moreover, he was a former FBI agent, which deeply concerned some of our more radical delegates. But he had a strong liberal record on the city council. Moreover, he was looking for a base and we were looking for a candidate. He promised to support our issues and we agreed to back him at the convention. I was chosen to give the nominating speech.

Minneapolis in 1969 was not the one-party town that it has become. The Republican Party was still a major force. It had not controlled the mayor's office for more than a decade, but it was well represented on the city council. The Republicans looked at the divided DFL and saw a real chance to elect a mayor. They chose a highly credible candidate: Dan Cohen, a moderate Republican who represented the silk-stocking Seventh Ward. And there was another threat to the DFL in 1969: Charles Stenvig, the president of the Minneapolis Police Federation, had announced that he was running as an independent. Stenvig had emerged as a leading champion of a hard-line position on law and order in the city. He had been highly critical of the way Naftalin had handled the Plymouth Avenue disturbances in 1967, and he appealed directly to working-class white people who believed that their problems were being ignored while blacks were being pampered and coddled. Few political observers believed that Stenvig could actually win, but his presence certainly complicated the race.

So the stakes at the March 1 convention were high. At issue was not just control of the DFL Party in the city but control of the city itself. The problem was that no one really knew which of the DFL candidates was in the best position to win an election against Dan Cohen and Charlie Stenvig. It was a tense and exciting day. I had by this time become a fairly effective political speaker, and I outlined the issues that Hegstrom would support. A candidate for mayor could not, of course, run on ending the war, but I talked about racial equality and justice for the poor, better police-community relations, affordable housing, and greater economic opportunity. None of the DFL candidates disagreed with any of these points, but I argued that Hegstrom brought to this agenda less baggage and a fresher approach than the candidates of the old factions. We held most of the McCarthy delegates for Hegstrom, and for the first few ballots the three candidates ran almost even. Then Dr. Salchert indicated that he wanted to meet

Hegstrom and the leaders of his campaign. He told us, to our total astonishment, that he planned to drop out of the race and throw his support to Hegstrom. There was no deal, no quid pro quo. Salchert simply explained that the convention was deadlocked, that he couldn't win, and that he could deliver his bloc of votes to us while he knew that we could never deliver our votes to him even if we had wanted to. He was willing to do what had to be done to stop McGregor. On the next ballot, Hegstrom was endorsed.

We were ecstatic, but now we had a campaign to run. McGregor reluctantly accepted the will of the convention, but we knew that Dan Cohen would be tough and we were beginning to worry about Stenvig. I was not, however, prepared for what happened next. The march on City Hall to protest the Morrill Hall indictments occurred four days after the convention. Immediately, George Thiss, the chairman of the Minnesota Republican Party, issued a statement suggesting that "[Spear] doesn't believe that justice should move along its normal course" and identifying me as "the number one man" in Gerard Hegstrom's campaign organization. "When one becomes attached as closely to a candidate as Spear is to Hegstrom," he concluded, "all his moves become suspect to the public as actually representing his candidate—in this case Gerard Hegstrom." Within a few days the Minneapolis newspapers were full of letters both defending and denouncing me and, by implication, Hegstrom. One of my students wrote supporting my statement that the march was a student initiative, not my idea. Hegstrom himself weighed in, distancing himself slightly from me by emphasizing his FBI background and his endorsement by Hubert Humphrey, while at the same time defending the rights of peaceful demonstrators. Probably the most damaging letter was ostensibly in support of Hegstrom and me. It called me a courageous leader who has admitted his radicalism, supported draft resistance, favored the legalization of marijuana, and opposed penalties for homosexuality. Hegstrom, the letter concluded, should "walk proudly beside Prof. Allan Spear throughout this campaign." The letter could possibly have come from an extremely naive supporter, but more likely it was planted by the Republican Party.

I was not, whatever George Thiss thought, "the number one man" in Hegstrom's campaign organization. Several professional campaign organizers were brought in to run the day-to-day operation. I learned

something in this campaign that would be reinforced by my later political experience. Professional campaign managers and consultants
are, with rare exceptions, absolutely useless in local and even most
statewide campaigns. They come in with preconceived notions about
how campaigns should be run and fail to grasp the nuances of the
particular political situation within which they must work. The Hegstrom campaign may have been hopeless—and obviously my activities
did not make it easier. But just about everything the campaign did
after the convention was counterproductive. The slogan, "Judgment Is
What It's All About," failed to connect either to the candidate or to the
basic concerns of the constituents. The lawn signs and graphic design
were far too arty to be effective. And the campaign focused exclusively
on Dan Cohen, even when it started to become clear that support for
Stenvig was growing. Nothing was done to persuade working-class
Democrats to stay loyal to the DFL rather than vote for Stenvig. I was
out of town on April 29. I voted in the morning, then flew off to give
one of my many talks on African American history at a nearby university. When I returned in the early evening, I called the Greenfields.
The news was devastating. Hegstrom had not survived the primary.
Even more shocking, Stenvig had come in first and Cohen had finished
second. Nothing changed between April and June, and Stenvig was
elected mayor.

I was also involved in several of the city council elections in the spring
of 1969, particularly in the wards where I had campaigned the previous year, the Second, the Sixth, and the Ninth. In the Second Ward,
the DFL endorsed Alpha Smaby, who, despite her loss in the legislative race in 1968, was still a popular and well-known figure in the
university community. The Second Ward did not include northeast
Minneapolis, where Alpha had been defeated by big margins the year
before, but it did include some lower-middle-class precincts outside
the university area. We nevertheless thought she would be a strong
candidate. She faced a young liberal Republican lawyer named John
Cairns, who capitalized on his lack of name recognition by planting
lawn signs that read "Who Is John Cairns?" But he ran an effective
campaign and our door knockers reported strong resistance to Alpha
whenever they ventured beyond the university community because of
her identification with the antiwar Democrats.

About a week before the general election, a brochure was distributed in the nonuniversity part of the ward that was a classic piece of red-baiting. It identified Alpha as the "Pink Lady," a term first used by Richard Nixon in his California Senate campaign against Helen Gahagan Douglas that focused on her left-wing positions and associations. Once again, the Republicans saw me as a political liability. Alpha was accused of having supported "Allan Spear who ran for the legislature on a platform of black revolution and surrender to communism." She was also attacked for her association with "Vance Opperman's red storm troopers." Alpha's supporters were, of course, outraged by the piece and accused the Cairns campaign of the worse kind of smear tactics. Cairns denied any knowledge of who put the literature out; I later came to know John Cairns as an honorable man and I believe him. But Alpha's campaign manager traced the piece to a printer in Wisconsin who identified the man who brought in the copy as one of Cairns's aides. This man went on to a successful career as a long-serving Republican elected official. Whoever was responsible, the piece did the Cairns campaign no harm. To our dismay, Cairns was elected to the city council and ended Alpha Smaby's political career.

We also thought we had a highly electable candidate in the Sixth Ward. The incumbent, Jens Christiansen, was a conservative Republican in a ward that was becoming more oriented toward young people and the counterculture. The DFL endorsed a candidate who was young but definitely not a product of the counterculture. Larry Schwanke was thoughtful and serious-minded, and while he had worked with the antiwar faction in 1968, he was not radical in politics or lifestyle. He seemed the perfect combination—young and fresh, yet not frightening to the older people who were still a significant part of the ward. He ran a good campaign and made no obvious mistakes. Yet the Stenvig wave overwhelmed him and Christiansen was reelected. In the Ninth Ward, on the other hand, we simply threw our opportunity away. The antiwar Democrats had made a deal the year before with a perennial party dissident named Tom McDonald. McDonald and his supporters went for McCarthy, despite no real commitment to the antiwar cause, and the McCarthy delegates agreed to support Tom for alderman in 1969. I became part of this deal when I accepted Tom's support for the legislature. As a result, I ended up giving an endorsement speech for him, probably the most embarrassing speech I ever had to give. McDonald was not a liberal and had no qualifications for public office. My speech, a masterpiece of verbal gymnastics, got him the endorsement, but he was eliminated in the primary.

In some ways, the results of the city election of 1969 were even more depressing than the 1968 results had been. In Minneapolis, the antiwar Democrats were operating on turf where we thought we could win. We endorsed, in most cases, plausible candidates, and yet we were totally wiped out. Minneapolis chose a right-wing police officer as its mayor and elected a city council with a twelve-to-one Republican majority. Later in the year, I attended a statewide DFL convention at the Hilton Hotel in St. Paul. At the end of the day, Lee and Marcia Greenfield and I were having a conversation at a reception held in a suite on one of the hotel's upper floors. I remember standing in front of a large floor-to-ceiling window with spectacular views over the city while Marcia made some snide remarks about one of the more conservative leaders in the party, Tom Kelm, whom we considered an old-time political boss. We were overheard by David Lebedoff, a young Minneapolis lawyer and party activist who was working with Kelm on state senator Wendell Anderson's campaign for governor. Lebedoff turned to us and started yelling. "Tom Kelm has more sense in his little finger than all of you people have put together," he shouted. Then he turned to me and wagged his finger in my face, pushing me up against the window so that I feared I would soon be flying off the twenty-second floor. "You, Allan Spear," he said, "are personally responsible for the election of Charles Stenvig. You think you are helping black people and poor people, but you are doing more to hurt them than anyone I know."

The next day Lebedoff apologized. "My father always told me that Jews can't hold their liquor and shouldn't drink," he said. "I should have listened to him." Nevertheless, his words stung. Even if he had been drunk, he had obviously meant what he said. And Lebedoff was no redneck. A thoughtful and intelligent man, he had written a book that I very much admired about the Keith-Rolvaag contest in 1966 and was in the process of writing another book about the McCarthy-Humphrey split in Minneapolis, which I ended up admiring less. How much truth was there in Lebedoff's accusation? Certainly it was hyperbolic. Many people and factors had created the discontent that had allowed Stenvig to win. The election was as much a backlash against the administration of Lebedoff's friend Art Naftalin as it was against the activities of the antiwar Democrats. At the same time, the perceived extremism of the McCarthy supporters had, without doubt, combined with fears of racial unrest to produce the conservative surge. The defeat of Alpha Smaby and Larry Schwanke, who were by no means extremists themselves, can only be attributed to their associations with the McCarthy movement. And while I was probably not as well known as Lebedoff seemed to think I was, I certainly combined many of the elements that the Minneapolis electorate was voting against: strong support of black activism; uncompromising opposition to the war; sympathy with student protesters; and an affiliation with the University of Minnesota. If they had known about my homosexuality, my villainy would have been complete. I was not about to change my ways, but I began to realize that the kind of politics that my friends and I were pursuing would have to become less incendiary.

There were other signs that I had become for the right wing a symbol of the leftist elite that was undermining traditional American values. The Twin Cities' first conservative talk radio show began broadcasting in 1969, hosted by an avid Stenvig supporter named Paul Helm, and I was a frequent target of his wrath. One day I tuned in and was startled to hear my own voice. Helm had secretly sent someone to tape one of my classes, hoping to catch me directing the students to go to a rally in support of the Morrill Hall protesters. I did mention the rally in class, but certainly did not tell the students whether or not they should go. Nevertheless, Helm leaped on this as evidence that I was using the classroom for political purposes. I contacted the university attorney's office, inquiring about the legality of secret recordings in the classroom, and the university sent Helm's station a letter warning them about the university's exclusive rights to classroom material. It didn't happen again. A short time later, a number of us at the university were contacted by *Life* magazine advising us that we were all on an FBI watch list. *Life* somehow thought this was interesting news and arranged to take a picture of University of Minnesota faculty members and students, gathered together on the steps of Northrop Auditorium, all of whom were presumably FBI suspects. After the passage of the Freedom of Information Act in the mid-1970s, I acquired my FBI files and found nothing particularly threatening in them. Almost everything the FBI knew about me was already a matter of public record; most of it consisted of newspaper clippings. But it has been a useful source in writing this memoir.

While white conservatives viewed me as a proponent of "black revolution," in the academic world I found myself struggling to maintain scholarly standards in the increasingly politicized field of African American studies. A ten-person committee met throughout the spring of 1969 to draft a report establishing the new curriculum in African American studies that the administration had agreed to at Morrill Hall. The committee included four students, four faculty members, and two "community representatives," one of whom was a university staff member. I went into the meetings believing that we should establish a program rather than a department. In university parlance, a program was cross-disciplinary, had a small core faculty, but drew most of its teaching staff from members of existing departments; a department was freestanding with a full faculty of its own. A program, it seemed to me, could better draw on the current resources of the university, would require fewer new hires in a highly competitive field, and could more quickly establish itself as a scholarly enterprise with respect throughout the institution. It is possible, of course, to see something self-serving in my position; my African American history courses could be incorporated into a program, whereas a department would likely hire its own African American historian. In any case, the majority of the committee, especially the black student representatives, insisted on a department. A program would connote second-class status and lack the autonomy that the black community wanted. A department, the final report stated, would include a full faculty, separate budgeting, and "the right to initiate the establishment of courses, set policy and hire staff."

All the committee members realized, however, that if the report were to be accepted it must not be permeated with ideas of black separatism. We needed to establish a curriculum that would reflect high academic standards and at the same time be sensitive to the needs of black students. The committee members developed respect for each other and generally we operated by consensus. Courses would be "open to all" and staff would be "inter-racial." And while African American studies would have departmental status, it was conceded that some of the staff could be affiliated with traditional departments. But there was also a recommendation that "every effort be made to staff this department with as many qualified black instructors as possible" and that "in certain areas the hiring of black instructors would be virtually imperative." Another statement, of which I did not approve, conceded that "in certain courses at certain times the nature of the subject being discussed may make it necessary for the class to divide into sections along racial lines." In short, the report, which was accepted with some reluctance by the College of Liberal Arts All-College Council, was a delicate balancing act. Whether the department would succeed was anyone's guess.

The committee had one last task before it broke up: to hire a head for the new department. This was perhaps the most important decision of all as the chair would establish the direction that the department would take in its formative years. Here the committee made its worse decision, one that almost destroyed the department before it was fully operating. Given the delicate balance on the committee between academics and black activists, it was understood that the chair would have the usual academic qualifications and would also be black. The problem was that there was a sellers' market for qualified black academics. Universities throughout the country were establishing programs and departments in African American studies and there were still relatively few black PhDs. We finally found one. He had a PhD in history and some teaching experience, but his résumé was thin and he never would have even survived the first cut if he were applying for a job in the history department. He was very unimpressive in the interview and I urged that we reject him and start the search over again. But I was outvoted and he was hired. As it turned out, he was not only incompetent, he also failed to show up for many of his classes and had a business on the side that he used his university position to promote. He became one of the very few tenured professors in University of Minnesota history to be fired for cause. He left the department in shambles. Fortunately it recovered. A series of able black scholars—John Wright in literature, Rose Brewer in sociology, and Geneva Southall in music—restored the department's reputation and gave it a permanent place at the university.

The tensions that accompanied the creation of the African American studies department were being reflected throughout the country.

I was still in demand as a visiting lecturer, particularly in the smaller colleges and universities of the Upper Midwest that did not have their own course offerings in African American history. But I also participated in workshops at summer institutes at the University of Wisconsin–Madison and North Carolina Central University, a historically black college in Durham. I was generally well received, but I was now beginning to notice the disappointment on the faces of black students when they saw that I was white.

I saw the most dramatic evidence of hardening attitudes, however, at a conference titled "The Black Man in America: 350 Years," held at Wayne State University in May to commemorate the anniversary of the arrival of the first slave ship from Africa to North America in 1619. The Wayne State conference is now seen as a landmark in the emerging schism between white and black historical scholars, and although I was a participant I was not a major player. I presented a relatively noncontroversial commentary on the work of the great black sociologist St. Clair Drake. The real fireworks came in the papers on slavery, particularly a paper by a young white scholar named Robert Starobin, which emphasized the process of accommodation that slaves made to the system. A black historian, Sterling Stuckey, and the black activist Julius Lester ripped into Starobin, questioning not only his findings but also his ability as a white scholar ever to understand the thought process of black slaves. I had long discussions over the next couple of days with several of my white friends, such as Eugene Genovese and Willie Lee Rose, about what this all boded for the future. We all thought Starobin's paper had serious flaws and that Stuckey and Lester had made some valid points. But we were taken aback by the vitriolic tone of the criticism and what it portended for cooperation and mutual respect among scholars.

I found one all-black constituency, however, that seemed totally untroubled by the color of my skin. T. Williams, a Minneapolis black community activist with a particular interest in the issues faced by black prison inmates, asked me if I would be willing to come with him to the federal penitentiary at Sandstone, in northern Minnesota, and talk to the Afro-American Prisoners Association about black history. I agreed and the two of us made a series of visits to Sandstone in late 1969 and early 1970. I never spoke to a more enthusiastic audience. These were men, most of them in prison for drug-related crimes, who were passionately trying to find out who they were and they were using their discoveries of the African American past to shape their own identities. Some were drawn to the Nation of Islam, some to Pan-Africanism, others to the radical thought espoused by Malcolm X in his last years and by the Black Panthers. Whatever their ideology, they eagerly absorbed what I told them about racial injustice and how black people had developed strategies to survive in a hostile world. It was to me an exciting example of how knowledge of the past could change people's lives. Unfortunately, I got carried away and tended to forget the unsmiling prison officials who watched everything from the back of the room. On one occasion, after Richard Nixon had done something I thought particularly egregious, I told the inmates that I wished they could change places with Nixon and his cronies; I would prefer having them in Washington and Nixon behind bars. I was soon informed that I was no longer welcome at Sandstone. The next year, I used my Sandstone experience to make a little fun of my somewhat stuffy colleagues in the history department. We were required to submit an annual activities report, more commonly known as a brag sheet. Under "Honorary degrees and other awards," I listed "Honorary Minister of External Affairs, Afro-American Prisoners Association, Sandstone Federal Penitentiary."

The summer of 1969 was, of course, the summer of the Stonewall riot, which has become the emblematic event in modern gay and lesbian history. As the historian Martin Duberman writes, this was supposed to have been "the moment in time when gays and lesbians recognized all at once their mistreatment and their solidarity." Recent historians, Duberman among them, have begun to debunk this idea. I can say only that I cannot even remember when I first learned about Stonewall. It was certainly not at the time it occurred and may not have been until some months later. In any case, the event did not leave much of an impression on me. Stonewall took place in New York, a long way from where I lived, and it occurred in a gay bar, an institution with which I never really identified.

My consciousness as a gay man was galvanized between 1969 and 1972, but it was not by Stonewall and it did not happen all at once. It began before Stonewall, in the spring of 1969, when I walked through the ground floor of Coffman Union where student groups set up information tables, and saw, to my astonishment, a table for a group called FREE, a rather tortured acronym for Fight Repression of Erotic Expression. FREE had been organized by an openly lesbian under-graduate named Koreen Phelps and was one of the first gay student groups anywhere in the country. This was the first time I ever saw gay people openly proclaiming their sexual orientation in public. I did not stop to inquire, but I was deeply impressed. The next fall, FREE be-came more visible on campus when it elected as its president a law stu-dent with a keen sense of publicity named Jack Baker. Over the next two years, Jack Baker and his partner, Mike McConnell, would bring the issue of gay rights into the public consciousness in Minnesota, first by attempting to marry, and then by Jack's election as president of the Minnesota Student Association. It was the courageous work of Jack and Mike and Koreen and a small group of pioneer gay leaders, culminating in the emergence of an openly gay caucus in the DFL in 1972, that would force me to come to terms with my sexuality.

The Morrill Hall takeover and the emergence of FREE were both signs that the University of Minnesota was beginning to change. Throughout much of the 1960s, while there were major campus dis-ruptions elsewhere in the country, Minnesota was relatively quiet. Some historians of the decade have suggested that the student pro-test movement began among privileged students at elite universities—Berkeley, Columbia, Harvard—and only later spread to the second-tier institutions. If so, Minnesota was definitely part of this latter phase of the movement. While student protest has been identified with the Viet-nam War and draft resistance, other issues also came into play. The Berkeley confrontation took place in 1964, before Johnson had esca-lated the war, and centered on free speech on campus. At Columbia, the conflict centered on the university's effort to build a gymnasium in an adjoining black neighborhood.

At Minnesota, too, the war was a catalyst, but students mobilized over a number of issues. And, as at other institutions, heavy-handed efforts to suppress dissent had a radicalizing effect and brought more students into the protest movement. When the county attorney brought charges against the leaders of the Morrill Hall takeover in the spring of 1969, thousands of students who had been indifferent to the original protest came to rallies in support of the "Morrill Hall Three." There was a new round of protests on campus in October when the

Morrill Hall case went to trial. But despite a two-week trial and hundreds of witnesses called by the prosecution, all three defendants were acquitted of the most serious charges. Two of the three were convicted of unlawful assembly, a misdemeanor, and the judge stayed their sentences and placed them on probation; no one went to jail. All of us who supported the "Morrill Hall Three" regarded the outcome of the trial a victory. But the stage was set for a series of major confrontations on campus in 1970 and 1972, provoked by the war but also involving racial tensions and competing visions for the development of the communities around the university.

Richard Nixon's decision to expand the war into Cambodia led to demonstrations at colleges and universities throughout the country in the spring of 1970. I was involved on two different campuses. I had been invited to spend spring quarter teaching at Carleton College in Northfield, Minnesota, forty-five miles south of the Twin Cities. Carleton is one of the outstanding small liberal arts colleges in the country, similar in many ways to Oberlin, and I eagerly accepted. Minnesota gave me a one-quarter leave of absence. I did not move to Northfield, since it was only a fifty-minute drive, and I commuted four days a week to teach my classes. It was a great experience as the classes were small and the students bright and eager. But with about a month left in the quarter, Nixon invaded Cambodia and four days after that, four students were killed by National Guardsmen during a demonstration at Kent State University in Ohio. Both the Carleton and the University of Minnesota campuses erupted and I soon found myself with a microphone in my hand at both places—Carleton in the morning, the university in the afternoon—urging students to protest but remain nonviolent.

At the University of Minnesota, the invasion of Cambodia occurred while many students were already protesting the proposed development of a fast-food restaurant in Dinkytown, the small commercial area that adjoins the East Bank campus. Students and local residents had a month earlier occupied a building that was targeted to be razed in order to build a Red Barn restaurant that residents believed would change the character of the neighborhood. The police cleared the site, hauling off demonstrators in paddy wagons, just two days after Kent State. I visited the Red Barn site and saw how, in the minds of many young people, the war, racism, corporate expansion, and the destruction of neighborhoods all seemed to be part of the same corrupt and unjust system.

After Kent State, the anger was so deep that it became clear at most American colleges that academic life as usual could not be quickly resumed. At Carleton, the decision was made by the administration to allow students to spend the next month doing organizational or political work instead of attending classes and not be penalized in their final grades. Some of my students took that option and several of them signed up to work in congressional campaigns. For those who remained, I continued to teach my classes. At the University of Minnesota, President Moos shut the university down for a day in memory of the Kent State students and then asked that everyone get back to business. The faculty was deeply divided. Some of my more conservative colleagues were appalled that outside events should have any impact on the life of the institution and demanded that everything continue as usual. I had been elected to the University Senate—previously the Faculty Senate, but now including student representatives—and bitter arguments took place in our meetings over how much the university should change its rules to accommodate activist students. Malcolm Moos's leadership now began to falter. He wanted to avoid confrontation with the students, but at the same time he did not want to alienate "key faculty members," as the conservative old guard was called, or, even more important, the Board of Regents and the legislature. It became hard to pin him down on anything and he was less and less accessible to people who wanted to discuss the situation with him.

A week after Kent State, two students were killed in a confrontation with police at Jackson State, a historically black college in Mississippi. With this incident, the major issues of the past decade converged. Black students who had watched the national outrage over the killing of white students at Kent State wanted to know whether there would be equal outrage over the killing of black students at Jackson State. On the Minnesota campus, black students demanded that the university shut down again, as it had in memory of the Kent State students. The night of the Jackson State killings, I was in Coffman Union with several colleagues from throughout the university. By that time, a small group of us, some of whom had met planning the first teach-in in 1965, all passionately antiwar and supportive of the student protests, had begun to meet informally to monitor what was happening on campus. We were disturbed that the university administration was not responding to the black students' demands.

I was delegated to call President Moos and ask him to meet with us. It was after business hours, so I called him at home. His wife, Tracy, answered the phone, and it soon became clear that she had been drinking. She reacted angrily to my request to speak to her husband. "It's Friday night," she said. "He's working hard all week. How dare you call him at home! Can't you let him get some rest?" I apologized but insisted that the situation was a critical one and that we needed to talk to him. There were, I said, potentially serious problems developing with the black student demands. "Problems?" she replied. "Don't tell me about problems. We have plenty of problems of our own. Why, we can't even get the boat started up at our lake place this year." I couldn't believe what I was hearing, but her husband must have heard it, too, and he got on the phone. He said that there was really nothing to meet about as there was nothing more he could do. "You can't turn the university on and off like a faucet," he said. I went back and reported the conversation to my colleagues. "My God," one of them said. "Don't tell the students about the boat or this place will blow up." Fortunately, the situation cooled off over the next few days.

In the winter and spring of 1970, I also became involved in the upcoming state elections. My political friends and I had no desire to take on any local races after the disastrous results of the past two years. But we certainly wanted to play a part in the open races for governor and U.S. senator. The incumbent Republican governor was not running for reelection, so the chance for the DFL to regain the governorship was bright. A divided party had lost it in 1966; if we could reunite, we could win it back in 1970. There were four major candidates: two state senators from St. Paul, Wendell Anderson and Nick Coleman; Hennepin County Attorney George Scott, the prosecutor of the "Morrill Hall Three"; and law professor David Graven, who had organized the ill-fated Sugar Hills conference in 1965. Graven had support from the goo-goo faction in Minneapolis, but had no statewide base. Scott never developed much momentum. The contest was really between Coleman and Anderson. Coleman had been one of the few elected officials who had supported McCarthy in 1968. Moreover, while most incumbent legislators had rallied around their colleague Jim Adams,

Coleman appeared at one of my "Spear Beer" fund-raisers at Dania Hall and spoke in support of my candidacy. Anderson, on the other hand, had been the chairman of the Humphrey campaign in Minnesota. That background would have been enough for me to support Coleman, but I also found him a far more articulate, intelligent, and thoughtful candidate than Anderson. My friends and I did what we could to elect pro-Coleman delegates in Minneapolis, where we found allies in the north side Rice-Salchert group, who liked Coleman's labor record and related well to his quick Irish wit. I did not run for state delegate because I had agreed to take a position teaching over the summer at Stanford University and would be in California by the time of the state convention.

While Coleman was a serious candidate with a real chance of winning, in the senate race my friends and I pursued the path of protest politics. Senator Gene McCarthy would have faced reelection in 1970, but he had announced shortly after the end of his presidential race that he would not run for another term. Hubert Humphrey, no longer the vice president and unsuccessful in his quest for the presidency, had come back to Minnesota, where he taught a class at the university and soon declared himself a candidate for the open Senate seat. Despite his association with Lyndon Johnson and the Vietnam War, Humphrey was still a popular figure in Minnesota and had easily carried the state in the presidential race. Moreover, with a Republican president leading the war effort, it was easier now for Democrats to oppose the war, and Humphrey's views were less bellicose than they had been during his vice presidential days. Nevertheless, although we realized that we couldn't beat Humphrey, the antiwar Democrats could not let his candidacy go unchallenged. We rallied behind a young man named Earl Craig, who had demonstrated real leadership potential over the past two years but had little statewide name recognition.

Earl Craig had come to Minneapolis to pursue graduate studies at the university. He had grown up in an affluent black family in St. Louis. A man with intellectual interests and refined tastes, he always seemed more comfortable in the community around the university than in the black community. He was certainly sensitive to racial slights and had, I think, a highly developed black consciousness, but his closest friends were white people who shared his interests. He was part of the McCarthy surge in the Second Ward in 1968 and shortly after the

Chicago convention helped organize the New Democratic Coalition, which was designed to carry on the ideals of the McCarthy campaign within the Democratic Party. I became the coordinator of the NDC for the Fifth Congressional District, and Earl was hired to be the state-wide executive director. Nothing much ever came of the NDC, and within a few years it had faded away. But it gave Earl a platform and he made the most of it. He spoke well and impressed people as deeply committed to his views, yet reasonable and not doctrinaire. When he indicated his willingness to run against Humphrey we were delighted and we organized to get as many votes for him as we could.

I followed the convention by long-distance telephone conversations from California. Humphrey, as we expected, was easily endorsed but Earl had done well. Even Humphrey had been impressed enough to try to find him a place on the ticket. He suggested to Earl that if he ran for lieutenant governor Humphrey would support him. The lieutenant governor was elected separately from the governor at that time, and Humphrey probably could have delivered. But Earl demurred as Rudy Perpich, another pro-McCarthy state senator, was already running for that office. Earl said that he would go on and run against Humphrey in the DFL primary, but he rejected the idea, urged on him by some of the more fervent antiwar activists, to run as an independent in the general election. In the governorship race, Humphrey did broker a deal. According to eyewitnesses, after hours of inconclusive balloting, Humphrey met with the three leading candidates; he looked at Ander-son and said, "Wendy, you're going to be governor," at Coleman and said, "Nick, you're going to be senate majority leader," and at Scott and said, "George, you're going to the state supreme court." All of this ultimately came true.

The party avoided the deep ruptures of 1966 and 1968 and went on to win the governorship, hold the U.S. Senate seat, and fight to a virtual tie in the state Senate. Humphrey easily defeated Earl Craig in the primary, and when I returned from California I focused my efforts on Rudy Perpich's race for lieutenant governor. Perpich was a Min-nesota original, a blunt-spoken dentist from the Iron Range, one of three politically active brothers, with strong populist inclinations that grew out of his background as a poor miner's son. I had a fund-raiser for him at my apartment, and even though the office of lieutenant governor had little inherent power, I was immensely gratified when he was elected. It was the first time since I had entered DFL politics that I was part of a winning campaign.

At about this time, I had a graduate student from West Germany who was active in left-wing politics in her home country. She commented to me one day that she was simply astonished by the ease with which American leftists jumped back and forth between the Democratic Party and organizations far to its left. In Germany, she told me, left-wingers would have nothing to do with the mainstream Social Democratic Party. I certainly could have been her prime example. While I was deeply involved in DFL politics in 1970, I was also busily organizing in support of one of the most radical groups on the American political scene—the Black Panther Party. Unlike the various Black Power groups that had emerged in the wake of the civil rights movement, the Panthers rejected racial separation and welcomed white support. They saw themselves as the successors to Malcolm X and spoke of an international revolutionary movement that transcended race and nationality. They rejected the nonviolent tradition of Martin Luther King and posed for pictures fully armed. Their most famous leader, Huey P. Newton, had the title of minister of defense. The Panthers became one of the principal targets of the FBI and other police agencies in the late sixties and early seventies and became involved in a series of violent shoot-outs that ultimately decimated their organization. White leftists like me saw them as victims of government harassment, as the front line in the battle against the repressive policies of the Nixon administration. In light of information about the Panthers that has been revealed over the past thirty years, I think now that I was naive. The Panthers, it seems clear, behaved in the manner of a criminal gang, many of them were involved with drugs, and their violent methods of retribution against wayward members were savagely brutal. I saw none of that at the time.

In the late winter of 1970, Bob Metcalf, who had remained my principal liaison with the radical left, suggested that Lee and Marcia Greenfield and I join him at a national conference in Chicago to protest the repression of the Panthers. The conference, which was held on March 7 and 8, was interracial, with a few Panthers in attendance, a larger group of black people who wanted to express solidarity with the Panthers, and a lot of white radicals, including a significant delegation from the

Communist Party. After we returned home, the Greenfields and I took the lead in establishing a local Black Panther support group, called Minnesotans Against Repression, which I chaired. We began planning a local event to call attention to the Panthers' plight. The event, an all-day conference held on May 23 called "The Black Panthers: Target of Repression," drew almost five hundred people to the First Unitarian Society. During the day, a series of workshops featured a virtual who's who of the local left. I spoke on the historical background of the Black Panthers, and my colleague in constitutional history, Paul Murphy, discussed the history of government repression in the United States. After a fund-raising cocktail party in the late afternoon, the evening plenary session featured Charles Garry, a white attorney from San Francisco, who was representing Black Panthers Huey Newton and Bobby Seale in criminal court in California. One real Black Panther, Bobby Rush from Chicago, came in for the day and was welcomed as a hero; Rush was one of the few Panthers who would successfully make the transition to mainstream politics and he currently serves in the U.S. House of Representatives.

We were enormously pleased with the attendance and the almost two thousand dollars that we had raised from the event. A few days later, after we had determined how much money we had cleared, someone came up with an idea that seemed brilliant at the time, a little risky in retrospect. I was about to go to San Francisco for the summer. Instead of mailing a check to the Black Panthers, I could deliver the money in person to the Panthers' national headquarters in Oakland. So a few weeks later, I found myself walking the bleak streets of the Oakland ghetto, the only white person in sight, looking for an address. I found an unmarked house, rang the doorbell, and heard a gruff voice on the intercom asking me who I was and what I wanted. I told them I had money for them. I was soon admitted, turned over the money, and had a cordial conversation about our activities on their behalf in Minnesota. They expressed their appreciation and I left.

I had agreed to teach two courses as part of Stanford University's eight-week Institute of American History. One was in African American history, the other in recent American history. The students were a mix of regular Stanford students, students from other universities who wanted to spend the summer in the Bay Area, and teachers who had come to the institute pursuing extra credits. The atmosphere was generally laid back. Classes met four days a week because, I was told, on Friday everyone headed for the beach. I was astonished by the number of students who brought their dogs to class; when the mailman walked by the door with his regular morning deliveries, the dogs all had to be restrained to prevent them from going after his ankles. The Stanford campus was a lovely place in the summer, and one special treat was an invitation to have dinner at the home of my former Yale professor, David Potter. Potter seemed to be thriving at Stanford, and when he went to his backyard to pick a fresh lemon for our gin and tonics, he commented on how different Palo Alto was from New Haven. Unfortunately, that was the last time I would see Professor Potter. Soon after, he was diagnosed with terminal cancer and within a couple of years was dead.

I had several black students in my African American history class and two of them challenged me with some points that I decided were completely valid. Despite my efforts to approach African American history from the perspective of the black community, I tended to ignore aspects of black life that I could not fully relate to. I have never been tuned into popular culture, whether black or white, so I knew little about black music, black storytelling, or black sports heroes. My students told me that I was omitting subjects important to black Americans, although they made it clear that their criticism was related to my presentation and not to my race. I decided that they were right and when I returned to Minnesota I began to read more on black popular culture. I never became an expert on it, but I did develop lectures on the emergence of jazz and the blues, the antecedents of what later became rap music, and the significance of the great black boxing champion Jack Johnson. I also came to realize that if I ever revised *Black Chicago,* I would need to add material on the evolution of black music and dance in the clubs and saloons of early-twentieth-century Chicago.

When I accepted the position at Stanford, I decided that I wanted to live in San Francisco for the summer. It would involve a daily commute over some of the most congested freeways in America, but this might be the only chance I would ever have to fully experience one of the country's most fabled cities. And although my gay consciousness was still undeveloped, I vaguely knew of San Francisco's reputation as a relatively open city for homosexuals. In the spring, I wrote to my friend Elizabeth Katz, who was living in the city, and asked her if she knew of an available apartment. Elizabeth had been a graduate student at Minnesota, one of the Mixers crowd, and we had even dated a few times although without much passion. She had been one of my brightest students, but had inexplicably failed her PhD preliminary exams. Demoralized, she dropped out of the PhD program, got a master's degree in library science, and took a job in San Francisco as a librarian. She told me that she in fact knew of a perfect place for me in the city. Friends of hers were going to Montana for the summer and wanted to sublet their spacious apartment on a tiny alley in the Mission district. If I were willing to care for their two cats, I could have it at a good price. I immediately agreed.

When I arrived, I found a perfectly adequate apartment in a run-down but colorful neighborhood. Balmy Alley, where it was located, has since become well known for its folk-oriented Latin American murals that cover every visible wall on its one-block length. The murals didn't exist in 1970, but the Latin American flavor of the neighborhood did, and once I gave the apartment the thorough cleaning it needed, I enjoyed living there. San Francisco in 1970 was three years past the famous "summer of love," but it was still the epicenter of hip culture. As soon as I unpacked my bags, my next-door neighbor invited me in for a joint and told me how he had just thrown the I Ching and learned that Charles Manson was Jesus Christ. Throughout the summer, I was offered marijuana everywhere I went and heard constant references to the occult. While I had been strongly attracted to the radical politics of the sixties and seventies, I found little appeal in the trappings of the counterculture. I smoked marijuana when it was offered to me, but was never excited by it. One reason may have been that I had never been a cigarette smoker and didn't know how to inhale. Years later, when Bill Clinton was ridiculed for saying that he had smoked marijuana but never inhaled, I believed him. For nonsmokers, inhaling does not come naturally. I also tried psychedelic drugs from time to time, but they never became an important part of my life. I was totally turned off, however, by the counterculture's embrace of the supernatural. I have never been able to understand how intelligent and well-educated people can believe in such things as astrology, witchcraft, fortune-telling, and psychic healing. In my mind, a critical attitude toward the political establishment ought not lead to a rejection of the entire Western tradition of science and technology that has been the great legacy of the Enlightenment.

When I arrived in Balmy Alley, I noticed immediately that the apartment's single bedroom was furnished with just one bed. It didn't take a genius to conclude that the two women from whom I was subletting were lesbians. And when Elizabeth arrived to welcome me, she told me that she had come out in San Francisco as a lesbian and that most of her friends were, in her words, "lesbian hippies." A few days later, she arrived at the apartment with a black eye. She had had a fight with her partner, who had hit her, and she needed a place to live. Could she stay with me? She moved in and stayed for the rest of the summer. From her I learned a good deal about lesbian life in San Francisco and met most of her friends. Some of them were, from my rather bourgeois perspective, pretty strange. On an uncharacteristically hot day, one of her friends came to the apartment to visit, complained about the heat, and then asked me casually if it would be all right if she took her clothes off. "All of them?" I asked. "Of course," she replied. I told her that I would not be comfortable with that. But I came to feel close to Elizabeth and enjoyed having her with me in a city where I knew no one. Toward the end of the summer, she suggested that we go camping together one weekend. I told her that I had never been camping, except for my unhappy experience in the Boy Scouts. She assured me that she would do the heavy lifting and I could just do the cooking. I agreed but insisted that there would be no dehydrated food; I would take a portable charcoal grill and cook steaks. We went to a campsite on a lake in Mendocino County. That night, as we talked under the stars, I told her that I was gay. She said that she was not exactly surprised. After all, she had just pitched the tents and I had cooked dinner—stereotypes, to be sure, but not without some basis in reality. She urged me to at least begin to explore my sexuality before leaving San Francisco.

I visited a few gay bars on Polk Street, which was still the center of gay life in San Francisco in 1970, and did not find them particularly appealing. But just a few days before I was scheduled to leave for home, I drove along Polk Street late in the evening to observe the action. A good-looking young black man waved at me and signaled for me to stop. I did and he got into the car. He suggested that we go to his apartment, which was nearby. His name was Brad and he was the first man with whom I ever had a fully consummated sexual experience. I enjoyed it, but I was awkward at it. When we finished, I apologized for my clumsiness and told Brad that this was the first time I had had sex with a man. He was astonished. "How old are you?" he asked. "Thirty-three," I replied. "What have you been doing all these years?" he asked. "Are you married?" I told him that I wasn't but that I had had a girlfriend and that I didn't think that I could live an openly homosexual life in Minnesota. "That's nonsense," he said. "You have only one life to live. Live it the way you want to live it." The next day I called Brad and asked if I could see him again. He said that he was busy. What had been a breakthrough experience for me had been just another one-night stand for him. I left San Francisco for the long drive home with his words ringing in my head: "You have only one life to live." One night as I was sitting alone eating dinner in Butte, Montana, I resolved that when I returned to Minnesota I would begin to explore the gay scene. But I didn't. Instead I plunged back into my busy life of academics and politics.

By the fall of 1970, the history department had changed significantly from what it had been when I joined it six years earlier. No longer did the conflicts center on personal alliances and relatively trivial issues. The department had become polarized around the issues that were dividing campuses throughout the country: student participation in decision making, non-Western studies, hiring practices, criteria for promotion. I had new allies in what some department members had begun to call "the radical caucus." Allen Isaacman had joined the department the year before as the first full-time professor of African history. A specialist in East Africa, he would eventually become one of the major scholars in his field. Stuart Wagner had been hired to supplement Stuart Schwartz in Latin American history, and Peter Carroll, a free spirit with wide-ranging interests, came in as a very unconventional American colonial historian. Allen, Stuart, Peter, and their wives, along with Stuart Schwartz and Al and Bonnie Jones, often got together with me for dinner and we became good friends. Stuart Wagner's wife, after divorcing him some years later, became a professional cookbook writer under the name of Jeannette Ferrary and credited me with first acquainting her with the pleasures of good food. Bob and Gene Berkhofer had left the university for Wisconsin and then, after two years, the University of Michigan, where Bob spent most of the rest of his career. So I now had a new grouping of social friends who were also generally with me on the divisive issues that faced the department.

The so-called radical caucus came largely from the American and third-world sectors of the department. The conservatives were mostly European, medieval, and ancient historians, with the exception of my friend Kim Munholland, a French historian who usually sided with the left. Some were older professors who were threatened by change. But the heart of the opposition came from a group of young men who had been recently hired and who shared an ideological conservatism. Most of them, coincidentally, lived in St. Paul and we began to refer to them as the St. Paul Tories. Not every issue was sharply divided. Many members of the department did not identify with either right-wing or left-wing factions and made decisions based on the specific issue before them. But the issues were far more ideological than they had been in previous years.

First, I led an effort to open up participation in promotion, tenure, and salary decisions to all members of the department. Previously, only those of higher rank could participate in these decisions; full and associate professors made decisions involving assistant professors; full professors alone judged associate professors. I was successful in persuading my colleagues that it would be more collegial for everyone to participate in these decisions. A committee on promotion, merit, and tenure made recommendations, but the entire department made the final judgment each year on how their colleagues should be rewarded. Second, my allies and I suggested that department meetings be opened to representatives elected by the history graduate students and by the undergraduate history majors and that students be included on search committees. This was a more contentious issue. Some faculty members thought student presence would chill discussion, and others were simply opposed to any action that would appear to be a concession to the student protest movement. One of my colleagues said, "The trouble with this department is that too many of its members care what students want." But we ultimately prevailed with the proviso that the students would leave during discussions of personnel matters and when students were being evaluated.

These changes were achieved with relatively little blood being spilled. Two other issues became more bitter. One was affirmative action in hiring, particularly the hiring of women. Until 1972, the history department was all male and all white. There had been two women in the department early in the century, but when they retired they were replaced by men. When I arrived, there was only a handful of women graduate students; one of them told me an incredible story of walking into a professor's office and asking him to supervise an independent studies course for her. His reply was, "I don't know what you are doing here anyway. You should be home having babies." This professor had left Minnesota by the 1970s, and I myself never heard views that blatant. When hiring decisions came up, no one ever said they were against hiring a woman. But if there was a woman candidate, there always seemed to be a man whom a majority agreed was better qualified.

The issue came to a head in 1971 when the central administration appropriated money for several new positions in the humanities and one was given to the history department. This came to be known as the sixteen-thousand-dollar position, as that was the sum made available for the salary. The field of specialization was left open, but there was a general understanding that we would hire in European history. There were many well-qualified candidates, among them an outstanding woman named Carla Phillips, who specialized in Spanish history during that nation's days of expansion. It was difficult to judge among the top candidates, and I argued that as I understood affirmative action, still a relative new concept, it should give an edge to an underrepresented group when all qualifications were relatively equal. Women could not have been more underrepresented. The young Tories were outraged that gender should even be discussed, and they quickly found a male candidate whom they preferred. At the interviews, Carla Phillips was superb. In a divided vote, the department offered her the job and she became a highly valued member of the department. But two years later, we went through the same struggle again when a position opened in medieval history.

Even more contentious were the issues surrounding evaluation, promotion, and tenure. We had adopted an open process for judging our colleagues but still had sharp disagreements on criteria. Decisions were supposed to be made on the basis of scholarship, teaching, and service. But clearly scholarship was, in practice, the most important. When I had joined the department, I was told that there was a one book/ two book rule—one book to become an associate professor, two books for promotion to full professor. The department now insisted that it had abandoned such a crude yardstick and looked at achievements more comprehensively. To be sure, several articles could now substitute for a book. But research and scholarship were still what counted. Teaching skill was hard to judge quantitatively, and service, which meant doing administrative and committee work and reaching out to the community, was not highly valued by all faculty members. In November 1970, I wrote a letter to the Committee on Promotion, Merit, and Tenure pointing out that the form that the committee distributed as the basis for the annual "brag sheets" was itself biased by an "almost exclusive preoccupation" with "research and scholarship." I argued that "the very fact that teaching and community service are relegated to a 'miscellaneous' category indicates the degree to which these criteria are regarded as afterthoughts." I went on to challenge the traditional notion of the academic professional as a scholar set apart from the general community. I said that I considered my community activities "as integrally related to my professional competence as are the scholarly activities of my colleagues." "I have attempted," I added, "to use my knowledge as a historian of black America to fight racism and injustice in American life. To me, this is the most important role that I can play as a professional historian." In conclusion, I asked "why those of us who choose to use our training as historians to attempt to effect change in the community [should] be judged any less sympathetically than those who choose to concentrate their time and energy on research and writing."

The issues I raised in my letter culminated in a case that centered not on me but on my friend Al Jones. University rules required that a decision be made to grant or deny tenure to an assistant professor within seven years after the awarding of the PhD. Al's seven years would expire in 1972, which meant that the decision would come in the spring of 1971 so that he would have a year's notice. Initially, I didn't think he was in serious trouble. No one had been denied tenure in history since I had come to Minnesota. In addition, Al had strong support from Clarke Chambers, the senior twentieth-century American historian with whom he worked closely. Clarke was a highly respected member of the department and with the death of Stuart Hoyt, early in 1971, was a leading candidate to become the next chair. I thought his opinion would carry great weight. To be sure, Al had not published a book. But his dissertation had been revised and was under consideration by several publishers, and I thought that would suffice. Most important in my mind, Al was known throughout the university as an outstanding teacher. His classes were packed and there were always lines in front of his door during his office hours. And he had made some unique contributions to the department. When the department decided that it needed to recruit black graduate students, Al was chosen, because of his experience at Tuskegee, to tour historically black colleges in the South to find qualified students to come to Minnesota. One of the students he identified, Quintard Taylor, went on to get his PhD and become a distinguished teacher and scholar.

The Promotion, Merit, and Tenure committee, however, came in with a recommendation that Al Jones be denied tenure. Part of the problem may have been the way he presented his case to the committee. Instead of pointing to the scholarship that he had done and to the very real prospects that his manuscript would soon be published, he argued along the lines that I had in my letter to the committee a few months earlier. He said that he saw himself primarily as a teacher and wanted to be judged that way. In my case, it had been a moot point; I was not up for anything. In his case, his future depended on it. The committee concluded that he had no commitment to scholarship and that he represented a poor risk for a lifetime appointment. At the full department meeting, those of us who supported Al tried to point out that he was an idealist who wanted to be evaluated on his own terms and that this should not be held against him. I emphasized the importance of his manuscript in a way that he hadn't. Clarke Chambers also spoke strongly on his behalf. But minds had been made up and Al was denied tenure. He and Bonnie stayed in Minnesota for one more year and then moved on. Ironically, his manuscript was soon published. But he never had another permanent full-time teaching job and spent the latter part of his career as an official with the United Church of Christ. We remained in touch over the years, but the circumstances of his departure contributed significantly to my growing alienation from the history department.

The outcome of the Al Jones case led to intensified discussions about departmental politics. My friends and I wondered why the conservatives always seemed to dominate the Committee on Promotion, Tenure, and Merit. In votes at department meetings we often prevailed. Yet in the multicandidate secret ballots that chose the committees, especially the important PMT committee, we always seemed to lose. Someone suggested that the young Tories, who often carpooled together to work, would decide on their favored candidates while riding together and vote as a bloc, while our votes were randomly distributed. Both sides can play that game, I said. I suggested that in the next year's election, we draw up a slate. We did so and passed it around to faculty members who we thought would be sympathetic. The entire slate was elected. But our opponents soon discovered what we had done; they were outraged and denied that they had ever done anything similar themselves. At a departmental meeting in the fall of 1971, we were forced to promise that we would never do that again. Professor Otto Pflanze, a specialist in German history and a noted biographer of Bismarck, wheeled around in his chair, looked me in the face, and said, "Spear, you're going to have to realize that the history department at the University of Minnesota is not the Hennepin County DFL."

But the election was not overturned and I served on the PMT committee for the 1971–72 academic year. The conservatives were waiting to pounce on us. When we submitted our report on salary recommendations, Bernard Bachrach, a medieval historian and the most aggressive of the young Tories, immediately filed a formal complaint with the chairman "concerning," he said, "what I believe to be the grossly unjust and discriminatory treatment I received." After talking about his myriad achievements and the failure of the committee to adequately reward him for them, he said that he could only conclude that he was a victim of discrimination because he has been "an outspoken opponent of the many efforts by the Radical Caucus which dominates the Merit Committee to lower academic standards and involve the Department in various political issues." He requested an official investigation and threatened that if he did not obtain satisfaction he would take his case to the dean and if necessary to the courts. The chairman, Clarke Chambers, asked the Committee on Academic Freedom and Responsibility to investigate. I served on that committee, too, but because I had been repeatedly named as one of the culprits in Bachrach's letter, I excused myself from participation. When the PMT committee had been elected that year, four of its six members had come from the "radical caucus" slate. But the two senior members had not. And when the most senior member, Tom Jones, a historian of ancient Greece who had been in the department for thirty-seven years, told the Committee on Academic Freedom that there had been a consensus on the salary recommendations and that politics had played no part in it, Bachrach's case collapsed. Professor Chambers wrote to Professor Bachrach that after reviewing the findings of the Committee on Academic Freedom, he had concluded that "there was no discrimination by the Merit Committee against any members of the Department on grounds of political or academic positions." This episode ended as I thought it should, but it had been bitter and divisive. We had come a long way from polite discussions about buying dishes for the Ford Room.

If academic politics was becoming unpleasant, I still found ample rewards as a teacher. I was now teaching almost exclusively in African American history. I had replaced the Race and Nationality course with a two-quarter upper-division undergraduate course in African American history. I continued to offer my graduate seminar and now tried to vary it by focusing on topics within African American history. In 1970 and 1971, for example, I did one quarter on the black urban experience in America and one quarter on black nationalism. Stuart Schwartz, Allen Isaacman, and I developed a one-quarter course on slavery in the Americas that we taught as a team. In the second year, we brought in a fourth colleague, Peyton McCrary, who had just joined the department to teach Southern history. The establishment of the Afro-American Studies Department had little effect on enrollment in any of my courses. I continued to draw large numbers of students, mostly white, but with a smattering of blacks. Occasionally black students would object to my formulation of issues with the clear implication that I was approaching the field as an outsider. We would then discuss it and move on. In my graduate seminar one year, a group of radical white students raised questions about my reading list and suggested that it included too few black authors and too few left-wing historians. I told them that I would be pleased to work with them on a supplementary list. Unlike some of my colleagues at other universities, I never had classes interrupted or faced heated confrontations. I ultimately decided to leave the field when I was elected to the legislature and could no longer devote full time to it. But I was not driven out.

One of the most rewarding aspects of my teaching during these years was supervising PhD students. This, too, was a responsibility that I gave up after becoming a legislator, but for a few years I worked with an outstanding group of graduate students, some of whom went on to illustrious careers. Joe Trotter and Earl Lewis completed their degrees after I went to the Senate, so I did not supervise their dissertations. But I was proud to have helped them get started. They both became outstanding black urban historians and, to my delight, revised some of the formulations that I had developed in *Black Chicago*. Quintard Taylor was my student and went on to became the leading historian of African Americans in the Pacific Northwest; he eventually became the department chair at the University of Oregon. Given the realities of the marketplace, the white students I worked with were less successful in finding academic jobs, but they still landed on their feet. Floyd J. Miller (who was called John) wrote the standard biography of the early black nationalist leader Martin Delany, and after teaching stints at Oberlin and Hiram he went to law school and had a successful career in labor law. Dan Cryer wrote a biography of Mary White Ovington, one of the white founders of the NAACP; he became a journalist and came close one year to winning a Pulitzer Prize. Mark Helbling, an American studies graduate student, found academic success at the University of Hawaii, and Gary Libman became a sports journalist and used his black history background to write some powerful pieces about racial discrimination in professional athletics.

In the summer of 1971, I made my last regular visit to Michigan City; I would not return until my uncle Lester's funeral twelve years later. My parents had made the bold decision to retire to Mexico. Five years earlier, they had sold the house where I had grown up and moved into a town house. With my brother and me both gone, they had no need for a big house and no desire to maintain a big yard. My father, who had never really found a good job after losing his position as an office furniture salesman in his early fifties, was now selling clothes at a menswear store in a new shopping mall on the edge of town. Since first visiting Puerto Vallarta ten years before, he had set his mind on retiring there and he conscientiously began studying Spanish, with some lessons from the local high school Spanish teacher (now, fortunately, a more competent one than the teacher I had studied with). My mother was not enthusiastic about the idea of moving to Mexico. She had many friends and an active life in Michigan City and would be moving to a foreign country where she knew no one, did not speak the language, and would need to come to terms with unfamiliar customs and traditions. But my father was insistent. He was tired of Michigan City and wanted to live in a warm climate. The usual retirement spots did not appeal to him: Florida was too Jewish; Arizona had no water; and a brief visit to south Texas convinced him that it was a haven for rednecks and yokels. Moreover, his economic situation made Mexico even more compelling. He had never had a pension plan, so when he was earning a good income he had saved money on his own for retirement. But after he lost his job, he was forced to use some of those savings, and the inflationary pressures of the Vietnam War era had taken its toll on what once had seemed like an adequate nest egg. His money, he reasoned, would go further and last longer in Mexico, which was still remarkably cheap by American standards, than it would in the southern United States. My mother finally agreed and in the spring of 1971, while my father was still working, she went to Puerto Vallarta to scout out apartments. She found one she liked, and in the fall she and my father moved there.

My visits to Michigan City were now replaced by annual trips to Mexico, usually over the winter holidays. After my first visit, I realized that life there was hard on my mother. My father seemed to be thriving. He had taken a small boat with him and was out on the water or on the beach every day. His Spanish had become proficient enough for him to chat away with the locals and he had become enamored with Mexican culture. He was also pleased to be able to afford things that he never could have done at home. My parents had a maid who came in every day, and when I arrived they had a welcoming party that included a mariachi band they had hired for the occasion. But my mother seemed isolated. Her Spanish was halting and she had made only a few English-speaking friends. Housekeeping, even with the help of a maid, was far more demanding than it had been in the

States. Marketing involved numerous visits to local purveyors—the fish market, the vegetable market, the meat market, the bakery. For the first several years, they were not even able to get telephone service and we could speak to each other only by agreeing on an appointed time when they would be at a nearby public phone. Most alarming, I thought, was their lack of access to good medical care. My mother had been diagnosed with scleroderma several years before and required specialized treatment. She saw a doctor in Chicago on her annual visits back to the States and found a doctor in Guadalajara who claimed some expertise in the area, whom they visited regularly. But getting to Guadalajara involved a bone-jarring, five-hour auto trip, or a quick but expensive flight, and the doctors in Puerto Vallarta were wholly inadequate. So, after five years in Puerto Vallarta, my parents moved to Guadalajara. My father was now becoming too old for the boat and the sun every day, and the need to be close to better medical facilities was becoming more apparent. But even there, I never felt that my mother got the medical treatment she needed.

I also made my third trip to Europe in the summer of 1971. Al and Bonnie Jones invited me to join them for two weeks touring Scandinavia. That was one part of Europe I had not yet visited, so I eagerly accepted. They were then going on to the Soviet Union, where I had recently been and had no desire to return, so I left them in Finland. I went to Great Britain for two weeks, where I toured England, Scotland, and Wales on my own, and then met Stuart Schwartz for several days in Paris and Amsterdam. Scandinavia was lovely, despite a lot of rainy weather. We flew into Bergen, toured the fjords, took the scenic railroad trip to Oslo, where we met a Norwegian professor who had just spent a quarter in Minnesota, and then went on to Sweden and Finland. When I had been in England nine years earlier, I had only seen London, so this time I rented a car and went everywhere—from Wales and the Lake District to the Scottish Highlands and Edinburgh in time for the festival, where I saw *King Lear*. In Paris, Stuart and I met Kim Munholland for dinner at the first three-star Michelin restaurant I had ever visited—Lasserre. The setting and service were magnificent and the food certainly good, although I thought the food tended to take a backseat to the pomp that surrounded it. When, a few years later, the nouvelle cuisine emerged and swept away much of the encrusted tradition surrounding French haute cuisine, I was definitely sympathetic.

Dinner at Lasserre cost a staggering thirty dollars; it was twice as much as I had ever paid for a meal and I considered it an enormous splurge. In Amsterdam, Stuart and I made the usual visit to the city's famous red light district, and Stuart told me he wanted to do more than window shop. He asked me if I wanted to join him. This was a repeat of my experience with Leon Waldoff in New Orleans sixteen years earlier and again I found a lame excuse. But the next day, I seriously considered telling Stuart the truth about why I had not wanted to hire a prostitute. I was coming closer to coming out, but was not quite there yet.

Events in Minnesota, however, were pushing me in that direction. In the spring of 1970, frustrated with his failure to get much publicity for FREE, Jack Baker had gone with his partner, Mike McConnell, to the office of the county clerk and applied for a marriage license. They took a retinue of reporters with them and when, predictably, the license was denied, they got the press coverage for which Jack had long been looking. Jack and Mike pursued the case in court, and although they eventually lost, they succeeded in making gay rights, and specifically gay marriage, a hot button issue in Minnesota. For Mike it had unfortunate consequences. A trained librarian, he had a contract for a job with the University of Minnesota library, but when the marriage case became big news, the university's Board of Regents withdrew the offer. This led to another lawsuit. It also led to the first gay rights demonstration that I ever attended. Hundreds of students, staff, and faculty members gathered in front of Morrill Hall to protest the regents' decision. I finally was beginning to see gay rights as a basic civil rights issue; this was job discrimination pure and simple and was no more permissible than racial discrimination. When the regents did not back down and Mike McConnell had exhausted his legal options, I called Richard O. Hanson, a longtime Hennepin County commissioner whom I had come to know through politics. "This is just not right, Dick," I said. "Can you do anything to help Mike find a job with the Hennepin County library system?" Dick said he would try. Mike did get a job with Hennepin County, which he had for the rest of his career. I have no idea whether my phone call had anything to do with it. Mike McConnell was fully qualified for the position and deserved the job for that reason alone.

Meanwhile, Jack Baker had found new challenges. In the spring of

1971, he ran for the presidency of the Minnesota Student Association, a position that on many campuses is called president of the student body. Once again, his keen sense for publicity served him well. He ran a high-profile and fearless campaign that didn't ignore student issues but at the same time never lost sight of what made him a unique candidate. He put up a poster with a full-length photograph of himself dressed meticulously as a young lawyer in a three piece suit—except that he was wearing a pair of high-heeled pumps. The caption read "Put Yourself in Jack Baker's Shoes." The poster became an instant collector's item and was reproduced in local and national newspapers. Jack's campaign resulted in the largest turnout ever seen for a student body election at Minnesota and he was easily elected. A year later, he became the first MSA president ever to be reelected to a second term. I followed all of this closely without getting deeply involved. But Jack was already planning activity on a new front that I would finally have to deal with directly. By early 1972, he had begun to organize a group of gay activists to go to their DFL precinct caucuses, run for delegate, and demand a gay-friendly DFL platform. He was now coming onto my turf and I would not be able to stay out of the fray. What ultimately happened made 1972 a turning point in my life.

7

THE TURNING POINT: COMING OUT AND GETTING IN, 1972

As I entered the new year, although I had become a player in the DFL Party, I had no realistic prospect for election to public office. And despite the stirrings of a gay rights movement in Minnesota, I had remained aloof, still deeply closeted to family and friends and without contacts within the emerging gay community. Both of these aspects of my life would change dramatically in 1972. I would take advantage of an opportunity to run for the state Senate and begin a twenty-eight-year career as a political official. And I would begin the process of coming out that would lead, two years later, to my emergence as the first openly gay man in elective office in the United States. I had not anticipated that either of these developments would occur in the way that they did, and I certainly would not have chosen for them to have happened simultaneously. But they transformed my life and made it far more fulfilling.

Most gay people who have come out describe what they have been through as a process. No one wakes up one morning and says, "Today I am going to come out of the closet." Instead, people come out in stages, first becoming comfortable with the idea of being gay, then confiding in a few trusted friends, then widening the circle, telling family, coming out at work, openly identifying with gay organizations and causes. Not everyone goes all the way. There are levels of "outness." I know people who are out with friends and family but not at work, and others who are out everywhere except with aging and vulnerable parents. Everyone's situation is different and I have always objected to efforts to "out" people involuntarily. Coming out is an intensely personal process, and everyone who goes through it must decide how to go about it.

I suppose I actually began coming out back in college when I confided in Jonathan Feinn. But after that, I did little more until my summer in San Francisco in 1970 and even that turned out to be a dead end. My coming out began in earnest in the spring of 1972 and continued for two and a half years until I gave an interview about my sexual orientation to the *Minneapolis Star* in December 1974. During that period I was out to many people but not to everyone. It was an experience that was at times confusing and frightening but also exhilarating as for the first time in my life I felt free to be myself. What gave my coming out an added dimension is that it occurred while I was running for public office and acclimatizing myself to my new position as state senator. It was a total coincidence that just three months after I had begun to tell my friends that I was gay an opportunity arose to run for the Senate. I was already in emotional overdrive about coming out and certainly did not need the frenzy of a hotly contested political campaign on top of that. But one lesson I had learned in my brief time in politics was that when opportunity presents itself, one must seize the time, as it might never come again. And so I did. This chapter tells the story of the most hectic year of my life.

As the year began, national politics was again dominated by the war in Vietnam. All our efforts in 1968 had come to naught. We had dumped Lyndon Johnson only to get Richard Nixon, who had continued the war for another three years and extended it into Cambodia. Yet Democrats remained deeply divided. Few fully supported Nixon's war policies,[1] but the fractures of 1968 had not healed. The left wing of the party questioned not only the Vietnam War but also the entire rationale behind America's anti-Communist foreign policy. The moderates and conservatives adhered to the basic ideology of the cold war. Moreover the social issues were more prominent than before, and older, conservative Democrats were uncomfortable with some of the causes being pressed by the left wing of the party: amnesty for draft evaders, legalization of marijuana and abortion, women's equality and, even in some circles, rights for gay and lesbian people. Senator Edmund Muskie of Maine, who had been Hubert Humphrey's running mate in 1968, was the early front-runner for the Democratic presidential nomination and had strong support from centrists, but there was also talk in Minnesota that Humphrey would run again.

---

1. Even Humphrey, when he announced his candidacy for president, said that if he had been elected in 1968, he would have ended American involvement in the Vietnam War. But in 1970, he had privately told Daniel Patrick Moynihan that he "wholeheartedly" supported Nixon's "course . . . in foreign affairs" (John M. Blum, *Years of Discord, 1961–1974*). This statement lends some credibility to the left wing's distrust of Humphrey.

There were several candidates on the left, but from the beginning, I decided to support Senator George McGovern of South Dakota. McGovern's strong record in the U.S. Senate, his firm opposition to the war, and his absolute personal integrity convinced me that he presented us with the best opportunity of nominating an antiwar candidate. Gene McCarthy was hinting that he, too, would run again, and some of my friends wanted to back him. But I was never tempted. I believed McCarthy had failed his supporters after the Kennedy assassination in 1968 and was simply too moody and self-centered to be a viable presidential candidate. McGovern became a candidate early in 1971, and by the summer I was a member of the executive committee of Minnesotans for McGovern. I traveled the state promoting his candidacy and helped host two McGovern visits to Minnesota in the fall of 1971.

By the time of the Minnesota caucuses, Muskie's candidacy was fading. His performance in New Hampshire, where he openly wept over an alleged insult to his wife, had resulted in a weaker than expected showing there. What we did not yet know was that Muskie, as the front-runner, was the target of an unprecedented array of "dirty tricks" being orchestrated by Nixon's campaign committee. Humphrey was now poised to replace him as the candidate of the center, and the Humphrey Democrats in Minnesota rallied once more behind him. On the left, there was some support for McCarthy and some for Shirley Chisholm, the feisty black congresswoman from New York, but most of the antiwar Democrats caucused for McGovern. So the lines were drawn once again as they had been in 1968—except that the rules had changed. A complicated proportional representation formula had replaced winner-take-all in the selection of delegates. The new system, called limited voting, was supposed to guarantee that each candidate would be awarded the number of delegates to which that candidate was entitled. In addition, affirmative action guidelines now demanded equal representation for women and fair representation for minorities.

The precinct caucuses were scheduled for February 22. In my precinct, a group of antiwar activists, supporting different candidates but united in our opposition to Humphrey, met two days before to plan strategy. My friends Lee and Marcia Greenfield, who in 1968 had lived across the river in Prospect Park, had recently moved into my precinct and the three of us emerged as the leaders of the anti-Humphrey group. Lee was a graduate student in the philosophy of science but he was working as a math instructor at the university, and he quickly mastered the ins and outs of the new limited voting formula. He explained that if each of us voted for a specific slate that he would provide, we could maximize our strength at the caucus. We didn't understand his reasoning, but we trusted him and, on caucus night, did what he told us to do. As a result, we won twelve of the fifteen allotted delegates, more than we would have won without his guidance. The *Minneapolis Star* ran a feature story on our precinct and quoted Martin Sabo, who had caucused for Humphrey, as muttering, "I've never seen such manipulation."

The Forty-second District convention, where state delegates were to be chosen, would be held in late March. I was out of town for two weeks in March. From March 12 to March 18, I went on the most luxurious junket of my life—and I had not even been elected yet to public office. The previous summer, I had received a letter out of the blue from the president of Dansk Design, who was also education chairman of the Young Presidents Organization, an association of company presidents under the age of forty. The YPO held an annual "University for Presidents," which usually emphasized business issues. But in 1972, when the group met in Acapulco, the theme would be "Dreams and Visions" and the goal would be to examine a "wide range of vital contemporary thought." The planning committee had asked student groups at universities throughout the country to nominate the outstanding teachers in their institutions and they had received my name along with that of Professor Mulford Sibley, my antiwar colleague in the political science department. I never knew what student group decided to nominate the two of us, but it was certainly not the College Republicans. YPO offered to pay first-class airfare for me and a guest to Acapulco, a room in a luxury hotel, and all living expenses. For that I would have to lead two seminars. It was irresistible and I immediately accepted. When I saw Mulford shortly thereafter, I asked him if he was going. "Oh," he said. "What do I have to say to a group of businessmen that would justify that kind of expense? I would feel guilty." Mulford's wife, Marge, overheard the conversation and said, "Mulford, you'll never take me to Acapulco on your own. We're going." They went.

I regretted that the invitation had not come a few years earlier when I could have taken Sally B. for a romantic week together. I now had no significant other. So I invited Stuart Schwartz to come along and he eagerly accepted. It was an incredible experience. The hotel, the Acapulco Princess, was the first of Acapulco's truly luxurious hotels, located just outside of the city with spectacular views over the ocean. We stayed in a suite, with the living room used for the seminars. On several nights there were parties around the largest of the hotel's several pools, with lavish buffets and endless tropical drinks. On other nights, we were free to eat in any of the hotel's five restaurants, including a high-end French restaurant, order what we wanted, and simply sign the bill. YPO picked up all expenses. One night, after spending several hundred dollars for dinner and signing for it, one of our companions commented that he wished he could take that "magic pen" home with him. The other professors who were invited included some of the most distinguished academics in the country and I met several historians whom I had previously known only by name: Jim Shenton and Eric Foner of Columbia, Warren Susman of Rutgers, and Jack Greene of Johns Hopkins. My two seminars were on the current racial crisis and on black capitalism. They seemed to have been well received. But the overall tone of the presentations had a left-wing edge that I think was a little more radical than most of the company presidents could handle. I had the impression that the experiment would probably not be repeated and that future seminars would once again emphasize business issues.

From Acapulco I went to Puerto Vallarta to spend a few days with my parents and then returned to Minneapolis just before the Forty-second District convention. I had missed the preconvention strategy sessions, but Lee and Marcia Greenfield filled me in. The antiwar Democrats had enough votes to win most, if not all, of the state delegate slots even without any of Lee's mathematical wizardry. But it was still considered a good idea to have a slate, and a meeting had been held to choose those who would be on it. I had been picked for the slate in absentia and both of the Greenfields were on it as well. In the spirit of affirmative action, an African American, an American Indian, and a Hispanic had also been slated as state delegates. But there was one startling bit of news. Three young men had come to the preconvention meeting, said that they were gay, and insisted that affirmative action also meant that there should be gay representation on the slate. Naively, all three of them ran for delegate, they split the vote, and none of them was chosen. Marcia was disturbed by this outcome. She thought the issue would come up again at the convention and that the slate should be adjusted to provide for gay representation. In retrospect, it seems clear to me that our friends and allies, the antiwar liberals, would never have allowed a slate to go forward without minority racial representation. But other than the Greenfields, most of them did not see sexual orientation as an issue of similar urgency.

The emergence of three openly gay men in the Forty-second District did not happen by accident. It was part of the strategy of an embryonic but rapidly growing gay movement in Minnesota that had begun with FREE at the university and attracted public attention with the Jack Baker–Mike McConnell marriage case and Jack's election as student body president. Although Jack and Mike remained key players, the movement soon developed a broader base. One group of gay and lesbian people had founded the first gay social service agency in the state, a drop-in and counseling center called Gay House. And another group had decided to make its presence felt in DFL politics. Gay people—mostly men—identified themselves at caucuses in many parts of Minneapolis and St. Paul in 1972, and at least a half dozen were elected as delegates to the state convention to be held in June in Rochester. There they planned to lead an effort to include a gay rights plank in the state party platform. In addition, they hoped to persuade DFL state legislators to support legislation that would include gay and lesbian people in the antidiscrimination provisions of the state Human Rights Act. One gay man, Mike Wetherbee, announced early in the year that he would be a candidate for the legislature himself. A lawyer for the Minnesota Civil Liberties Union, Wetherbee was a credible candidate, and although he never had a realistic chance of winning, he put enough pressure on the incumbent, Tom Berg, who had a large gay constituency, to convert Berg into a strong proponent of gay rights.

I was not sure how to react to this development. Until the spring of 1972, I could observe the gay movement from the sidelines. But when it entered the DFL caucuses, I knew that I could no longer avoid direct involvement. I went to the Forty-second District convention excited about what was happening but also confused about what I should do. Shortly after I arrived at the Bell Auditorium on the university campus, where the convention was held, one of the gay delegates, Jim Anderson, came up and introduced himself to me. He was very young with long, flowing blond hair and a boyish face that looked almost angelic. Known as Andy, he would later become a prominent figure in the local community as the coproprietor of the Saloon, Minneapolis's first gay-owned gay bar. Andy approached me very formally. "Mr. Spear," he said, "we understand that you support gay rights and we want to ask you some questions about your position." I was terrified. I thought that they somehow knew about me and that I was going to be forced out of the closet. I went with Andy to the back of the room and he introduced me to the other two gay men—who were also very young—Tom Schuster and John Foster. They were in no way threatening and simply asked me for help in their effort to secure a gay state delegate and pass a gay rights resolution. I promised that I would do what I could.

Before electing state delegates, the antiwar delegates met as a group to discuss the slate that had been drawn up a few days earlier. We constituted about 80 percent of the convention and were clearly in the driver's seat. The question was whether the slate would be reopened so that a gay state delegate could be added. Most of the leadership opposed any tinkering with what had been previously agreed to. At this point, I saw Marcia Greenfield, who was sitting next to me, get up and ask the three gay men to come with her to the back of the room. They conferred for a few minutes and when she returned, she was immediately on her feet. "It is important," she said, "that we leave here with good feelings and that everyone feel fairly represented. For that to happen, we must have a gay delegate on our slate. Therefore I withdraw as a candidate for state delegate in favor of Jim Anderson." When she sat down, I leaned over to her and said, "I should have done that." She told me later that she did not understand why I said that. Andy, who had been designated as the candidate by the three gay men, was elected as a state delegate. Marcia went as an alternate.

Marcia had saved the day. Years later, when both Lee and Marcia were among the strongest nongay supporters of the GLBT movement, many people assumed that they were drawn into it because of their friendship with me. But when Marcia withdrew as a candidate that afternoon she did not know anything about my sexual orientation. She had, on her own, come to an understanding that was shared by very few straight liberals at the time, namely, that GLBT people were a minority group and that gay issues were serious civil rights issues and could not be cavalierly dismissed. I was both grateful to her for what she had done and, at the same time, felt terribly guilty for having sat there like a log terrified of becoming too involved. Moreover, I was deeply moved to see three young men get up at the convention and say that they were proud to be gay while I could not muster up the courage to say a word. When I went home that night I realized that I could no longer go on like this. I decided to call Tom Schuster, whom I somehow saw as the most approachable of the three gay men at the Forty-second District convention. I told him that I would like to get together to discuss gay issues so that I could learn more about them. I told him nothing more than that on the phone and he told me later that he suspected nothing else. We agreed to meet a few days later for a drink at the Black Forest, a German restaurant and bar in south Minneapolis.

I was a nervous wreck the day I was scheduled to meet Tom and it was not until we got to the Black Forest that I was sure I would actually do what I had planned to do. After a few minutes, I told him. I had not asked to see him just to learn more about gay issues. I wanted him and the other members of the gay caucus to know that I, too, was gay. I was deeply in the closet, I said, and would probably not come out. But I would work with them in any way I could to help advance the gay cause. Tom was warm and sympathetic and asked me if I wanted to meet other gay people. I said that I did and he invited me to go with him to the downtown gay bars the next weekend.

That Saturday, I went with Tom to Sutton's Place, then the leading gay bar in Minneapolis, located on North Seventh Street on what is now the site of the Target Center. We also visited the Happy Hour, the only part of the Gay Nineties complex that was then gay (the main room of the Gay Nineties featured a female strip show). Both bars were slightly seedy, but it was nevertheless exciting to be among gay people for the first time in my own city. Tom introduced me to a number of people, including Steve Endean, who would later become one of my best friends. Steve was active in the DFL but was supporting Humphrey so I had little to do with him that year; but in 1973 we forged a strong working relationship that lasted for the rest of his life. I also ran into Larry Bye, another DFL activist, whom I already knew but didn't know was gay. Larry and I had worked together on the McCarthy campaign in 1968. He was as surprised to see me at Sutton's as I was to see him. Two years later, Steve, Larry, and I would found Minnesota's first gay political organization, the Minnesota Committee for Gay Rights.

Over the next few weeks, I met with other gay rights activists. I visited Jim Anderson and talked about how we could work together at the state convention. I met with Jack Baker in his office at the university. Jack was pleased that I was working with the gay political activists, but he urged me to come out. "You don't have to stay in the closet anymore," he told me. "Things have changed." True, there had been changes since 1969, and Jack Baker had played a major role in bringing them about. But there was still a long way to go. After all, Jack's partner, Mike, had lost a promised job because of his high-profile gay activism. And there was even some uncertainty as to whether Jack would be allowed to take the bar exam when he graduated from law school. State law said that entry into the bar was restricted to persons of "good moral character" and there was case law suggesting that homosexuality in itself presumed a lack of "good moral character." In my case, the barrier to coming out was psychological rather than career-oriented. I had a tenured position at the university and didn't expect to lose it. I even knew, intellectually, that most of my friends were prepared to accept my sexual orientation. Nevertheless, as I told Howard Brown when he interviewed me two years later for a book he was writing about gay men in America, "In the back of my mind, I still felt that my whole world would fall apart. The need to conceal my homosexuality had been such a part of me for so long that I couldn't imagine living without it. After all, a lot of my life had been built around keeping that secret."

Nevertheless, once the closet door was ajar, I began to open it wider. I decided to tell my straight friends. Over the next month, I held what I would later describe as "an almost comical series of melodramatic little dinner parties" at which, "sometime between dessert and coffee," I would spring my confession on my guests. Lee and Marcia Greenfield were first. After Marcia's performance at the convention, there was not much doubt about how they would react. Not only were they sympathetic, they also told me that they felt closer to me because I had shared with them something so personal. I told Dick and Carol Flynn, who since 1968 had become not just political allies but personal friends as well. Dick had some concerns about the political repercussions, but they were totally supportive and demonstrated that support in many ways over the next few months. Al Jones was perhaps the most emotional in his response. He had known me the longest of all of my current friends, and we had spent a lot of time together over the years. He was totally positive but he needed to recast many of the experiences we had shared in the light of this new information about me. I was concerned about Stuart Schwartz. We had traveled together frequently over the past several years and I feared that he might find himself compromised as news about me got around. But he took it all in stride and a couple of years later I was the best man at his wedding. Leo and Vi Giovannini were of an older generation and had working-class backgrounds, and I wasn't sure if they would be able to deal with this issue. But when I told them, they simply said, "That's OK. It makes no difference in our regard for you." Only one person broke off relationships with me when she learned that I was gay—my cleaning lady. She told me that "homosexuality is not part of God's plan" and that she could no longer work for me. I found a new cleaning lady.

The most difficult question I faced was how to handle my family. Telling my parents was still, in my mind, out of the question. I thought that they would be simply devastated. Moreover they lived a long way from me and visited only once a year. I didn't think they needed to know. But I very much wanted to tell my brother and sister-in-law. I had no doubt that they could deal with it and that it would be immensely affirming for me to let them know. They were spending the academic year in Rome, and international telephone calls were in those days too costly and the connections too poor to use for anything other than emergencies. So, on May 8, I wrote them a five-page, single-spaced letter that, today, provides the best documentation I have of my state of mind in the spring of 1972. It is, I think, worth quoting at some length.

I started out by telling Richard and Athena that I was gay and "finally coming to grips with it." I told Richard that he had probably sensed it years ago. I then explained that "I am such a political person that my coming out could only occur in a political context, and that is exactly how it did occur." After describing what had happened at the Forty-second District convention, I said:

Here I was, almost thirty-five years old, having suppressed my gayness for almost twenty years, confronted with bright, articulate (and often beautiful) young boys who knew what they were and were in no way ashamed of it. I could only, in all honesty, come to one conclusion. All of my political activities were fraudulent if I could not liberate myself. What was the use of engaging in everybody else's liberation movement, if I was too scared to identify with my own liberation movement?

I then talked about my friendship with Jonathan Feinn, tried to explain my relationship with Sally B., and told Richard and Athena about my tentative explorations of the gay world in San Francisco in 1970. Then I said:

I am only beginning to understand what happened to me this spring. I think that what happened was, in the profoundest sense of the word, political. . . . I have read a lot about the psychodynamics of black liberation and women's liberation. Only now do I have some sense of what personal liberation is all about. I have seen it in other people—blacks who suddenly came to realize what had happened to them, how they had been fucked over. Women who suddenly came to the same conclusion. . . . Well, that is what has happened to me. I have come to the conclusion that there is nothing basically wrong with me, but there is something wrong with a society in which I cannot be what I want to be. And what I want to be is not simply a gay person. It is still hard for me to say to anyone simply that I am gay—because that is an oversimplification of what I am. Why can't I be what I want to be in all of my human complexity? Why can't I be straight when I want to be, gay when I want to be, without making any apologies for either?

But I recognized the personal dimension of my actions as well:

What I am doing now requires building a wholly new kind of personal relationship. . . . It's like learning how to date all over again. . . . I want to think that I can build stable gay relationships. But it requires all kinds of psychological gymnastics on my part right now. How does one court a man to whom one is very much attracted? I'm learning—but it's a bit mind-blowing to have to learn this at my old age.

Then I came back to the political dimensions of coming out:

I feel for the first time in my life, I have done something genuinely radical—in the existential sense. I've finally come to grips with myself and the oppression I myself have undergone. There is a ridiculous sense to all of this—that after having championed everyone else's liberation movement, I have finally found my own. . . . I don't equate the oppression of gays with the oppression of blacks or of Indians or of Chicanos. But it is oppression nonetheless. The gay has a choice that the black does not have. He can reveal himself or not reveal himself. . . . The gay that reveals himself faces external oppression; the gay that stays in the closet faces . . . internal oppression—the inability to be oneself—perhaps the worst oppression. The black at least has the support of his family. The gay must hide his identity even—and most importantly—from his own family. But it is changing. . . . I want to do everything I can to support this movement so that other people aren't going to have to go through twenty years in limbo without revealing themselves even to those whom they love the most.

Finally, I made two predictions about my future behavior that totally misjudged how quickly events would move over the next two years. First I said:

I have not yet made any public political statements about my gayness. I am not sure if I ever will, although it may very well come. . . . I am publicly identifying with the issues of the gay movement. And I came to the conclusion that I owed close friends a disclosure. But surely I don't have to tell the world about my sexual predilections. Other people will figure it out in their own good time. Let them. . . . I feel no more compulsion to flaunt than to hide.

Then I said:

> Let me rest your mind about one thing. . . . The only people
> that I know that I must never reveal this to are Esther and
> Irving. Sure, I'd like to—it would be the ultimate liberation at
> this point. But it would also be the ultimate self-indulgence.
> There is no way that they could come to terms with it. They
> would probably ultimately put on a good front, but it would,
> literally, break their hearts. . . . I simply love them too much
> to allow them to be hurt. I'll do what must be done even if
> means some painful deceptions on my part.

I attached to the letter a memo that I had penned the following
day. It said: "I wrote this letter at 3:00 this morning, a little bit high.
Reading it over in the sober light of mid-day, I realize it is somewhat
frenetic. I almost tore it up. But I didn't—and finally decided to mail
it. I hope you'll understand."

A few days later, Richard and Athena both replied with separate
letters. Richard told me that contrary to what I had surmised, he never
sensed that I was gay. "Perhaps I was blind, or family ties disguise
what one otherwise would see, or you were an excellent bluff—or,
what must be the case, all three factors hid your impulses from me."
Therefore, my letter had come as a total surprise. But "it was so open
and honest that I feel much closer to you than ever before." He went
on to agree with my decisions not to tell our parents as they "never
could understand" and to proceed cautiously with any public coming
out. He ended by saying that "I only can admire the courage it must
have taken at a mature age to make the break, and be sad that it took
until 1972 to make it possible." Athena wrote an equally warm and
accepting message. She confessed that until recently she had held "a
lot of the prejudices perniciously spread by society" and was "conde-
scending toward homosexuality and considered it a pejorative thing."
But even before she had read my letter, she had rethought her views
as a result of "internal maturing and questioning of set notions." She
told me that she liked my letter a lot and respected me more than ever.

In my May 8 letter to Richard I noted, amidst all of the personal revelations, that "Nixon, tonight, just made his speech announcing the

mining of Haiphong Harbor." I went on to comment on "the astounding fluidity of this political year, a year, like 1968, that can fluctuate between the depths of despair and the exhilarating heights of hope." I expressed wonder that while "Nixon is virtually destroying Southeast Asia" and "Wallace is making unprecedented inroads into the mainstream of Democratic politics . . . McGovern—who represents the only hope for change—is the frontrunner for the Democratic nomination." Within a day, my attention was diverted from my personal journey to the ongoing struggle over Nixon's policies, as the University of Minnesota campus erupted into its most serious confrontation of the Vietnam War era.

As in 1970, opposition to the war was conflated with local issues involving the development of the communities adjacent to the university campus. Two years before it had been the protest against the Red Barn in Dinkytown. In 1972, antiwar demonstrators combined with opponents of a proposed "New Town in Town" in the Cedar-Riverside neighborhood on the west bank of the Mississippi. The conflict in Cedar-Riverside was a particularly interesting one as the enemy was not a big right-wing corporation but a well-intentioned old-style liberal who never really understood why the young people who lived in the area did not embrace her plans. Gloria Segal was the wife of a wealthy doctor in suburban St. Louis Park. In the late sixties, with grown children, time on her hands, and money to invest, she began searching for a venture that would make sense financially and at the same time be consistent with her liberal Democratic politics. Someone introduced her to Keith Heller, an accounting professor at the university's business school, and the two formed a partnership to buy up and redevelop the dilapidated residential area surrounding the West Bank campus. Soon they unveiled their plans.

Urban renewal had evolved since I first learned about it in New Haven in the 1950s. Heller-Segal did not propose razing slums and replacing them with highways and commercial buildings. Instead, they envisioned a dense urban neighborhood of high-rise apartments, retail businesses that would serve the residents, and a full array of social services. Gloria Segal invited me to her office shortly after my 1968 legislative race, to which she had donated free campaign headquarters. I found her a warm and appealing person. She served me a piece of her delicious homemade poppy seed cake and instead of chastising me for not supporting her efforts, she told me gently how "disappointed" she was in me. It was something my mother might have said. She then showed me the blueprints and assured me that the "New Town in Town" would be racially and culturally diverse and that there would be subsidized housing to make sure that all income levels would be represented. To emphasize her empathy with the cultural radicalism of the time, she even proposed that at the heart of the development there would be an open-air bazaar where itinerant vendors could sell handicrafts and works of folk art.

The problem was that neither the young people nor the older residents of Cedar-Riverside wanted to live in densely packed high-rise apartment buildings. They liked the old, funky little houses that filled the neighborhood. They realized that many of the buildings needed repair, but they advocated rehabilitation of what existed rather than replacement with something totally different. Several of the neighborhood leaders hired professional consultants and eventually came up with an alternative plan to rehabilitate as many houses as possible and to replace those that were beyond repair with "infill"—new houses that would fit into the existing scale and architecture of the area. In my 1968 campaign, I had supported this emerging plan and continued, as one of the political leaders of the community, to be one of its major advocates. Yet Heller-Segal went ahead and by the spring of 1972 had begun work on Phase I of their project: six buildings, called Cedar Square West, that would contain the first 1,300 of a projected 12,500 new housing units. Secretary of Housing and Urban Development George Romney was scheduled to be the guest of honor on May 9 for the dedication of the new buildings.[2]

Two protests, one against the war and one against Cedar Square West, began that day on opposite sides of the campus and ultimately

---

2. Only Phase I of the project was ever completed. Legal challenges from the neighborhood group forced delays, and eventually federal funding for this kind of development dried up. The old neighborhood, as it was called, was rehabilitated along the more modest lines advocated by the local activists. Phase I, Cedar Square West, never fulfilled its expectations. Physically unappealing, it did not attract the diverse residents that Gloria Segal had envisioned. It instead played the role that the Cedar-Riverside neighborhood had historically filled—a first home for new immigrants, this time not Scandinavians but Somalis.

merged. When students on the East Bank had finished listening to speeches denouncing Nixon's war policy, someone suggested they march across the river and join the protest already in progress in Cedar-Riverside. It was not hard in those days for left-wingers to make connections between seemingly disparate causes. One antiwar demonstrator urged the group to confront Romney because "he represents the president." Another said, "You don't have to reach too far to find a tie between urban renewal and war. They are both making life miserable for everyone." Romney was late for the dedication (and when he did finally arrive, he took one look at the demonstrators and returned to Washington), and so the target became the police who were guarding the construction site. "U.S. out of Southeast Asia . . . Cops out of the West Bank," the crowd shouted. Demonstrators began, in hippie fashion, throwing marshmallows at the police, but it soon escalated to eggs and then rocks. The police retaliated by using Mace and arresting a dozen or so demonstrators, including Congressman Fraser's daughter.

The next day, the center of action returned to the East Bank campus and the violence escalated. I was now in the thick of things—drawn to antiwar protest like a moth to a candle. I saw my role as both a supporter and an observer. As in 1970, I was part of a group of radical faculty who spoke at the rallies, urged students to oppose the war and resist the draft, but also cautioned against violent tactics that would invite police retaliation. The situation in Minneapolis was particularly volatile with a mayor, Charles Stenvig, who had no great love for the university and thought disorder on campus should be treated no differently from disorder anywhere else. We witnessed an illustration of that on May 10. After another antiwar rally on the mall, a group of students decided to storm the university armory, where the ROTC cadets trained. They succeeded in tearing through the fence and threatened to enter and occupy the building. President Moos, who had handled these situations calmly in the past, was out of town, in Ottawa, Ontario, on what was described as a business trip. His surrogate was a relatively low-ranking university official named Gene Eidenberg, who panicked and asked Stenvig to send in the police. Stenvig was only too happy to oblige. The police used tear gas grenades and a machine called a Pepper Fogger to disperse the students. Inevitably, these tactics brought out more students, who were now outraged over what they saw as police brutality. Thousands of demonstrators moved from the armory to Washington Avenue, the main street running through campus, and erected a barricade, made up primarily of construction material, that closed the avenue to traffic. Stenvig then sent in a helicopter to spray gas from above and asked Governor Wendell Anderson to send in the National Guard. The governor said he had no alternative but to comply with the mayor's request. Eidenberg, seeing what he had wrought, now tried to stop the use of gas and call off the National Guard, but it was too late. Stenvig would not even accept his telephone calls.

I was not gassed, but it was a close call. I was in front of Coffman Union when the helicopter approached and when I realized what it was about it do, I started to run. I got away in time but fell, ripping the entire front of my pants. That was the extent of my "war wounds." My faculty allies and I were furious that it had come to this. We had expected this response from Stenvig but were appalled by Eidenberg's actions and dismayed that Moos had not been here for such a crucial point in the life of the university. Moos returned from Canada late that night and went into an immediate session with the regents. The next day the Twin Cities campus assembly met; this group consisted of the University Senate members affiliated with the main Twin Cities campus. The assembly was deeply divided: on the one hand, a coalition of students and left-wing faculty pushed a series of resolutions demanding that the police and National Guard leave campus and that students be allowed to spend the rest of the quarter working for peace; on the other hand, the faculty conservatives, led by law school professor Carl Auerbach, a close associate of Hubert Humphrey's, tried to kill the resolutions with endless quorum calls. President Moos was at the meeting and I confronted him directly. "It seems to me," I said, "that whatever your business was in Ottawa, it was not as important as providing leadership when it was needed here. Why didn't you return earlier?" Moos told us how difficult plane connections were from Canada's capital city and said that he had come back as soon as he could.

Meanwhile, the demonstrations ebbed. Stenvig met with Moos and agreed to consult him before taking further action. The police stopped using gas. Gene McCarthy appeared at a rally on-campus and urged students to maintain the barricades for a few more days. But at dawn the next day, the police removed the barricades. Few demonstrators had been present at the time, but when they realized what had happened they returned and threatened to erect the barricades anew. Moos himself, visibly trembling, met with the demonstrators and personally urged them to leave Washington Avenue. "I am with you on the war," he assured them. "But don't blow this." By the afternoon of May 12, most of the protesters were off the street. I wondered if the entire crisis could have been avoided if Malcolm Moos had been on campus from the beginning.

Throughout the spring, the seemingly endless series of DFL conventions, caucuses, and planning meetings continued. My new identity as a champion of gay issues, although not yet an openly gay man, colored a number of my experiences at these events. The most painful, by far, came at a meeting held prior to the Fifth Congressional District convention to choose a slate of antiwar delegates to the national Democratic convention in Miami Beach in July. The new party rules assured that the Minnesota delegation would be better balanced than it had been in 1968, but a majority would still be going for Humphrey. The antiwar Democrats needed a slate and needed to be well organized to gain maximum representation. Some of the delegates would be chosen at the congressional district convention in May, the remainder at the state convention in June.

I went to the meeting with two goals. First, I hoped to become a national delegate myself. I had been a leader of the McGovern campaign in Minnesota and a hardworking party activist. I thought I had a good chance. Second, I wanted the slate to include an openly gay delegate. I was not yet open, so I would not count. The leading contender was Jack Baker. Both of these goals ran up against one of the new rules that I had long championed—representation for women and members of racial minorities. As at the Forty-second District, it was understood that our slate would include at least one African American, American Indian, and Hispanic and that half of the delegates would be women. I never believed that representation for the emerging gay and lesbian community should conflict with this. In fact, I saw it as complementary. As I explained in my letter to my brother, I thought that my new self-awareness was possible only because of what I had learned from the African American search for identity and from the consciousness-raising emphasis of the women's movement. Terms such as "the personal as political" and "identity politics" were not yet in frequent usage, but they were concepts that I was clearly moving toward. Yet to some African Americans, the gay movement was a threat to African American civil rights. As they saw it, mostly privileged white men were claiming minority status and ripping off the hard-won rewards that belonged to struggling racial minorities.

At the meeting, several of the openly gay state delegates spoke in favor of Jack Baker's candidacy for national delegate. One, a good-looking, articulate young man named Lowell Williams, gave the most insistent speech, arguing that gay and lesbian people in particular needed representation because they faced oppression comparable to that of other minority groups and did not even have the legal protection of the state human rights law. This infuriated an outspoken black delegate named Randy Staten, who interrupted Williams and shouted at him, "Sit down and shut up, you filthy little faggot." Carol Flynn, whom I had come out to just days before, was immediately on her feet. "Mr. Staten," she said, "you are the one who should sit down and shut up. That language is unacceptable." It was a gutsy thing for a white woman to say under the circumstances, but it worked and Staten sat down. Still, the atmosphere remained tense.

It soon became clear that no openly gay delegate would be on the slate. I continued to think that I might make it and concocted a plan in my own mind. If I were chosen, I would come out and instantly give the slate its openly gay delegate. But by the time we had provided places for the women and the racial minorities, there was no slot for me either. It was probably just as well, since I was not yet ready to handle a public coming out. I met with the gay delegates and we decided that something needed to be said to express our disappointment. I agreed to do it. I got up and said that I thought the slate was incomplete without gay representation and that I still hoped this could be remedied at the state convention. Most of the people in the room did not want to hear any more about this issue. My remarks were greeted by hisses and even a few comments implying that my views had racist overtones. Earl Craig, my closest African American friend in the DFL, walked by a few minutes later, looked at me, and in a loud stage whisper said, "Racist." The look on my face must have told him that I was in no mood to be teased. He immediately flashed a grin and put his arm on my shoulder. The support I received from Carol and Earl and the rest of my friends was heartening, but it was nevertheless a traumatic day.

The rise of the women's movement had led not only to an insistence on parity in the election of party delegates but also to a change in the designation of party offices. Since women had entered politics in 1920, most parties throughout the country had created positions, at each level, for a chairman and a chairwoman. The original idea was to assure recognition for women, but as it developed, the chairman became the person who made the decisions while the chairwoman organized the work details, especially those involving clerical tasks or the preparation of food. At a special constitutional convention in 1971, the DFL decided to end this practice and replace the chairman and chairwoman with a chair and associate chair. These two positions would still have to be filled by persons of different genders, but there would be no assumption that the chair would be a man. This change did not come without opposition. One rural Democrat asked in frustration, "How can we do away with our chairwomen? Who will brew the coffee and bake the beans?" The new system would begin with the 1972 state convention, so the Fifth Congressional District convention, meeting a month earlier, would still elect a chairman and a chairwoman.

My friend, Joan Campbell, wanted to be Fifth District chairman. Joan had gone through a few rough years after I first met her at the Mixers back in 1964. A nurse at the University Hospital, she had supported her husband, Gregg, while he worked toward his PhD in American history. Then, just as he was about to finish his graduate work and take a job in California, Gregg announced that he wanted a divorce. Joan was deeply hurt, but she recovered emotionally, dedicated herself to raising her daughter, and became increasingly involved in the DFL, working in every campaign that came along. Everyone conceded that she would be a good chairman. The problem was that since the terminology had not yet changed, electing a woman as chairman would leave the chairwoman position to a man.

Shortly before the convention, John Salchert, the north Minneapolis politician who had withdrawn in favor of Jerry Hegstrom at the 1969 city convention, invited Joan, me, and a few of our friends to his house for a meeting. He pointed out that we had been allies before and should remain allies now. He had a proposition for us. Carl

Baby Allan with his father's mother, Grandma Jen.

Irving Spear with sons Richard and Allan, 1945. Courtesy of Richard Spear.

Allan, Esther, and Richard on a fishing trip to Canada, 1947. Courtesy of Richard Spear.

Allan with his parents, Irving and Esther, crossing the Straits of Mackinac by ferry, 1953. Courtesy of Richard Spear.

The Spear family aboard the Aldick, a thirty-four-foot Chris-Craft, in the marina at Michigan City. Richard holds Paleface, the family's cocker spaniel. Courtesy of Richard Spear.

High school graduation,
June 1954. Courtesy of
Richard Spear.

On the Isla de La Roqueta, Acapulco, Mexico, during a monthlong
trip with Richard in 1960. Courtesy of Richard Spear.

Allan and his parents attend Richard's wedding in Oberlin, Ohio, on June 11, 1965.

The cover of the first Spear campaign brochure, 1968.

University of Minnesota student–faculty anti–Vietnam War leaders on the steps of Northrop Auditorium on campus, c. 1971. Allan is in the middle row, far right. Also in the photograph are Mulford Sibley (back row, far left), Grover Maxwell (back row, third from left), Mahmoud El-Kati (back row, far right), David Noble (middle row, second from left), Joe Kroll (middle row, center right), David Lykken (front row, far right), and Don Olson (front row, second from right). Photograph by Lee Balterman for Time-Life.

Allan with his parents during his 1972 campaign for state Senate.

With Rep. Karen Clark and former Minneapolis City Council member Brian Coyle in the Minneapolis Gay Pride Parade, c. 1983.

Celebrating with Rep. Karen Clark after the gay rights bill passes the Minnesota legislature, 1993.

Allan addresses his colleagues in the Minnesota Senate.

*With President Bill Clinton at the White House at a meeting of
gay rights leaders in 1999.*

*Allan with
Wisconsin U.S.
Representative-Elect
Tammy Baldwin,
December 1998.*

*Allan with former Rep. Ann Wynia, Rep. Karen Clark, and
U.S. Rep. Barney Frank at a fundraiser for Clark, 1994.*

Allan and his partner, Junjiro Tsuji, with his brother and sister-in-law, Richard and Athena Tacha Spear, December 1996.

With Kathy O'Brien, Marcia Greenfield, Lee Greenfield, and Jun Tsuji at Clogher Head, Dingle Peninsula, County Kerry, Ireland, September 2007. Courtesy of Jeff Loesch.

Feeding friends—a favorite pastime.

Jun and Allan at Gallerus Oratory, Dingle Peninsula, County Kerry, Ireland, September 2007. Courtesy of Jeff Loesch.

Kroening, one of his close allies, wanted to be chairman. If we would support Carl, his group would support Joan for chairwoman. Essentially, he had offered us nothing. The antiwar Democrats had a clear majority in the Fifth District and we could elect Joan without him. And Joan was not about to accept the clearly secondary position of chairwoman. I put it to John Salchert directly. Let's just reverse that, I suggested. I told him that if his people would support Joan for chairman, we would support Carl Kroening for chairwoman. John was simply outraged. "How dare you suggest such a thing!" he shouted. "Carl is a real man. He would never agree to that." At the convention, Joan was elected chairman and we found another man whose masculinity was not threatened by the title of chairwoman. Later on, I would serve with Carl Kroening in the state Senate. We never had a good relationship and, although he was not there that night at John Salchert's house, I am sure that he heard what I proposed and I suspect that it always affected his attitude toward me.

A few weeks later, I was invited to a very different kind of meeting at the home of our incumbent county commissioner, Richard O. Hanson. Dick Hanson had served on the Hennepin County board since his initial appointment by Mayor Hubert Humphrey in 1948. He was an old-fashioned liberal, supportive of the county's welfare programs, unafraid of raising taxes for what he thought were just purposes, and convinced that new, often lavish, public buildings always constituted progress. But he knew nothing of the new politics that had emerged in the DFL since 1968, especially ideas involving community control, the rights of the poor, and affirmative action. His district was overwhelmingly DFL and for years he had faced no serious opposition. But in 1972, deciding that Dick Hanson's days were numbered, the north Minneapolis DFL group recruited a candidate against him. They chose a young man named Dick Miller, who, they thought, was just hip enough to draw some votes from the new Democrats while at the same time maintain solid support from labor and the north side. Dick Hanson didn't know where to turn for help. He had no organization of his own and knew none of the newcomers in the party. He called Forrest Harris, one of the few older party stalwarts who had built bridges to the antiwar Democrats. Forrest told him to call me.

I asked about a dozen people to join me in meeting with Dick Hanson. He lived in the heart of Dinkytown in an old-fashioned, rather fussy house that he had shared with his mother until her death a few years earlier. As we talked, I began picking up signals. My gay identity was still too new for me to have developed a keen sense of what is sometimes referred to as "gaydar," but even I could figure out Dick Hanson. He was in his early fifties, had never married, had a vacation home in the Hollywood Hills, served us coffee out of dainty bone china cups, and at one point, referring to something confidential, said that it was "strictly between us girls." When we left the house, a young woman in our group said, "You know, I think Mr. Hanson is a homosexual." We all agreed that he probably was but that it made no difference one way or another. We decided to support him for reasons of political strategy. If Dick Miller were elected, the position was likely to belong to the north Minneapolis Democrats for years to come. Dick Hanson, on the other hand, was nearing the end of his career and, when he retired, we could replace him with someone from our group. Moreover, while his liberalism was from an earlier generation, and he was a Humphrey supporter, we could find no reason to dump him for a challenger who was no more liberal than he was.

At the county commissioner district convention a few weeks later, I gave the principal speech for Dick Hanson. I borrowed heavily from Gene McCarthy's famous speech for Adlai Stevenson in 1960 and told the delegates that we must not turn our backs on this man who had championed liberal causes before many of us had even thought about politics. Dick Miller came into the convention believing that he had the 60 percent support needed for endorsement. Over five ballots, he never reached that level and we finally adjourned without an endorsement. Dick Hanson was pleased with the results—the best he could have hoped for—and grateful to me and my friends. Over the next few weeks, we met several times for dinner and came out to each other. He invited me to visit him in the Hollywood Hills (or the "Swish Alps," as he called them) after the elections were over. In the meantime, Dick Hanson was totally dependent on my allies to run his campaign. Denis Wadley, a long-time liberal activist from the university area, who had become part of our antiwar group, agreed to serve as campaign manager and we all worked to distribute Dick's campaign brochures. He was a nice man but a terrible politician. He was too elitist to knock on doors for himself, and when we succeeded in dragging him to community meetings, he invariably showed up, even in poor neighborhoods, in finely tailored suits and Italian silk ties. Yet somehow his incumbency and perhaps his Scandinavian name carried him through and he was reelected. What we did not yet know was that our involvement with Dick Hanson would lead to a serious rift in the south Minneapolis liberal coalition a few years later.

After my unsuccessful legislative race in 1968, Jeff Spartz, who had worked on my campaign and was rapidly emerging as one of the most effective political leaders in our group, asked me if I would try it again. Yes, I said, but not in the Forty-second District as it had been drawn in 1968. I would run, I told him, if two things happened: if the voting age were lowered to eighteen and if the university community were united into a single legislative district. I saw the university as my political base, I explained, and I needed the student vote. And I could not win so long as the West Bank and East Bank campuses were in different districts. In 1971, the U.S. Constitution was amended to lower the voting age to eighteen. Redistricting was a longer and more complicated story.

Minnesota was a textbook example of why the U.S. Supreme Court decided in the early 1960s to require states to regularly reapportion their legislatures. There had been no general reapportionment between 1913, when the state had been mostly rural, and 1966, when more than half of the population lived in the Twin Cities metropolitan area. The legislature blithely ignored a state constitutional requirement that it reapportion itself every decade. The result was a legislature dominated by rural, conservative interests. This was compounded by the lack of party designation on the legislative ballot. The idea of a nonpartisan legislature had been adopted as a reform in the early twentieth century, but ultimately it worked to the advantage of Republicans.

The legislature did not function in a nonpartisan manner. The parties endorsed legislative candidates and, once elected, the legislators divided into "conservative" and "liberal" caucuses that coincided with their party affiliations. Without party designation, candidates who would ultimately become part of the "conservative" or Republican caucus would frequently win in districts that otherwise elected Democrats. The DFL won control of the House for a few years in the 1950s, but the Senate had been in Republican hands continually since 1860. The DFL came closest in 1970, when it took thirty-three Senate seats to the Republicans' thirty-four.

The Supreme Court decisions of 1962 and 1964, which established the "one man, one vote" principle, required states to reapportion after each census. If legislatures failed to do it, the federal courts would do it for them. The Republican-controlled legislature passed a reapportionment plan in a special session in October of 1971, but at the urging of Martin Sabo, who was now House minority leader and Governor Wendell Anderson's closest legislative ally, the governor vetoed the bill. The Eighth Circuit Court then appointed a panel of three judges to draw up a plan. In December, the panel made an announcement that struck the political community like a bombshell. Their plan, they said, not only would redraw the district lines, it also would reduce the size of the legislature, from 135 to 105 in the House and from 67 to 35 in the Senate. There had long been a sense among government reformers that Minnesota's legislature was too large, but no one expected its size to be reduced by judicial fiat. Nor had the U.S. Supreme Court specifically authorized the lower courts to take such action. The panel argued, rather lamely, that reducing the size of the legislature was necessary to meet the "one man, one vote" test without cutting across county and municipal boundaries. Senate leaders of both parties immediately said they would appeal to the U.S. Supreme Court, and there was concern that a long appellate process might prevent any plan from being adopted in time for the 1972 election.

Legislators and potential legislative candidates lived in a state of uncertainty throughout the winter and spring of 1972. In late January, the federal court panel revealed the new district lines for its smaller legislature. Predictably, many long-term incumbents were thrown together in the same district. And the general analysis was that the plan favored the Republicans. Then in late April, the U.S. Supreme Court heard the appeal that had been brought by the Senate leadership and ruled in its favor. The lower court, it held, had exceeded its power in reducing the size of the legislature. The panel was ordered to come up with a new plan "promptly." Now there was utter confusion as legislators who had bought houses or rented apartments in what they thought were their new districts didn't know where they would be running in the fall. The panel tried to calm fears by assuring that it

would have a new plan by early June and that the deadline for establishing residency in a district would be extended from May 7 to June
26. The panel revealed its final plan on June 2. The size of the legislature would remain the same, except the House would now have 134
members instead of 135. All Senate districts would be divided into two
House districts; there would be no more two-member at-large districts
such as I had experienced in 1968. And the pundits agreed that this
plan was far more favorable to the DFL than the one that had been
thrown out in April.

I was attending another one of our endless antiwar caucus meetings on June 3, the day after the new district lines were released, when
Jeff Spartz ran up to me, clutching in his hand the map of the plan,
which he had just seen for the first time. "Well, Allan," he said to me,
"both of your conditions have been met. You have the eighteen-year-
old vote and now you have a district that includes the entire university
community. What are you going to do?" We looked at the map together, focusing on the Fifty-seventh Senate District. House District 57A,
where several DFLers were already running, included the East Bank
campus, the faculty and student neighborhoods surrounding it, and
a slice, but not all, of working-class northeast Minneapolis. House
District 57B included part of the old Forty-second District—the West
Bank campus, Cedar-Riverside, the area adjacent to downtown, and
the senior citizen high-rise apartment buildings—but it no longer contained the Ninth Ward working-class neighborhoods where I had been
badly beaten four years before. Both Martin Sabo and Jim Adams
lived in 57B, but we soon learned that Jim would move, leaving the
district a safe one for Martin. What Jeff and I had our eyes on was the
Senate seat. Yes, there was a resident incumbent—Jack Davies, who
had represented the Forty-second District for over a decade. But Jack,
who had been a vocal opponent of reducing the voting age, would
not be a strong candidate in the East Bank student neighborhoods.
Within a day, he announced that he would move to run in the district
immediately to the south. There would be no Senate incumbent in the
Fifty-seventh.

I faced a dilemma. I had wanted another chance to run for the
legislature ever since my defeat in 1968. Now it presented itself. Here
was a district where I had a chance to win, and, if successful, I would
go not to the House but to the more prestigious Senate. But I had just

started to come out. How could I reconcile my new gay identity with what would undoubtedly be a hard-fought legislative race? As far as I knew, no openly gay person had ever served in elective office anywhere in the United States. In fact, the conventional wisdom was that of all possible revelations none was more damaging to a politician than a hint of homosexuality. The most popular political novel of the 1950s, Allen Drury's *Advise and Consent,* had suggested that the only way out for a political official accused of homosexuality was suicide. I had not yet come out to Jeff Spartz, but now we needed to talk. I told Jeff that I was gay, that I was in the process of coming out, and that I had no intention, even if I ran for the Senate, of going back into the closet. He asked me if that meant that I would run as an openly gay candidate. He told me frankly that he didn't think that would go over well in the senior citizen buildings or in northeast Minneapolis. No, I told him, I would not run as a gay candidate. But I would insist on including gay issues in my platform. And if anyone asked me directly if I were gay, I would not deny it. He told me that he thought that was a reasonable compromise and he was ready to support me. I had similar conversations with a number of other political leaders in the district over the next few days.

I knew that I did not have long to make a decision. Other candidates would emerge soon and I wanted to be the first to announce. Moreover, with a June 26 residency deadline looming, the endorsing convention would have to be held within two or three weeks. Two days later, I sent a letter to the delegates in the new district announcing my candidacy. I was forthright in putting myself forward as the candidate of the left. "The new redistricting plan," I said, "places the entire university community together, for the first time, in a single senatorial district. This gives us a unique opportunity to elect a progressive senator. . . . I believe that my record in DFL politics, in university affairs and in the struggle for peace and liberation [qualifies] me for this position." After reviewing my credentials, I stated that "I am strongly committed to basic change in the American political structure. I favor not only complete withdrawal from Southeast Asia, but an end to all American military involvement abroad and a rededication to the creation of a decent society at home." I ended by focusing directly on what would later be called the "hot button" issues: "I would work for the repeal of all abortion laws and for the end of the oppression of women and gay people." A prominent Democrat from northeast Minneapolis called me as soon as he received the letter, warning me that I was making a big mistake taking on abortion in heavily Catholic northeast. But I made it clear that I was going to run for the legislature on my own terms.

The next weekend was the DFL state convention, for which I had been preparing since February. Now I wished that I were not a delegate. I needed to start work on my campaign. Moreover, DFL conventions were notoriously divisive and whatever I did I was sure to make new enemies. By the time we met in Rochester on June 9, George McGovern had virtually wrapped up the Democratic presidential nomination. George Wallace's surprisingly strong campaign had ended on May 15, when a gunman had gravely wounded him and left him paralyzed. That left Humphrey as McGovern's only viable opponent, and McGovern's narrow victory in California, which had not yet adopted proportional representation, gave him a large bloc of delegates that put him over the top in most counts. But I realized when I arrived at the convention that Minnesota's Humphrey supporters were just as irreconcilable as the antiwar Democrats had been four years earlier. They were determined to do whatever they could to thwart McGovern's march toward the nomination, and many of them refused to support him even after he was the party's nominee. So every issue at Rochester was hard fought. Not knowing that I would be a legislative candidate, I had made commitments that put me in the thick of it all. I served on the nominations committee, which chose the slate of party officers, a position that was almost guaranteed to create animosity among those who were not picked. And, of course, I had promised to work with the gay caucus to get a gay national delegate or alternate and to win approval of a gay rights plank in the party platform.

The presence of the gay caucus was to many of the old-line Democrats the ultimate in the insults they had been forced to endure since 1968. One elderly, labor-oriented DFLer told my friend Dick Flynn that accepting the blacks and the women had been hard enough, but he was never going to give in on this one. A prominent Humphrey delegate in Rochester, seeing me speaking with the gay delegates, asked me, incredulously, "Are those people actually practicing homosexuals?" It was as though the convention had been invaded by aliens. At the antiwar coalition caucus, we managed to get an openly gay man chosen as the last alternate on the Minnesota delegation to the national convention. Through some curious twist in the voting, it was not Jack Baker but Lowell Williams. Jack was obviously unhappy, but he couldn't object too much as Lowell was his protégé. Lowell went to Miami Beach as one of only three openly gay delegates or alternates in the entire country.

The real fireworks came over the platform. The Humphrey Democrats had a working margin at the convention, although not a large one, and they managed on the first day to pass a rule requiring that any platform plank would require 55 percent approval from the delegates. This they thought would keep anything too incendiary out of the platform. It worked in the early going, and the convention was not able to agree on any plank involving abortion. But by Sunday, the Humphrey delegates, many of whom lived in northern and western Minnesota, left early for the long drive home. In the last hours of the convention, three planks were approved that represented everything the conservative Democrats feared: legalization of marijuana; unconditional amnesty for draft evaders; and full rights for gay people, including the right to marry. The gay rights plank passed just before the required time for adjournment. I did not speak on the issue. I did what was necessary at the time; I ran around the floor urging people not to speak so that we could come to a vote before the final gavel came down. We just made it. After we adjourned, I went out to celebrate with the gay delegates. For Jack Baker and Mike McConnell, it was particularly gratifying that the gay rights plank included gay marriage. That was their major issue, but it was a radical departure for the time.

The reaction to what was immediately dubbed the "Rochester platform" was sharp and swift. The Republicans were gleeful and promised to tie every DFL candidate in the state to the issues of marijuana, amnesty, and homosexual marriage. The DFL leadership, believing that the platform seriously jeopardized the party's chance to win control of the legislature, tried to implement damage control. Tom Kelm, Governor Anderson's chief of staff, challenged the gay rights plank on the grounds that a quorum was no longer present when it was approved, and he vowed to get it removed from the platform. He was not successful. Dave Roe, the president of the state AFL-CIO, had perhaps the most colorful statement: "This is how these people get their jollies. They don't give a damn about electing a DFL legislature or retaining Democratic congressmen." The platform even received national attention. A week after the convention, Arthur Schlesinger Jr. came to town representing McGovern, and as a historian and a local McGovern leader, I was given the pleasant task of taking him out to dinner. The first question he had for me was how the Minnesota DFL could have adopted a platform that included homosexual marriage. Later in the summer, I received a letter from the DFL Senate caucus that had been sent to all DFL-endorsed candidates for the Senate. It urged me to send a registered letter to my Republican opponent advising him that I had repudiated the Rochester platform and would bring a campaign ethics complaint against him if he or his party tried to identify me with it. After I was elected, I learned that I was the only DFL Senate candidate in the state who did not follow this advice.

When I returned from Rochester, I found out that I would have strong opposition both at the endorsing convention and in the general election. The Fifty-seventh District convention had been scheduled for June 25, just two weeks away. My opponent would be Fran Naftalin, the wife of former mayor Art Naftalin and an impressive person in her own right. I had known her for a number of years and liked her. She had been active in various social service agencies and the year before had been elected to the Minneapolis Library Board. She was warm, charming, and intelligent and had a well-known name. Besides, no woman served in the Minnesota Senate and Fran's candidacy would obviously appeal to delegates who thought it was high time to break that barrier. Art Naftalin had been a close associate of Hubert Humphrey's, and both Art and Fran were identified with the Humphrey wing of the party—which gave me an advantage in the fervently antiwar university community. But many of the party leaders thought I couldn't win and that, with my radical politics, I would fritter away what should be a safe DFL seat and possibly cost the party control of the Senate. Martin Sabo, in particular, urged Fran to run for the endorsement.

The fears about my electability loomed larger when it became clear that John Cairns would be the Republican candidate. Cairns was the young Republican lawyer who had beaten Alpha Smaby for the Second Ward city council seat in 1969. Since then, he had been a hardworking and effective member of the council and prided himself on working across party lines. He identified with the Rockefeller wing of his party and was active in the Ripon Society, a national organization of liberal Republicans. At one point in his city council career he had even left the Republican caucus and tried to form a bipartisan majority caucus with DFL aldermen. When he ran for reelection in 1971, his only opposition came from the right and most Democrats supported him. I was among those. Therefore, at a time when party designation did not appear on the ballot for the state legislature, John Cairns would be able to run on his record and downplay his association with the Republican Party. His ward made up more than 40 percent of the Fifty-seventh District, which gave him instant name recognition. He would have a good chance of winning even in an overwhelmingly Democratic district.

I busied myself calling delegates and by the time of the convention thought I had a good chance of winning. But it is notoriously difficult to get a hard count when running for an endorsement in Minnesota. What is sometimes referred to as "Minnesota nice" often leads to a false sense of confidence. Delegates hate to say bluntly, "No, I will not support you," to a fellow Democrat whom they know and will likely work with in the future. So they hedge their answers. I learned that anything short of a definite "Yes, you have my vote" should be counted as a no. Still, when I walked into Mayo Auditorium at the University Medical School on June 25, I liked what I saw. Most of the delegates were wearing my stickers, and they roared with approval when I was introduced. As I did in my introductory letter, I emphasized my ties to the antiwar movement, the McGovern campaign, and the "new politics" that had emerged in the DFL since 1968. I didn't quite call Fran Naftalin a creature of the old politics, but I hinted at her family ties to Humphrey and the historic split in the DFL by evoking the name of the Farmer-Labor governor of the 1930s, Elmer Benson, who I told the delegates was at that very moment lying gravely ill just above us in University Hospital. I touched lightly on issues, but my major argument was that while many districts could elect a conventional liberal like Fran, only the Fifty-seventh had the opportunity to elect a "true progressive" who would bring the ideas of the "new politics" to the state Senate. I was endorsed with more than 65 percent of the vote on the first ballot. Fran Naftalin was gracious in her defeat and immediately told me that she would not challenge me in the September primary.

The real fight at the convention came in the contest for the House seat in 57A, the East Bank portion of the district, and it was a fight that would plague me throughout the campaign. The two leading candidates for the open seat were both assertive, highly articulate, somewhat abrasive, Jewish, and from New York City. Phyllis Kahn held a PhD from Yale in biophysics, was a research associate at the university, and was married to a mathematics professor. She had been active in the emerging women's movement, and when Fran Naftalin failed in her Senate bid, many of us believed that delegates who wanted a woman on the ticket would quickly endorse Phyllis. But her opponent, Matt Stark, had a devoted following, too. Matt worked at the university in a counseling position, but was best known as the president of the Minnesota Civil Liberties Union. He was closely identified with human rights issues and his supporters argued that he had a longer and deeper commitment to these issues than Phyllis had. I found Matt overbearing and hoped that Phyllis would win, but I had strong supporters on both sides so officially stayed out of it. To my dismay, the convention deadlocked and neither candidate was endorsed. Even the primary decided nothing as it was nonpartisan, and in the heavily DFL district, Phyllis and Matt came in first and second, respectively, postponing a final decision until November. Throughout my entire campaign, I had to tread carefully to make certain that I would not antagonize anyone on either side of this hard-fought and bitter race.

Now I should have gotten to work and begun to organize my campaign. But I had one more convention to attend. I had been working my heart out for McGovern for over a year and watched him climb, improbably, from a long shot to the almost certain Democratic presidential nominee. Even though I was not a national delegate, I wanted to be in Miami Beach to see it finally happen. I was able to stay at the same hotel as the Minnesota delegation, rooming with Kenny Enkel, who made national news by telling the conservative columnist Robert Novak that he had come to Miami Beach to fulfill his longtime dream: to get even with Hubert Humphrey for his "purge" of the left wing of the DFL Party in 1948. Novak used this as an illustration of the irrationality of the McGovern delegates. I attended all of the meetings of the Minnesota McGovern caucus and even managed, in that time of more casual security, to get on the convention floor during a couple of the evening sessions.

That week in Miami Beach, I also made my first contacts with gay leaders from other parts of the country. Lowell Williams took me along to all of the meetings of gay delegates, alternates, and various hangers-on. I met Lowell's two counterparts, Jim Foster from San Francisco and Madeline Davis from Buffalo, New York. Jim, Madeline, and Lowell were the first openly gay people ever to be delegates or alternates to a national political convention. They spoke to the convention in favor of a gay rights plank, but the McGovern leadership, which didn't want to deal with this issue, kept the plank out of the platform and scheduled the speeches for three in the morning when no one was watching. I also met Troy Perry, the founder of the gay-oriented Metropolitan Community Church, and perhaps the most dynamic of the early gay leaders. I would come to know Troy better a few years later as I became more involved in the gay movement. One afternoon, Lowell invited me to accompany him on a protest march of gay and lesbian people through the streets of Miami Beach ending at the convention center. I went and marched for about a block. The protesters carried signs proclaiming "Gay Is Good" and other slogans of the day and chanted rhymes such as "Two, four, six, eight, gay is just as good as straight." I was not ready for this kind of activism and found it extremely embarrassing. I apologized to Lowell and left the march.

McGovern, of course, was nominated, but the convention was a disaster. This was the first national convention held under the new rules, and it was far more diverse and open than any previous convention had been. But the McGovern people could not maintain any kind of discipline. Humphrey and Wallace delegates were treated rudely and went home angry. Everything ran behind schedule and key events, such as McGovern's acceptance speech, occurred long after prime time. To top it all off, McGovern chose a running mate who was not properly vetted and he was forced to replace him two weeks later. By the end of the summer, the enormous optimism about McGovern had given way nationally to a sense of resignation among antiwar activists that Nixon's reelection was inevitable. But in my district in Minneapolis, enthusiasm for McGovern—and hatred for Nixon—never flagged. As I finally settled down to the business of putting my campaign together, my task was clear. I needed to tie myself to McGovern and to the Democrats and convince the voters that my vision for a new and more decent society was consistent with McGovern's. At the same time, I could not let John Cairns, despite his liberal ideas and personal decency, escape the reality that he was running as a Republican, on the Nixon team, and would caucus with the Republicans in the state Senate.

Lee Greenfield met me at the airport when I returned to Minneapolis. He told me that he had rented a storefront on University Avenue, near the St. Paul city line, to serve as our campaign headquarters. Most legislative campaigns in Minnesota did not even have headquarters; they were run out of houses. But none of the key players in my campaign owned their own houses yet, and we knew that we would be running a labor-intensive campaign with volunteers coming and going at all hours of the day. We could not do that out of one of our apartments. Lee had found a good space for us, easily accessible and well located, and by the end of July it was bustling with activity. There had been no doubt from the beginning that Lee would be the campaign manager. He and I shared the same political values, I trusted his political judgment, and I knew that he was totally loyal to me. Moreover, his job at the university gave him flexible hours and he could put in the time that would be necessary to keep the campaign going.

Another half dozen people soon came to form the inner circle of my campaign. Jeff Spartz was, next to Lee, the most deeply involved. I was never as close personally to Jeff as I was to Lee. I was sometimes put off by his ambition and drive. But at a time when many antiwar Democrats were political dilettantes, Jeff mastered the political game and was determined that we were going to start winning elections. He believed that by electing me to the Senate, and electing Linda Berglin to the House in the neighboring district, we could begin to establish a liberal base that could dominate south Minneapolis for years to come. Some years later, when much of Jeff's vision had been realized, political observers began to speak of a "Spartz machine." That was always something of an exaggeration as we were far too unruly a group to ever behave as cogs in a political machine. But Jeff Spartz does deserve credit for bringing an ethos of hard work, discipline, and tempered pragmatism to what had previously been an exercise in political futility.

Jeff was joined in the campaign by his friend from the Ninth Ward,

Tony Scallon, a stocky, rough-hewn, tough-talking young man who shared our progressive values but preferred to keep them hidden under the demeanor of a hardened political realist. One of the chief strategists was Andy Kozak, whom I had previously known as a graduate student in history at the university. A working-class kid from Pennsylvania, Andy soon found politics more rewarding than academics and worked in the Rudy Perpich campaign in 1970 and later for Governor Wendell Anderson, becoming an assistant to Tom Kelm. Andy tried to move the campaign toward the DFL mainstream, but at the same time he respected me and knew that he could not make me into something that I was not. Joan Campbell was in the office every day working hard. But I sensed that despite her well-developed political skills and her new position as Fifth District chairman, Joan was not always included in decision making by the men who were running the campaign. All of us were fully committed to women's issues, and Jeff and Tony later took justifiable pride in the role they had played in electing a number of women to elective office, yet old habits died hard. Marcia Greenfield's role in the campaign was more directly challenging to some of the guys. Unlike Joan, who was easygoing, Marcia was a sharp-edged, aggressive woman who had a strong opinion about everything. She particularly annoyed Tony Scallon, who finally told me that he would stop working on the campaign if he had to deal with her. I never told Marcia what Tony had said, but she sensed the problem and started doing her work at home rather than at the headquarters. She wrote most of the campaign literature, and that was a task that could be done anywhere.

I have always been puzzled by the public perception of politics as a cynical business. In fact, my experience is that most people are drawn to politics for idealistic reasons. The tangible rewards are not great. Not a single person who has ever worked in any of my campaigns was ever paid anything for their efforts. And yet dozens of people put in twenty, thirty, forty hours a week, after working at a regular job, as volunteers, because they believed that my election would make a difference. To be sure, some of the major players in my 1972 campaign gained valuable experience that would help them establish successful political careers of their own. Lee Greenfield became a state legislator, Jeff Spartz was elected to the Hennepin County Board, Tony Scallon and Joan Campbell served on the Minneapolis City Council, and Andy Kozak worked as a political aide and later a lobbyist. But most of the people who put in time had no political ambitions of their own. A particularly interesting case was my campaign treasurer, Joe Altholz. Joe was my colleague in the history department and usually opposed me on the issues that divided the department. He supported the war and Hubert Humphrey and even told me that he would have preferred Fran Naftalin as the Senate candidate. But I needed a totally responsible, obsessively organized person to take on the job of handling campaign finances and making sure that proper procedures were followed. I decided that anyone who spent much of his life cataloging Victorian periodicals would be methodical enough to do this well. Joe agreed to take it on and did a terrific job with a time-consuming and thankless task.

It is interesting to note that none of the key players in my campaign were gay. And there were only a few gay people among the volunteers who came in every day to stuff envelopes and collate literature and go out and knock on doors. I had developed a loyal group of supporters among the antiwar activists and liberal Democrats in the university community. Many of them knew that I was gay and didn't care. But the district did not include the heavily gay neighborhoods around Loring Park, and not many gay people came across town to work in the campaign. The gay issue came up only sporadically. In mid-August, the *Advocate,* the leading national gay newspaper, published an article about my campaign, identifying me by name and describing me as a gay candidate. In today's world, the *Advocate* article would be instantly posted on every Republican blog in the state. But in 1972, no one seemed to have noticed it. John Cairns certainly knew that I was gay, but never used the issue. Some door knockers did report that they had run across hostile voters who had referred to me as "Spear the queer." And we learned that the very conservative Republican alderman from the Sixth Ward, Jens Christiansen, had gone into the senior citizen buildings spreading the word about my sexual orientation. But he did not seem to have had much impact. One day, when I was knocking on doors in one of the senior buildings, a woman asked me how I stood on the DFL platform plank advocating gay marriage. As I struggled to answer, she immediately shot back, "Oh well, I guess it doesn't make much difference. The way we've messed up marriage, they couldn't do much worse."

Of all the people who worked to elect me in 1972, perhaps the most important was Martin Sabo. Martin and I had been feuding since 1968, when he had run a joint campaign with Jim Adams and assured my defeat. We lived in the same precinct and clashed in the precinct caucuses in 1970 and again in 1972. He had not wanted me to be the DFL Senate candidate, and when I defeated Fran Naftalin for the endorsement he told me frankly, "You were not my first choice for a running mate." But at the same time, he said that now that I was the DFL candidate, I would have his full support. "This is different from 1968," he added. "Then you were running against another Democrat. Now you are running against a Republican. I don't want John Cairns or any other Republican representing this district in the Senate." Martin kept his word. He did not give me just token support. Most of the senior citizen buildings were in his half of the district and he was enormously popular there. He went with me through every one of those buildings, knocking on doors, introducing me to the residents, and urging them to support me. In addition to benefiting from my association with him, I learned a great deal from him about campaign techniques. He taught me to keep it short, avoid discussions about issues, make sure they know who you are, and get on to the next door. If they are hostile, don't argue—just thank them for their time and walk away. The only thing I could not emulate was the little pitch he would give in Norwegian to anyone whose name identified him or her as a "Norskie."

Perhaps the toughest part of a legislative race for a nonincumbent was raising money. Although we had no paid staff, we needed money to pay rent on the office, to print literature and lawn signs, to send out mailings, and to place ads in community newspapers and in the university paper. A few years later, Minnesota would adopt a system of public financing that would relieve some of the burden. And when I became a legislator, I developed contacts with lobbyists and trade groups that helped with contributions. But there was no public financing in 1972, and I had no special interests willing to give me money. In fact, the special interests were rallying behind the Republicans to prevent a DFL takeover of the Senate. I did receive some help from the

DFL Senate caucus, but for the most part I was on my own. We sent out fund-raising letters to every liberal list we could get our hands on. And we had a continual series of fund-raising events. We had graduated beyond the "Spear beers" of 1968. Now most of our fund-raisers involved food. Jeff Spartz dug a pit in his backyard and roasted a whole pig to raise money for the campaign. And we spit-roasted beef, Texas style, at a Pedernales River barbecue.

The most spectacular fund-raiser, however, was organized by Marcia Greenfield and held in late July at a comfortable house in St. Paul that Al and Bonnie Jones were renting for their last year in Minnesota. Marcia was particularly enthusiastic about combining her two major passions—politics and food. She and I had, for several years, teased each other about how we were going to fight the revolution and still have access to fully equipped kitchens. We both believed that nothing in left-wing politics precluded eating well. So one of Marcia's first campaign projects was to organize an haute cuisine fund-raising dinner. Some women, at this time in history, would have regarded this as a "retreat to the kitchen" in the face of male hostility. But to Marcia, cooking was a creative activity second to none, and she never saw it as anything to apologize for. She was now in her Julia Child phase and the menu reflected that. The first course was coulibiac, described as "layers of boneless salmon, seasoned with dill and mushrooms, covered with veloute sauce and herb-seasoned crepes, encased and baked in a brioche dough." This was followed by *gigot d'agneau farci, viroflay*—braised lamb with mushroom and spinach stuffing seasoned with basil. Dessert was charlotte russe, a ladyfingers mold filled with Bavarian cream, served with a raspberry sauce. Each course was accompanied with the appropriate French wine. This entire repast cost what we thought was the exorbitant amount of twenty-five dollars and we easily sold out. I am not sure how much money we made, but it was a wonderful dinner.

Despite all the enthusiasm and high spirits, the campaign, by the end of the summer, looked like another losing proposition. One of my biggest disappointments was my failure to get any of the major labor endorsements. I could understand that in 1968, when I was running against a labor Democrat who was himself a union member. But in 1972, I was running against a Republican lawyer and I expected at least some support from labor. Two things worked against me. First, John Cairns had built good ties with labor during his three years on the city council, supporting the public employee and building trade unions on many of their bread-and-butter issues. Second, labor hated McGovern. Nationally, most of the major unions either withheld their support or, in a few cases, even endorsed Nixon. My identification with McGovern was almost as toxic to labor in 1972 as my identification with McCarthy had been in 1968. One after another, the major union endorsing groups—the Central Labor Union of the AFL-CIO, the Teamsters, the UAW, the Building Trades—came out for Cairns. I was left with a few minor endorsements. I got the left-wing mavericks at United Electrical again. I was endorsed by a local at the university, made up mostly of hospital and food service workers. And in an endorsement that became particularly useful later in the campaign, I received the nod from the railroad brotherhoods.

The low point of the campaign was the primary in early September, for which there was really no need at all. As the system worked before we adopted party designation in legislative races, the primary winnowed the field down to two; if there were only two candidates to begin with, there was no primary. John Cairns and I were the only serious candidates for the office. But Cairns sensed that as the better-known of the two of us, he was starting as the front runner and would be ahead at the time of the primary. So his campaign urged another candidate to run, setting up a primary, in order to demonstrate publicly his front-runner status. This was a common practice and there was nothing unethical about it. And it paid off for Cairns. He led me 3,500 to 2,300, a margin of over 20 percent. That would be difficult to make up. The Sunday after the primary, the Fifty-seventh District DFL held a fund-raising event that I dutifully attended. But I was clearly dispirited. A young man named Doug Legg came up to me and asked me what was wrong. I told him that I was discouraged by the primary results. He told me that he had broken down the results by precinct and that he thought I was being too pessimistic. The students, he pointed out, were not yet back on campus and the heavily student precincts had barely registered in the primary. I would make up hundreds of votes there. And the dynamic would be different in November, when many more people would come out to vote in the presidential race. He proved right in just about every particular. But

I didn't pay too much attention at the time. Perhaps it was because Doug Legg was only nine years old.

It was hard to get back in the groove after the primary. The start of the fall term at the university might have been good news politically, but it meant that I had classes to teach on top of my campaign tasks. Moreover I was in a funk about my romantic life. Perhaps the hardest thing about coming out at the age of thirty-five was learning how to develop same-sex relationships. I was so excited about my new openness that I tended to rush into things, come on too strong, and scare off potential partners. I desperately wanted to make up for lost time, and each rejection was hard to take. I had a particularly difficult relationship with Barry B.,[3] a man I had known in the DFL for a number of years and who I discovered was gay when I began coming out. We began seeing each other and within a short time I told him I was in love with him. He told me very honestly that he liked me as a friend but was not in love with me and did not see a romantic relationship in our future. But I couldn't accept it and for the next year I futilely pursued him. In late September, after he had given me the first of several firm rejections, I went to Lee and Marcia Greenfield's apartment and told them I didn't see how I could continue the campaign. I was going to lose, my love life was a mess, and I couldn't concentrate on anything. They calmed me down and Marcia gave me a frank assessment of my situation. "You're acting like you are going through adolescence all over again," she said. "It is like the adolescence you never had. But you are thirty-five years old. You have to start acting your age." They went on to persuade me that the campaign was still winnable, even if the man I thought I loved was not.

Political campaigns are so amorphous and multifaceted that it is rare to be able to say that on such and such a date at such and such a place a campaign turned around. But I can say that with virtual certainty about my 1972 campaign. It turned around on October 12 when George McGovern visited Minneapolis and spoke to a crowd of more than twenty thousand people on the University of Minnesota campus. We had known for several weeks that McGovern was

---

3. This name has been fictionalized.

coming, and Lee Greenfield and I thought it was essential that I be on the platform with him. Lee and I asked the local McGovern committee if I could introduce him. No, they said. They were looking for a much bigger name—someone like Senator Mondale or Governor Anderson. Well, could I give a warm-up speech? They wouldn't promise that either; after all, I was just one of many legislative candidates. Yes, I argued, but I was running in the university district and I had been one of the earliest McGovern supporters in the state. Still, there was no promise.

Then, Lee and I learned that the advance man from the McGovern campaign would be Gary Dotterman, whom we had met a year before. Gary had come to Minneapolis in the fall of 1971, representing something called the "Dump Nixon" campaign, an attempt to repeat the "Dump Johnson" effort of 1967–68. He had met with a number of antiwar activists, and we had then taken him to the airport. His plane was several hours late because of the weather, and so we drank with him at the airport bar and got to know him. A short time later he went to work for the McGovern campaign. When we heard that he would be coming to Minneapolis to prepare for McGovern's visit, Lee immediately called him. He responded warmly. He remembered Lee well and, yes, of course he would make sure that I was on the platform with McGovern and had a chance to say a few words. But it would probably be limited to one minute. We were thrilled. We knew that despite all our efforts, many people in the university community still did not identify me with McGovern and that a personal appearance with him could make a crucial difference. Some years later, Gary Dotterman had become a gay activist in Boston, and I told him how, without knowing it, he had helped elect the first gay senator in the country.

The crowd that day was enormous. Despite polls that showed McGovern trailing Nixon in almost every state, he was still in the running in Minnesota and the young people at the university had not given up hope. The podium was set up on the plaza in front of Northrop Auditorium and the mall was completely filled with people all the way to Washington Avenue and beyond to the steps of Coffman Union. I saw Gary Dotterman as I walked up to the Northrop plaza and he motioned me to come over. "McGovern's plane is late," he said. "In fact, it still hasn't landed. It will be at least an hour until he gets here. We are asking all of the warm-up speakers to help us kill time.

Do you think you could speak for ten minutes?" Boy, could I ever. I had never been so happy to hear about a late plane. I had prepared remarks for just one minute, so I immediately began reformulating in my mind what I would say. When my time came, I was ready.

My speech that afternoon was, in terms of my own career, probably the most important I ever gave. From what people told me later, it may also have been one of the best. Because of the circumstances, I had nothing written down and it was all off the top of my head. But I can remember much of it. I never mentioned my own campaign. I knew that I was there for McGovern and that to talk about myself would be an abuse of the opportunity that I had been given. I talked about the war and how we needed a new president if we were going to end the war. The heart of the speech was a rhetorical device I had come up with centered on the name "the Committee to Re-elect the President." Why, I asked, was it not called "the Committee to Re-elect Richard Nixon"? "Doesn't the man have a name?" I shouted. "Were the Republicans ashamed to even utter the name of Richard Nixon?" And then I took off. "Well, I'd be ashamed, too, if I were supporting a man who . . ." and then, one after another, I recited the misdeeds of the Nixon administration. After three or four minutes of that, I noted that we did not call our campaign "the Committee to Elect the Junior Senator from South Dakota." That was, of course, because we were proud to speak the name of George McGovern, the man who . . . And I then rattled off a list of McGovern's many virtues. I ended by urging the students to let their studies go for a few weeks, to give up their usual activities, and to spend all of their time to help put McGovern over the top.

When McGovern arrived he gave his standard stump speech, which I thought was fine, and the crowd roared its approval. But many people told me afterward that my speech was more memorable. And the next day as I began door knocking again, I immediately sensed a change. More people now recognized me. "Oh sure," they would say. "I saw you at the McGovern rally." Or, "That was a great speech you gave for McGovern." Our literature and ads featured pictures of me with McGovern. And my identification with McGovern played into the theme we were developing that party affiliation really was important. Unlike the Minneapolis City Council, where John Cairns had served successfully, the state legislature was dominated by the leadership of the majority caucus; and if the Republicans retained control, the legislature would continue to be run by probusiness, antienvironmental, antilabor interests. John Cairns's individual views on these subjects would be less important than his vote to establish the Republicans as the majority caucus.

We had to be careful not to go too far with the partisanship. John Cairns fought back. He argued in an ad in the university newspaper, the *Minnesota Daily,* "Mr. Spear . . . offers you the proposition simply stated that you ought to support him because of a label. . . . He asks for your support, not because he offers any record of success, or even interest in the essential problems he will deal with, but because he carries a label. . . . I submit to you that the problems Minneapolis and the university face at future legislative sessions will be solved only by progressive leadership rather than by mere partisanship." I did, of course, try to offer more than mere partisanship. For seniors, I promised better nursing home regulation, expanded bus service, tax relief on Social Security benefits, and price controls on drugs. In labor-oriented northeast Minneapolis, I talked about increases in workers' compensation, the right to strike for public employees, and better consumer protection. I also vigorously opposed a freeway that would have cut through several neighborhoods in northeast, displacing hundreds of residents. While I would never compromise on abortion, I did make one gesture to Catholic voters by promising to support an income tax credit for tuition to parochial or private schools. And in the faculty neighborhood of Prospect Park, I stressed my academic credentials. One stuffy retired professor told me bluntly at his doorstep that he was supporting John Cairns because "he went to Carleton and Duke." "But," I replied, "I went to Oberlin and Yale." He promised to reconsider.

My most intense pitch was to the university students. I was convinced that only a large student turnout would make up for my lack of labor endorsements and Cairns's edge in experience. I had to convince the students not only to vote but to vote on campus rather than back home. Of course, many Minnesota students were commuters and they were lost to us. But we concentrated on the dormitories and the apartment buildings around campus and mounted a vigorous voter registration drive. I was barred by university regulations from going door-to-door in the dormitories, and I sharply challenged the kind of paternalism that I said this represented. I spoke repeatedly about the representation I would provide for students in the legislature. Some of the issues I emphasized were those important to many young people in the early 1970s: water and air pollution; tenants' rights; the development of rapid transit. But I also focused on matters specific to the University of Minnesota. Legislators, I argued, heard only from administrators, who all too often put the university's priorities in the wrong order. I would represent not Morrill Hall but students, civil service employees, and faculty who often don't share the interests of administrators. I supported reduction in tuition, a university budget that placed priority on teaching programs, and an expanded role for students and civil service employees in governing the university. I also emphasized my opposition to the kind of commercial development in the university community that was epitomized by the Red Barn in Dinkytown and Cedar-Riverside West on the West Bank. My colleague Hy Berman told me of a conversation he had with President Moos that fall in which Moos expressed his hope that I would not be elected. "I am afraid," he said, "that Spear will try to reform the university from the floor of the Senate."

While I learned to emphasize different issues when speaking to different constituencies, I never hid my basic commitment to human rights issues, which I always considered the core of my political identity. In my basic campaign brochure, which was distributed everywhere in the district, I described myself as "long active in efforts to end all forms of discrimination based on race, circumstance or life style." I cited my support for inclusion of gay people in the state human rights law, ratification of the Equal Rights Amendment, and the repeal of all restrictive abortion laws. The liberal political group Americans for Democratic Action, in a letter sent to the district, conceded that "John Cairns came off better than Spear in his knowledge of the intricacies of tax matters and high finance," but "Allan Spear's views on human rights issues are not only better than Cairns', they are more enthusiastic." It is in these matters—"questions of privacy, life style, and victimless crimes, for example"—that most legislators are weakest and outspoken leadership is most needed. The *Minnesota Daily* in its editorial endorsement of me picked up on this theme: "Spear is a sincere and uncompromising advocate of human rights. Unlike other candidates, he does not avoid controversial issues such as abortion, gay rights and penal reform. The state Senate has had a conspicuous and unhealthy dearth of concerned civil libertarians. . . . Spear is determined to be a vanguard voice."

Many of those who worked on my 1972 campaign went on to spend years in politics, but they still remember the last three weeks of that campaign as the most exciting they ever experienced. We knew that we were gaining ground, but we had no scientific polling. Door knockers came back and reported enthusiastic response. Informal polling of a few key precincts added to the encouragement. But each day there was a new crisis to respond to. The Cairns campaign or the Republican Party or the AFL-CIO would come out with a piece of literature and we would leave nothing unanswered. One aspect of the campaign that everyone remembers was the battle of the sample ballots. With no party identification on the official ballot, each campaign tried to use sample ballots to identify its candidate in the most favorable way. We used the DFL sample ballot extensively while Cairns tried to avoid the Republican sample ballot as he did not want to be identified with Nixon. On the other hand, he distributed labor sample ballots and, to our great distress, even used one, put out by the United Auto Workers, that featured a picture of him next to a picture of McGovern.

We resorted to some rather creative variations on the sample ballot. First, we put out our own labor sample ballots even though I had no major labor endorsements. One we boldly labeled the "AFL-CIO LABOR BALLOT" and then put in small type below "AFSCME LOCAL 1164," which was the small university local that had actually endorsed me. Local 1164 was affiliated with the AFL-CIO, but the heading was obviously misleading. When Bob Metcalf saw it, my former campaign manager, who had now graduated from law school and begun practice as a labor lawyer, told us we were asking for a legal challenge. We made a rubber stamp reading "AFSCME LOCAL 1164" and stamped that name once again on the ballot, but the AFL-CIO soon put out a "Special Bulletin" warning the working men and women of District 57 to "not be misled by last minute attempts to confuse you through circulation of another ballot." We then put out a second ballot under the label of "District 57 Labor Committee," bearing the imprimatur of the railroad brotherhoods. This one was straightforward enough, but it caused us an internal problem as the brotherhoods had endorsed me but had also endorsed Dick Miller over our friend Dick Hanson for the county board. Dick Hanson frequently dropped by our campaign headquarters, and when we saw him coming we quickly hid the "choo-choo" ballots, as we called them, away in a file cabinet.

In addition to getting my name out there in as many ways as we could with the Democratic candidates, we also wanted to get Cairns's name associated with the Republican ticket. The Republican Party printed a sample ballot, but Cairns mailed it very selectively only to known Republicans, and none of us had ever actually seen it. Jeff Spartz offered a cash reward to anyone who would come in with one. We finally got hold of it and put out a single-sheet piece of literature that simply reproduced the DFL sample ballot on one side with my picture together with McGovern, Fraser, and Mondale, and the Republican sample ballot on the other side with Cairns's name following those of Richard Nixon and Spiro Agnew. Above the two ballots was just one word: Compare. Some of my campaign workers also engaged in a more questionable effort to identify Cairns with the Republicans. My lawn signs included the words "DFL-Endorsed"; Cairns's signs omitted any reference to party. So one night, very late, a few of my more reckless supporters went out with a stencil and a can of spray paint, found the lawns displaying Cairns signs and stenciled the words "GOP-Endorsed" under his name. When I asked who did it, Lee Greenfield told me that I didn't need to know.

But one borderline activity I was fully aware of. We called it vacuuming and it consisted simply of going through a neighborhood and picking up the opposition literature. The classic political film *The Candidate,* starring Robert Redford, has a memorable scene portraying vacuuming. It is the morning of Election Day; the opposition meticulously places a last-minute reminder to vote for the other candidate on every doorknob, and within minutes the workers for the "good guy" descend en masse, ripping each piece of literature off doors and throwing it away. Questionable as it is, it is standard political procedure. When we learned that a hostile piece was being distributed in a particular neighborhood, Jeff Spartz would issue a "vacuuming alert" and sometimes within a few minutes we would have the literature picked up. And when we went out with our own literature, we always cleaned up the doorsteps of whatever opposition brochures we found there. I learned how to do this in the senior high-rises from Martin

Sabo. Often when we were talking to a constituent at the door, Martin would spot a piece of literature on the floor that the resident had not yet seen. He would put his foot on it and when the conversation was over simply slide it out into the hall where we could pick it up after the person closed the door. I called this the "Sabo shuffle." Once during the campaign, my mother came to visit and help out. I took her with me to a senior citizen building where after working one floor together we then split up. She saw me picking up opposition literature and looked shocked. "I'm surprised at you, Allan," she said. "I didn't think you would do something like that." I told her that we just didn't want the residents to see that particular sample ballot. After we finished working the building and went back to the car, my mother opened her purse. It was stuffed full of opposition sample ballots. "OK," she said. "Now what do I do with these?"

About a week before the election, polls began to show that although Nixon would probably carry Minnesota, the DFL had a good chance of winning control of the legislature. The business community was particularly concerned about the Senate, where for over a century Republican majorities had stopped populist and progressive measures from passing. A committee of business leaders ran an ad in the Twin Cities daily newspapers warning the citizens of Minnesota that putting the DFL in charge of the Senate could lead to unwise regulatory schemes and confiscatory tax policies that might damage the state's business climate. We immediately leaped on this and ran an ad in the *Minnesota Daily* featuring pictures of the most curmudgeonly looking corporate CEOs we could find accompanied by the question "Why Are These Men Afraid of Allan Spear?" We then once again made the point that my election might prove crucial to DFL control of the Senate and the opportunity to pass the very kind of progressive legislation that these businessmen feared.

By election night, the signs were good that we had turned it around. The campaign workers gathered in Jeff Spartz's apartment clutching beer cans labeled "Spear's Beer" when, at 8:15, the telephone rang with the first results. I had carried my own precinct. My precinct—moderate, middle-class, dominated by homeowners—had been considered the bellwether; I had lost it badly in 1968. "On the basis of that," Jeff said, "I'd say that he has won the election." I wasn't there yet. Too nervous to sit still, I was out in the district collecting results.

By the time I arrived at Jeff's, favorable results were pouring in and it was clear that Jeff was right. According to the *Minnesota Daily,* I "wore the expression of a blissful child on Christmas morning."

In the end, I won by a thousand votes, 11,454 to 10,459. I attributed my victory to my association with McGovern, who won the district by almost three to one. Jeff Spartz told the *Daily* that he had been worried about the sample ballot that associated Cairns with McGovern and by Cairns's "vote the man, not the party" appeal. "Allan seemed to have poor name identification," he explained, and "Cairns spent a lot more money on his campaign." But, he added, my speech at the McGovern rally and the repeated leaflet drops had overcome the name identification problem. I added that we were still twenty-five hundred dollars in debt, but now that we had won, that amount would not be hard to raise. Later in the evening John Cairns called and congratulated me. He never ran for public office again, but had a successful legal career. As the Republican Party became too conservative for him, he became a Democrat and supported me in my later political campaigns. He has told me on several occasions that I did him a favor beating him in 1972 as it freed him up to make money in the private sector. But I'm sure it didn't seem that way at the time. He was quoted in the *Minnesota Daily* as saying, as the results came in, "Too many kids voted."

After the celebration at Jeff's apartment, we drifted downtown to the Leamington Hotel, where the DFL was holding its victory party. It was another scene of jubilation. Despite McGovern's overwhelming loss throughout the country, the DFL had won control of both houses of the Minnesota legislature. All the concerns about the "Rochester platform" had come to naught; either the social issues did not trouble the voters as much as the party had feared or, more likely, few people pay attention to party platforms anyway. In addition, some major barriers had been broken. In suburban St. Louis Park, Bob Lewis, a popular veterinarian, was elected as the first black member of the Minnesota Senate. And the lone woman legislator, Helen McMillan of Austin, was joined by four new women House members, including Phyllis Kahn, from my district, and Linda Berglin, from the neighboring district to the west. Whether my election was a breakthrough was a matter of interpretation. I was not yet openly gay and the local press made no reference to my sexual orientation. But my election was reported in the *Advocate* as a gay victory and many people knew. It did not seem to have had much impact on the outcome. There was some surprise among old-line DFLers about my victory, but it had more to do with my reputation as a radical. Someone who was in a suite at the Leamington with Fritz Mondale reported to me that when the results came in from the Fifty-seventh District, Mondale said, "Oh my God, if we can elect Spear, we can elect anyone."

The next day I received a telegram from Nick Coleman telling me that the organizing meeting of the first DFL Senate majority caucus in history would be held Thursday evening at the Criterion restaurant in St. Paul. I held it in my hands for a few minutes, hardly believing that I was really going to be there as a member. There were thirty-eight of us, four more than the bare minimum but still a slim working majority given that several of the DFL senators were rural conservatives who would often vote with the Republicans. As I met my new colleagues, a number of them told me that they were both pleased and surprised that I had won. We were all asked to introduce ourselves and say a few words. A number of the newcomers told about how they had overcome the odds and won in historically Republican districts. When my turn came, I said, "I pulled one of the biggest upsets of all. I come from a 65 percent DFL district and won with 53 percent of the vote and everyone seems surprised that I am here." It was a self-deprecating remark that had the intended effect of demonstrating that, as politicians go, I was relatively modest. But in fact, I was immensely proud of what I had achieved. In four years, I had gone from being a political novice to winning a seat in the state Senate. And I had managed to balance a difficult political campaign with the stress of coming out as a gay man. How I would continue to balance my personal and political lives was the major challenge that lay ahead of me.

8

ENTERING THE SENATE AND LEAVING THE CLOSET, 1973–1974

I began my dual-track career as a politician and an academic when the legislature convened on January 2, 1973. Prior to that year, the legislative session had been limited constitutionally to 120 days, meeting every two years between January and the third week in May. But a constitutional amendment approved in 1972 allowed those 120 days to be spread over two years. Sessions would still end in May, but they would be held annually rather than biennially. Legislators would remain part-time employees, but the commitment would be significantly greater than it had been in the past. I had always intended to keep my position at the university as I did not have the financial security to give up a tenured teaching position for the uncertainty of a political career. I asked the university for a two-quarter leave of absence for the 1973 session. The sessions in the second year of each biennium were expected to be shorter, and I anticipated that a one-quarter leave would be adequate then. At the time, I saw this as a temporary arrangement as I had no idea how long I would remain in the legislature. But in fact this became the pattern of my career for the next twenty-eight years.

The 1973 legislature marked another significant departure in Minnesota's political history. In 1860, two years after Minnesota became a state, Republicans gained control of both houses of the legislature. Over the next century, Democrats, sometimes in coalition with third parties, would win back the House of Representatives from time to time, but the Republicans would maintain their majorities in the Senate for 112 years. After 1913, the legislature was nominally nonpartisan, but G. Theodore Mitau, the leading expert on Minnesota politics in the first part of the twentieth century, refers to it as a "nonpartisan partisan legislature." The Republican members organized as the "conservative caucus" and maintained tight control of the committee structure and the legislative agenda. With their dominant role in the Senate, they successfully blocked proposals that they considered, in Mitau's words, "too costly, too liberal, too untried or too dangerous." These included measures strengthening the governorship, increasing taxes, expanding government services and regulation, supporting organized labor, and moving government into new socioeconomic areas such as housing and public transportation.

The DFL victory in 1972 was therefore a momentous event in Minnesota's political history. For the first time since the earliest days of statehood, the Democrats, now in the form of the DFL Party, had won majorities in both houses of the legislature and, with a DFL governor, Wendell Anderson, would be in a position to enact the dozens of proposals that had been blocked for so many years by Republican legislative leadership. My first term in the Senate was by far the most productive as measured by overall legislative achievement. We passed Minnesota's first minimum wage law, provided increased benefits and coverage under the workers' and unemployment compensation systems, and gave public employees the right to strike. We made the income tax more progressive and created an income-adjusted property tax, popularly known as the circuit breaker, to provide relief for low- and middle-income people. We enacted a wide range of consumer protection laws: open dating of perishable foods; generic drug substitution; no-fault automobile insurance; and protection against unscrupulous door-to-door salespeople. We effectively regulated nursing homes for the first time and began a state-funded catastrophic health insurance program. We moved the state into new areas such as childcare services and land-use planning. We passed several bills dear to the hearts of my student constituents: lowering the age of legal majority to eighteen, creating a student regent at the University of Minnesota, and decriminalizing the possession of a small amount of marijuana. And we challenged the political system that had kept us out of power for so many years, ending the concept of the nonpartisan legislature by placing party designation on the ballot, limiting campaign contributions, and establishing partial state funding for legislative and statewide campaigns.

It was, of course, an exciting time for a Democrat to begin a legislative career, and for the first few months it seemed almost like a dream that I was actually a part of all of this—that I had a vote and could make a difference. Yet, while I participated actively in the discussions and debates about many of these bills, I was not a key player. In part, this had to do with my status as a freshman senator. I had good committee assignments: health, welfare, and corrections; labor and commerce; and education. But I was not a committee chairman and was not on the committees that made the most crucial decisions—finance and taxes. I also faced a problem that went beyond my lack of seniority. Several of my freshman colleagues were the chief authors of some of the major bills of the session. John Milton, for example, carried the minimum wage bill and Steve Keefe authored the campaign reform bill. A bill was generally assigned either by the DFL leadership or was brought to a particular legislator by the lobbying group that had developed it, such as the AFL-CIO or a consumer advocacy group. I was rarely asked to carry a major bill. It wasn't that anyone doubted my ability. I was nimble in debate and a good speaker. But I brought with me to the legislature a reputation as a wild-eyed radical from the university community. The fear was that my name as the chief author of a bill would immediately stigmatize it as a crazy, irresponsible proposal and make it more difficult to pass. It would take me a number of years to overcome this image and become a truly effective legislator.

Still, I had plenty to keep me busy as I learned my new job. First, I had to get to know my colleagues. They were a remarkably diverse lot. The DFL caucus ranged ideologically from me on the left to Charles R. "Baldy" Hanson, a crusty banker from southern Minnesota, who was a Democrat in name only and rarely voted with the caucus majority except on organization. Baldy chaired the Labor and Commerce Committee and tried to kill some of the major DFL proposals of the session. His committee was jokingly referred to as Forest Lawn because it seemed to be the graveyard of so many bills. In the end, some of the bills that died there were revived on the floor, but it was frustrating, as a member of the committee, to watch Baldy in action. He was a legislator of the old school who would have been more at home with the Republicans. He would use his power as chair to filibuster to death any bill that was opposed by the business lobbyists. Then I would watch him, when the committee meeting ended at noon, blatantly approach the lobbyist he had just helped and ask him to take him to lunch at the best restaurant in St. Paul.

Two other conservative DFLers ultimately become my principal legislative nemeses. Florian Chmielewski represented a district near Duluth; an accordion player, he made a good living leading a polka band that played gigs in small towns throughout northern Minnesota, the Dakotas, and Manitoba. An almost comical figure with an ill-fitting wig who would often appear on the legislative floor in the brightly colored polyester jackets that he wore at his polka performances, Florian was nevertheless dogged in his defense of the right to bear arms and in his opposition to abortion and gay rights. Elected at twenty-one, Wayne Olhoft was the youngest member of the Senate. His worldview was shaped entirely by his fundamentalist Lutheran upbringing, and although he was smoother than Florian, Wayne was equally rigid on issues he considered moral imperatives. Baldy focused most of his attention on business and economic issues. When I emerged in the Senate as a strong champion of woman's and gay issues, it was Florian and Wayne whom I most often battled.

I had allies, too. I felt particularly close to Bob Lewis, the veterinarian from St. Louis Park who was the Senate's only black member. I had known Bob before we were elected; he was a good friend of Rosalie and Milt Goldstein's, and we had spent many evenings together at their house. Bob and I agreed on all of the major issues. But more important, I was drawn to his temperament. He had fought hard to get where he was—a black man from a poor family who had built up a successful veterinary practice in an affluent suburb and was elected to the legislature by an almost all-white constituency. But although he took life seriously, Bob had a keen wit and an ability to see the humor in almost any situation. He knew when to compromise, but when he was asked to do something that violated his principles, his answer would be "No way, José," and that was the end of it. Bob was clearly on his way to becoming a leader in the Senate when, early in his second term, he died suddenly of a heart attack.

There were two other freshman senators with whom I worked closely. John Milton was from the northern St. Paul suburbs, an able and articulate man of about my age who shared my liberal views but represented a far more conservative district. Although he had to agonize over his votes more than I did, he usually came down on the side of principle and I strongly admired him for it. Steve Keefe had a very different political problem. He represented the district just west of mine—the poorest and probably the most liberal in the state. He was articulate, able, and ambitious and on most issues took strongly progressive positions. But he was uncompromising in his opposition to a woman's right to choose to have an abortion. I never understood whether this stemmed from personal beliefs or from promises he had made to certain constituent groups, but he never changed his position and, as the abortion issue intensified over the decade, it ultimately cost him his political career.

My most important ally was the majority leader, Nick Coleman. Nick was one of the most engaging and talented people I have ever met in politics. On the Senate floor, no one could match his debating skills or his ability to skewer an opponent with the appropriate one-line comeback. His most difficult job was to keep the caucus together without the arsenal of rewards and punishments that legislative leaders at the federal level have at their disposal. He had to persuade DFL senators to vote with the caucus "for the good of the order," as he put it, and usually got the votes he needed. When he failed, he did not accept defeat easily. Old legislative hands still talk about the night Nick lost a vote on the floor and kicked in the glass on the front door of the Capitol. Nick was not a disengaged leader who sacrificed his own agenda to manage the caucus. He carried major bills and strongly pushed his own ideas, which were in transition in 1973. Nick was an Irish Catholic from St. Paul with close ties to organized labor, and he had generally been an economic liberal but relatively conservative on social issues. Yet he had been an early opponent of the Vietnam War and had begun to question some of his previous views. Moreover, he had recently left his wife and was dating a reporter from the *Minneapolis Star* named Deborah Howell, who broadened his perspective. It was Deborah, whose brother was gay, who made Nick an early champion of gay rights. I am not sure when Nick first realized I was gay, but he was from the beginning helpful in every way. He tried to steer me away from some of my more radical tendencies, without asking me to make compromises that he knew I would find unacceptable. He taught me a great deal about how to be an effective legislator.

My other legislative mentor was Jack Davies. When Jack was the senator from the old Forty-second District, he had been part of the Humphrey group and we had not gotten along well. But after redistricting he had moved, so we were no longer rivals, and after my election he did everything he could to be helpful. He was a law professor who had been in the Senate for fourteen years and had mastered the rules. I soon learned that I could accomplish very little in the legislature without learning how the place operated and I began going to him frequently for advice. He never expected that the "wild-eyed radical from the university" would become a stickler for procedure, and he was pleased to tutor me in the ways of the Senate. Jack was also the chairman of the Judiciary Committee. I did not initially serve on it but increasingly I saw that many of the issues that interested me most—civil rights, criminal procedure, women's and gay rights—were handled there. After my first two years, I asked to be appointed to judiciary and served there for the remainder of my legislative career, eventually becoming the first nonlawyer to chair the committee. Jack influenced me both in how I approached the issues and, after becoming chair, in how I ran the committee.

If the DFL senators were ideologically diverse, so too were the Republicans. The right wing had not yet established the hegemony within the Republican Party that it has today. Most were economic conservatives, and some of the rural Republicans who had previously been in leadership positions seemed to be in virtual shell shock as they watched the DFL-controlled Senate pass the bills that they had blocked for so long. But on social issues, many of the Republicans were more moderate than some of the firebrands within our caucus. On abortion, there were almost as many pro-choice Republicans as there were Democrats. And on many issues, Republicans worked with the DFL leadership to make sure the Senate functioned efficiently and the work got done on time. Some Republicans, like Harmon Ogdahl from southwest Minneapolis, George Pillsbury from the western suburbs, and Bill McCutcheon from St. Paul, were frequently coauthors of DFL bills. There was little of the obstructionism that I witnessed in my last years in the Senate when many Republicans seemed determined to shut the place down if they couldn't get their way.

If there was ideological diversity, however, there was very little racial diversity and absolutely no gender diversity. Other than Bob Lewis, all the senators were white. And all sixty-seven members were men. Just off the Senate floor was a restroom with a sign on the door reading "Senators Only." There was no need to say that it was a men's room. When I retired from the Senate in 2000, I was asked many times what I considered the most significant change I had seen over my twenty-eight years. I answered without hesitation that it was the coming of female senators. The all-male Senate had the feel of a men's club. The lobbyists, too, were men and they often met the senators at smoke-filled St. Paul bars where deals were cut and decisions were made. When female senators arrived, interest groups began hiring female lobbyists and meetings were more likely to be held in offices at the Capitol. The issues we considered also began to change. Child care, sexual assault, child abuse, and a whole range of social issues that had been ignored for years were now placed on the agenda. The changes came gradually. The first female senator was elected in a special election in 1974—Nancy Brataas, a Republican from Rochester. A janitor's closet near the Senate chamber had to be quickly converted into a restroom for women. From then on, in every election cycle, the number of women increased until, by the time I retired, they constituted a third of the members. They made the Senate a very different—and better—place than it had once been.

The other most visible change over my years in the Senate was the professionalization of the legislature's operation. In my first term, I shared a two-room suite of offices with three other senators. Two of us sat at adjoining desks in the same room, giving us no privacy when we met with constituents or lobbyists. Even this was far better than the situation with our House colleagues, who were all in one large room separated by crude dividers. My officemate and I shared a single secretary. Other than that, we could draw from a small pool of lawyers and committee administrators who would help us draft bills. By the time I retired, every senator had a private office and at least one staff member of his or her own. In addition, the legal and administrative staff had expanded significantly and included many extremely able people with many years of service, who, even more than the senators, provided the Senate with its institutional memory. Moreover, the coming of computers had vastly streamlined what had, in my early years, been a cumbersome process of printing, amending, reprinting, and distributing bills as they made their way through the legislature.

If my principal problem as a new legislator was my reputation for radicalism, I did little in my first months to alleviate it. The first bill I introduced was a resolution putting the Minnesota legislature on record in favor of withdrawal from the Vietnam War. The president of the Senate was somewhat puzzled as to what committee should hear the bill because, as Jim Rice had caustically pointed out to me when I first ran for the legislature in 1968, there was no committee on foreign relations. The bill was assigned to the Committee on General Legislation, whose mostly conservative members were not thrilled by it. Nick

Coleman helped me get it out of committee, but even his silver tongue could not save the bill on the floor. This was my first floor debate and it was a baptism by fire. The Republicans had a field day chastising the DFL majority for wasting the Senate's time with an issue over which the state had no constitutional jurisdiction. Moreover, they pointed out that President Nixon was on the verge of a deal with North Vietnam and that the timing for this kind of resolution could not be worse.

I had my hands full with some members of my own caucus as well. Conservatives like Baldy Hanson and Florian Chmielewski were predictably hostile. But the final motion to lay the bill over and effectively kill it came from a less expected source. Hubert H. Humphrey III, known as Skip and the son of the former vice president, had been elected to the state Senate from a northern Minneapolis suburb. Although a conventional liberal Democrat on most issues, he had accepted his father's views on the Vietnam War and it was he who led the effort to defeat my bill. It seemed almost inevitable that my antiwar efforts would once again be thwarted by a Humphrey. Skip and I would later become political allies, but we did not get off to a good start.

In later years, when I became an old legislative hand, I viewed efforts such as my antiwar resolution with skepticism. There is little evidence that legislative forays into national and international affairs have ever had much effect, and I came to the conclusion that they were generally a waste of time. But given my background and the expectations of my constituents, there was little doubt that I would begin my legislative career with this issue. And I continued throughout the session to look for ways to bring the Vietnam War into the debate. In the 1972 election, the Minnesota electorate had approved a constitutional amendment authorizing a bonus for veterans of the Vietnam War. I had supported this measure and worked as a legislator on the bill to implement it. Contrary to what later became common belief, I never witnessed hostility within the antiwar movement to the troops themselves. The hostility was reserved for those who sent them to Vietnam. But when the bonus bill came to the floor, I introduced an amendment to extend it to conscientious objectors. I did not include draft evaders—those who broke the law—but only those whose religious or philosophical beliefs made them legally eligible for alternatives to military service. Nevertheless, the amendment elicited fierce hostility. One Republican senator said that he was glad it had been offered before lunch because if it had been after lunch, he would have thrown up. The amendment received a grand total of five votes.

My continuing opposition to the Vietnam War also led to one of the more memorable experiences of my first year in the legislature. In those days before there were restrictions on treats from lobbyists, each legislative session began with a flurry of receptions hosted by groups with business at the legislature. Among those that I attended was one hosted by the Honeywell Corporation, which had been a frequent target of protest by antiwar activists for its manufacture of cluster bombs and other antipersonnel weapons for use in Vietnam. At the reception, I was introduced to James Binger, Honeywell's chairman, and I commented to him that I had previously seen him at Honeywell shareholder meetings. He smiled and told me how pleased he was that I was a Honeywell stockholder. "Well," I replied, "I own only one share and I bought that just so that I could protest Honeywell's immoral policy of manufacturing antipersonnel weapons." Binger didn't flinch. "You know," he said, "we should get together for lunch to discuss that issue. You'll hear from me soon." I left certain that I would never hear from him again.

But just a few weeks later, I was invited not just for lunch but to a dinner party at the Binger estate on Lake Minnetonka. I accepted, sent my best suit to the cleaner, and mentally prepared for a stressful evening. As I drove up the long driveway that night, I could not help but notice that my old Chevrolet looked rather shabby compared with the cars the other guests were parking. I really felt out of place when, as I walked to the door, a woman rolled down her window and asked me, "Boy, are you the car park attendant?" Yet it was a surprisingly pleasant evening. There were about sixteen people at dinner, some bearing familiar names like Pillsbury and Dayton. Jim Binger briefly explained to me why he believed that Honeywell had an obligation to produce the weapons that the government requested. I disagreed, but we were polite to each other and found that there were other issues on which we were not nearly as far apart as I would have imagined.

When I returned to my car at the end of the evening, I discovered that it had been snowing for several hours. I tried to back the car out but the wheels spun in the freshly fallen snow. So I returned to the house and asked Binger to call someone for help. "No need to do that," he replied. "I'm sure we can push you out." He turned to the other guests, who had not yet left. "George, Don, let's give him a hand." I wish the scene that followed had somehow been preserved on film. There, outside the Bingers' stately home, stood several of the wealthiest and most prominent men in Minnesota pushing a beat-up old car plastered with the iconic bumper stickers of the 1960s and 1970s: "End the War Now," "Free Huey," and so on. They got the car moving, I thanked them, and went on my way, having learned that the upper crust was not quite as stuffy as I had supposed.[1]

While I gradually lost my enthusiasm for pursuing foreign policy in the state Senate, another early interest evolved into one of my major legislative concerns. My attraction to prison issues had begun a few years earlier with my visits to the federal prison at Sandstone, and I had developed a view of the correctional system that was held by many radicals in the late 1960s and early 1970s. Prisons, as I saw it, were primarily instruments of social control used by a repressive society to keep down rebellious elements, particularly minority groups. I didn't doubt that there were people in prison who were guilty of serious crimes, but I tended to be naively susceptible to the stories I heard from inmates who proclaimed their innocence. And I thought many who were guilty had been driven to their crimes by economic and social conditions caused by the very system that was now so severely punishing them. I had talked vaguely of prison reform during my 1972 campaign, and after my election I was approached by a group called the Prisoners Union, who asked me to work with them to help change the system. The Prisoners Union believed that inmates did not lose all of their rights upon conviction, and they hoped to organize the prisoners, along the lines of labor unions, to stand up to the prison authorities and maintain their autonomy as individuals. Its immediate agenda included guaranteeing the rights of inmates to form voluntary organizations; due process in parole hearings; conjugal visits for prisoners so that they could continue to have intimate sexual lives with their partners; and the right to communicate at will with the press. I agreed to take on those issues.

Shortly before the start of the session, I joined several members of the Prisoners Union in a visit to the Minnesota state prison at Stillwater.

---

1. The story of my evening at the Bingers' was published, in a slightly different form, as an opinion piece in the *Minneapolis Star Tribune* on November 20, 2004, following Jim Binger's death.

We had an appointment with the warden, an experienced correctional official named Bruce McManus. The warden was understandably suspicious of us. He listened politely, but then pointed out the practical problems of implementing our proposals. He also made it clear that he thought we had a hopelessly idealistic view of the character of the inmates with whom he dealt every day. I saw him as a tough prison boss out of whom we would never get much. He did not seem too impressed with me either. When I told him that I had been recently elected to the legislature, he replied coldly, "When you become a senator, I will treat you with the respect your position deserves." I would never have guessed that Bruce McManus would ultimately become a close and trusted friend. We both evolved over the years and eventually developed very similar views about correctional issues. Long after I have all but forgotten the people in the Prisoners Union, Bruce McManus and his wife frequently have dinner with my partner and me and we still discuss how we can make prisons more humane and effective.

When I became a member of the Senate Committee on Health, Welfare, and Corrections, I asked the chairman to assign me to the subcommittee on corrections. There were only five members, three of whom were Democrats (my friends Bob Lewis and John Milton, and I). Hence the three-member majority on the subcommittee consisted of perhaps the three most liberal members of the Senate, and even some of my more controversial Prisoners Union bills were approved. This deeply frustrated one of the Republican members, Bob Brown of Stillwater, who represented many of the people who worked at the prison. One morning, when the subcommittee met at eight o'clock to consider one of my bills to protect the rights of inmates, he brought in several prison guards, their uniforms caked with blood, who had been working all night to quell a disturbance at the institution. We avoided a direct confrontation and laid over the bill for the day. When my bills did pass the subcommittee, they were usually defeated or heavily amended in full committee or on the floor. The conjugal visit proposal was shot down when prison officials pointed out that few inmates were legally married and that, under the bill, the state would end up providing facilities for nonmarital sexual activities that were still officially illegal in Minnesota. I did pass a version of the press access bill, but it was so watered down that I don't think it ever really had much impact.

The most controversial prison bill I passed in my first session did not come from the Prisoners Union. Judge Neil Riley of the Hennepin County District Court was cofounder of a volunteer group called Amicus. Members of Amicus, all successful people in the community, met with inmates in the prisons to provide them with support and guidance and, upon their release, help them adjust to life in the free world. Judge Riley came to see me to discuss the plight of first-degree murderers. Other prisoners were eligible for parole at any time the parole board thought they were no longer a danger to society. But inmates convicted of first-degree murder could not even be considered for parole until they had served at least seventeen or, in some instances, twenty-five years. Judge Riley said that this group of prisoners was actually among the least likely to recidivate and that they should be treated like all other inmates. He asked me to introduce legislation to repeal the minimum sentence requirement. In light of later efforts to toughen sentences, especially for violent crimes, it is hard to believe that this proposal got anywhere. Even in my liberal district, it was controversial. A leaflet was distributed in one neighborhood headlined with the words "Citizens Arise"! "Did you know," its anonymous author asked, "your state senator Spear has sponsored a bill that would permit 1st degree murderers to run free? . . . If you disagree with this bill call [him] to register your disapproval." And indeed a number of constituents did call. Since this was a sentencing bill, it was heard in the Judiciary Committee, which amended it so that instead of repealing the minimum sentence, it reduced it to ten years for some types of convictions, fifteen for others. In that form, it passed the legislature, only to be vetoed by Governor Anderson. The governor realized that the bill would make Minnesota's most notorious murderer, T. Eugene Thompson, convicted in the early sixties of killing his wife, eligible for parole during Anderson's term of office. That was the last thing the politically cautious governor wanted to deal with. I was furious and wrote him an angry letter calling the bill "a very modest measure that had the support of nearly every responsible person working in the corrections field." I would have been horrified had I known that two decades later I would be the chief author of a bill increasing the minimum sentence for first-degree murder to thirty years.

Although I was generally bypassed as the chief author of the major reform bills of the session, I did successfully write one significant bill, even though it took me two years to get it passed. Minnesota, like many states, had a divorce statute that required an adversarial procedure: one party needed to bring a charge against the other—cruelty, abandonment, adultery—and prove it in court, even if both parties wanted to end the marriage. This was cumbersome and expensive and often created additional animosity. States were beginning to look instead toward "no-fault divorce," in which the only requirement would be a stipulation that the marriage was irretrievably broken and it would not be necessary for one spouse to prove a charge against the other. I was asked by a group of social workers at Hennepin County to carry the legislation and I agreed. When one skeptical legislator asked me why I was carrying this bill when I had never even been married, I replied that that status gave me a certain measure of objectivity.

The divorce bill turned out to be much more difficult than I had anticipated. I learned that family law was immensely complicated, not only in terms of its legal entanglements, but also because of its deep emotional implications. The ending of a marriage engenders some of the most intense hatreds I have ever seen, particularly, I think, because it involves a relationship between people who had once been in love. No one objected much to no-fault divorce when there were no disputes over children or property. But in contested cases, it was extremely difficult to come up with a formula that everyone thought was fair. We had to deal with lawyers, judges, women's groups, men's groups, children's advocates, and religious organizations that thought making divorce easy would trivialize marriage. I got the bill through the Senate and into conference committee, but a story in the *Minneapolis Star* just days before the end of the session, which referred to the plan as "postcard divorce," doomed it. We had to go back to the drawing board, rework the bill, and pass it in the 1974 session. It was the first in a series of measures that converted traditional divorce into "marriage dissolution" and moved toward less adversarial ways of dealing with such thorny issues as child custody, child support, alimony, and visitation.

One of the most controversial issues I had raised in my campaign was reform of the state's highly restrictive abortion law. In the 1971–72 session, a bill had been introduced modeled after the law that had been passed in New York, which would allow abortions in the early stages of pregnancy and under certain circumstances. But the Minnesota bill had gone nowhere, and a well-organized antiabortion advocacy group, Minnesota Citizens Concerned for Life, had emerged to make certain that the next legislature would be equally unsympathetic to abortion reform. Despite the DFL victory, the pro-lifers (as they called themselves) had large majorities in both houses and in both party caucuses. There were only twelve senators among sixty-seven who were solidly pro-choice. Then, just three weeks after the legislature convened, the U.S. Supreme Court handed down its famous decision in *Roe v. Wade,* which invalidated Minnesota's abortion law and those like it in other states. This completely reversed the playing field. It was now those of us on the pro-choice side who wanted to preserve the status quo and our opponents who hurriedly drafted and introduced bills. Many of us thought naively that the issue was now basically settled. I remember a conversation just a few days after *Roe* was handed down in the office of Lieutenant Governor Rudy Perpich. Rudy's two younger brothers, Tony and George, were both state senators and were among the small pro-choice minority. Rudy summarized what most pro-choicers at the time believed. He predicted that most of the current opposition to the Supreme Court decision would die down quickly and that within a few years the availability of abortion services would be generally accepted. Ironically, nine years later, Rudy himself would reverse positions and run successfully for governor on a pro-life platform, totally abandoning the position that he and his brothers had long held.

In fact, the pro-lifers had just begun to fight. They introduced a new abortion regulation bill, presumably designed to meet the standards of *Roe v. Wade.* But, as those of us in opposition pointed out, it went far beyond what the Court allowed and, although it easily passed the legislature, was promptly ruled unconstitutional. The pro-lifers also introduced a resolution memorializing Congress to approve a constitutional amendment overriding *Roe v. Wade* and outlawing abortion everywhere in the country. That too passed, but it was as meaningless as my antiwar resolution had been. Those of us who opposed these bills had mixed emotions. Because of the Supreme Court decision, our position was the law of the land. But it was frustrating to continually lose by votes of fifty-five to twelve or, perhaps, depending on the specific issue, fifty-two to fifteen. Even among the pro-choice minority, only three or four of us were willing to debate the issue on the floor of the Senate: Bob Lewis, George Perpich, on occasion George Pillsbury, and me. Bob was particularly skillful. When Wayne Olhoft, unmarried and presumably a virgin, began to discuss the details of pregnancy, Bob would pepper him with questions about female physiology that Wayne was totally unprepared to answer. His face would literally turn purple as he stumbled to find the proper vocabulary. For me, debating the abortion issue gave me invaluable experience in thinking on my feet and developing rebuttal skills. At the end of the day, the pro-choice legislators often retreated to a downtown St. Paul bar called Fiorito's to lick our wounds. There we would be joined by our allies in the feminist movement, who greeted us as heroes. Among them was a group of women who had just organized a feminist caucus within the DFL, women who would profoundly affect the future direction of the party—Jeri Rasmussen, Koryn Horbal, Cynthia Kitlinski, and Yvette Oldendorf.

The feminists did have one significant legislative victory in 1973: Minnesota ratified the Equal Rights Amendment, which had been approved by Congress and sent to the states the year before. Opposition to the ERA had not yet crystallized and the measure passed both houses by large margins. The result was similar in other states that year, and it looked as though it would take just a few years for the ERA to become part of the U.S. Constitution. During my election campaign in 1972, I had knocked on the door of an elderly woman in a working-class neighborhood in northeast Minneapolis, who told me, much to my surprise, that she was a former legislator. When I asked her when she had been elected, her answer was even more astonishing: "Nineteen twenty-two." Her name, I learned, was Myrtle Cain and she was one of four women who had been elected to the House that year—the first time women had been eligible to run for office. As the youngest and most stylish of the four, she had been described in the newspapers as "the flapper legislator." She had served only one term and had successfully authored one bill—a measure aimed at the Ku Klux Klan that prohibited people from appearing in public with their faces covered. In 1924, she went to Washington, D.C., to work with Alice Paul, the suffragist and women's rights leader, in the first effort to pass the Equal Rights Amendment. On the day the Minnesota Senate ratified the ERA, almost fifty years later, I invited Myrtle Cain to sit with me on the Senate floor and I introduced her as a special guest of honor. No one at that time anticipated the fierce struggle ahead that would ultimately result in the failure to ratify the ERA.

I did not take the initiative on gay issues in my first two years in the legislature. I had not yet decided how I would handle my own sexual orientation. Some of my colleagues, especially those from Minneapolis, must have known that I was gay. But no one ever discussed it and I never brought it up. Outside the legislature, however, my gay contacts were expanding. Much to my frustration, I still had difficulty developing romantic liaisons. I visited the gay bars, where I was now often recognized, but although people were eager to talk to me, at closing time I usually went home alone. I occasionally approached men who attracted me sexually, but all too often I heard the line "I really respect you but I'm not interested in you that way." I did, however, have an expanding circle of gay friends. Most notable was Steve Endean. I had met Steve the previous year but had dismissed him as a Humphrey hack. With the election over, we saw more of each other and I learned of Steve's deep commitment to gay issues. Steve was one of the first people in Minnesota who understood that to be effective the gay movement would need to sever its ties with 1960s-style radicalism and enter the mainstream. A moderate Democrat himself, Steve loved the political process and wanted to use it to advance the gay cause. He believed that the kind of dramatic, publicity-generating actions that Jack Baker had initiated were no longer effective and served only to irritate people. He liked to quote a critic of the movement who said that "the love that dares not speak its name has now become the neurosis that doesn't know when to shut up." It was time, he thought, for systematic, long-range, strategic planning.

Unlike me, Steve Endean was totally out. He had told his family that he was gay—a difficult and painful process—and had an active and, to my eyes, promiscuous sex life. A short, compactly built man, Steve was not strikingly handsome, but he was pleasant-looking and had no trouble finding sexual partners. He was particularly interested in black men, something that struck me as a kind of reverse racism, but Steve insisted that it was no different from a preference for blonds. Steve was ten years younger than I, but he became a mentor on gay issues. He wanted me to come out, but he never pushed me, understanding that I would have to do so at my own pace. We talked a lot about his plans to advance gay rights in Minnesota. Steve had already begun to organize what he first called the Legislative Gay Rights Caucus and, by 1973, the Gay Rights Legislative Committee. He held some meetings and had a long list of endorsers, but only a handful of people had become active. Steve had two goals at the legislature: repeal of the state's century-old sodomy law, which made anal or oral sex a gross misdemeanor; and the inclusion of gay people in the state human rights law, prohibiting discrimination in employment, housing, public accommodations, and public services. Before approaching the state legislature, however, he wanted to pass antidiscrimination ordinances in the cities of Minneapolis and St. Paul, which were more politically liberal than the state as a whole. Steve hoped that I would gradually come out and become a key player in these efforts.

For a while, however, in 1973, it looked as though the legislature was going to get ahead of us. Both sodomy repeal and gay rights came to the floor that year, brought there by legislators whom we had done relatively little to influence. Gary Flakne was a Republican member of the House of Representatives from Minneapolis. Like most urban Republicans, he was a political moderate. He was also a lawyer with a strong libertarian streak, and he found ludicrous the Minnesota laws that criminalized private, consensual sexual activity, not only anal and oral sex but also fornication and adultery. These laws, he pointed out, made criminals of a large percentage of adult Minnesotans and were wholly unenforceable. Their existence could only breed disrespect for the law itself. Flakne introduced legislation to repeal all these statutes. Strictly speaking, this was not a gay rights issue. Fornication and adultery were heterosexual practices and even the sodomy law made no mention of the gender of the participants; it was as illegal for a married couple to have anal or oral sex as it was for two men. Still, when the press and other legislators spoke of Flakne's bill, they emphasized that it would legalize gay sex. And that became the focus of opposition to the bill—primarily from conservative religious groups. The bill nevertheless passed both the House and Senate Judiciary committees and became the subject of spirited debate on the House floor. In the end, it failed. Many legislators acknowledged in private that the bill made sense, but they could too easily envision the opposition literature in their next election: "Representative X supports anal sex between two men!" In my twenty-eight years in the legislature, we were never able to repeal these laws. They were still on the books when the United States Supreme Court ruled all such legislation unconstitutional in 2003.

Once defeated in the House, the bill to repeal the consensual sex laws never made it to the full Senate. So I merely watched the House debate from a distance. But the Senate soon confronted gay rights directly, and it was difficult for me to remain on the sidelines. No freestanding bill to bar discrimination against gay people was introduced in either house in 1973. But Nick Coleman carried a bill to update various aspects of the state human rights law. It was what, in legislative parlance, is called a "housekeeping bill," a generally noncontroversial piece of legislation brought to the legislature by a state agency to clean up the statutes that govern it. Usually, the authors of such bills merely get them through the legislative process in the form that the agency has requested. But Nick had other ideas. Sensitized to the gay issue by his girlfriend, Deborah Howell, he saw the state human rights department's bill as a vehicle to extend legal protection to gay people. When the bill was heard in the Senate Judiciary Committee, he offered an amendment to add the term "homosexual orientation" to the list of protected classes that already included race, religion, nationality, and sex.[2] The department was totally unprepared for this development and didn't know how to react. On the one hand, this was not an issue it was ready to take on. Yet it was difficult for a human rights department to oppose an extension of the principle of human rights, especially when it is coming from its own chosen author, who also happens to be the majority leader. The Judiciary Committee, too, with some reluctance, acquiesced to the wishes of the author and passed the bill, with the author's amendment, on to the full Senate.

Steve Endean and I were stunned. We had seen statewide human rights legislation as something that would come in a few years. Now

---

2. The term "homosexual orientation" was improper on two grounds. First, the use of the word "homosexual" was objectionable to many gay people because of its clinical tone. Jack Baker was so incensed over Nick Coleman's use of the word that he compared it to a black civil rights bill that spoke of "nigger rights." I thought this was hyperbolic, but I agreed that it was not language I would have chosen. Second, the term was not parallel with the words used to describe the other protected categories in the human rights law: race, sex, religion, nationality, and so forth. All of these words referred to the bases on which one could not discriminate, not the groups against which one could not discriminate. Hence it was race rather than not being white; sex rather than being a woman. To be parallel, the term should have been "sexual orientation" rather than "homosexual orientation." Steve Endean and I were both aware of this defect but decided not to confront Nick Coleman with it unless it looked like the bill was about to pass. The difference was more than semantic. Under the Coleman language, it would have remained legal for a gay place of business to discriminate against straight people. With the term "sexual orientation," discrimination was banned in both directions.

we had a bill on the floor of the Senate authored by the majority leader. To be sure, there was no guarantee it would pass the Senate, the House companion did not include the gay rights amendment, and it was not certain that if the amendment stayed on the bill, the governor would sign it. No state had yet passed anything like this. But because of Nick Coleman's initiative, we were further along than we had ever hoped to be. We met with Nick and offered him assistance, and Steve brought over a few people to lobby key senators. But we had no real organization and it was going to be up to Nick to handle things. When the bill came to the floor, the Senate became almost eerily quiet. Usually there is continual hubbub of conversation and people moving around on the Senate floor even during debate, and the presiding officer must periodically use his gavel to ask for order so that the speakers can be heard. But when Nick brought up the gay rights issue, there seemed to be a sense that this was serious and that everyone should pay attention. Nick was eloquent, but not always well informed. The issue was new to him and he had no expertise on gay life. I had decided that I was not prepared to get involved in the debate as I did not see how I could do so without coming out. I was later ashamed of myself for what I came to see as an act of cowardice. But I did send notes to Nick advising him on answers that he might give to questions that were asked during the debate.

Passing gay rights in 1973 was an uphill battle. The department had quietly lobbied against Nick's amendment. Bob Brown, the same Republican senator who had opposed my prison reform bills, moved to delete all references to "homosexual orientation."[3] The Brown

---

3. I learned many years later that Bob Brown's brother was gay. I had previously known Ricardo Brown within the gay community, and he had worked on several of my campaigns. But I had never connected him to Senator Bob Brown. Dick Brown, as I knew him, was ten years older than I and wrote a fascinating memoir about life in St. Paul's only gay bar in the years immediately following World War II. I wrote a foreword when the University of Minnesota Press published the book in 2001 under the title *The Evening Crowd at Kirmser's*. Unfortunately, Dick did not live to see the book published. I do not know whether Bob Brown knew about his brother's sexual orientation when he led the floor fight against Nick Coleman's gay rights amendment. I suspect that he did not as, in my experience, nothing is more effective in changing attitudes toward gay people than the knowledge that a close family member is gay.

amendment passed thirty-eight to twenty-four. But Nick was not ready to give up. He was, after all, the majority leader and he knew how to twist arms. The next day he moved to restore the gay rights provisions, excluding teachers and other employees of educational institutions. He had determined that this was the most sensitive issue for his colleagues and that without this exclusion, no gay rights bill could pass. If I had been the author of the bill, I would not have done what Nick did, as I believed that the exclusion of teachers reinforced the most damaging misconception about gay people—that we preyed on children. Moreover, teachers were an important part of our community and perhaps the most in need of job protection. Nevertheless, Nick's calculation was correct and the amended gay rights provision was restored to the bill on a vote of thirty-two to thirty-one. In the end, however, the House, which had never even discussed the issue, failed to concur and gay rights was removed from the bill in a conference committee. After the session, I wrote a letter to Nick Coleman:

> I want to express to you my very special appreciation for your
> efforts to include gay people in the human rights act. Although
> we ultimately failed, I think that the very fact that gay rights
> were seriously discussed in this session of the legislature was
> a major step forward. And, so far as I know, the Minnesota
> senate was the first state legislative body to act favorably on a
> gay rights measure—which should be a matter of some pride
> despite the final outcome. . . . What I most appreciated, Nick,
> was that, as majority leader, you had absolutely nothing to
> gain by putting your prestige on the line for as volatile an
> issue as this. The fact that you did it nevertheless is, to me, a
> real indication of your deep commitment to human values. . . .
> As you know, Nick, this is an issue that I am close to person-
> ally and, as you sensed, it was not easy for me to sit through
> some of that debate. But your constant commitment to the
> issue, and the unerring sensitivity with which you handled it,
> more than made up for the ignorance and contempt on the
> other side.

Hence I virtually came out to Nick Coleman. But it would be a year and a half before I fully emerged from the closet.

On the last day of the session, I realized as I never had before how much I loved being a member of the Senate. The day began at nine in the morning and didn't end until seven the following morning. During those twenty-two hours, we passed most of the major budget bills for the biennium, spent hours while the leadership tried unsuccessfully to round up enough votes to pass a highway bonding bill, and listened to speeches that were, alternately, brilliant, inspiring, foolish, demagogic, and just plain boring. I scurried about throughout the afternoon and evening trying to put out the fires that had endangered my no-fault divorce bill, until I finally realized that it would have to wait another year. It was an inefficient, often frustrating, and in many ways crazy way to run state government. And yet it was an unbridled expression of representative democracy as legislators from a wide variety of backgrounds, most of them not professional politicians, came together to work out their conflicting ideas about how to run the state. And we ended up passing some truly significant bills. There were those who hated the intensity and pressure of the last days of the session and burned out after a term or two. But I found it enormously exciting and I was eager to master the process so that I could become a more skilled legislator. It was not, however, just the gamesmanship of it that I enjoyed. Especially during those heady early days of DFL control, I believed that I was part of a major reform effort that would tangibly improve the quality of life in Minnesota.

After the session, I took a few weeks off and drove to the West Coast. Unfortunately, I had still not given up in my efforts to pursue Barry B., despite his insistence that he was not interested in me romantically and wanted only to be a friend. I learned that he planned to be in California when I would be there and invited him to meet me in Los Angeles and drive with me to San Francisco. Predictably, it was a disaster. In Los Angeles, we stayed with Dick Hanson at his house in the Hollywood Hills. It was a lovely setting and Dick took us around to his favorite haunts. We also spent a few days with my old graduate student friend, Norman Zimmerman, and his wife, who were now living in Laguna Beach, and visited Disneyland stoned on whatever drug was fashionable that year. But the relaxing times were spoiled by continuing conflict between Barry and me over the nature of our relationship. By the time we left for San Francisco we weren't even speaking to each other. We reconciled temporarily and went out to the bars I knew on Polk Street and in the newly developing Castro area. But while Barry picked up young men at the bars, I had eyes only for him. Finally, we parted, as I headed toward home and he stayed on for a while in San Francisco.

I clearly needed to talk to someone about my inability to handle my relationship with Barry. I tried to find my friend Elizabeth Katz, one of the first people I had come out to when I had been in San Francisco three years earlier. I learned that she was on a farm near Yakima, Washington, picking apples. So I drove to Yakima with no address for her other than a postal box number. The Yakima post office helped me find her on a kind of hippie commune, several miles outside town. We talked all night. She was pleased with how far I had moved along in the coming-out process since we had last seen each other. But when I told her about Barry, she said, "You have to learn to take no for an answer and move on." She was right, of course and eventually I did. But the hardest part of the coming-out process for me was realizing how difficult it would be to find a partner with whom I could share my life.

With the legislature in adjournment for the rest of the year, I went back to the other major activities of my life—party politics and teaching. The Minneapolis DFL was poised for a major comeback in the 1973 city elections. The Watergate scandal boosted Democratic prospects throughout the country, and in Minneapolis voters were beginning to tire of the one-dimensional leadership of Charles Stenvig. In the Second Ward, John Cairns, having failed to move to the state Senate, had announced that he would not seek reelection to the city council and most observers thought the DFL would win this seat. Five candidates emerged to seek the party endorsement. I had known since late the previous year that Jack Baker wanted to run for Second Ward alderman. His major problem was that he lived across town in the Seventh Ward. Yet his most likely constituency, university students, was concentrated in the Second and so he decided to move in order to run. He asked me if I would support him. I told him bluntly that I would not and I encouraged him not to run. I explained that among the other candidates were people with extensive party and community experience in the Second Ward and that, unlike Jack, several of them had been key players in my campaign. Moreover, I told him that the delegates would resent an outsider moving in to run and that he could not win. Jack did not take my advice and was upset by my lack of gay solidarity. My failure to support him began what ultimately became a permanent rupture in our relationship.

Jack Baker and I were clearly moving in opposite directions politically. I believed that the dramatic and courageous actions Jack had taken in earlier years—his attempt to marry Mike McConnell and his audacious campaign for student body president—had played a major role in gaining attention for a movement that had not previously been taken seriously. But I also agreed with Steve Endean that these advances now had to be consolidated and that could only be done by winning a place at the table, electing gay people to office, changing the laws, and gaining acceptance for gay rights as a legitimate civil rights movement. My own career pattern reinforced these convictions. I was no longer the outsider I had been in 1968. I had become fascinated by party politics and by the legislative process and thought we could make progress by working within the system rather than standing outside it and protesting. Jack Baker had little interest in this kind of politics. He was willing to use the DFL Party to advance his cause, but he didn't care about the party itself. When he came in fourth among the five candidates at the DFL endorsing convention, he announced that he would run as an independent in the general election, enhancing the possibility that a Republican could win the seat. I wrote a letter to the *Minnesota Daily,* supporting the DFL-endorsed candidate, Tom Johnson, and attacking Jack for "casting himself in the role of a spoiler." Jack was infuriated by my letter, and I learned that he told several people in the gay community he would not have his name dragged in the mud by a "closet case." I took this to be an indirect threat to "out" me.

I regret many things about my break with Jack Baker. There was blame on both sides. While there was no way I could have supported him for alderman given my political position at the time, I think in retrospect that I was unduly harsh with him. The letter to the *Daily* was overkill. It was at least in part self-serving of me to publicly repudiate the more militant leadership within the gay movement. As I began to move toward the political mainstream, I made myself look more reasonable by discarding former allies who remained on the fringe.

On the other hand, as the decade went on, Jack became more idiosyncratic and alienated many of his former supporters. He opposed all the efforts Steve Endean and I launched at the legislature to pass gay rights legislation, either because the bills were not inclusive enough or because he did not approve of the wording. He became a key adviser to my Republican opponent in 1976 and participated in some attacks on me that bordered on gay-baiting. He began to refer to heterosexuals as "breeders" and started a religious organization for gay people that he called "the Church of the Chosen People," of which he was the "Prime Archon." It reminded me of the religion that Jonathan Feinn and I had invented when we were fifteen years old—but this was being carried on by adults! By the 1980s, Jack had become embittered about the direction the movement was taking and withdrew completely from gay politics, retreating into his still-strong relationship with Mike and a law practice that was never as successful as he had hoped. He even refused to meet with journalists and historians who wanted to interview him about his significant early contributions. Although he stayed in the Twin Cities, we never saw each other. I was pleased, however, when I retired in 2000, to receive a cordial note from him congratulating me on my years of service to the gay and lesbian community.

In November 1973, a young north Minneapolis Democrat named Al Hofstede defeated Stenvig for mayor and the DFL won eleven of the thirteen city council seats. Tom Johnson in the Second Ward was among them. Although Stenvig would come back two years later for one more term as mayor, the DFL would never again lose its majority on the council. Increasingly, Minneapolis would be a one-party city with most of the issues fought out within the DFL rather than between the parties. When Steve Endean saw the results on election night, he was practically salivating. Not only was the city council heavily DFL, it was overwhelmingly liberal. He was certain that with a little work and organization, Minneapolis could become one of the first large cities in the country to pass an ordinance banning discrimination on the basis of sexual orientation. By the spring of 1974, Steve had almost single-handedly lobbied the ordinance through the council and persuaded Mayor Hofstede to sign it.

Meanwhile, I had gone back to the university to resume my teaching job. I had some decisions to make as, for the immediate future at least,

I would be in residence only part-time. The first was whether I could continue to carry the responsibility for the department's undergraduate and graduate offerings in African American history. Up to this point, I had resisted the idea that only black scholars should teach in this field. I was confident of my mastery of the subject and of the broad perspective I brought to it. But I realized this was a responsibility that required a full-time commitment, and I was no longer able to provide it. I spoke with Clarke Chambers, now chairman of the department, and suggested that the department begin a search for a full-time scholar in African American history. The tacit assumption was that this person would be black. During the terms I was in residence, I would teach twentieth-century American history. This subject always attracted a large number of students, and while several professors were already sharing responsibility for the course, there was a need for another, as Al Jones had never been replaced and Professor Chambers was limiting himself to graduate seminars. The search for an African American historian was more difficult than I had anticipated. It had become a sellers' market as universities throughout the country competed for the relatively few black scholars in the field. Not only did the department have trouble finding an appropriate person to hire, it also subsequently had trouble retaining qualified people in a city that was not exactly a center of African American life and culture. Over the next twenty-eight years, I stepped in from time to time to teach African American history when there was no one else on the staff to do it. But most of my teaching now centered on twentieth-century American political and social history.

I also made a second difficult decision regarding my career in the history department. I came to the conclusion that I could no longer be a successful teacher of graduate students and, in particular, a supervisor of PhD dissertations. Although my graduate seminar and my relationship with my doctoral students had been exceptionally rewarding, I believed that to teach someone to be a cutting-edge scholar it was necessary to be one. Graduate teaching is a collegial effort in which professor and student learn together. It was clear to me that while I was in the legislature I was not likely to do much original scholarship. I could keep up with the secondary literature, which I would have to do for my undergraduate lecture courses. But I would not be working with primary sources, and at a time when computer technology was first becoming an important tool of scholarly research, I would not be abreast of the latest methodology. Moreover, I would simply be absent from campus too much to give PhD students the attention and supervision they needed. So while I finished working with my dissertation students who had already begun their work, I did not take on any new students and I stopped teaching a graduate seminar. I was obviously putting my academic career on a back burner. Someday, I thought, I would come back to it. But for now, I needed to devote as much time and energy as I could to the challenge of learning how to be an effective legislator.

Despite my unhappy experience with Barry B., I did not give up in my pursuit of a romantic relationship. I continued to go to the gay bars, particularly Sutton's, where if nothing else developed, I could always visit with Steve Endean at the coat check counter. But I was more successful in making new friends than in meeting potential partners. One evening late in 1973, I met Mark Snyder at Sutton's. Mark had just come to the university to take a position in the psychology department. Only twenty-six, he already had a PhD from Stanford and was beginning what would turn out to be a highly successful academic career. He was good-looking and charming and I hoped at first that something would develop between us. But when Mark made it clear that he wanted only to be a friend, I had learned enough by that time to accept his decision. We have remained close friends for the past thirty years.

My initial exhilaration with the openness of the gay bars, however, was wearing off. They were uncomfortably smoky and the deafening disco music was not my style. Moreover, despite my desire for companionship, I found the overt sexual competitiveness of the bar scene—the "meat rack," as it is often called—totally unappealing. I much preferred entertaining friends at home, and in the fall of 1973 I bought a house of my own where I could do that in comfort. Located just a block down the river road from the duplex where I had been living for six years, my new house was designed in the Craftsman style of the early twentieth century. It had a lot of dark wood, a stone fireplace, a built-in buffet and china cabinets, and a breakfast room overlooking a fenced-in backyard. There was a huge master bedroom upstairs with a wonderful view of the Mississippi River gorge. I had been thinking for some time of buying a house and a few years earlier had made an offer on the duplex where I lived, but at that time I could not secure the financing. Now I was in a better financial situation and had no trouble completing the purchase. My new house was so close to my old one that I didn't even need to hire a moving company. My friends and I got some hand trucks and rolled everything down the street. After Marcia Greenfield helped me set up my new kitchen, I looked at her and said, "Well, now I'm set. I don't need to ever do this again. This house is perfect for me. I can stay here the rest of my life." I had not counted on the exigencies of politics.

Throughout that fall, I was becoming increasingly involved in the gay movement. I saw a lot of Steve Endean and he always had some new idea to advance the cause and told me what I could do to help. I wanted to do what I could, but I was gradually coming to the conclusion that if I was going to be a gay rights activist, I would have to come out. I was in an awkward situation—going to gay rights meetings, advocating for the cause, yet not being fully open about my own sexuality. My silence on the Senate floor during the gay rights debate in the spring had been the most conspicuous example of my discomfort. As I thought through my situation, however, I realized that if I were to publicly come out, I would first have to overcome what in my mind was the highest barrier of all—telling my parents. When they had visited in the summer, there were several occasions when they almost learned the truth. They overheard telephone conversations that I was having with Steve Endean and had trouble understanding why I was spending so much time working with a gay man on gay issues. I reminded them that as a white man I had spent years working on black issues, and, yes, they admitted, that was true. Still, I couldn't keep up this pretense forever. I wanted desperately to get it out and get it over with. The question was how I could do it with the minimum of tears and anguish.

I finally decided that I would tell my parents when I visited them in Puerto Vallarta in December. My brother and sister-in-law would not be there then. I had made plans to meet them in Yucatán after I left Puerto Vallarta, and they were then going to visit our parents in early January. I did not tell Richard and Athena what I planned to do as I was certain they would try to talk me out of it. After all, I had assured them the previous year that I wouldn't do this. But my consciousness was evolving quickly, and once I had decided, I was determined to go ahead. I went through the scenario dozens of times in my mind. I needed somehow to get across the point that there was something missing in our relationship, that it was not their fault but had to do with my holding something back, and that I needed to tell them the truth about myself if we were to have an open and honest relationship. In other words, I was telling them I was gay, not to hurt them or blame them for anything, but because I loved them and cared about them and did not want anything to stand between us.

My plan worked—up to a point. I was not sure until the very end that I would go through with it. I steered the conversation around to some of the strains I perceived in our relationship and then, as I had planned, told them there was something they needed to know about me. My mother then said, "Well, I only know of one thing it could be and I hope to God it's not that." That was not the response I had hoped for, but I plowed ahead. "Yes," I said. "It is probably what you are thinking." Until that moment, my father had not been as intensely involved in the conversation as my mother; he had been lying on the floor, listening but not saying much. Now he sat bolt upright as he realized what was coming next. I told them I had known I was gay since I was a child but had only in the past few years been able to come to terms with it. I also told them that Richard and Athena knew and fully accepted it. And I emphasized how difficult it was for me to keep this kind of secret from them as it made our relationship more distant. My mother cried and they were both visibly upset, but they immediately assured me that they loved me regardless of what I was and that they would certainly love me no less because of my sexuality. I asked them if they had suspected and they said that they might have had it not been for my affair with Sally B. That then led us into a discussion of the complexity of human sexuality—or, at least, of mine.

Overall, I thought my parents handled it well. We continued to talk about it during my remaining days in Puerto Vallarta. They were probably more upset than they let on to me, but they certainly did everything they could to assure me that they would think of me no differently than they had before. My father pursued one line of questioning that startled me, although it probably shouldn't have. He had always had a lively interest in sex and its various permutations and a day or two after my revelation he started asking me about the details of gay sex: "What do you do? How do you do it?" I really didn't want to talk about that and, frankly, I was not a great expert on it. But I answered his questions as well as I could. At the end of the week, I flew to Mérida to meet Richard and Athena; from there we had made arrangements to go on to Chichen Itza and Uxmal to see the Mayan ruins. I told them what I had done, and while they were surprised, they did not chastise me for having done it. But when they arrived in Puerto Vallarta, they had a lot of hand-holding to do. Our parents expressed concerns to them that they had not wanted to discuss with me. My mother was particularly worried about the unhealthiness and tawdriness of the gay lifestyle (fortunately, AIDS had not come along yet) and what would happen to me in my old age. She also realized for the first time that, with Richard and Athena still childless, she was not likely ever to be a grandmother. Richard and Athena tried as much as they could to allay their concerns.

It was for me a huge barrier to have crossed. I felt far freer than I ever had before. I still didn't know when or how I would come out publicly, but there was no longer much doubt in my mind that I would at some time do so. I knew that whatever I did and whatever inner doubts they might have, my parents would support me. A couple of years later my parents were visiting Minneapolis during a conference that Steve Endean and I had organized. One of the speakers was a leader of a relatively new group called Parents and Friends of Gays and Lesbians (PFLAG). My parents came to hear her, and during the discussion that followed her speech, my mother got up and talked about how proud she was of her son and how proud all gay parents should be of their children. I was, for my part, enormously proud of her. My mother said on several occasions that the one thing she might have trouble handling would be visiting me if I had a male partner living in the house. I told her that we would cross that bridge when we came to it, and unfortunately she died before I met my life partner. But my father did visit me after Jun came to live with me in 1982, and he was fully accepting. In fact, one of the major concerns that he and my mother had shared was now alleviated: he knew that I would not grow old alone.

When the state constitution was changed to permit annual sessions of the legislature, it was anticipated that the second year of each biennium would be a short "cleanup" session. Because the state remained on a biennial budget, in the second year it would be necessary only to tweak the budget so that it covered unforeseen developments. And bills that had not been completed in the first year could be passed in the second. Later on, the second-year sessions grew in length and complexity until they were almost indistinguishable from the first-year sessions. But in 1974 we generally stuck with the original plan. We finished the session by March, and most of the bills were either responses to new issues or measures that followed up what we had done the previous year. For example, the growing Watergate scandal had created a demand for campaign ethics reform throughout the country. We passed a comprehensive bill that placed limits on campaign contributions, established a system for the public disclosure of contributions and expenditures, and provided partial public funding for legislative and statewide candidates.

I finally worked out a satisfactory compromise on the no-fault divorce bill and passed it into law. I continued my work on prison inmate issues and passed what I think in retrospect was my most constructive effort in that area. I was convinced that the high rate of recidivism among offenders was due, at least in part, to the difficulty ex-felons had in finding employment. The state of Minnesota itself contributed to this situation in its hiring and licensing practices. State statutes governing the regulated professions specified that a person must be of "good moral character" to be licensed, and the licensing boards often interpreted this to include any criminal conviction regardless of its nature. My bill prohibited discrimination in hiring and licensing by public employers and licensing boards on the basis of criminal record unless the offense were directly related to the occupation involved. Hence a conviction for medical malpractice should prevent someone from being licensed as a physician but not as a watchmaker. Later, I tried to extend this bill to include employment in the private sector, but I was unsuccessful. And in the fervent anticrime climate of the 1990s, even the limited and, I thought, sensible provision that had passed came under frequent attack.

While I was often criticized over the years for caring more about criminals than I did about victims, I was in fact the author of one of the first victims' rights bills to pass the Minnesota legislature. Before the rise of the feminist movement, probably the most underreported crime in the United States was rape, particularly rape by an acquaintance or, as it was often called, "date rape." Women who reported that they had been raped were often not believed and were treated by law enforcement and medical personnel with callous insensitivity. Representative Arne Carlson and I successfully passed a bill in 1974 which required the Department of Corrections to develop a plan to aid rape victims by providing female counselors, notifying victims of their rights, and requiring sensitivity training for county attorneys, police officers, and hospital employees. In ensuing years, this modest first step grew into a full-fledged statewide program that gave immediate assistance to rape victims and contributed to a heightened consciousness about the nature and frequency of the crime of sexual assault.

I also carried a controversial piece of labor legislation that grew out of the bill we had passed in 1973 allowing public employees to strike. That experience taught me once again the need to learn the rules of the Senate. In 1971, the teachers in Minneapolis, members of the Minnesota Federation of Teachers, an AFL-CIO union, had gone out on a strike that was at that time in violation of state law. When they returned, they were subject to harsh penalties, in some cases the loss of their salary for the remainder of the school year. The Minneapolis school board had agreed, as part of the settlement, that if state law were changed to permit public employees to strike, they would reimburse the teachers for these losses, in effect making the change in law retroactive. We did change the law in 1973, but it still required separate legislation to allow the teachers to be reimbursed. I carried the bill for the Minneapolis teachers' union. Many rural legislators, especially Republicans, strongly opposed it and thought it an outrage to reimburse public employees who had committed an illegal act.

I brought the bill up during an evening session without noticing that many of my supporters were not on the floor. I thought I had enough votes to pass the bill, but when the time came I was several votes short. Senate rules allow a bill to be reconsidered if the motion is made by a senator who had voted on the prevailing side. Therefore, I changed my vote to "no," anticipating that I would move to reconsider the next day when my supporters had returned. But Senator Joe Josefson, a seasoned Republican legislator from southwestern Minnesota, was ready for that. He moved to reconsider immediately. A bill can be reconsidered only once, so had we reconsidered immediately and defeated the bill again, it would have been dead. I looked to Nick

Coleman in panic, not knowing what to do. Nick saved me. He moved that the Senate adjourn before we could consider the Josefson motion. The next day, I had my votes in place, moved to reconsider, and passed the bill. I never again brought an important bill to a vote without first counting heads to make sure that I could pass it.

In addition to our standing committee assignments, legislators were given the opportunity to serve on a variety of commissions that consisted of both elected officials and appointees from the communities affected by the commission's work. I chose to join the Indian Affairs Commission, which dealt with the legislative concerns of Minnesota's substantial Indian population. Despite my background in the history of American racial minorities, I knew very little about the life and culture of American Indians. My failure to deal with this subject had been the most gaping hole in my course on race and nationality in American history. Indians did not fit well into the models that I had constructed to deal with African Americans and European and Asian immigrants, so I tended to ignore them. My work on the Indian Affairs Commission helped fill some of the gaps in my knowledge. We visited most of Minnesota's eleven reservations. I learned of the divisions between the seven Chippewa (or Ojibwe) reservations in northern Minnesota and the four Sioux (or Dakota) reservations in the southern part of the state; the difference between the one closed reservation, Red Lake, which was not subject to state law, and the other reservations; and, perhaps most important, the conflicts between the urban Indians who had left the reservations for Minneapolis, St. Paul, or Duluth and those who remained on their ancestral homelands.

If the historical experience of Indians was substantially different from other minorities, there were some ways in which their experience was similar. The majority society had reduced them to a state of almost unrelieved poverty and had tried relentlessly to suppress their culture. The militancy of the 1960s had spread to the Indian community and Minneapolis became the center of the best-known national Indian protest organization, the American Indian Movement (AIM). Like many groups of its type, AIM often pursued unrealistic goals and used superheated rhetoric. But I sympathized with its efforts to restore pride and self-sufficiency to a people who had been made dependent on the whims of often uncaring bureaucrats. The more conservative reservation Indian leaders felt threatened by AIM and the urban communities that supported its approach. This led to a deep schism on the Indian Affairs Commission, where I found myself usually allied with the urban Indians, some of whom were my constituents. Eventually, the reservation leaders won and succeeded in passing legislation removing the urban representatives from the commission, transforming it into the Indian Affairs Intertribal Board. With my Indian constituents no longer allowed to participate, I resigned from the board, but I continued to work on Indian issues. In my second term, I authored the American Indian Language and Culture Act, one of the legislative achievements of which I remain most proud.

Throughout the winter and spring of 1974, Steve Endean and I, along with our friend Larry Bye, a gay man who had been active in DFL politics for a number of years, began plans to organize a new statewide coalition to support gay rights. Steve had come to realize that his Gay Rights Legislative Committee was not adequate to sustain a long-term effort to affect political and social change in the state. He conceived of a permanent organization with an adequate funding base, a statewide membership, and strong alliances outside the gay and lesbian community with civil rights, civic, and religious groups. While volunteers would continue to do important work, Steve thought it essential that the new group have a salaried staff who would assume the ongoing responsibilities of running the organization. "If we are going to be serious about this," he insisted, "we have to establish it on a professional basis." Steve was frank about wanting the executive directorship for himself. He had never really had a full-time job and used his position as the coat check person at Sutton's to recruit volunteers for his gay rights activities. He could not do that forever. He wanted to devote his life to gay rights, but at the same time realized that someone was going to have to pay him for his work.

Larry, Steve, and I tentatively called the new organization the Minnesota Committee for Gay Rights (MCGR) and brought together fifteen or twenty people whom we knew for a series of planning meetings. Most, but not all, of the organizers were gay. I brought in Lee and Marcia Greenfield and Dick and Carol Flynn. The gay people included many of those who had been working with Steve on his successful effort that spring to pass the Minneapolis gay rights ordinance. My new friend, Mark Snyder, also participated.

Our informal organizing committee decided to launch MCGR formally with a conference in the spring featuring one or more national speakers. Our first choice was Dr. Howard Brown, one of the founders of the newly organized National Gay Task Force (NGTF). Howard Brown had been one of the first well-known professional people in the country to come out. A physician prominent in the field of public health, he had been health services administrator for New York City under Mayor John Lindsay. His announcement that he was gay made the front page of the *New York Times*. On February 4, I wrote to Dr. Brown:

> I am one of several gay Minnesotans who are attempting to organize a new gay rights organization in this state. We have been deeply impressed by the work of the National Gay Task Force and are frankly modeling our approach after yours. Like the Task Force, we hope to attract professional people and individuals with resources and skills who have not previously participated in gay rights activities. We see ourselves as principally a civil rights group with the following aims: inclusion of gays in state and municipal human rights statutes; repeal of laws restricting sexual activity among consenting adults; the election of public officials who take pro-gay positions; and the dissemination of accurate information on gay life styles to the general community.

I then invited Dr. Brown to be the keynote speaker at our conference in the spring.

Howard Brown accepted my invitation, and we scheduled the conference for May 11 at a student center just off the university campus. But our planning ran into two problems that were indicative of the internal struggles that plagued the early gay rights movement in Minnesota and elsewhere. The first involved the tension between those who still favored a confrontational approach and those who wanted to move toward the mainstream. Despite the conflict between Jack Baker and me the preceding year, Jack came to a couple of the early MCGR organizing meetings. But it was clear that he was not comfortable with the direction in which we were going. In late April, we printed a flyer announcing the conference and distributed it to various organizations and institutions that we hoped would circulate it. The flyer included the words "The First Real Step Toward Building a Viable Movement for Gay Rights in Minnesota." Jack and his allies saw this as a direct repudiation of the contributions that they had made. I received a letter from Tim Campbell, who had recently moved to the Twin Cities, and who in the coming years would replace Jack Baker as the leading proponent of the confrontational style in gay politics. Tim reviewed the many things that had already been done for gay causes in Minnesota and said that it was "blatantly false" to suggest that none of these activities have been "viable or part of a movement for gay rights." I apologized for unnecessarily causing hard feelings and admitted that the claim in the flyer was "undoubtedly exaggerated." We promised to stop distributing the flyers and to alter those that we could still locate to delete the offensive language. It had been a mistake on our part, but it exposed an underlying conflict that went well beyond the wording of a flyer.

The second tension developed between gay men and lesbians. Most of the organizers of the conference were men. Of the twenty-nine names on MCGR's first mailing list, only four were women and when we established committees, all were chaired by men. We invited a man to be our sole keynote speaker. Larry, Steve, and I were aware of the problem, but we simply did not know how to reach out to the lesbian community. In the early days of the gay rights movement, gay men and lesbians knew very little about each other. Pre-Stonewall gay life had been primarily social, and gay men had wanted to be with other men, lesbians with other women. The politicization of the movement created a need to work together, but the divide was difficult to bridge. I simply didn't know many lesbians. The only women I knew to invite to the MCGR organizing meetings were the straight women I had worked with in the DFL. But gradually, we began hearing from lesbians about the male domination of MCGR. Why were so few women involved? Why was there no woman keynote speaker? Were we exclusively a gay male organization? Belatedly, Larry, Steve, and I tried to bring some lesbians into our planning activities. Steve recruited Kerry Woodward, who ultimately became one of the leaders of MCGR. Larry sought advice from his friend Colleen Zarich. They urged us to invite a prominent woman to join Howard Brown as one of the keynote speakers. We invited Phyllis Lyon from San Francisco, one of the founders of the pioneer lesbian organization, Daughters of Bilitis, and coauthor of the book *Lesbian/Woman*. She agreed to come, but she fully understood the circumstances of her invitation. In her address to the conference, she noted that "male gay activists too often approach lesbians for support but not cooperation. They say, 'We have this program we'd like you to join in on.' Well, that's not really planning together." She had described perfectly what we gay male activists in MCGR had done.

Despite our mistakes, the conference was a success. More than two hundred people attended. I briefly addressed the conference and explained the mainstream emphasis of our new organization:

> We are a very traditional civil rights organization. Marches have their place, but they are not our major thrust. Our emphasis will be on political action—lobbying and education to create a positive attitude toward the extension of full civil rights to gay people. This is a gay rights organization, not a gay organization, and we expect people who are not gay to play an important role in these efforts.

For me, perhaps the most rewarding part of the conference was getting to know Howard Brown. He gave a splendid speech, recounting his years in the closet and his very public coming out. He said that his only regret was not coming out earlier. Howard stayed at my house that weekend and we had long conversations about my own situation. He told me that I was brave to be as open as I was and said that he was impressed to get my letter written on Senate stationery. I confessed that I had typed it myself at home rather than dictate it to my secretary, but he said that didn't matter, that everything happened incrementally. He formally interviewed me for his forthcoming book about the experiences of gay men in America, which would be published the following year as *Familiar Faces, Hidden Lives*. Howard assured me he would conceal my identity, but by the time the book appeared, I was out and I was identified by my real name. The example of Howard Brown had helped push me in that direction.

As we moved to put MCGR on a permanent footing, we tried to absorb the lessons we had learned when planning for the conference, particularly the importance of inclusiveness. The women who had joined us and helped bring in Phyllis Lyon had now formed a women's caucus within MCGR and served notice that they expected to play a fully equal role in the organization. Larry Bye sent out a memo in late May urging that the board be fully representative of women, racial minorities, and nongays. Kerry Woodward and I became cochairs and a number of women joined the board, but many women were suspicious of an organization that still seemed male dominated. And it was extremely difficult to find people of color who were willing to become involved. We hired Steve Endean as the coordinator and rented a small office. Steve was given a salary, but it was dependent on our ability to raise money, and that was by no means a certainty. Nevertheless, Steve got to work right away, established a series of task forces, and by the end of the summer had chalked up another significant victory. The St. Paul city council followed the action of its Minneapolis counterpart and passed an ordinance extending human rights protection to gay and lesbian people.

While we were working to bridge the divisions between gay men and lesbians, the rupture between the militants and the moderates showed no sign of healing. Tim Campbell was now emerging as the principal spokesperson for those who favored a confrontational approach. Originally from Texas, Tim had come to Minnesota to teach French at Southwest Minnesota State University at Marshall. His contract there had not been renewed, and while I never learned the details, his openness as a gay man and his proud flamboyance apparently entered into that decision. Tim then came to the Twin Cities, where he quickly allied with Jack Baker. His priorities were somewhat different. While Jack focused on gay marriage, Tim was particularly concerned with sexual liberation, cross-dressing, and the rights of transgender people. But he shared with Jack a commitment to an "in your face" approach to politics and a disdain for the kind of "within the system" tactic that Steve Endean and I were advocating. After the successful effort in St. Paul, Tim wrote to Steve, congratulating him on the outcome, but criticizing a flyer Steve had posted in the gay bars urging people who came to lobby not to "be so flamboyant as to alienate possible supporters." "We know," the flyer had continued, "that gay people don't fit those tired stereotypes that some straights label us with." Tim replied:

> You are seemingly uncomfortable with Gays whose style
> differs from your own. Some Gays do fit the stereotypes, at
> least in appearance. I see that behavior as a non-verbal way of
> saying: "We have a right to be ourselves. We refuse to hide our
> gayness." . . . I value their courage and style.

Meanwhile, Jack Baker and his partner, Mike McConnell, opened an attack on me for my failure to publicly come out. I had agreed to be a featured speaker at the 1974 gay pride celebration held in Loring Park, a popular gay meeting spot a few blocks from downtown Minneapolis. This was not the first gay pride event in the Twin Cities—there had been one or two before—but it was the first I attended, and I let the organizers know that I would speak openly as a gay person. I still did not see this as a public coming out as gay pride celebrations in those days were largely community events and I thought I would be primarily addressing other gay people. But the National Gay Task Force learned that I would be speaking and I received a call from Ron Gold, the NGTF's communication director. He told me he thought the national television networks would cover the coming out of a state senator at a gay pride event, and he wanted my permission to tip them off. I refused to give it. I said I was coming out in my own way at my own pace and was not prepared for a coming-out speech on national television. He was disappointed but accepted my decision. I gave the speech, it received little publicity, and I thought that was the end of the incident.

A few weeks later, I received an angry letter. While it was signed by Mike McConnell, its style reflected that of Jack Baker. Mike said that while visiting New York, he had been "deluged with questions about why we have a 'closet case' speaking for the movement in Minneapolis." He said that he was "exceedingly embarrassed." He went on to tell me that the leaders of the National Gay Task Force had been stunned by my refusal to let them contact the press, and they wanted to know whether I would continue this "policy of repression of media coverage" as cochair of the Minnesota Committee for Gay Rights. The next day I received a letter from Ron Gold, disassociating himself from the tone of Mike's letter. He indicated that he had not even spoken to Mike McConnell, but had told Jack Baker about the incident and had specifically told him not to use the information to trash me. He stated that while he was disappointed in my decision, it was mine to make and he did not share the view that not desiring national publicity made me a "closet case."

My reply to Mike McConnell reflected my outrage at what I considered a mean-spirited and untruthful letter as well as my internal conflict over how open I should be about my sexuality. I told Mike that I considered his letter "a totally unwarranted intrusion by you into my private affairs," and in light of the letter I had received from Ron Gold, his characterization of the NGTF leadership's attitude toward me was "at best a gross exaggeration and at worst a lie." I added:

> I have no intention of becoming a national symbol—as a "gay senator." I am not a one-issue person and I do not wish to become so totally identified with the gay movement that I lose my effectiveness on other issues. At the same time, I consider myself an openly gay person. I am open with my family and with my straight friends and colleagues, and, as you well know, I was open in the speech I gave on Gay Pride Day. It somehow has not occurred to me that one is a "closet case" unless he comes out on CBS Television!

I concluded by affirming my respect for the contributions that Mike and Jack had made to the gay movement. But, I said, their style was not my style, and if the gay movement stands for anything, "it should stand for a willingness to respect the life styles chosen by other gay people. I only regret that that respect cannot be mutual."

I was not going to be rushed into publicly coming out in a manner not of my choosing. A two-minute feature about an openly gay senator in Minnesota on national television news would not have been an appropriate format, and Jack Baker and Mike McConnell's behavior in this incident was inexcusable. At the same time, my position could not be maintained forever. I could not simply choose when I wanted to be identified as gay and when I did not. Sooner or later, an unfriendly reporter was likely to "out" me and it could very well come in an unflattering way. My problem was compounded by the fact that I had no models to follow. Other than two women who held minor local offices in the student district of Ann Arbor, Michigan, no openly gay person had ever served in an elective position in the United States. I was impressed by what Howard Brown had done, but he had never been an elected official, and when he came out, he no longer even held appointive office. My district was liberal, and some of my constituents already knew I was gay, but I still had no real way of knowing what the reaction would be if I came out publicly. Moreover the concern that I expressed in my letter to Mike was a legitimate one: would I become so identified as the "gay senator" that I would not be taken seriously when I worked on other issues?

Another episode during the summer of 1974, however, paved the way for the manner in which I did ultimately come out. While Steve Endean was lobbying to pass the gay rights ordinance in St. Paul, he asked me to call Nick Coleman and find out if Nick could try to persuade a couple of council members to vote with us. I made the call and Nick promised to do what he could to help. Nick then said to me, "While we are on the subject, I'd like to ask you a question. Are you yourself gay?" I had almost come out to Nick the previous year, but had never done so directly. I answered, "Yes, I am." Then he asked, "Have you thought about coming out publicly?" "Yes," I replied. "I've thought about it. But I haven't decided whether to do it." I was sure that Nick was going to advise me against it. The seasoned veteran was certain to tell the promising rookie not to do anything rash that might ruin his career. Instead Nick said, "Well, that will be your decision. But if you decide to come out, Deborah would really like to do the story." The reference was to Deborah Howell, the city editor of the *Minneapolis Star,* who was soon to become Nick's wife and who was largely responsible for turning Nick into an advocate for gay rights. Nick went on to tell me how important it would be for me to maintain control over a story like this as it could easily turn sensationalistic. "I can assure you," he said, "that Deborah will give you the story you want." I made no commitment that day, but at least I knew now how I would proceed if I made the decision to come out.

Meanwhile, I returned to the university to teach in both the spring and fall quarters of 1974. As I was no longer in residence full time, I had hoped to be less involved than I had been in academic politics. By this time, the polarization of the campus seemed to be easing up. American troops had been withdrawn from Vietnam, departments had been established in not only African American studies but also American Indian and Chicano studies, and there were no more violent confrontations of the sort that had torn the university apart in 1970 and 1972. Yet conflict continued in the history department, particularly over the hiring of women. When Carla Phillips joined the department in 1972, I thought that would be the end of it; Carla was an exemplary scholar and colleague and would, I assumed, make it easier to hire women in the future. But the next year, when we searched for a medieval historian, we fought the issue once again. In my mind, the most promising candidate, regardless of gender, was Kay Reyerson, a PhD from Yale who had studied with the distinguished medieval economic historian Robert Lopez. But the conservatives in the European section managed to find a man they liked better, and when a majority of the department voted to make an offer to Kay, the conservatives stormed out of the room in anger, slamming the door behind them. Kay, like Carla, turned out to be an outstanding addition to the department, but even then one of the professors who had opposed her appointment commented grudgingly, "We just lucked out on that one." In other words, hiring a woman meant taking a chance; if she was good, it was sheer luck.

In the fall of 1974, I became involved in a more difficult case. I had been appointed equal opportunity officer for the department and one of the cases I was watching was that of Carol Gold, an untenured faculty member in her third year at the university. No decision needed to be made yet on retaining Carol, but already some of my colleagues had decided that she did not meet department standards. One of my feminist friends told me once that the first women to break barriers were usually so much better than the men they competed with that they could not be denied. But, she warned, the going gets tougher when average women compete with average men. Carla Philips and Kay Reyerson had been exceptional candidates. Carol Gold was simply a competent historian— as good as most of her male colleagues but not a superstar. She had not yet completed her dissertation, and while her pace was slow, it was not unprecedented. In the past, the department had waited five years before using an uncompleted dissertation as a cause for termination. Nevertheless, the Committee on Promotion, Merit, and Tenure (PMT), now back in the hands of the conservatives, recommended that she be terminated after her third year.

I suspected that the decision was not made solely on academic grounds. Unlike Carla and Kay, who were dignified and "ladylike" in their demeanor, Carol was outspoken and brash. She was completing her graduate work at the University of Wisconsin, and she was very much a product of the radical political and cultural ethos that prevailed in Madison in the late 1960s. She rubbed a lot of our more staid colleagues the wrong way. I called her adviser at Madison, who told me that her dissertation was "very imaginative but concrete social history" and that she needed only to complete an introduction and conclusion to fulfill the PhD requirement. That confirmed my belief that Carol was being terminated more for personal than for academic reasons.

I could not attend the October meeting when Carol's case was to be decided. Instead I wrote a letter to the chairman of the department that was circulated to other members. I learned later that my letter, rather than Carol herself, became the major issue at the meeting. To be sure, it was not the most tactful letter I have ever written. I said:

> I have underestimated the ability of the department of history
> to force internal confrontations. . . . Has Ms. Gold's posture as
> a dissenter within the department influenced the decision of the
> committee? Is it simply coincidental that the only recommenda-
> tions for termination that have been made in this department in
> the past decade have been handed down in the cases of individ-
> uals who have refused to play the "academic game" in the tradi-
> tional sense? And finally, and most disturbing, is the committee
> setting different standards for a woman than they would for a
> white male? . . . As equal opportunity officer of the department,
> I would certainly be forced to raise the question of possible sex
> discrimination with central administration if the recommenda-
> tion of the committee were upheld by the full department.

The vote to terminate Carol Gold was a tie, eighteen to eighteen; the chairman, Clarke Chambers, cast the deciding "no" vote and Carol was retained for another year. The PMT committee insisted that my letter had questioned its integrity, and its members resigned en masse. Gradually, most of them returned to the committee. But the chairman, Otto Pflanze, was adamant. He demanded that the department censure me and said he would no longer participate in the affairs of the department if it did not. I was not censured, but at the next meeting, I was asked to apologize. I said that I regretted the harsh tone of the letter and had not meant to question anyone's integrity. But I continued to maintain that the questions I raised were legitimate ones. Professor Pflanze considered this inadequate and he never again attended a department meeting or served on a committee. Two years later, he left the department for a position at Indiana University, where he also became editor of the *American Historical Review.* I never knew whether I drove him from the department or whether he just accepted an attractive offer.

A year later a majority of the department found Carol Gold's dissertation inadequate and she was terminated. She found another job but filed a complaint against the department charging sex discrimination. I testified on her behalf before the university's judicial committee. Ultimately, her case became part of a class action suit filed in U.S. District Court on behalf of several dozen women who alleged discriminatory treatment at the University of Minnesota in violation of federal law. Known as the *Rajender* case, after the lead plaintiff, a woman who had been denied a permanent appointment in the chemistry department, it resulted in a large out-of-court settlement in 1980. The university agreed to pay up to ten million dollars to the aggrieved parties; Carol Gold received a share of that amount. The settlement also called for a strong affirmative action policy, including an automatic preference for hiring women for faculty positions in all university departments. Ironically, this went further than what even the most radical members of the history department had ever suggested. *Rajender* finally laid the issue to rest. By the time I retired in 2000, more than a third of the members of the history faculty were women and today the number approaches 50 percent.

After the Carol Gold case, I more or less withdrew from the affairs of the history department. I had enough battles to fight at the legislature, in the political arena, and within the gay and lesbian movement. I didn't need the intense and highly personal kind of conflict that I had been so often involved in at the university. What made it particularly discouraging was that my principal antagonists were not a fading old guard; they were men of about my age who would be at the university as long as I would be. I was willing to fight battles for things that really mattered. But increasingly, the issues at the university seemed less important to me than the other causes I had taken on. I was reminded of the cynical remark that "academic politics are so bitter because the stakes are so low." Consequently I took on few committee assignments, attended department meetings sporadically, and did only what I had to do to meet my responsibilities to my students. I continued to maintain a few friends in the department, such as Stuart Schwartz and Allen Isaacman, but I rarely saw my other colleagues socially. Obviously all these factors affected the choices I made about my career. When, from time to time over the next couple of decades, I thought of not seeking reelection to the legislature, the prospect of returning full time to the history department helped deter me.

The 1974 elections were relatively uneventful in Minnesota. Governor Anderson was easily reelected and the DFL, benefiting from the Watergate scandal and the resignation of Richard Nixon, increased its already hefty margin in the state House of Representatives. In the Senate, where we enjoyed four-year terms, we watched from the sidelines. But the election that most intrigued me occurred far from Minnesota. I read with great interest of the election of Elaine Noble, an open lesbian, to the Massachusetts House of Representatives. Elaine was the first openly gay person to be elected to a state office anywhere in the country, and from the accounts I read in the gay press, her district was similar to mine. She represented inner-city Boston and her constituents were a mix of university students, senior citizens, and working-class people in fading neighborhoods. I had not yet met Elaine, but her example inspired me. If I did come out, I would have company, even though she would be a thousand miles away.

On Thanksgiving weekend of 1974, I went to New York to speak at the conference of a new national gay organization, the Gay Academic Union. Howard Brown invited me to have Thanksgiving dinner with him and several of his friends and to spend part of the weekend at his townhouse in Greenwich Village. The conference itself was held at New York University on Washington Square, and unlike the gay caucuses that later emerged in the various academic professional organizations, it focused not on empirical scholarship but on theories and ideas about gay liberation. I spoke about my own experiences and how I thought gay people needed to relate to electoral politics. Most of the participants were more radical than I was, and some of the presentations I found downright silly. I remember one speaker, a man, who maintained that a male erection, whatever the context, was an act of violence against women, and that if gay men wanted to develop coalitions with women they would have to learn to have sex without having erections. I was also shocked when Howard Brown, whom I considered a true hero of the gay movement, got up to speak and was greeted with scattered boos. He was obviously too main-stream for some of this group. In fact, the most rewarding part of the weekend was seeing Howard again and having long discussions with him and some of his friends. In the struggle that was going on in my own mind about coming out, nothing was more encouraging than seeing stable, successful professional gay men who were open about their sexuality.

When I returned from New York, I had a long discussion with Steve Endean. Many of the things that had happened over the past three years had been beyond my control. But one thing that still was in my control was the timing and circumstances of my coming out. If I waited too long, I might lose control of that, too. More and more people knew that I was gay. In the next election cycle, if not before, someone was sure to ask me about it publicly and it might not be in a situation that would allow me to present my sexual orientation in a positive way. If my major concern was not to be pigeonholed as a "gay senator," timing was also important. I had now been in the Sen-ate long enough to have established myself as a multi-issue person. I had carried labor legislation and prison reform legislation, worked on Indian affairs, and even carried a major bill involving the singularly heterosexual matter of divorce. And my next election was still far enough in the future that my coming out would not likely dominate it. Most important, I was personally ready to do it. I had crossed the barrier with my parents a year before. Now my friendship with How-ard Brown and the example of Elaine Noble had convinced me that I would not be marginalized by coming out. Steve was delighted with my decision. I picked up the phone and called Deborah Howell at the *Minneapolis Star*. We made an appointment for lunch at a downtown Minneapolis restaurant called the Normandy Village on December 5.

I thought the interview went very well. Deborah knew enough about the issue to ask the right questions and she learned what she needed to know about me in a relatively brief period of time. When we were finished, she said, "I'm going to offer you something I've never before offered the subject of an interview—a chance to read what I've written before it's published. That violates normal journalistic practice, but this is a special case and I want to get it right." When I did read her draft, I found nothing I wanted her to change. I asked her when the story would appear. She said that it would be the following Monday, December 9. Then I asked her where in the newspaper it was likely to appear. There was a brief pause before she said, "Oh, you've got to be kidding. On the front page, of course."

Minneapolis still had two newspapers in 1974. They were both owned by the same company and operated out of the same building, but they had separate staffs and nominally competed against each other. The *Tribune* came out in the morning, the *Star* in the afternoon. On Monday, I asked a number of my friends to come to my house around noon, when the *Star* hit the street. I knew that I would be getting a lot of phone calls, I had no way of judging what the range of reaction would be, and I needed moral support. Steve Endean, Mark Snyder, the Greenfields, and the Goldsteins all came. Someone brought a *Star,* hot off the press. There just under the fold on the first page was the bold black headline: "State Sen. Allan Spear Declares He's Homosexual." Even with all of my careful preparation, seeing those words in that place sent shivers up my spine.

The story itself, however, portrayed me in a wholly positive manner. It began:

Allan Spear is a 37-year-old freshman member of the Minnesota Senate, a DFLer.

Allan Spear is an associate professor of history at the University of Minnesota, a respected specialist in Afro-American history.

Allan Spear has a doctorate degree from Yale University and has written a book on the making of the Chicago black ghetto.

Allan Spear has long been active in DFL, civil rights and peace causes and ranked as the most liberal state senator in an Americans for Democratic Action survey.

Allan Spear also is a homosexual.

And, as of today, he doesn't care who knows it.

Deborah then went on to explain why I had chosen to come out. She gave three reasons: (1) I no longer wanted my homosexuality to be whispered about; (2) I wanted to be able to speak as a gay person on gay rights issues without any ambivalence; and (3) I wanted to be a role model, to let other gay people know that they can succeed in teaching and politics even in the American heartland and not just in San Francisco and Greenwich Village. She also discussed my fear that being openly gay would overshadow the other things I did and what impact it might have on my constituents. "I think that most of the people in my district," I said, "are concerned with issues and my performance as a senator. . . . I have served the district as well as I can. Primarily I am a representative of the district. Quite secondarily, I am a spokesman for gay rights." After summing up the various steps I went through before deciding to come out, the story ended with a quotation that all of my friends had heard many times: "[For years] I've been trying to do something about everybody else's oppression. It took me a long time to realize I'd been oppressed by society's attitude and now I want to do something about it."

The telephone rang all afternoon and evening. I received only one hostile call, from an elderly constituent who had voted for me and now felt hurt and betrayed. Otherwise the calls were wholly supportive—many from friends, of course, but others from people I didn't know, both gay and straight, who congratulated me for my courage and wished me the best. The next day, I started receiving letters and telegrams from all over the country. What I hadn't realized, even after Deborah Howell had assured me that I would be coming out on the front page, was that my story would be national news. But the wire services picked up the article and short versions of it appeared everywhere, from prestigious journals like the *New York Times* and the *Los Angeles Times* to small-town papers that ran the Associated Press release. There was even a piece in the German newsmagazine *Der Spiegel.* Hastily, I called relatives in other parts of the country so that they would hear the news from me before they read about it in their local papers. My parents knew, of course, but I was sure that they had not spread the word to other family members, and I did not want any of my aging aunts and uncles to die of shock.

The mail I received over the next several weeks included every possible kind of reaction. National gay leaders such as Howard Brown and Troy Perry wrote warm and encouraging letters. There were moving messages from less visible gay people who applauded me for my courage and expressed the hope that someday they would be able to do what I had done. "Whatever the consequence," wrote a man in Pittsburgh, "you've given gay people a sense of tremendous pride, relief and involvement." A man in San Francisco wrote that "it will be of use to all of the young brothers still in their parents' homes to see that for one man being gay is not the nightmarish toothache, compulsive and desperate, only to be played out in the shadows with eyes and heart closed." Several parents of gay children wrote to tell me that the example I had set was a great comfort and encouragement to them. An old friend from graduate school, whom I had not seen in years, sent a congratulatory telegram and commented on "those bittersweet Yale days [when] we talked . . . and never heard one another." Many of the local DFL politicians, including the governor, pledged their continuing support for my career, and even a few Republicans sent good wishes. There were predictable responses from the other side as well. Most of the negative letters came from conservative Christians who predicted a dire fate for me on judgment day. Some of them had read about me in an evangelical paper called *The Sword of the Lord,* which headlined its item "Depravity at the Top!" and described with horror how a state senator had "announced to the world that he is a pervert." I received numerous copies of a little illustrated religious tract called *The Gay Blade,* which warned of the biblical admonitions against homosexuality and implored gay people to mend their ways before it was too late. These messages, of course, went unanswered, but I replied to everyone who had responded positively and carefully kept a list of the names and addresses of those who might be potential contributors to my 1976 reelection campaign.

I was most interested in how my colleagues in the Senate would react. I had called my closest allies—Bob Lewis, Steve Keefe, John Milton—before the *Star* story had appeared and knew that they would be supportive. And, of course, Nick Coleman had himself been involved in the coming-out process. But when I attended a DFL Senate caucus a few days later, most of my colleagues said nothing. It was obviously not an issue that they were comfortable discussing. I learned that at a meeting of the DFL caucus steering committee, Baldy Hanson had offered a resolution appropriating a hundred dollars to any member of the caucus who was a homosexual so that he could go to a psychiatrist and get cured. Nick Coleman shut him up and quickly moved to the next item on the agenda. When I heard this story, my reaction was, "What a cheapskate! You can't even get into a psychiatrist's door for a hundred dollars." And a few weeks later, Florian Chmielewski wrote a letter to the *Duluth News Tribune* calling my coming out "a maneuver on behalf of secular humanism, a religion which denies the existence of God and glorifies pleasure." My announcement, he warned, "should sound the alarm to every Minnesota citizen who believes in maintaining our Judeo-Christian ethics."

I was determined that these isolated expressions of hostility were not going to discourage me. I was wholly comfortable with what I had done and felt better about myself than I ever had in my life. I would never again have to be ambivalent about who I was. I was now proudly and affirmatively gay.

9

THE FIRST STRUGGLE FOR GAY RIGHTS, 1975-1978

I returned to the legislature in January 1975, prepared to play a more open role in the effort to pass gay rights legislation. Steve Endean and I, however, decided that it would still be best strategically for Nick Coleman to be the chief author of the human rights bill. For me to take over the bill now would give credibility to the very idea I was hoping to dispel—that I would become simply the "gay senator." Moreover, as majority leader, Nick gave the issue a legitimacy that it still sorely needed. In the House, the chief author would be John Tomlinson, an able and respected legislator from St. Paul, who seemed totally committed to the issue. Both Nick and John were willing to let Steve and me call the shots. We planned the strategy, did the lobbying, and advised them on their presentations. Even though I was not chief author of the bill, I was deeply involved in every step this time as I had not been two years earlier. With our successes in Minneapolis and St. Paul behind us and with a gay rights organization in place, Steve and I thought we had a good chance of becoming the first state in the country to pass gay rights legislation.

The session had just begun when I received distressing news. Howard Brown, who had done so much to inspire my decision to come out, had died suddenly at the age of fifty. I had known that Howard had serious heart disease but assumed it was under control. One day, however, friends arriving at his town house for a dinner party found that he had died in his sleep the previous night. I accepted the invitation to come to New York to speak at the memorial service that was held for him on February 17. I spoke warmly about a man whom I had known for less than a year but whom I had come to consider a trusted friend. He was the first accomplished professional person I had ever met who was openly gay, and his example helped convince me that coming out would not limit my career. I told Howard's friends at the service that in the manuscript for his forthcoming book he had referred to me by the pseudonym "John Brainerd." But now, in part because of Howard, "John Brainerd" no longer existed; I could proudly be Allan Spear. At the reception after the service I met many of the prominent people, both gay and straight, who had been part of Howard's circle—Congressman (and future mayor) Ed Koch, the historian Martin Duberman, and Los Angeles gay activist Morris Kight. Morris invited me to be the grand marshal of the gay pride parade in Los Angeles that summer, an honor that I readily accepted.

I had thought that in New York I would meet the other person who had directly affected my decision to come out. Representative Elaine Noble had been invited to join me in speaking at the Howard Brown memorial, but she had not been able to make it. I met her, however, the next month at a Midwest conference of the Gay Academic Union in Ann Arbor, Michigan. I will never forget my first encounter with Elaine. I had left Minneapolis late on a Friday afternoon, going directly from my office to the airport, and when I arrived I was taken to the lecture hall on the University of Michigan campus just in time for the evening session of the conference. I walked in wearing the same dark suit, white shirt, and tie I had been wearing all day and confronted an audience that did not appear to know that the sixties had ended. Ann Arbor was still a center for student radicalism and the counterculture, and the scruffy young people in the auditorium included a sizable contingent of men dressed in what was commonly referred to as "genderfuck." These men were wearing women's clothes, but unlike drag queens, they made no pretense of looking like women; dresses were often combined with beards and conspicuously hairy chests. I knew immediately that my remarks, including my usual emphasis on the need to work within the mainstream in order to win a seat at the table, would not go over well with this crowd. When I told them that they would need to change their appearance before they could effectively lobby legislators, they began to boo me.

I was the first speaker of the evening and was followed by Elaine Noble. She wasted no time. She picked up the portable microphone, walked to the edge of the stage, and looked directly at the men in "genderfuck." Pointing the microphone at them, she said, "If any of you motherfuckers boo me, you're going to get this right up your ass." She then went on to give a speech with a message very similar to mine. But there was not a peep out of the audience. Afterward, Elaine told me that she had had a lot of experience in Boston confronting the militant wing of the gay movement and that she had little tolerance for their disruptive tactics. Over the next several years, Elaine and I were in frequent contact, sharing experiences with one another, and both of us faced problems in dealing with those within our own community who saw us as "sellouts" to the establishment. Elaine stayed in the Massachusetts legislature for only four years. When she left in 1978, a difficult redistricting contributed to her decision. But she also told me that she was "quite confused about all the shit I must take from the local crazy gay people." She added, "I don't have to tell you that—you have your own gay nuts out there." Elaine Noble was an important pioneer in the history of the gay movement, and I regret that she did not receive the respect that she deserved. She was an important source of support for me in the days just after I came out.

My confrontation with our own "gay nuts" came soon enough. In preparation for our legislative effort, the Minnesota Committee for Gay Rights (MCGR) held a number of meetings early in 1975 to involve the gay and lesbian community in our activities. It became immediately clear that we had an internal fight on our hands. Tim Campbell insisted that any bill we introduced include as part of the definition of the protected category the words "having or projecting a self-image not associated with masculinity or femininity." This language, he said, was necessary in order to include transvestites and transsexuals and also those he referred to as "obvious gays"—people "who would have difficulty passing for straight." Steve Endean and I, after consulting with our authors, concluded that including language of this type would doom the bill. Passage of gay rights in any form in 1975 was an uphill battle. An attempt to include transgender people, as they would later be called, using language that was subject to varying interpretations, would make that battle impossible to win. I asked Tim and his allies, who included a number of transgender people, to help us pass a basic bill first and then, I promised, I would come back in another year or two to try to make the bill more inclusive. That offer was rejected and Tim hastily organized a new group to counter MCGR, which he called the Coalition of Concerned Gays and which included among its members Jack Baker and Mike McConnell and a particularly fervid young man named Thom Higgins.

The bill had its first hearing in the House Judiciary Committee in late March. In his presentation, John Tomlinson tried to anticipate the opposition from both directions—from those who opposed any legal protection for gay and lesbian people and from those within the gay community who thought the bill was too narrow in its scope. He pointed to the precedents that had been established in Minneapolis and St. Paul; although the ordinances in Minnesota's two largest cities were still relatively new, they were working well and there had been no barrage of frivolous cases. Moreover, many of the state's largest private corporations had adopted policies forbidding discrimination on the basis of sexual orientation without negative consequences. The problem, Tomlinson emphasized, was a real one. A national survey had indicated that 9 percent of gay people had lost a job at one time or another once their employer learned of their homosexuality. Why, he asked, was this any different from a person losing a job because of age or race or sex? "People should be judged on their individual merits, not lumped together into a group. If a person does poor work, he should be fired, but not because he is old, black, or gay." As for transvestites and transsexuals, Tomlinson argued that the bill protected them if they were discriminated against simply on the basis of their identity. But it would not preclude an employer from establishing dress codes requiring men to wear men's clothing and women to wear women's clothing while at work.

We had arranged for a strong lineup of witnesses that included psychologists, clergy, parents of gays, and civil rights leaders. The opponents were heavily weighted toward religious fundamentalists who viewed homosexuality as a violation of biblical law. Tim Campbell then testified in favor of his amendment and argued that without it, the bill would have a major loophole and bring relief only to middle-class white gays who could pass as straight. Tomlinson opposed it and said that while no one should lose a job for cross-dressing outside the workplace, cross-dressing on the job "would be very disturbing to the atmosphere and relationships at work." Thom Higgins then testified about the rights of gay people to marry and adopt children and the need for compulsory gay sex education in the schools. These were exactly the issues we were hoping to avoid, and Steve Endean and I could see our support melting away. The committee adjourned without voting on the bill, but we were no longer certain that we had the votes to pass it out. Steve Endean met over the next several days with committee members to assess our support. We now had to assure nervous members that the bill did not in fact do what Campbell and Higgins wanted it to do, and to make that perfectly clear, we agreed to an amendment that would completely remove references to public accommodations and services, limiting the bill's coverage to employment, housing, credit, and educational opportunities. With that compromise, the charges of "sellout" from Campbell's contingency intensified.

Before the second hearing, in early April, Tim Campbell called a press conference in the men's room adjacent to the House chamber. There he denounced the House leadership, MCGR, Endean, Tomlinson, me, and everyone associated with the bill for selling out the gay community. Meanwhile, several of his transvestite allies invaded the women's room, insisting on their right to be there and terrorizing some of the female legislative staff members. Finally, Tim chained himself to a railing in the Capitol and announced that he would go on a hunger strike to protest what was being done to the bill. Many of these tactics were, I think, dreamed up by Thom Higgins. Campbell, although a militant, was a man of serious demeanor who always presented his ideas earnestly. Higgins, on the other hand, saw politics as street theater and seemed more interested in simply stirring things up than in long-range consequences.

At the next hearing, the militants tried to disrupt the proceedings, and Capitol security was forced to remove them from the room. The bill passed out of committee in its amended form, on a close vote, but all the talk now at the Capitol was not about the bill itself but about the tactics of the "gay crazies" and the division within the gay community. Steve Endean and I did what we could to repair the damage. Both Minneapolis newspapers published strong editorials hailing the bill as a moderate and sensible reform and castigating the protesters for putting the future of the bill in doubt. On the national level, the *Advocate* ran an editorial in the form of a fable that spoke of the "fairy crazies [who] said that the law would have to be changed so that men could dress like ladies—all the time, if that's what men who wanted to dress like ladies wanted." On the other hand, the editor of the *St. Paul Pioneer Press* wrote that "the homosexuals always manage to live up to every stereotype we have stamped them with" and that their antics probably assured the defeat of their bill.

Most of the action on the gay rights bill in 1975 occurred on the House side. We had a much larger DFL majority in the House than we did in the Senate and thought we could pass it there first and create momentum. But it didn't turn out that way. When we finally had a hearing in the Senate Judiciary Committee in early May, the bill was in serious trouble in the House. The militants stayed away and we passed the bill out of committee on a very close vote of seven to five. Nick Coleman, as the chief author, presented the bill, but I was a member of the committee now, so I answered many of the members' questions. In the meantime, Tim Campbell turned his attention to the upcoming debate on the House floor. He decided that he could best embarrass the DFL liberal establishment, including Steve Endean and me, by finding a Republican to introduce his amendment to extend protection to transvestites and transsexuals. Incredibly, he found one—Arne Carlson, a liberal Republican representative from Minneapolis and future governor of Minnesota. Carlson gave a sincere and well-reasoned speech exposing many of his colleagues for the first time to the still relatively new idea that transsexuals were women trapped in men's bodies and deserved civil rights protection. But we knew that the amendment would have little support, and John Tomlinson was forced to oppose it. After it was defeated, it soon became clear that the entire bill was going down. The next amendment, offered by a conservative legislator, removed teachers and all other educational employees from the protections offered by the bill. We considered this a killer amendment, yet we did not have the votes to stop it. Even with that amendment, the bill was defeated on a vote of fifty-one to sixty-eight. Once the bill was dead in the House, Coleman had no choice but to withdraw it from consideration in the Senate.

The events of the spring left the local gay and lesbian community deeply divided and demoralized. Steve Endean never missed an opportunity to blame Tim Campbell and Thom Higgins for our defeat. I believed we would have lost the bill even if they had stayed away, but nevertheless I shared his anger at their tactics. Foolishly, I accepted a challenge from Jack Baker to debate him on a talk radio show. Jack and his partner Mike McConnell had made some effort to reconnect with me after I came out in December, even inviting me to their house for dinner. But during the session, they had been strongly supportive of Campbell and Higgins and made it clear that they blamed me and Steve for all that had gone wrong. It was a mistake on my part to take this internal dispute into a public forum, and I gained nothing from arguing with Jack on the radio. At the end of the program, he announced that he would be supporting my opponent in the 1976 election and was confident that I was going to lose. In fact, he had picked out my opponent. Steve Carter, a young straight university student, was Jack's protégé and his successor as president of the Minnesota Student Association. Jack and Thom Higgins were already plotting a campaign against me modeled on Jack's successful campaigns for MSA president.

Despite my deep involvement in the gay rights bill, I continued my interest in a wide range of legislative issues. I began work in 1975 on two projects that would occupy much of my time and energy for the remainder of the decade: bilingual and bicultural education and reform of the parole system. Both grew out of long-standing concerns that preceded my election to the legislature.

My entire view of American history had been shaped by my belief in the multicultural nature of American society, and I had always rejected the notion, often expressed through the image of the melting pot, that minority cultures needed to assimilate in order to be truly American. I much preferred the social historian Carl Degler's metaphor of the salad bowl—each ingredient could maintain its integrity even as it was mixed together. The bilingual and bicultural education bill that I introduced in 1975 reflected that view. It had been developed by the Minnesota Department of Education and was intended primarily for the Hispanic and American Indian communities, both of which experienced distressingly high dropout rates in the public school system, in some areas as high as 40 percent. The bill would establish ten pilot programs scattered throughout the state. Four would be bilingual, intended for children with limited English-speaking ability, who at that time in Minnesota were primarily Hispanic. Instruction would be in both Spanish and English, and instead of being suddenly immersed in a language they did not comprehend, students would be gradually taught English language skills while at the same time learning about their own language and culture. The other six pilot programs would be for American Indians, for whom the problems were not primarily linguistic. Here the goal would be to make the curriculum more relevant to Dakota and Ojibwe cultures and enhance the self-identity and self-esteem of Indian youngsters. I did not see the bill as separatist. Ultimately, both Hispanic and Indian children would have to become skilled in English and learn how to function in a white Anglo-majority

American society. But I did not think this reality required them to give up their own cultural legacies.

When I started working on this bill, I believed it had broad support. The governor had included funding for the pilot programs in his budget. There had been considerable input from the Indian and Hispanic communities, as well as the educational establishment. And a recent U.S. Supreme Court decision had ordered the San Francisco school system to provide equal educational opportunities for children without basic English language skills. But I soon ran into difficulties on two fronts. First, there was a rift in the always-divided Minnesota Indian community. Indian educators had, in recent years, established several alternative Indian schools outside the public school system, and they protested that my bill limited the pilot programs to public schools, hence excluding them. They came to me with their objections when we were already in the middle of the session, and I could not understand why they had not tried to shape the bill in its early stages. It was hard at that point to accommodate them and the disunity hurt the bill. At the same time, a number of my colleagues, including several prominent DFL senators, objected to the very premise of the bill. Jack Davies, usually an ally, said that "the bill sounded like the native American and Chicano communities were trying to preserve their separateness instead of trying to overcome the handicaps of a separate culture." I knew I would have trouble when even liberals saw separate culture as a handicap. While the bill passed out of the Education Committee, it ran into strong opposition in the Senate Finance Committee. Even after we had trimmed the funding and reduced the bill from ten to five pilot programs, it was defeated in a Senate Finance subcommittee. It would take me two more years to pass the bill.

I had taken on a new committee assignment in 1975 as a member of the Judiciary Committee. In part, I wanted to be closer to the action on gay rights, abortion, and the wide range of civil rights and civil liberties issues that had always engaged my interest. But I had also come to realize that the most important criminal justice issues were determined in that committee. In the Health, Welfare, and Corrections Committee, we dealt with prisons (or the back end of the system, as it was sometimes called) but not with the process that took people there. Law enforcement, courts, and sentencing were all in the jurisdiction of the Judiciary Committee. I became particularly immersed in the issues of sentencing and parole. Like most states at the time, Minnesota had an indeterminate sentencing system in which the statutes established only the broadest parameters (e.g., five to twenty years) and judges had wide discretion. This led to disparities among individual judges and regions of the state and, most disturbingly, disparities that seemed to be based on the race and economic status of the defendant. Moreover, the parole system made the sentences themselves virtually meaningless. A defendant might be sentenced to "up to twenty years," but the parole board could let him out whenever it thought he was ready to rejoin society. And that judgment was very difficult to make.

I visited the prisons frequently in my early years in the legislature, and while I remained a bit too credulous in accepting stories told to me by inmates, I did gradually develop a more realistic understanding of the system. I was particularly appalled by what I saw when I sat in on parole board meetings, which my status as a legislator permitted me to do. The parole board was made up of citizens appointed by the governor, a few of whom had criminal justice experience but most of whom did not. They were part-time appointees and had far more cases to hear than they could adequately handle. Although well meaning, they had no real guidelines for their decisions. Often, they acted on hunches. An articulate inmate who had joined a number of rehabilitative programs while in prison could easily snow them. A timid or frightened inmate might appear hostile and would be rejected even though he could be a good risk. I came to believe that there had to be a better way.

The impetus for reforming the indeterminate sentencing and parole system came from all over the political spectrum. Conservatives thought the parole board was too soft, and when a parolee committed a new crime, the board was castigated for its woolly-headedness. Liberals like me disliked the lack of uniformity and due process and the seeming capriciousness of the system. Moreover, we thought it discriminated against the poor, the less educated, and the nonwhite. We all were drawn to what criminologists at the time referred to as the "justice model," which centered on determinate sentencing. Nationally, its leading advocate was a University of Chicago professor named Norval Morris. In Minnesota, it was supported by David Ward, a sociologist at the University of Minnesota. Morris came to Minnesota to speak and Ward was a frequent visitor at our committee meetings.

They both argued that it was time to scrap the "rehabilitative model" that had dominated the American criminal justice system since the turn of the century. A progressive idea based on the concept that criminality was like a disease that could be cured, it simply hadn't worked. Instead, they argued, offenders should receive and serve like sentences for like offenses, with consideration given to prior criminal histories. Their punishment, in other words, should fit their crime and their past behavior, but not their record in prison or their perceived readiness to rejoin society. This could best be done by establishing fixed sentences or at least guidelines for each crime and abolishing the current system of parole. This would obviously be a big change for Minnesota that could not be accomplished in one session. Senator Jack Davies appointed a committee to study the issue and I was one of its members. It became one of my major issues over the next several years.

While bicultural education and criminal sentencing policy represented the kind of broad, challenging issues that drew me and kept me in the legislature, I also came to realize that they were not necessarily the keys to being reelected. The legislature was a very parochial place. Each senator represented about seventy thousand people and wanted to know how everything the Senate did affected those people. There were hundreds of local bills every session that were of intense interest to a few people in a single district but didn't matter much to anyone else. While this was certainly the way representative democracy was supposed to work, it also had a definite downside. It was often difficult to develop policies that might be good for the state as a whole if they required short-time losses for particular constituencies. In the 1970s, for example, we had too many state hospitals for the mentally ill and the mentally retarded, but it was a struggle each time we tried to shut one down as it meant a loss of jobs in the neighboring community. On the other hand, we built colleges in remote parts of the state that were represented by powerful legislators but never attracted a student body large enough to sustain them.

I tried to avoid that kind of parochialism as much as I could and, in fact, was sometimes criticized by local officials for not doing enough for Minneapolis. I believed that my constituents were smart enough to want me to keep my eyes on the long-term needs of the state and not just "bring home the bacon." Yet many of them lived in vulnerable neighborhoods and had needs, too, and if I were to represent them well I had to look after those local concerns. Two neighborhood issues occupied a good deal of my energy in the early seventies, and a third one emerged in the middle of the decade.

The first involved the interface between the University of Minnesota and its surrounding community. The university was continually expanding, often buying up residential property and holding it for several years while it developed its plans for the area. It could be a difficult landlord and rarely consulted with the increasingly assertive neighborhood associations. I tried to intervene on several occasions with the university's vice president in charge of the physical plant, but he simply brushed me aside. I came up with a tactic to at least get his attention. High on the university's legislative priority list was funding for a new law school. I had no doubt that this was a real need and I had no quarrel with the proposed location. But I knew the vote in the Senate would be close as a lot of money was involved, and I also realized that, given my connection to the university, my opposition to the new school was likely to sway a number of my colleagues. So when the measure reached the Senate floor, I argued that it needed further study and moved to delete it from the larger bill of which it was a part. My motion prevailed and the Senate version of the bill went to a conference committee without funding for the law school; the House version was still intact, so the proposal was by no means dead. Within the next few days, I was deluged with messages from the university asking me how I could have done such a thing. I replied that I wanted the bill to mandate a land use plan for the Minneapolis campus developed with neighborhood input that would guide university expansion. With that provision, I would withdraw my opposition to the law school. In the end, I got the land use plan and the university got the law school.

The second issue involved a freeway through northeast Minneapolis. Most of the interstate highway system through the Twin Cities had been completed by the time I went to the legislature. Its impact had been devastating on many communities. Interstate 35W tore south Minneapolis in half while I-94 destroyed the venerable, predominantly black Rondo-Dale community in St. Paul. Affluent, well-educated neighborhoods had learned to fight the system; Prospect Park, in my district, had succeeded in changing the route of I-94 and preserving the heart of the community. But once-stable working-class neighborhoods were severely damaged by broad highways running directly through them.

In the 1970s, highway officials in Washington and St. Paul wanted to build one last link—a short freeway designated I-335 that would link I-35 in northeast Minneapolis with I-94 in north Minneapolis. Designed as a bypass of downtown Minneapolis, it would require an expensive new bridge across the Mississippi, wipe out a large swath of northeast Minneapolis, and be of no benefit to the people who lived there. Although much of the land had already been acquired, a determined group of local residents came together to fight the plan. Unlike Prospect Park, lower northeast was a working-class neighborhood, and the anti-highway forces included a wide range of people— housewives, senior citizens, young people, hippies, and union members. They learned organizing skills as they went along. To their advantage, public opinion on freeways was shifting. The gasoline shortage of the early seventies raised questions about the unlimited expansion of superhighways, and a renewed interest in stable urban communities had cast freeway construction as one of the villains. I introduced a bill to place a moratorium on new freeways in the Twin Cities and found allies in St. Paul, where neighborhoods were fighting the completion of I-35E, and in south Minneapolis, where there was opposition to a freeway in the Hiawatha Avenue corridor. We passed the bill, and at the same time, Congressman Don Fraser and Senator Walter Mondale expressed their opposition to I-335 to federal officials. In the face of this opposition, plans for the freeway were dropped.

My involvement in fighting university expansion and freeway construction had won me a lot of friends in the community, including people who had never supported me before. One last neighborhood issue also helped me broaden my coalition, even though it did not have as positive a conclusion as the first two. As early as 1971, Minneapolis business interests had begun to talk about a new downtown stadium. They had never been reconciled to the decision made in the late 1950s to locate major league sports in suburban Bloomington. Moreover, Metropolitan Stadium had been built for baseball and was too small and improperly configured for football. In the spring of 1973, the Minneapolis City Council approved a plan to build a domed stadium for the Vikings in the downtown warehouse district, not far from where an open-air Twins stadium would be built thirty-four years later. I attended a meeting shortly after my election where this idea was presented by DFL city council members Lou Demars and John Derus, and much to their dismay, I sided with the vast majority of the people in the audience who objected to a public subsidy for millionaire sports team owners. The stadium would have been built, despite widespread public disapproval, had Mayor Stenvig not vetoed the proposal. Antistadium forces then collected enough signatures to force a referendum on a city charter amendment requiring public approval for any project costing more than $15 million. When that provision passed in June of 1973, it ended any possibility that the city of Minneapolis could fund a new stadium.

Stadium proponents now turned their attention to the legislature. Between 1975 and 1979, every legislative session included a struggle over whether to build a stadium and where to build it. The idea of a football-only stadium gave way to proposals for a multiuse stadium that could accommodate both the Vikings and the Twins. And the Minneapolis warehouse district location gave way to a plan to build the stadium in Industry Square, an underutilized stretch of land adjacent to two active neighborhoods in my district, Elliot Park and Cedar-Riverside. Bloomington meanwhile intensified its efforts to keep the teams, either in a new suburban stadium or in a remodeled Metropolitan Stadium, and the Twins and Vikings upped the ante with periodic threats to move their franchises to other cities. I stood with my neighborhood groups in opposing a stadium in Industry Square. While I had general philosophical opposition to this kind of public subsidy for private enterprise, regardless of location, I sometimes found myself in an alliance of convenience with the Bloomington Chamber of Commerce. For the first couple of years, we managed to defeat various stadium proposals. But by the latter years of the decade, we found ourselves battling an unstoppable force.

Within a few days after the end of the 1975 legislative session, I was off on the most ambitious trip I had ever taken. Several months before, I had been approached by Fred Ptashne, one of the old left-wingers I had met during the McCarthy campaign, and asked if I were interested in going to China. Fred and his wife, Millie, once friends of the Soviet Union, had now become starry-eyed about Maoist China and were among the first Americans to travel there after Nixon's visit in 1972. China was not yet open to commercial American tourism, but the U.S.–China Peoples Friendship Association, in which the Ptashnes were active, organized "friendship tours" and sent select "delegations" to see the myriad achievements of the new China. A Midwest delegation would be going in May, and they hoped that I would be part of it. I readily accepted.

For three weeks, twenty-two of us toured China, visiting Beijing, Changsha, Guilin, Guangzhou, and Shanghai. It was a fascinating trip and when I compare the China that I saw in 1975 with what tourists see today I realize how dramatically the country has changed. China was in the last stages of the Cultural Revolution, Mao was still alive (although in very poor health), and most Chinese led drab lives, dressed in blue or gray "Mao" suits, lived in dilapidated housing, and crowded the streets with bicycles. Consumer goods were scarce and expensive, and no ordinary Chinese owned an automobile. We saw some of the standard "sights" of China—the Great Wall, the Ming tombs, the Forbidden City—and none of them disappointed. But much of the tour was devoted to visiting social and cultural institutions. We were taken to communes, collective farms, hospitals, child-care centers, schools, factories, and housing projects. Some of this was interesting, but after a while it began to wear thin. The places we were taken, while genuine enough, were clearly selected to make good impressions on foreign visitors. The routine was usually the same. We toured the facilities, then sat down for tea while the "responsible person" answered our questions with pat and well-rehearsed answers. Then we were entertained by singing and dancing children who were cute and endearing but also well rehearsed and who always ended their performance waving Chinese and American flags and singing to our enduring friendship.

Fortunately, our group included several people who spoke Chinese well, and with their help we were able to do some things on our own. I roomed with Ted Farmer, my University of Minnesota colleague in Chinese history, who was making his first trip to the Chinese mainland. Ted, Marilyn Young, another Chinese historian, and I would often get up early in the morning, before our first organized activity, and go out and talk to people on the streets. The Chinese we met were as curious about us as we were about them. Especially in Changsha and Guilin, where Western visitors were rare, we were stared at and often surrounded by locals. I was particularly amused one day as I tried to take a picture of a Chinese family without being observed and noticed one of them surreptitiously taking a picture of me. No one we talked to complained about the regime, so I am not sure why the officials tried to keep us under such tight reins. But our guides clearly did not like us being out on our own and tried to discourage it. They also resented our taking pictures of what they called "the old China"— people plowing fields with water buffalo or carrying burdens on bamboo sticks, for example. They couldn't seem to understand why that seemed more picturesque to us than the model housing projects that they showed us with such pride.

In the end, I came back with mixed feelings about China. Much of the countryside was beautiful; in fact, the sugarloaf mountains around Guilin are among the loveliest places I have ever been in the world. The cities, though dilapidated, were vibrant and the street life was exciting. The food, even at the hotels where we ate most of our meals, was far better than the Chinese American food I was used to. And the people were enormously hardworking and resourceful. But the representatives of the regime that we met—the "responsible people" at the various institutions, our guides, the tourist officials—seemed distrustful both of us and of their own people. Moreover, although the people we met were not the regimented "blue ants" that cold war America had taught us to expect, what we learned about cadre schools and reeducation was chilling to anyone who valued human freedom. We felt certain that vast changes lay ahead, especially as the Chinese had increasing contact with the consumer culture of Japan and the West, but none of us could have foreseen the capitalist explosion that transformed China over the next generation. In any case, the Minnesotans in our group were all in great demand as speakers over the next several months. Travel to China in 1975 was still unusual and everyone wanted to hear about it. So I put together a slide show, donned the Mao jacket and cap I had bought at Shanghai's Number One Department Store, and shared my impressions with church groups, schools, and whoever else wanted a glimpse behind the bamboo curtain. It was a welcome change from talking about gay rights.

For three weeks in China, questions of sexuality were laid aside. I told my traveling companions that I was gay, but saw little point in raising the issue with the Chinese. The one occasion when it came up in a discussion, a woman in Shanghai told us that homosexuality was so unheard of in the new China that young people didn't even know the meaning of the word. From this world of denial I plunged directly back into the heart of gay America. After a few days of rest in Honolulu, I went on to California, where I had agreed to be the grand marshal at the Los Angeles gay pride parade. First, I met Steve Endean, who was vacationing in San Francisco, and was introduced to his gay activist friends there. Jim Foster, the founder of the Alice B. Toklas Memorial Democratic Club, the core of San Francisco's gay political establishment, invited me to his house for dinner; there I also met Bill Kraus, a major community leader until his death of AIDS in the early 1980s. Jim and Bill listened empathetically as Steve and I told them how Tim Campbell and Thom Higgins had undermined our efforts to pass gay rights legislation. They had their own struggle in San Francisco, they told us, with a relative newcomer to the city who was trying to get elected to the Board of Supervisors, San Francisco's city council. He wanted everything at once, and if he were elected, they believed, he would undermine the incremental progress they had made with years of hard work. His name was Harvey Milk. That was the first time I had ever heard of him.

Steve also introduced me to George Raya, who lobbied on gay issues at the California legislature. George suggested that we go with him to Sacramento to see the legislature at work. He had just succeeded in securing the repeal of California's consensual sex laws, the first such repeal that was not part of a general revision of the criminal code. We spent the day with him visiting both houses and I was introduced on the floor as a distinguished out-of-state guest. Then I headed to Southern California and met Mark Snyder, who was in Los Angeles visiting Dick Hanson. Dick had sold his hillside house and bought a condo in West Hollywood, and we both stayed with him for a few days.

My schedule for gay pride weekend was tightly packed. On Saturday, I drove to San Diego, where I was the featured speaker at the first gay parade and rally ever held in that rather conservative city. The next day, back in Los Angeles, we went first to the Metropolitan Community Church for a special service celebrating the repeal of the consensual sex laws. Troy Perry managed to make a Sunday worship service an occasion of high drama. The gay pride parade or, as it was officially called, Christopher Street West, was held in the afternoon. I asked Mark to ride in the parade with me as I knew it would be a bit overwhelming. And it was. Unlike San Diego, where the crowds were sparse, Hollywood Boulevard was jam-packed with spectators on both sides. I rode in my own open car with my name on the side; in front of my car and behind it were floats carrying drag queens from what were called the "imperial courts." I was greeted with cheers and applause—and a few catcalls from antigay hecklers—when the crowds realized that I was an openly gay elected official, something that California did not yet have. After the parade, I spoke about my coming-out experience and the importance of gay political involvement. In all, it was a heady experience. But I soon heard from my mother about it. She had talked to her sister—the same one whom I had called a racist thirteen years before—who now lived in Los Angeles and she had made a point of telling my mother that she had seen me on television in a parade with a bunch of drag queens.

Back in Minneapolis, my life was not quite as exciting. Once again I struggled with the gap between my public and private lives. As a public figure, I was riding high. My coming out had gone according to plan and I seemed politically secure. I was comfortable in my position as an openly gay elected official and welcomed the national attention that I was receiving. A cover story in *Time* magazine on gay America in the late summer featured me prominently. And I continued to be a respected figure in the liberal community in Minnesota as I had been before I came out. Yet I had very little success in finding a compatible partner. Gay mythology would have it that the 1970s, just before the AIDS epidemic, was a time of unbridled promiscuity and endless sex. It was for some gay men. But it wasn't for me. I was no longer young and I had never been physically attractive, so sex did not come easily. Moreover, promiscuity was not what I was looking for. Yes, I would have liked more sex than I was having. But I was really a monogamist at heart. I was looking for someone with whom I could settle in, someone who would share my life.

I had several relationships in 1975 and 1976, but none of them lasted very long. Each was instructive in its way. One taught me what it was like to be the pursued rather than the pursuer. Usually, I was the one trying to attract a younger man. But in this case, an older man was very much interested in me, and although he was intelligent and kind and tried very hard to please me, I was not attracted to him and was soon bored with the attention he lavished on me. I understood all too well the hurt he felt when he finally realized I had rejected him. The other relationships were with younger men who ultimately dropped me. One was much too young for me. Both of us were embarrassed when I took him to a legislative reception and a lobbyist asked me if he was my son. "Mr. Right" remained elusive. I continued to go to the bars from time to time, but I did not usually enjoy myself and I almost always went home alone.

The year ended with another trip overseas. After Al Jones left Minnesota, he did not succeed in finding another tenure-track academic position. He taught for a year at Iowa State and then took a job with the United States Information Agency (USIA). Following several months of training in Washington, he was, to his delight, assigned to the American embassy in Paris. He and Bonnie suggested that I come to visit them over the holidays and meet their new baby. So after I submitted my grades for fall quarter I headed for Paris. Once again, I found myself in love with French food. Al and Bonnie lived on a market street, and it was wonderful to shop with her at the various specialty shops and cook dinner together. I had never been to Europe during the winter before and was intrigued by the availability of game—the whole birds and rabbits hanging from the ceilings of the meat markets. After a week in Paris, I took the train to Marseilles, where I was hosted by Al's French USIA colleague, Ramon García, who lived in the country near the seaside town of Cassis. It was Christmastime and we indulged in lots of foie gras and champagne. Then I rented a car and toured Provence. The highlight for me was a magnificent dinner at the three-star Michelin restaurant Baumanière in the little Provençal town of Les Baux.

The 1976 legislative session was again basically a wrap-up session, and my most time-consuming project was working on the determinate sentencing bill. We had had numerous interim hearings and ultimately passed a bill that significantly narrowed the range of sentences a judge could impose in felony cases and reduced the options for parole. This system, we argued, would provide more consistent justice throughout the state and guarantee a kind of "truth in sentencing," allowing the public to know what it could expect when an offender went to prison. At the same time, we also provided more alternatives to imprisonment, allowing the less serious offender to be punished in the community with a combination of jail time, probation, and community service. This approach had widespread support in the legislature and passed both houses easily. But unexpectedly Governor Anderson vetoed it. The reason he gave was that his staff had discovered a technical flaw in the drafting of the bill. I suspect there may have been more to it. In retrospect, it was a risky proposition. The sentences determined in the 1976 bill were reasonable ones, but once we had given the legislature the power to set sentences and taken discretion away from judges, there was no guarantee what would happen in the future. In the 1980s and 1990s, when fear of crime escalated into panic, there would have been no limit to the draconian sentences the legislature imposed. As it was, the governor forced us back to the drawing board in 1977, and by that time the experts in the field were talking less about determinate sentences and more about sentencing guidelines. Under this plan, a commission appointed by the governor, rather than the legislature itself, would establish guidelines that restricted but did not eliminate judicial discretion. Minnesota enacted a guidelines system in 1978 that served it well and became a model for other states.

For most politicians, the important thing about 1976 was that it was an election year and there were presidential contests in both parties. I did not become as deeply involved as I had been four years earlier. I had my own reelection to think about as well as some other vigorously contested local elections. Moreover, the differences among the various Democratic candidates were not as clear-cut to me as they had been during the Vietnam War. I would have gladly supported Teddy Kennedy, but he took himself out of contention very early. Fritz Mondale would have had virtually unanimous support among Minnesota DFL activists despite his position on the war in 1968, but he too decided not to run. I would have been less forgiving with Hubert Humphrey, who was tempted to try again but ultimately stayed out of the race. Of those who did run, I obviously opposed George Wallace and I had little use for Henry "Scoop" Jackson, the hawkish senator from Washington State. But my constituents were divided among such liberal luminaries as Morris Udall, Fred Harris, Birch Bayh, and Jerry Brown and I could have easily supported any of them. I had a slight preference for Udall, but decided to remain neutral. When Jimmy Carter came seemingly out of nowhere to win the nomination, I knew little about him. But I had no trouble supporting him, especially after he chose Mondale as his running mate.

Of more immediate concern to me were the local races, particularly a county commissioner race that threatened to split the political alliance that had elected me four years earlier. When my friends and I agreed to support the reelection of Dick Hanson in 1972, we thought Dick was nearing the end of his political career and that someone from our group would soon replace him. But no one, of course, told Dick about this expectation. Sometime in 1975, he told me that he intended to run for reelection the following year and that he did not anticipate serious opposition. In the meantime, he and I had become personal friends. I found him something of a political anachronism, but he was charming and generous and fun to be with. When Lee Greenfield lost his instructorship at the university and needed a job, Dick eagerly hired him as his administrative assistant, and Lee, too, soon became his good friend and loyal aide. But early in 1976, Jeff Spartz announced that he was running for Dick's seat. Jeff had been elected to the Minneapolis Park Board a few years earlier and was now eager to move up to a more responsible and better-paying position. He reminded us that our support for Dick in 1972 had been opportunistic and that we never anticipated that we would support him indefinitely. Moreover, Jeff identified Dick's weaknesses. Dick was elitist, he was unsympathetic to community involvement in decision making, and he rarely listened to his constituents. He had been the chief proponent of the new office tower the county had constructed in downtown Minneapolis. While Dick was enormously proud of it, many ordinary citizens thought it was too expensive and too luxurious. Jeff assured us that this would be a major issue in the campaign.

Lee and Marcia and I were in a quandary. Jeff Spartz had been one of our key political allies since 1968. Many of the things he said about Dick Hanson were at least partially true and we knew they would resonate among many of our supporters. Yet Lee worked for Dick and felt a strong sense of loyalty to him. And Dick was my friend and I found it hard to betray him. We tried to talk Jeff out of running but were unsuccessful. Then Lee sounded out Dick to determine whether there was any chance he would gracefully retire. No, he told Lee, and he was sure he could win as he had four years before. I tried for a while to stay neutral in the race, but Lee and Marcia became deeply involved and it was hard for me to stay out. A couple of weeks before the endorsing convention, I came out for Dick and agreed to give the nominating speech for him at the convention. But I told Jeff that if he were endorsed, as I expected he would be, I would support him in the primary and general election. This time my speech was not enough to carry Dick through. Jeff was a far stronger opponent than Dick had faced before and he took full advantage of Dick's vulnerabilities. He pointed to the county commissioners' offices on the top floor of the new county building with their rosewood paneling and private showers and accused Dick of wasting taxpayers' money on such indulgences. He also criticized Dick for the amount of time he was in Los Angeles and assured the delegates that he would be spending his time not in California but in the neighborhoods of the district. He was easily endorsed.

Lee and I again tried to persuade Dick to drop out of the race. I think that if at that point Jeff had come to him and personally sought reconciliation, Dick might have done it. But Jeff immediately geared up for a primary and continued the attacks; Dick was angry and insisted on carrying on. I kept my promise and officially supported Jeff as the endorsed candidate of the party. But Lee managed Dick's campaign, and when he asked me for advice, I gave it to him. The biggest coup the Hanson campaign could manage was to get the support of Hubert Humphrey and persuade Humphrey to appear at a fund-raiser on Dick's behalf. This was a friendship that went back thirty years, and Humphrey was not about to abandon Dick because of the endorsement of a political party that had not been particularly cordial to him in recent years. But even this support was not enough. Jeff was elected in November. Dick Hanson's political career was over, but the Spartz-Greenfield split, as it was commonly called, was not. After 1976, the group that had come together in south Minneapolis in 1968 to oppose the war began to move in different directions. Jeff and his friends developed a strong base in the working-class sections of the south side and, while remaining liberals, became more mainstream in their orientation. The Greenfields and I retained our base in the university community and became more identified with liberal positions on social issues. Alliances shifted in subsequent years, but we were never as close to Jeff Spartz as we had once been.

With Lee Greenfield busy running Dick Hanson's campaign, I asked my old friend Joan Campbell to be my campaign manager. We had known since the previous year that Steve Carter would be my opponent and that he would run a vigorous campaign. Just twenty-six years old, he had succeeded Jack Baker as president of the Minnesota Student Association in 1973. But he had not served his full term. He had resigned after being accused of misusing MSA funds to promote a Republican candidate for mayor and to hire Jack Baker as a consultant and of withdrawing his entire personal stipend for the year less than two months after taking office. Despite this record, Carter hoped to put together a coalition of young people and traditional Republicans to defeat me. The difficulty of forging this kind of a coalition led to one of the most bizarre campaigns I have ever seen. I was never in any danger of losing. But I was subjected to a constant barrage of personal attacks and accusations that revealed less about me than it did about the immaturity of Carter and the people around him.

The first sign that this campaign would be unconventional came when the Carter campaign proposed an agreement that we have no lawn signs. I was delighted. Lawn signs are expensive and unsightly and they take a lot of work to put up and maintain. But on the local level, where television advertising is not feasible, they provide a new candidate with the best way of introducing himself to the electorate. They had been essential to me in 1972 when I was less well known than John Cairns. Now it was Steve Carter who needed them, yet he was prepared to give them up. We readily agreed. It soon became clear why. When Jack Baker had been elected MSA president he had flooded the campus with clever flyers that he tacked up on telephone poles, trees, and bulletin boards. It was cheap and, in the confined setting of a university campus, highly effective. Carter now intended to use this tactic in his Senate race in lieu of lawn signs. The problem was that a Senate district was vastly larger than a campus and did not have the same kind of foot traffic. Few people even noticed his flyers. Moreover, what was clever to university students did not necessarily appeal to a more diverse public. Several of his flyers impressed me as being well conceived. One featured a drawing of him as "Mr. Peanut" and the caption "The other Carter wants a seat in the senate—Give him a crack at it," an obvious allusion to the Democratic presidential candidate. But others were repellant. One was so obnoxious that it was barely off the drawing board when it was withdrawn. Under the caption "Steve Carter for state senate—even if he doesn't act the part" was a drawing of a row of men in suits and hats and down on hands and knees, each kissing the ass of the man in front of him.

The contradictions within the Carter campaign were clearest in its handling of the gay issue. On the one hand, Carter was a protégé of Jack Baker's, Baker was a key figure in his campaign, and Carter had the support of a number of the gay militants who thought I had sold out on the gay issue in the 1975 legislative session. Yet Carter was the Republican-endorsed candidate and wanted the support of traditional Republicans who didn't support any kind of gay rights and were unhappy they were represented by an openly gay senator. How could he gay-bait me and at the same time criticize me for not being gay enough? He came up with what he must have thought was a brilliant strategy. He filed a complaint against me with the newly created Minnesota Ethical Practices Board, charging that I had illegally taken an in-kind contribution from the Minnesota Committee for Gay Rights. The charge was frivolous and was dismissed before the election. But for the month it was being processed Carter was able to say that I was "under investigation" for ethical misconduct and reproduce the MCGR newsletter that supposedly represented the illegal contribution, reminding everyone at the same time that I was a gay activist. He also distributed a tabloid-style newspaper in which an anonymous interviewer asked him whether his opponent's homosexuality would be an issue in the campaign. His answer was worthy of Richard Nixon at his most disingenuous:

> No, I don't think Spear's affectional preference will have much bearing on the way people vote. However, I feel that Spear has caused a great deal of infighting within the gay community and he has used the gay press and an organization he founded—the Minnesota Committee for Gay Rights—to undermine my campaign. . . . In my door knocking around the district some people have complained that they felt Spear should have announced his preference before he ran for

legislature rather than after he won. But I don't think Spear's gayness will come up as an issue unless he continues to bring it up.

The piece of literature that I found most troubling, however, came out late in the campaign and was attributed to a previously unknown group called "The Gay Imperative" led by the irrepressible Thom Higgins. Steve Carter denied any connection to the group, but Jack Baker was listed as an officer, so it is hard to believe that there was no collusion. An 8 x 10 flyer printed on card stock, the piece on one side consisted entirely of a close-up of my face that had been doctored to make me look unshaven, shadowy, and sinister. Printed across my forehead was the caption "Would you let your baby kiss this man?" On the other side was a series of accusations detailing how I had sold out the gay community. Some were highly distorted versions of what happened; others were made up out of whole cloth. Even my name was misspelled. The piece was used in two ways. It was distributed at gay bars in an effort to discredit me within the gay community. And it was posted on telephone poles in some of the more conservative parts of the district with only the picture side visible. Here it seemed to me was hypocrisy at its peak. The same piece of literature was used first to attack me for being disloyal to gay people and then, by exposing only the scurrilous picture and its homophobic caption, to resurrect the old stereotype of gay men as seducers of the young. Higgins was obviously delighted when he heard how upset I was about this piece because he then spread the word about his next project. He said that he planned to go into northeast Minneapolis on Halloween night and distribute lollipops to all of the children with a little tag attached to each one reading "Suck on this—from Allan Spear." This would have been illegal on several grounds and I doubt that he ever seriously considered it. But it is indicative of how warped the man's mind was.

Carter engaged in more conventional attacks as well. His last piece of official campaign literature included several accusations that were patently untrue. Some involved a convoluted reading of my voting record in the Senate. But the most serious one was that I was "double dipping at the public trough" and had collected my salary at the university while the legislature was in session. I had been particularly scrupulous about that and had made certain I was not paid by the university when I was not in residence. I called my lawyer friend, Ken Enkel, and took him my tax records; they clearly proved my point and we filed charges of false campaigning with the Hennepin County attorney. Carter was forced to withdraw his literature and publicly admit that it was inaccurate. Even before then he was perceived as running a negative and unconstructive campaign, something a "good government" district like mine didn't like. This final false accusation ended whatever chance he may have had for an even respectable showing in the election.

For my part, I said little about Steve Carter except to defend myself from his attacks. Some of my supporters brought up his dubious record as student body president, but I never mentioned it myself. My literature focused on my record in the legislature. In addition to the conventional brochures we indulged ourselves with a couple of pieces that would probably not have passed muster at a campaign school. One, printed on newspaper stock with a Gothic masthead resembling that of the *New York Times,* was so thick with type that only a political junkie would have read it all. The other was a reproduction of an old Thomas Nast cartoon of "Mr. Moneybags" with the caption "Don't let special interests get control of our state legislature—re-elect Allan Spear" and then, "Allan's only special interest is you, ask any tycoon." The campaign itself was far lower key than it had been four years earlier. We had no storefront headquarters, no daily activities. Every week a group of volunteers would gather at my house and we would go out and knock on doors. Without lawn signs to worry about, and with a nettlesome but less formidable opponent, there was less to do. It was a good thing as I fought a lingering case of hepatitis through much of the campaign, and while I was never critically ill my energy level was considerably reduced. My campaign manager was a nurse in real life and made certain that I did not overdo it.

In the final returns, I defeated Steve Carter with 15,035 votes to his 6,302. When I was asked at gay political conferences in future years about how coming out affected my political career, I had a ready answer. I ran in the closet in 1972, I said, and received 53 percent of the vote; I came out two years later and was reelected with more than 70 percent of the vote. There was a bit more to it than that, but that line never failed to get a round of applause. My reelection campaign had received a lot of attention in the national gay press. Many people saw it as an important test of the political viability of openly gay officials. But there was also dismay that the first two openly gay state officials in the country—Elaine Noble and I—were both the victims of vicious attacks from within our own communities. I received a telegram from Elaine and from the two cochairs of the National Gay Task Force just before the election assuring me that "gay people throughout the nation support you and are hoping for a strong victory for you and for all of us on election day." But the divisiveness continued and it was not limited to Minnesota and Massachusetts. Shortly after my reelection Jim Foster, whom I had met in San Francisco the previous year, called to tell me that they were likely to elect that city's first openly gay supervisor in the 1977 city elections. The leadership of the Alice B. Toklas Club was supporting Rick Stokes, a moderate, well-qualified gay lawyer. But he was facing a vigorous challenge from Harvey Milk, who, as Jim had told me previously, represented the same kind of confrontational militancy that I had been battling in Minnesota. Would I endorse Stokes? Knowing nothing more than that about San Francisco politics, I agreed. I would subsequently learn that I should keep my nose out of local races two thousand miles away.

The Democrats reached their peak of post-Watergate electoral success in the 1976 elections. In the state Senate, we went from thirty-eight seats to forty-nine out of a total of sixty-seven—a margin big enough to make up for the frequent defection of a handful of conservative DFLers from rural districts. In Washington, we now had a Democratic president and, more important for Minnesotans, a Minnesota DFLer as vice president. Fritz Mondale's election created a vacant U.S. Senate seat, giving Governor Anderson the opportunity to appoint a replacement who would serve until the 1978 election. There was immediate speculation that the governor would appoint himself—or, more technically, resign as governor and allow the lieutenant governor to succeed him and then appoint him to the Senate. I remember discussing this possibility with Martin Sabo, who was close to Governor Anderson, and pointing out to him that, historically, governors who had arranged for their own appointment to higher office had been defeated in the next election. Voters saw it as unseemly and self-serving. Sabo dismissed my argument, insisting that Anderson was in such a strong position politically that he could weather any dissatisfaction.

Within a few weeks, Rudy Perpich had become governor and Wendell Anderson was off to Washington. And soon enough we would learn how quickly overconfidence and arrogance could bring down a political party that had seemed almost invincible.

While I had real reservations about Anderson's self-appointment, I was delighted that Rudy Perpich was now governor as I had always seen him as more progressive than Anderson. With large DFL majorities in the legislature, I looked toward another round of real accomplishment, including, I hoped, a gay rights bill. Perpich started out like a house afire. He had never expected to be governor and he planned to make the most of it. Minnesota had never had a governor quite like him. He was the first governor from the Iron Range, the first Catholic, the first non-Scandinavian since 1915. The son of a miner, he spoke bluntly, had no pretensions, and was full of ideas, although it soon became clear that he was not always able to distinguish between good ideas and bad ones. He worked at a furious pace and never seemed to sleep. The first time I asked for an appointment, I received a message that the governor would see me at 10:30 p.m. I called his office and told his appointments secretary that there must be some mistake, that this must be 10:30 a.m. No, she assured me, it was no mistake. The governor was scheduling appointments every day until midnight. This high level of energy led to constant press attention. There were big stories when he unplugged the coffeemakers in the executive offices in order to save energy and personally stopped speeders on the freeway. And some of his more eccentric proposals, such as a chopstick factory in northern Minnesota and publicly financed bocce ball courts, garnered more headlines. But after a while I began to wonder if the substance would match the style. The legislative achievements of 1977 and 1978 were no match for what we had done earlier in the decade.

Steve Endean and I were determined to try again on the gay rights bill. This time, we decided, I would be the chief Senate author. With four years of experience and a landslide reelection behind me, I was sufficiently established to take this topic on without anyone seeing me as a one-issue politician. And no straight legislator, no matter how sympathetic, could bring to the bill the same perspective that I had. We also decided that the election had made the Senate much friendlier than it had been before and that we would start the bill there rather than in the House. We still faced some fierce opposition within DFL ranks. Baldy Hanson had been defeated by a more liberal DFLer, but Florian Chmielewski and Wayne Olhoft were back and they were now joined by another religious right-winger named Mike Menning, who had moved over from the House. Of all of the adversaries I faced over my years in the Senate, none repelled me more than Menning. Chmielewski was something of a clown and Olhoft, with all of his religious fervor, was indubitably sincere. But Menning struck me as a real-life Elmer Gantry, a self-serving charlatan who used religion to advance his own political career. Curiously, all of the most outspoken opponents of gay rights were Democrats. Most of the Republicans opposed the bill, but they seemed perfectly willing to leave the heavy lifting to Chmielewski, Olhoft, and Menning.

Steve and I feared that once again we would be undercut by the militants within our own community. We planned to introduce basically the same bill that we had gotten to the floor in 1975. It included protection in employment, education, and housing, but not public accommodations and services, and did not include explicit protection for transvestites and transsexuals. But this time, for reasons that I never knew, our gay antagonists stayed away. Perhaps they had been shocked by my decisive reelection or perhaps they were just burning out. In any case, Jack Baker quarreled with the language of the bill but no one from the gay or transgender community came to the Capitol to disrupt our efforts. Once we realized this, we were optimistic about our chances. Steve had worked hard to build an effective support group. The Minnesota Committee for Gay Rights now had lists of people throughout the state—both gay and straight—who favored the bill and were willing to call their legislators on its behalf. Steve had targeted districts with undecided legislators where, he was convinced, we could mobilize constituents to persuade them to vote for the bill. He had also carefully trained a team of eleven lobbyists—all well informed, polite, and well groomed—to come to the Capitol and personally visit every legislator. MCGR had not totally fulfilled the hopes we had had for it when we began it in 1974—it still had no steady funding base and it tended to lurch from crisis to crisis without much presence between legislative sessions. But the gender divisions had been tamped down and there was a core of able, hardworking

people in its leadership. We thought it would serve us well in the upcoming legislative struggle.

For a while, it appeared that our optimism was justified. I secured
endorsements for the bill from all of the major DFL office holders in
the state—from Governor Perpich on down. We also put together a
list of organizational endorsements that reached well into the mainstream of civic life: the League of Women Voters, the Mental Health
Association, the Minnesota Council of Churches, the two major teachers' unions, and the leading metropolitan newspapers. When the bill
received its first hearing in the Senate Judiciary Committee, I was able
to present it as a moderate measure, assuring my colleagues that it
had nothing to do with marriage or adoption rights and would not
interfere with employers' rights to insist on codes of dress or behavior
on the job. A vote for this bill, I asserted, was not a vote in support
of homosexuality but an affirmation of the premise that all people
have the right to education, housing, and employment that is based
on their qualifications and not their private lives. I shared my personal experience of living in the closet for fifteen years of my adult
life, "terrified that being found out would jeopardize my job, my personal and family relationships and my standing in the community."
Once again, I presented an impressive list of witnesses that included
a Roman Catholic priest, a Lutheran minister, and the mother of a
gay son. The opposition testimony was predictable, but there was one
disappointment that did not bode well for the future. Steve Endean,
who had been raised a Catholic, had tried very hard to persuade the
relatively moderate archbishop of St. Paul, John Roach, at least to stay
neutral on the bill. But he had apparently failed in that effort, for the
archdiocese testified against the bill. Nevertheless, our committee vote
was overwhelmingly positive. All the Democrats and all but three of
the Republicans voted to send the bill to the Senate floor.

The Judiciary Committee was more urban and more liberal than the
Senate as a whole, and we knew that the vote in the full Senate would
be much closer. We also knew that Menning and Olhoft were actively
working to line up votes against us. It was at this very time—April
1977—that the religious right, inspired by the singer Anita Bryant, was
organizing to repeal a gay rights ordinance in Miami/Dade County,
Florida. Involvement in politics by Christian fundamentalists was still

a relatively new phenomenon in American life and the Miami referendum was the most dramatic early example of how effective it could be. Using the slogan "Save Our Children," Bryant and her allies organized through churches and prayer groups in hope of defeating a proposal that had not even seemed controversial a few months earlier. In Minnesota, we soon witnessed a similar juggernaut. Menning and Olhoft communicated regularly with their counterparts in Florida and soon had fundamentalist churches in Minnesota ready to launch a campaign against our bill.

Nick Coleman was never at a loss for strategic ploys. One evening in early May, the Senate met late debating one of the end-of session omnibus appropriation bills. Everyone was fidgety, hurrying up the speakers, anxious to complete work, and go home. Nick came over to me and said, "Allan, are you prepared to take up the gay rights bill after this debate ends?" "Tonight"? I replied incredulously. "It's almost midnight." "Yes," he said. "We'll bring it up when they are too damned tired to fight it." So after we voted on the appropriations bill and everyone was slamming their books shut in anticipation of adjournment, Nick announced that we were moving on to an even more controversial bill and yielded the floor to me. I've never heard as much groaning. I presented the bill and waited for what I anticipated would be a barrage of amendments. In fact, my allies on Senate counsel staff had warned me that every conceivable kind of crippling amendment had been drafted and was awaiting introduction. To my amazement, none was offered. Perhaps Nick's strategy had worked. There were some questions and fervent speeches from Senators Menning, Olhoft, and Chmielewski. When Senator Olhoft argued that unlike race and sex, currently covered by the state human rights law, homosexuality was a matter of choice, I countered that "growing up in a small town in Indiana in the 1950s, the last thing I would have chosen to be is gay." After about an hour of debate we moved to the vote. There were thirty-two ayes and twenty-seven nays. When I asked Wayne Olhoft why he had offered no amendments, he said, "We thought we had the votes to kill the bill outright. We miscalculated."

There was one catch. This was not a final vote. The arcane rules of the Senate call for two votes in the full body—a preliminary vote on second reading in what is called the "committee of the whole" and then a final vote on third reading. Near the end of the session, the process is often bypassed by placing a bill on "special orders" and avoiding the committee of the whole. But we hadn't done that on the gay rights bill, and we would need one more vote to pass the bill out of the Senate. Moreover, while a bill can pass the committee of the whole with a majority of those voting, final passage requires a majority of the entire Senate. My bill received thirty-two votes that night; it would ultimately require thirty-four. Of the eight members who had not been there to vote, I would need to have two of them with me on final passage and not lose any of the votes I already had. As I studied the roll call, I was certain I could do that.

In the next three days, I witnessed the religious right in action. Our opponents were obviously well prepared; they merely gave the signal and the phone calls and letters began pouring in. Some of my colleagues told me that they received more calls on this issue in just a few days than they had on every other issue the entire session. Some of their constituents told them that they had been alerted by their telephone "prayer trees" or had received personal calls from their pastors. Many of the callers recited passages from Leviticus or told the story of Sodom and Gomorrah. We had support from the mainstream Protestant denominations—Episcopalians, Methodists, Presbyterians, the largest Lutheran group—but they were no match in effectiveness for the fundamentalists allied with the Roman Catholics. Not only was I unable to pick up the additional votes that I needed, I also began to see my support melting away. Several senators came to me to tell me that I could no longer count on them. A Republican senator from St. Paul who had supported my bill in the Judiciary Committee and in the committee of the whole was particularly apologetic. "I really wanted to support you on this," he said, "but I will just be killed in my district if I do." Senator Tim Penny, later a United States congressman, who had just been elected to the Senate in an upset victory in a conservative rural district in southern Minnesota, had told me that he had prayed with his pastor over this issue and had given me his commitment to support the bill. He assured me that he would not back off but asked me to please not force him to vote for the bill again if I didn't have enough votes to pass it.

It soon became apparent that I could not pass the bill. The organizing effort of MCGR, good as we thought it was, paled compared to the clout of the opposition. As I often said when I described this experience in talks to gay and liberal groups, Minnesotans responded more readily to out-of-context quotations from the Bible than they did to evocations of the Bill of Rights. I decided not to make my allies take another tough vote on an issue we couldn't win and I moved to withdraw the bill. At the same time, I gave perhaps the bitterest speech of my entire career in the Senate. I attributed the bill's demise to "bigots" and said that it was particularly sad that the campaign of vilification that had been waged against it was the work of "people who called themselves Christians." "I had always believed that Christianity had something to do with loving one's neighbor as oneself," I continued, "demonstrating concern and care for one's fellow man, showing respect for individuals for what they contribute to society, not what they happen to be. I believe those who've led the campaign against this bill have distorted and cheapened the message of Christianity." Those remarks were aimed at Menning and Olhoft, but I also spoke directly to those who had abandoned me when the going got tough. "Many of you have come to me and said, 'I'm with you in my heart but can't take this pressure any more.' I can understand that, but can't admire it. The bottom line in this job is having the courage and the guts to stand up for what you believe."

When I finished, I immediately walked off the Senate floor as I knew that I was losing control of my emotions. Steve Endean was waiting for me in the foyer and steered me into an empty room where no one would see us. There I broke down and cried for several minutes. I had tried to treat gay rights as another legislative issue that I cared deeply about but would deal with rationally and dispassionately. Obviously, I couldn't do it. This was personal to me and to who I was in a way that no other issue would ever be. It was deeply hurtful when colleagues whom I otherwise respected failed to support my basic human rights. Mike Menning even had the audacity to come up to me and assure me that his position on the bill was "nothing personal," just an ideological difference. I wanted to spit in his face.

Others in the community responded even more viscerally. Gay Catholics, in particular, were offended by what they saw as a betrayal by Archbishop Roach. The position of the fundamentalist Protestants was expected. But Roach was a humane, thoughtful, highly respected Catholic leader who, many of us hoped, would see the simple justice of our position. Even nominal support for the bill on his part could have been an effective counterweight to our religious opposition. Ironically, just a week after the bill's defeat, Roach was scheduled to receive a brotherhood award from the National Conference of Christians and Jews at a gala dinner in the ballroom of a downtown Minneapolis hotel. For many gay people, this was like rubbing salt in the wounds. As Roach rose to receive the award, two men emerged from the audience and one of them ran to the podium and heaved a chocolate cream pie directly into the archbishop's face.

When I heard about this incident, my initial reaction was that it must have been the work of Thom Higgins and that its consequences would probably be negative. But in fact, one of the two men involved was Dennis Miller, an active member of MCGR and one of the lobbyists whom Steve Endean had recruited to work on the bill at the Capitol. Dennis, I knew, was no "crazy." Moreover, Dennis had been encouraged in his efforts by a Jesuit priest named George Casey who served as chaplain of Dignity, an organization of gay Catholics, and who had been outraged by Roach's gutlessness. In the end, Father Casey paid dearly for his involvement; he was transferred to a distant post and never heard from again. In his farewell letter to me, he was unbowed: "We will win," he said. "God damn the bigots, everyone!" Contrary to what I would have anticipated, however, Archbishop Roach was moved in the right direction by his ordeal. He had been troubled to learn that his actions had caused enough pain to precipitate this kind of a violent response and he began to rethink his position. This was a case in which the confrontational approach I usually oppose turned out to have positive results.

At the end of the session, Steve Endean flew immediately to Miami to work on the Dade County referendum that was scheduled for June 7. During the three weeks he spent there, he called frequently and told me that it did not look good. It was, in fact, worse than anyone anticipated. The antigay forces won with almost 70 percent of the vote. Jubilant, Anita Bryant announced that she would take her movement nationwide and work not only against future efforts to enact gay rights but to repeal ordinances that already existed. Minneapolis and St. Paul were among her target cities. The Minneapolis city charter did not allow for initiative or referendum, so any repeal effort would have to come from the city council, an unlikely prospect given the political makeup of the council. St. Paul, however, did allow for citizens to place initiatives on the ballot by petition. Immediately,

Menning and Olhoft announced the formation of a Minnesota branch of Bryant's Save Our Children organization, and although neither lived in St. Paul, they pledged that they would bring Bryant in to help if there were a drive to repeal the city's gay rights ordinance. Jack Baker, relatively quiescent for the past year, now sprang back into action and announced the formation of the Target City Coalition, using Bryant's own terminology and basically daring her to try to mess with gay rights in Minnesota.

While gay rights was by far the most emotionally draining issue that I faced in 1977, I continued to work on a wide array of causes in the legislature. Some were continuations of what I had begun during my first term. Having failed to pass a bilingual and bicultural education bill in 1975, I tried again. I let another senator, who represented the St. Paul Hispanic community, handle the bilingual program for students with limited English-speaking ability, and I focused on a separate bill that we called the American Indian Language and Cultural Education Act. This time I included nonpublic alternative Indian schools and I made certain that the appropriations would be equitably divided between the urban Indian communities and the reservations. With these provisions, I had united support among Minnesota's Indians, and with strong support from Governor Perpich the bill passed with relative ease.

The Indian education bill was just one example of a lesson that I was rapidly learning as I worked to be a more effective legislator. It was not enough simply to draft and introduce a good bill and then hope for the best. It was necessary to bring together every group that might have an interest in the bill and try to work out differences before the bill even had its first hearing. Total agreement would not, of course, always be possible. But differences could at least be minimized and I would know what sticking points remained and be prepared to deal with them. When the Indian alternative schools opposed my bill in 1975, I lost it; when they were brought into the process, I passed it. I had a similar experience with the knotty issue of adoption records.

Traditionally, the birth records of adopted children were kept sealed on the grounds that adoption represented a new beginning, that the adoptive parents were the real parents, and that reopening the past benefited no one. But increasingly, adoptees, when they became adults, wanted to know who their birth parents were and wanted an opportunity to find them. Two organizations of adult adoptees, LINK and LEAF, advocated for total access to birth records even when birth parents had been promised confidentiality. Most adoption agencies and many adoptive parents bitterly opposed this. Legislators had been working unsuccessfully for several years on a solution. I agreed to take on the issue. I brought everyone together and insisted that we were going to work out a bill that everyone could live with. We spent hours behind closed doors. There was a lot of shouting and many angry exchanges. But I insisted that there was going to be a bill and eventually we agreed to a plan. Birth parents would retain the right to remain anonymous. But if they agreed to be revealed to their adult children, a state welfare worker would arrange a mutually satisfactory way for them to meet. With the agreement of all interested parties, the bill passed easily. I received many letters from people who said their lives were transformed by their ability to discover their biological origins. Not all searches, of course, were successful. But the bill worked reasonably well and demonstrated that it was possible to resolve even thorny and emotional issues in ways that respected the rights of all of the people involved.

I pursued a similar strategy with another bill that I carried—to add age as a protected category to the state human rights law. This was not as straightforward an issue as providing human rights protection for gay people. There were some forms of age discrimination that society generally accepted. Minimum ages for positions of great responsibility were written into the U.S. Constitution. Senior citizen housing seemed a benign kind of discrimination as were special discounts at movies and cultural attractions for people over sixty-five. Moreover, mandatory retirement was a complex and difficult issue. For certain jobs that required finely honed physical skills—police officers, airline pilots, prison guards—it probably made sense. But should office workers and teachers who were willing to work into their senior years be forced to retire? All of this required careful discussion with a myriad of interested parties. What we really wanted to eliminate was capricious discrimination in employment aimed at people in their forties and fifties. Eventually we passed two narrowly drafted bills that applied to employment only. The first, approved in 1977, exempted mandatory retirement. A year later, we came back and banned mandatory retirement, with exceptions for jobs requiring special physical skills. As I worked on this issue, I thought often of my father, who had lost his job at the age of fifty-two and was told repeatedly, when he sought another position, that he was too old.

It was customary at the end of each legislative session for each legislator to send out a newsletter summing up the achievements of the session and bragging about the number of bills he had sponsored that had become law. I usually followed this tradition, but as my career went on I came to realize that toting up bills passed was a poor measure of legislative achievement. Sometimes, defeating bills was just as important. For example, after the 1973 abortion decision, I supported the status quo on abortion and therefore spent a lot of time and energy trying to kill the annual attempts to weaken *Roe v. Wade*. Similarly, in the 1970s, one of my major legislative goals was to stop the proposed stadium in Industry Square, which most of my constituents strongly opposed. In 1976, despite an all-out effort to pass a stadium bill by the business community, the labor unions, the governor, and the Minneapolis newspapers, we had been successful. But in 1977, the pro-stadium forces found a winning strategy that we were unable to thwart.

The problem stadium proponents faced was that even while they were able to muster legislative majorities for the concept of a new stadium, they could not agree on the particulars. That had been their undoing in 1976 when, each time the bill was heard, the location of the proposed stadium would change from Minneapolis to Bloomington to "no site specific" and the funding mechanism from a hotel tax to a cigarette tax to a liquor tax. In 1977, on the other hand, weary of seeing each session dominated by this issue, Martin Sabo and Nick Coleman agreed on a simple formula: the legislature would establish a seven-member commission to choose a site, the stadium would be financed by revenue bonds, and if the revenue fell short, the difference would be made up with a 2 percent metropolitan-wide liquor tax. Minneapolis senators were divided on the bill. Steve Keefe was the chief author, despite his representing a district that overwhelmingly opposed the whole concept. Jack Davies and I led the opposition. Jack was philosophically against government subsidies of this kind, and while I shared that view, my motives were also parochial. I was convinced that the commission would choose the Industry Square site, which my constituents saw as disruptive of their neighborhoods.

This bill, however, passed. As Davies put it, "Those people just kept pushing and pushing and pushing. You had to beat them 100 percent of the time. If you lost just once, the project would be authorized." When Governor Perpich appointed the commission, I was certain he had stacked it in favor of the Minneapolis site. But they had eighteen months to make their decision and there was still one more act to be played out.

By the end of the session, I was deeply involved in the city elections. This was the year when it became apparent that Minneapolis was becoming a one-party DFL city. Stenvig had made a surprise comeback in 1975, but now he was convincingly beaten by former mayor Al Hofstede and no one but a DFLer would ever again occupy the mayor's office. A few Republicans retained their seats on the city council and some of the elected city boards, but they were generally moderates with views almost indistinguishable from those of their DFL colleagues, and their numbers also now began to diminish. The real action was within the DFL, and as the party became more dominant in the city, it also became more deeply divided. Not only did the old split between the north side/labor faction and the south side/good government faction continue, but the division on the south side that had developed the year before in the Hanson-Spartz race showed no sign of healing. I was soon in the midst of two city council races in my district that divided sharply along those lines.

In the Second Ward, where I lived, Tom Johnson, after four years in office, had announced that he would not seek reelection and instead would prepare to run the following year for the position of Hennepin County attorney. Naomi Loper, a southeast Minneapolis community leader and environmentalist, entered the race with the support of most of the Spear-Greenfield group, while Jeff Spartz and his allies rallied behind a brash, outspoken political activist named Judy Corrao. As was often the case in races of this kind, there was little difference between the two candidates on issues. But the two women brought very different styles to the campaign. Loper was more mature, thoughtful, careful in her words. Corrao was more articulate, more voluble, sometimes careless with the facts. Even apart from my factional loyalties, I much preferred Loper and thought she would be a better council member. But the "Spartz machine," as it was now called, flexed its muscles, outorganized us, and secured an easy endorsement for Corrao. Loper settled for the consolation prize, an endorsement for a seat on the park board. In the fall, both were elected. Corrao won over token opposition. Loper, running citywide, eked out a narrow victory with a campaign that was run with compulsive thoroughness by Marcia Greenfield.

The other hotly contested council race involved the incumbent Sixth Ward alderman, Earl Netwal. In 1973, Netwal had defeated a conservative Republican of limited ability whom we had been trying since the midsixties to get off the council. Only twenty-four years old at the time, long haired, and scruffy, Netwal had been seen by most Democrats as a sacrificial lamb. But in the DFL sweep of that year, he was a surprise winner. Unfortunately, although well intentioned, he was unprepared for the office and had trouble resisting the blandishments of the lobbyists and favor seekers who stalked city hall. He was already in trouble in his first term and I met with him in 1975 to tell him that I would reluctantly support his reelection but that he would have to improve his performance and demonstrate his ability to stand up to the special interests. He didn't. In 1977, he was indicted for taking campaign contributions and illegal payments from a businessman in his ward who had applied for a liquor license from the city. While Earl was never convicted on this charge, he was still under a cloud. But he sought reelection and the Spartz group stuck with him.

My allies, disillusioned with Netwal, rallied around the chairperson of the Cedar-Riverside neighborhood association, a woman named Jackie Slater. Slater was perhaps the most unconventional candidate I have ever supported. She was a Roman Catholic nun, a member of the Sisters of St. Joseph, who saw her mission as social change and justice. She lived with another nun in the community, wore conventional street clothes, and held liberal views that she certainly had not cleared with the Vatican. When the church ruled that priests could not hold public office and forced Massachusetts congressman Robert Drinan to resign, I asked Jackie if this would affect her. "No way," she replied. "Only when the church gives us the same privileges and responsibilities as priests can it make the same demands on us." So, strangely enough, while my friends were "pieing" the archbishop, I was supporting a nun for city council. Slater and Netwal deadlocked at the endorsing convention and went on to the primary. There she turned out to be the perfect candidate. Who could better contrast with an incumbent accused of being involved in shady dealings than a Roman Catholic nun? Jackie was elected and served six years on the city council.

The other city election that I followed closely in 1977 occurred not in Minneapolis but in San Francisco. Even before Election Day, I realized that I had endorsed Rick Stokes for supervisor without knowing enough about San Francisco politics. This was the first city election held along district lines. Harvey Milk had run twice before and lost, but those had been at-large elections and he had run citywide. Now he was running to represent a district centered on the Castro neighborhood, the recently emerged center of gay life in San Francisco. And Harvey had a real base in the Castro. He was a popular, gregarious community leader who knew everyone and seemed far more accessible than the able but somewhat buttoned-up Rick Stokes. Jim Foster had been correct in describing Harvey Milk's approach as brash and confrontational; he loved street theater and converted otherwise mundane issues into high drama. But beyond that, comparisons with my antagonists in Minnesota stopped. He was more pragmatic than ideological, and there was always a long-range strategy behind his actions. When he won the November election, I called to congratulate him and welcome him to the still-exclusive club of openly gay elected officials. And I somewhat sheepishly apologized for my endorsement of his opponent. "Don't worry about it," he replied. "I know exactly how it came about. And now we need to work together." He wrote to me two months later to tell me that he was supporting a gay candidate running for public office in Chicago. "Maybe you can join us and help," he said. Then he caught himself, remembering that I knew something of the perils of endorsing candidates in other cities. "I know! I know! . . . Anyway, I hope I have not stepped into what you did." Even with Harvey's support, the candidate in Chicago did not win.

Everyone who was committed to gay rights realized by the beginning of 1978 that we were facing some difficult times. During the first few heady years after Stonewall, continual progress seemed inevitable. After all, we reasoned, we were on the side of history. As African Americans and women had gradually moved toward greater acceptance into American society, so too would we. Each year another city or two passed a gay rights ordinance, another corporation announced a nondiscrimination policy, another state repealed its sodomy law. It was agonizingly slow, but we never questioned the direction in which we were moving. Now with Anita Bryant's victory in Miami, we couldn't be so sure. Bryant toured the country throughout the fall of 1977 and the spring of 1978 helping to organize conservative Christians around the gay issue. We were now on the defensive and would have to struggle to keep the hard-fought gains we had made over the past decade.

I was back on the lecture circuit now and visited a number of smaller cities in the Midwest where barely emergent gay communities and a few liberal allies were feeling that they were under siege. Some were the same places I had visited a decade earlier teaching the lessons of African American history—Sioux Falls, Indianapolis, Fargo, Mankato, St. Cloud. Perhaps my most memorable visit was to Topeka, Kansas, in December of 1977. Anita Bryant was coming to town and the gay people of Topeka needed to do something to counter her. They were not ready to go out and picket her rally; none of them were willing to have their faces on television. So they decided to have an alternative event across town in the Unitarian Church and invited me to be the featured speaker. We started with a press conference, and when I asked whether a local person would introduce me, I was told sheepishly that I would have to introduce myself as even the organizers who had brought me to town were closeted. During the talk itself, the cameras were allowed only at the back of the room and only my face could be televised. Yet despite these restrictions, we got fantastic publicity. The Topeka newspaper gave me equal billing on the front page the next morning with Anita Bryant—even though her crowd was many times larger than mine. We had clearly succeeded in letting the people of Kansas know that hers was not the only view on the issue of gay rights.

Anita Bryant never debated the issue, so I never actually appeared with her. But my Senate colleague Florian Chmielewski was willing to take me on, and later in the winter of 1978 we spoke jointly in St. Cloud about gay rights in the Minnesota legislature. I am not usually left without an answer to anything, no matter how preposterous, but that night Florian left me speechless. He told the audience that he did not believe that I was really gay. After all, he said, Senator Spear is an intelligent man, he went to Yale, he is a professor, he couldn't possibly be a homosexual. He is just saying this, he suggested, for political reasons, to help a cause he believes in. After looking at him for a moment or two with my mouth agape, I finally asked, "Florian, what would I have to do to prove to you that I am really gay?" I thought for a few seconds of making that question more explicit, but then decided to leave well enough alone. After all, why pull on the noose, when an opponent is hanging himself? But I think this episode shows how deeply seated stereotypes can be. I did not fit Senator Chmielewski's vision of a homosexual. I was not a street person, I was not effeminate, I did not have limp wrists. Instead I was middle aged, well educated, and rather staid looking. So rather than modify his stereotypes, Florian concocted an utterly ludicrous proposition that it was somehow to my political advantage in the Midwest of the 1970s to pretend to be gay.

Not only did 1978 portend to be a bad year for gay rights, it also did not bode well for the DFL Party in Minnesota. Hubert Humphrey had been diagnosed the previous year with inoperable cancer and on January 13 he died at the age of sixty-six. I had never forgiven Humphrey for being on the wrong side of what I thought was one of the great moral issues of our time—the Vietnam War—but I recognized the tremendous impact he had had on progressive politics in the country as a whole and, especially, in Minnesota. The DFL would badly miss his leadership. Moreover, his death gave Governor Perpich a second appointment to the U.S. Senate and both seats would be on the ballot in November of 1978. This meant that the party would have two Senate seats to defend at the same time, both of them held by appointed incumbents. And one of those incumbents, Wendell Anderson, had already seriously compromised his popularity by the manner of his appointment. Perpich did the best he could with the second appointment. He picked Humphrey's widely admired widow, Muriel, with the general understanding that she would probably hold the seat only until November and allow the party to choose Humphrey's permanent successor. Even before Humphrey's death, Congressman Don Fraser had expressed interest in the seat. A distinguished legislator with a strong base in the Twin Cities area, Fraser was considered too liberal by many rural Democrats, especially northern Minnesotans, who distrusted his environmentalism and his support of gun control. His candidacy assured a bitter fight within the party.

On the day of Humphrey's funeral, the dominos began to fall. Fraser immediately announced that he would be running for Humphrey's Senate seat and would not, under any circumstances, be a candidate for reelection to the U.S. House of Representatives. I was having dinner with Lee and Marcia Greenfield that night when Martin Sabo called. He would be a candidate for Fraser's House seat and hoped for our support. We promised him that he would have it, and when he hung up, our discussion immediately turned to Martin's seat in the Minnesota House. "Well," I said to Lee and Marcia, "which one of you is going to run?" They told me that they would discuss it that night and let me know in the morning. When I called the next day, the answer was "Lee." Marcia decided that she did not have the temperament to be either a candidate or a public official and could be more useful behind the scenes. "Lee," she said, "will be the better candidate and the better legislator." "Fine," I replied. "I'll be his campaign manager." So we reversed our positions of six years before, and I managed Lee Greenfield's campaign for the Minnesota legislature.

Lee and I knew that the real decision in this heavily liberal district would be made at the DFL endorsing convention, and there was only one potential opponent who really worried us. Earl Craig had been a major figure in liberal circles for the past decade, and although he had not done well in his statewide race against Hubert Humphrey in 1970, he was a hero in the Fifty-seventh District. Moreover, many of the delegates would welcome the opportunity of adding to the tiny number of black members of the Minnesota legislature. Earl considered it for a while and then decided not to run. Confidentially, he told me why. I had known for some time that Earl was a closeted gay man, but we had never discussed it. Now he acknowledged it to me and said that he bowed out of the race when he realized that as a legislator it would be much harder for him to live a secret life. "But why," I asked him, "couldn't you come out? You'd be running in a district that has already accepted an openly gay senator." He replied that the district might accept him as a gay man, but he didn't believe the black community would. And he wanted to maintain his position as a respected leader among black Minnesotans. Given my loyalty to Lee Greenfield,

I was pleased that Earl did not become a legislative candidate, but I did not agree with his reasoning. Ultimately his decision to remain in the closet would have tragic consequences.[1]

With Earl out of the race, Lee had relatively clear sailing. He immediately got to work and began calling delegates to the endorsing convention on May 6. The Spartz-Hanson division once again came into play. One of Jeff Spartz's closest friends, Scott Dickman, announced his candidacy as did a third candidate, a young community activist named Sheldon Mains, who declared his independence from political factions. But this district, centered on Cedar-Riverside and the West Bank university campus, was really our turf. And Dickman proved to be a poor candidate, somewhat gruff in his manner and hard for delegates to relate to. Lee was far warmer personally and his liberal commitments were unquestioned. His work with Dick Hanson and, after Dick's defeat, as a health planner for Hennepin County gave him knowledge of the issues, especially health care, which would become his specialty in the legislature. It was soon apparent that he had a solid lead. Still, when we came to the convention, we expected the process to involve several ballots. Instead, Lee was endorsed on the first ballot, Mains came in second, and Dickman third. Dickman now referred to us as "the Southside Machine." After the endorsement, there was no serious contest. Lee easily beat a token Republican candidate and went on to serve in the legislature for twenty-two years. I was, of course, delighted to have one of my closest friends as my colleague in one-half of my Senate district.

But Lee Greenfield's election was just about the only good news of 1978. The year did not otherwise go well for the DFL. And even before the fall elections, we faced a serious challenge to gay rights in the city of St. Paul. Anita Bryant's nationwide campaign led to petition drives to force popular votes on recently enacted gay rights ordinances in three cities—Wichita, Kansas, Eugene, Oregon, and St. Paul. We learned just before the first of the year that Pastor Richard Angwin of Temple Baptist Church in downtown St. Paul had organized a group called Citizens Alert for Morality and had sent 150 volunteers door-to-door throughout the city seeking signatures to place a referendum

---

1. Earl Craig was murdered in 1992 by a young man he picked up.

in the spring election ballot. By mid-January, Angwin had the signatures he needed and we knew we had a fight on our hands. No one
among the gay rights leadership underestimated the importance of the
St. Paul referendum. When we had lobbied the city councils and the
legislature, we had told elected officials that despite the high-decibel
opposition they would hear, most Minnesotans believed in fundamental fairness and a pro-gay rights vote would not hurt them politically.
But we had never had a popular vote on the subject and had no way
of really gauging public opinion. Now there would be a vote, at a time
when the tide seemed to be turning against us, in a city that, while
probably more liberal than the state as a whole, had a strong working-
class and Roman Catholic base. If we lost in St. Paul, it would be a
long time before we could pass gay rights at the legislature.

Steve Endean recognized that the campaign to save the St. Paul ordinance could not be run through the Minnesota Committee for Gay
Rights. We would need an ad hoc local committee that would frame
the issue in broad human rights terms. Steve immediately formed a
group called St. Paul Citizens for Human Rights (SPCHR), and since
he lived in Minneapolis, he asked Kerry Woodward, the cochair of
MCGR, to head it. Soon the new committee succeeded in lining up
a veritable who's who of St. Paul civic life in opposition to repeal. It
included Mayor George Latimer, both of the U.S. senators, most of
the city council and legislative delegation, labor leaders, prominent
members of the clergy, and leaders of the business community. Probably the biggest catch was Archbishop John Roach, who, while not
explicitly telling Catholics how to vote, said that "it is a matter of
injustice when, due to prejudice, [homosexuals] must suffer violation
of their basic human rights." SPCHR emphasized in its literature that
the ordinance had been on the books for four years and was working well. "The city hasn't been taken over by gays. . . . Gay men and
women have gone on leading their private lives, knowing that if they
should become the target of discrimination they would at least have
legal recourse. So why not leave well enough alone?"

Throughout the spring, I was busy with the legislative session and
the Greenfield campaign and was not involved in the St. Paul effort
on a day-to-day basis as were Steve Endean and Kerry Woodward
and our friend Larry Bye. But in April Steve had a major assignment
for me. SPCHR had been invited to participate in a debate on the

most popular news show on Twin Cities television: *Moore on Sunday.* Dave Moore was the dean of local newscasters, an almost iconic figure who had been presenting the news every day on WCCO-TV since the earliest days of television. Now nearing the end of his career, he had branched out with a weekly magazine-type show that allowed him to focus in more detail on one or two major issues. He had decided to devote his entire show on April 23, two days before the St. Paul election, to the gay rights referendum and he settled on a format modeled after a national public television program called *The Advocates.* Each side would choose an advocate who would appear in a courtroom-like setting, select and question witnesses for his or her side, cross-examine the opposition witnesses, and make a final summation to the jury—which was the viewing audience. Citizens Alert for Morality had chosen as its advocate Roger Magnuson, a young, conservative lawyer with the Dorsey firm, one of the top legal firms in the state. Steve wanted me to be the advocate for SPCHR. "Steve," I protested, "you're asking me to go into what is basically a trial against a hot-shot lawyer with a premier firm and I don't even have a law degree." "You're the only one who can do it," he insisted. "You know the issues and you know how to debate. You don't need to be a lawyer." I agreed to be the advocate.

We taped the show in the council chambers at St. Paul city hall on the Thursday before it was to air. Dave Moore presided. We had spent a great deal of time discussing who our witnesses should be. We would have time for three and decided that we should have a clergy person, a mental health professional, and someone identified with the human rights community. Our man of the cloth was the Reverend James Nelson, a professor at United Theological Seminary in a Twin Cities suburb, who had recently written a book on biblical views of homosexuality. He would refute the idea that gay people are an abomination in the eyes of God. Ora Lee Patterson, a black woman who chaired the St. Paul Human Rights Commission, would link the gay cause to the human rights cause in general and to the black struggle for justice in particular. And finally we needed a psychiatrist or psychologist who could attest that homosexuals were normal people and not predators with designs on children. Here we landed our biggest fish. We flew in Dr. John Spiegel, the former president of the American Psychiatric Association, who had written that there was no evidence to support the thesis that homosexual teachers might affect the sexual orientation of their students or that homosexual seduction of a student is any more likely to occur than heterosexual seduction. My job was to ask our witnesses the right questions, cross-examine the opposition, and tie it all together.

Our witnesses were excellent both in answering my gentle questions and in responding to Magnuson's challenges. I was relieved when I saw that Magnuson's witnesses were all identifiable right-wing Christians, including Pastor Angwin, already identified with his cause. I didn't see how they could sway anyone not already committed. But Magnuson himself was very effective. As I tried to keep the discussion focused on human rights and fairness, he continually steered the argument to sex, to what homosexuals actually did in bed. He knew, as did we, that this aspect of gay life was what made many heterosexuals most uncomfortable. When Rev. Nelson said that he believed God approved all expressions of sincere, committed human love, Magnuson asked him whether he thought God approved of anal sex. And when we got to the summation I saw that Magnuson had a large cardboard mock-up of something that he was prepared to hold up to the camera. When I saw what it was, my heart sank. Earlier in the spring, Steve Endean had called my attention to a small classified ad that had appeared in a Twin Cities alternative newspaper. It had been placed by Jack Baker and Thom Higgins's Church of the Chosen People, perhaps their most outrageous undertaking, and called for young men to join them for initiation rites that included a "prostate rub." "I just hope our opponents don't find this, " Steve said. But they did and it was an enlargement of that ad that Magnuson held up in his peroration. "They might say they are interested only in job protection and don't want to recruit. But here is clear evidence to the contrary," he said. I responded by pointing out that every group has its fringe and that the Church of the Chosen People was not representative of the gay community. But I knew that Magnuson had made an effective closing argument.

Everyone said that I did well in the debate and that I had held my own against Roger Magnuson. But I couldn't help but feel that, once again, carefully planned efforts had been undermined by the irresponsible behavior of a few loose cannons within the gay community. In the end, the results were not close. We lost the referendum by a vote of almost two to one—and the next month also lost overwhelmingly in Wichita and Eugene. We were all bitterly disappointed. As I left what had been billed as a "victory party" at a St. Paul hotel on election night, I saw several people holding up signs for the opposition and, completely losing my cool, began yelling obscenities at them. We held an impromptu march around the Capitol promising that we would not go away. But we knew that our goals were now further away than ever, that it would be years before we could mount another viable statewide drive for gay rights legislation. Steve Endean told me that he was moving away. He could no longer continue to put his heart and soul into a battle that, in Minnesota at least, no longer seemed possible to win. He moved to Washington, D.C., and within a few months became the executive director of the Gay Rights National Lobby, a relatively new national organization that was attempting to establish a gay presence on Capitol Hill. In the wake of the St. Paul defeat, and without Steve to spur it on, MCGR withered away and within two years was dead. We would continue to introduce gay rights bills at the legislature and we made one serious effort in the mideighties to repeal the state's consenting adults laws. But it would be another fifteen years before we were able to organize another major campaign to provide statewide human rights protection for lesbian, gay, and—by that time—transgender people.

10

SETTLING INTO A LEGISLATIVE CAREER, 1978-1982

When I insisted that I was a legislator who happened to be gay rather than a gay legislator, this was not just political rhetoric. I honestly saw myself as a person with a wide range of interests and many causes with which I identified. In this I clearly differed from many gay activists, including my friend Steve Endean, who saw gay rights as the major focus of his life. And yet, between 1972 and 1978, my effort to forge a gay identity was so emotionally intense that it always seemed at the center of my consciousness. My personal coming out, the decision to go public with my sexuality, and the two intense struggles at the legislature over gay rights bills—all these occupied an extraordinary amount of my time and energy. After 1978, circumstances changed. I was now an openly gay man, but this was now more or less taken for granted at the legislature and I was no longer struggling with it. Moreover, the chances of significant legislative action on gay issues were much reduced and I necessarily had to place them on a back burner. While I remained active in the gay movement, I began to forge a legislative career around other concerns and to cultivate other aspects of my identity.

For example, in addition to being one of a very small group of gay and lesbian elected officials, I also identified with the growing number of 1960s radicals who had now decided to work within the system. A few of us had been elected to office; in Minnesota, that number included, in addition to myself, Linda Berglin, Phyllis Kahn, and now Lee Greenfield. Others held appointive office within government and many more took academic jobs or worked for labor unions, policy institutes, environmental groups, or neighborhood associations. It had been a significant transformation in just one decade. Some sixties radicals, to be sure, burned out and ended up living marginal, self-absorbed, often drug-dependent lives. Others went on with careers in the private sector, barely acknowledging the radicalism of their youth. But a large number, recognizing that protests and demonstrations were no longer effective and that change would not come overnight, altered their tactics without abandoning the principles that had brought them into politics in the first place. The generation of the 1960s would continue to have a major impact on American society for years to come.

In an attempt to organize the progressives (a term most of us now preferred to radical) who held public policy positions, a group called the National Conference on Alternative State and Local Public Policies had begun to meet annually in 1975. The first two conferences were held in cities with great symbolic significance. Both Madison, Wisconsin, and Austin, Texas, had been centers of 1960s radicalism, and both, in the early 1970s, elected mayors who had emerged from that movement. At the third conference, in Denver in 1977, we decided that we would meet in the summer of 1978 in Minneapolis or St. Paul. I had attended all the conferences and immediately became part of the local planning committee for the Twin Cities event. Since the meetings attracted six hundred to seven hundred people, most of whom needed housing, we generally rented small college campuses with dormitory and dining hall facilities. We held the 1978 conference at Concordia College in St. Paul. The planning itself was a difficult process that left several bruised egos. But the conference was well attended and lively. For many, the highlight was the opportunity to meet Tom Hayden and Jane Fonda, who were the celebrities of the group. Tom had just run for the U.S. Senate from California in a campaign that was designed more to call attention to issues than to win. But he was already planning a more realistic campaign that would land him in the California legislature in the 1980s. His was perhaps the most remarkable transformation—from defendant in the notorious Chicago Seven trial to an effective member of the California Assembly and, later, the California Senate.

I found the most rewarding part of the alternative policy conferences to be the people whom I met. Several would be friends and allies for years to come. I first met Barney Frank at one of the early meetings, and he was the opening-night featured speaker at the St. Paul conference. Barney was then a Massachusetts state representative and was not yet out of the closet. We talked about many issues, but gay rights was not among them. He already exhibited the combination of idealism and pragmatism that would later be his trademark and had little tolerance for radicals who insisted on all or nothing. At a panel on welfare issues, someone suggested that there were people without children and without disabilities who nevertheless needed help.

Barney replied that anyone who thought Americans were ever going to support welfare for able-bodied, childless people were out of their minds; "if we ever get socialism in this country," he quipped, "it will come in on a wheelchair." I also met another closeted gay politician at the alternative policy conferences, but he was far less circumspect than Barney. David Clarenbach was a young state representative from Madison, Wisconsin, who, when we first met in Denver in 1977, told me immediately that he was gay. When I asked him why he didn't come out given the liberal nature of his constituency, he replied that it would be hard on his family and that it would probably thwart his ambition to go to Congress some day. Over the years, as we saw each other from time to time, I tried to nudge him toward the closet door, but I was never successful. Curiously, David successfully steered the first statewide gay rights bill in the country through the Wisconsin legislature in 1982, while he was still closeted. Only after he lost his bid to go to Congress did he finally come out.

My own contribution to the St. Paul alternative policy conference was a speech titled "The Minnesota Populist Tradition." It was a somewhat strange subject for me as I have never considered myself a populist. In studying and teaching American history, I always found myself more drawn to the urban-based, pragmatic progressives than I was to the rural, somewhat woolly-headed populists. The original idea was to feature me together with former governor Elmer Benson, who certainly did think of himself as a populist, but Benson, old and in fragile health, was unable to make it. So I ended up on my own, debunking the idea of populism as it had come to be understood. I outlined the many ways in which the word had been abused, including the absurd idea that right-wing figures like George Wallace and our own Charles Stenvig were populists. And I provided a capsule history of the Minnesota Democratic-Farmer-Labor Party and how it transformed the rural populism of the early twentieth century into a rural-urban, left-wing coalition in the 1930s. Finally, I pointed out that despite the state's progressive tradition, Minnesotans faced the same problems as other Americans. Contrary to the notion that we were a role model for good government, "we're only a little better than the rest of the country" and face the same threats from a resurgent right wing.

Only one more alternative policy conference was held. By the end of the decade, the group that attended had become too diffuse and it was difficult to find unifying themes. Moreover, simply organizing the annual meetings consumed too much time and energy. The group itself held on as a resource for information and a place to share new progressive policy initiatives on the state and local level. But by the 1980s, the ex-radicals had begun to lose their identity as a special group. We had become a part of the body politic.

The rather pessimistic assessment of Minnesota politics that I included in my speech to the alternative policy conference was fulfilled all too soon. The DFL Party went into the 1978 elections hobbled by one unpopular U.S. senator and a divisive fight for the other Senate seat. At the state convention in June, Congressman Don Fraser had been challenged by my state Senate colleague Doug Johnson, a feisty Iron Ranger who was liberal on economic and labor issues, but sharply dissented from Fraser's views on gun control and the environment. Fraser had aroused sharp hostility in northern Minnesota by championing a proposal to limit motorized vehicles in the Boundary Waters Canoe Area, a high priority for environmentalists but anathema to those who lived nearby and wanted to use their motorboats and snowmobiles. Fraser was endorsed and Johnson did not carry his campaign further. But another candidate did. Robert Short was a wealthy businessman who had made his fortune in the trucking and hotel businesses and had long been a thorn in the side of the DFL establishment. A conservative Democrat who dissented from the Humphrey-Mondale tradition, he was perhaps as much motivated by his love of being a maverick as he was by his ideology. He soon announced that he would run against Fraser in the primary, and with money to finance his own campaign, he had to be taken seriously. Meanwhile, some members of the liberal wing of the party exacerbated the division by supporting a primary challenge to Senator Wendell Anderson by a St. Paul lawyer named John Connelly. Anderson had political problems resulting from his self-appointment, but Connelly couldn't win and could only weaken Anderson even further.

I strongly supported Don Fraser and was confident that he would win the September primary. The last week was a flurry of door knocking, rallies, and meetings; everyone I knew was supporting Fraser. The problem was with the people I didn't know. The state was sharply divided geographically, and in rural areas, particularly in northern Minnesota, which voted heavily in DFL primaries, Short was running well. DFL election night parties were traditionally held at the Leamington Hotel in downtown Minneapolis. But Short owned the Leamington, so on September 12 we gathered at the nearby Holiday Inn and cheered as the early returns from the metropolitan area came in overwhelmingly for Fraser. I noticed, however, a few of the old politicos standing in silence. Quietly, they told me that they were worried, that Fraser's margins might not be big enough once the "canoe vote"—as the late-reporting precincts from northern Minnesota were called—started coming in. I went home after midnight still thinking that Fraser had won. The next morning I awakened to the news that once the rural votes were counted, Short had eked out a narrow victory. I had become used to winning over the past few years. This defeat was devastating and it turned out to be disastrous for the DFL party.

The Republicans were poised to take advantage of the DFL's woes. Rudy Boschwitz, a self-made millionaire who had built up statewide name recognition over the years as the result of a series of unconventional ads that had promoted him as much as they did his business, took on the tarnished Anderson. David Durenberger, a lesser-known but attractive Republican activist, was recruited for what was originally seen as the more difficult job of beating Don Fraser; the primary result made him a real contender. And in their biggest coup, the Republicans persuaded Al Quie, a highly respected congressman from southern Minnesota, to oppose Rudy Perpich for governor. In the few weeks between the primary and the general election, I worked on what little still had to be done to assure the election of Lee Greenfield to the legislature and Martin Sabo to Congress. I enthusiastically supported the reelection of Rudy Perpich and, with some reluctance, the reelection of Wendell Anderson, who had easily beaten John Connelly in the primary. But I never supported Short, and for the only time in my adult life, I voted for a Republican, Dave Durenberger. Many liberals in the party did the same and Short's candidacy was doomed. On election night, the only thing we had to cheer about in my corner of Minnesota was the easy election of Greenfield and Sabo. The Republicans won both U.S. Senate seats: not only did Durenberger win but Boschwitz handily beat Wendell Anderson, who had gone from being a popular governor to a generally reviled senator in just two years. The state Senate was not up for election that year, for which DFL members were grateful, but in the House, the Republicans went from a deep deficit to a sixty-seven/sixty-seven tie. And, most surprising to me, Quie defeated Perpich. Rudy had been a dynamic governor and, despite a few foolish ideas, had not seemed to be in deep political trouble. But he was the victim of a DFL Party that had simply come apart at the seams.

The best news on election night came from the West Coast. The antigay crusade, which had begun the previous year in Miami and had seemed almost unstoppable in the spring of 1978, finally met its match. Seattle became the first American city to defeat a referendum to repeal a local gay rights ordinance and it did so by a convincing margin of 63 percent to 37 percent. Even more dramatically, California had defeated the statewide Briggs Initiative. Directly inspired by Anita Bryant's victory in Miami, state senator John Briggs had proposed a measure that would have barred gay people—and in fact anyone who advocated gay rights—from teaching in the public schools. Polls had initially shown strong support, but public opinion turned around when Ronald Reagan opposed the initiative as an unwarranted infringement of basic rights of privacy. Interestingly, it was the privacy issue that had also been used successfully in Seattle. Steve Endean, now attempting to build the Gay Rights National Lobby into a viable organization, suggested to me that we might need to rethink some of our strategic assumptions, that the right to privacy seemed a more effective approach than the human rights argument we had used in St. Paul.

Three weeks later, on November 27, I was driving from the Capitol to the university with my radio tuned to the news on our local public radio station. What I heard was so shocking that I had to pull my car over the side of the road and stop for a few minutes before I could drive again. Harvey Milk and San Francisco Mayor George Moscone had been assassinated in their offices in city hall and the perpetrator was city supervisor Dan White. Over the next few days, the entire story of Dan White's relationship with Milk and Moscone and his twisted motives would emerge. But to me it was the tragic conclusion to a year that had seemed a bit like a roller coaster but with more dips than high points. Not only did I mourn the death of one of the very few openly gay elected officials—a man whom I didn't know well but had come increasingly to respect—but I also feared for my own safety. To be sure, the circumstances of the San Francisco tragedy were very special ones. Nevertheless, I realized that my visibility as an openly gay man in public office gave me a certain vulnerability. I had generally laughed off threatening letters. One handwritten note, which arrived several times in slightly different versions and was signed with the obviously falsified name of the sheriff of Stearns County in central Minnesota, warned me that "if we ever catch sight of you in this area we will kill you with pleasure." Suddenly this didn't seem quite so comical. Minnesota had long prided itself as having a state Capitol accessible to the people and thus provided little in the way of security. Anyone could easily walk into my office with a gun without being stopped. I didn't want a Capitol ringed with armed guards and metal detectors and never pushed for changes. But after the murder of Harvey Milk I felt a little less secure.

Following the defeat of the St. Paul referendum, a group of Minnesota activists, primarily lesbians, had come up with the idea of reaffirming the gay rights movement with a high-visibility march in Washington, D.C., in the spring or summer of 1979. My own experiences had made me skeptical of the effectiveness of this kind of political activity. It had worked once, famously, during the black civil rights struggle, but that was only after the movement had developed critical mass over a period of many years. The peace marches, on the other hand, had done little to end the war in Vietnam. I doubted that the policy makers in Washington would pay much attention to a gay march. Steve Endean, in fact, thought it would make his work of lobbying members of Congress even harder. But gradually, the Minnesota group convinced people in other parts of the country that it was a good idea. With the assassination of Harvey Milk, the march took on a new urgency and became the dramatic response that many in the gay community thought was necessary. Recognizing that the march was going to happen, I became a member of the steering committee. But I never became deeply involved in the planning, and when the march finally took place, on October 14, 1979, I did not attend.

The 1979 gay march on Washington was the first of four such events that would take place over the next quarter century. I did attend the second and third—in 1987 and 1993. My view of these activities evolved slightly over the years, but I still believe that there was considerable merit in my initial lack of enthusiasm. I cannot see how any of the marches had a direct impact on policy decisions affecting gay people. All of them were largely ignored by the powers that be in Washington. Moreover, the marches involved enormous investments in time and energy that, in my mind, could better have been used for less dramatic but more effective lobbying efforts, particularly on the state and local levels. Yet I must admit that being in Washington for two of those marches, and being surrounded by one hundred thousand or more gay and lesbian people rallying for a common cause, was exciting and inspirational. I think the most positive effect of the marches was not how they influenced the policy makers but how they influenced the participants. They created a sense of solidarity and purpose in the community that more mundane activities simply could not equal. For that reason alone, they may have been worthwhile.

The 1979 legislative session confronted me with a new reality. For the first time, I served under a Republican governor and with a House of Representatives that was not DFL controlled. With the House deadlocked, the two caucuses had been forced to reach a power-sharing agreement: the Republicans chose the speaker, while DFLers chaired the three most important committees. Only the Senate remained fully in DFL hands. The DFL regained control of the House after just a year. But Governor Quie stayed in office until 1982, and during his tenure state government was far more contentious than it had been during my first six years in office.

By this time, my own attitude toward my legislative career was beginning to change. Initially, I was just thrilled to be there and didn't think much about moving up the hierarchy of influence. Moreover, as an ultraliberal and an open gay man I did not seem a likely candidate for legislative leadership. But gradually, my politics began to move a bit more toward the mainstream and my sexuality lost its novelty. And I no longer assumed that I would be in the legislature for only a short time. I was becoming less and less committed to my academic career, and the prospect of going back to the university full time no longer had much appeal. So I began to think more about my future as a state senator. After the 1976 election, I had become vice-chair of the Commerce Committee, which was chaired by Senator Robert Tennessen. This gave me an opportunity to wield the gavel from time to time, which was valuable experience but entailed no real power. I was now, however, able to choose my own staff assistant rather than simply be served by a secretary from the Senate pool. And I soon learned that dealing with staff often required considerable tact and sensitivity.

In the late seventies and early eighties, when I was allowed only one staff member, I hired, in succession, two people that I had come to know through politics—Paulette Will and Don Jorovsky. The advantage of this arrangement was that Paulette and Don not only could deal with the secretarial and administrative tasks of the office, they also could handle political issues for me. Overtly political activities were not, of course, supposed to be conducted in legislative offices. But it was hard to draw a clear line between constituent services and good politics. Keeping constituents informed, handling their problems, getting me prepared for events in the district, or, when necessary, representing me in the district were all part of the job. But such activities were also what got a politician reelected. Randomly assigned Senate staff who knew little of my district couldn't do those things. People like Paulette and Don could. On the other hand, if I didn't like the work of a staff member who was assigned to me, I could easily have that person replaced. With a politically active staff person I had to tread lightly or risk a blowup in the district. So I learned to work through problems with staff and to treat them with respect. Don Jorovsky worked for me for four years, managed my campaign in 1980, then went on to another Senate job. A complete political junkie, he is still the person I talk to almost daily to exchange the latest gossip from the world of politics.

The 1979 session was the first in my legislative career in which DFL ideas about taxation and spending were sharply challenged. During the previous six years, the state usually enjoyed budgetary surpluses, and programs dear to the hearts of liberals were adequately funded. The House and Senate often disagreed on particulars (Martin Sabo and Nick Coleman were never close), but there were few basic philosophical differences and we always finished our work on time. But with a Republican governor and a Republican speaker everything changed. The Republicans had long argued that the surpluses were the result of the galloping inflation of the decade that pushed taxpayers into higher brackets even when their incomes were not increasing in real dollars. Their solution was indexing the income tax to allow for inflation, which had the effect of sharply reducing state revenues. To pay for this, they demanded cuts in the state's relatively generous system of social service programs. This resulted in the first special session of my time in the legislature. It would not be the last.

The most contentious issue of 1979, and the one that occupied most of my time, was once again the stadium. On December 1 of the previous year, the stadium commission had voted to build a domed, multipurpose stadium on the Industry Square site in Minneapolis. The outcome was no surprise, but the commission had carefully considered the alternatives and the final vote was four to three, so it was hard to argue that it was all a setup. Nevertheless, the opponents were outraged and had no intention of giving up. The 1977 bill had given the commission the final authority to make the decision and issue bonds without further legislative action. But within days of the start of the 1979 session, two St. Paul legislators had introduced a bill to repeal the 2 percent metropolitan liquor tax that was to have backed up the bonds. Without the tax, the stadium would be effectively dead. The tactic was a shrewd one. Once a Minneapolis site had been chosen, legislators from the rest of the metropolitan area resented the notion of their constituents paying a tax for a stadium that would not directly benefit them. Moreover, a number of pro-stadium legislators had been defeated in the 1978 elections, and legislators increasingly viewed the issue as a politically unpopular one. And, of course, even the Minneapolis delegation was not united as Jack Davies and I enthusiastically supported the repeal effort.

The debate reached a new level of intensity in the spring of 1979. On the one side were some of the most powerful forces in the Twin Cities—the business community, the newspapers, the unions—who had finally put together a plan that they thought had settled the issue. In opposition was a motley collection of groups with a variety of motives. Citizens Opposed to the Stadium Tax (COST) was organized by St. Paul bar owners who didn't want to collect a tax that would go to Minneapolis. Save the Met, led by a quirky but charming young man named Julian Empson, was made up primarily of baseball fans who thought their favorite game should be played outdoors. And Minnesotans Against the Downtown Dome (MADD), the group I most identified with, had its base in the Elliot Park and Cedar-Riverside neighborhoods. Its most effective spokesperson was a young veteran of the antiwar movement named Brian Coyle, who would in a few years represent these neighborhoods on the Minneapolis City Council. I was attending rallies and marches in opposition to the stadium several times a week during this period and spirits were high. Our optimism was justified. By early April, the liquor tax repeal had passed both houses of the legislature and was signed by Governor Quie.

Our victory, however, was temporary. Faced with threats that the Vikings would leave Minnesota, the legislative leadership quickly put together a new package that accepted the commission decision on a Minneapolis location but replaced the metropolitan liquor tax with a hotel and liquor-by-the-drink tax restricted to the city of Minneapolis. On the last day of the session, the bill narrowly passed both houses. Even then, our fight was not quite over. Nick Coleman, who had helped put together the final bill, felt betrayed by the stadium commission's interpretation of the statute in its dealings with the teams and the bonding companies. Together with minority leader Bob Ashbach, long a stadium opponent, and Bob Short, who hated the hotel tax, Nick sued the commission in an attempt to stall the bond sale. And Jack Davies launched a campaign to secure signatures on a petition to repeal the Minneapolis tax through a city charter amendment to be placed on the November ballot. I helped Jack with his petition drive and almost joined Nick Coleman's lawsuit—until I learned that I would be personally liable for costs if we lost. But neither of these last-gasp efforts worked, and in October of 1979 the bonds were sold and construction began on a stadium that was scheduled to open in time for the 1982 baseball season.

Amy Klobuchar, who would go on to become a United States senator, published a book in 1982 about the stadium controversy based on a senior thesis she had written while an undergraduate at Yale. While she attempts to be careful in her judgments, she clearly admires the stadium commission for its ability to build a stadium on time, under budget, and without scandal. It is true that the Hubert H. Humphrey Metrodome—as it came to be called—did not become the costly white elephant that stadiums in other cities often were. Moreover, some of the fears of the neighborhood groups were not realized; traffic and noise were relatively well contained and, other than the construction of a new hotel, little changed in Cedar-Riverside. But I still think I was right in opposing the stadium. I have never found a justification for public subsidies of privately owned sports teams that would not apply equally to any privately owned business. The promise that the stadium would lead to development of underused land in the Industry Square area was never fulfilled; not until the Guthrie Theater relocated nearby twenty-five years later did vacant lots fill up with condominiums, markets, and restaurants. The commission members and staff were proud of staying within a remarkably low budget, but, as the old saying goes, they got what they paid for. Sportswriters from other cities have continually remarked on the building's poor design and lack of amenities. Finally, authorizing a stadium did not achieve what legislators wanted above all: laying the issue to rest so that we could concentrate on more important business. Within fifteen years of the opening of the Metrodome, the Twins were asking for a new stadium, followed within a few years by a similar demand from the Vikings. The Metrodome was as unsuitable for baseball as the old Bloomington stadium had been for football, and other cities were abandoning the multipurpose concept and building separate facilities for each sport. My last session in the legislature was dominated once again by the stadium issue.

While my involvement with the stadium grew out of the special needs of my district, I also began in the late seventies and early eighties to work on a series of issues that related more directly to how I wanted to define myself as a legislator. I always saw myself as a champion of the poor, the disabled, and the abused, and I welcomed the opportunity to carry bills that directly addressed these concerns: changes in the guardianship law; due process in the commitment of those with mental illness; state-subsidized child care; and mandatory reporting of abuse of children and vulnerable adults. Many of these bills were brought to me by advocacy groups, and I had help from well-organized constituencies in shaping them and getting them through the legislature. But they were often complicated and required negotiations with a wide range of interested parties and, in some cases, took several years to pass.

I first introduced a mental commitment bill, for example, in 1976. Based on the concept that no one should be involuntarily committed to a mental institution without full due process, it was strongly opposed by many psychiatrists and some families of the mentally ill, who believed that it would hamstring their efforts to make decisions for their incapacitated relatives. After repeated efforts, the bill finally passed as the Hospitalization and Commitment Act of 1982. In 1979, I introduced a similar law that would protect the legal rights of people about to be placed in guardianship or conservatorship; it passed the following year. The vulnerable adults bill was brought to me by a woman named Jeanette McDougal, whose mentally and physically handicapped daughter had been seriously injured by what she believed was abuse in a nursing home. The bill, which became law in 1980, after long negotiations with the nursing home lobbyists, required all health-care professionals and educators to report to the appropriate authorities any evidence of abuse or neglect they witnessed in a nursing home or a facility for those with mental or developmental disabilities.

I also became the leading spokesman in the Senate for the Minnesota chapter of the National Federation of the Blind. Here, I soon learned, I was entering into territory far more perilous than my efforts on behalf of people with mental illnesses and disabilities. The blind were deeply divided over the nature of their condition and how they should respond to it. Advocates of the traditional approach saw blindness as a handicap to be overcome and sought funding for sheltered workshops that would provide training and jobs, at subminimum wages, for people who, they believed, could not otherwise be employed. Federation members with whom I worked, on the other hand, saw blindness more as an identity and believed that the blind, given the opportunity, could do most things that sighted people could do. They believed societal attitudes toward the blind were patronizing and resented the notion of sighted people making decisions for the blind. They favored training, too, but emphasized the importance of learning Braille, using canes, and becoming self-sufficient so that they could take jobs at full salaries. I was particularly involved in efforts by the federation to influence the policies of the Minnesota State Services for the Blind, which generally followed the traditional approach. I soon learned that a similar division existed within the deaf community. I found the debate itself fascinating, although I was frequently put off by the level of vitriol between the competing factions. But then I remembered how the disputes between Jack Baker, Tim Campbell, and me must have looked to well-meaning straight people.

I made another foray into foreign policy at this time too, although,

I think, with greater justification than my anti–Vietnam War resolution of the early seventies. In 1978, Phyllis Kahn and I introduced a bill that would prohibit the State Board of Investment from purchasing stock in any corporation that operated in the Republic of South Africa and engaged in practices that would be considered discriminatory under the Minnesota Human Rights Act. South African divestiture, as it came to be known, was part of an international response to the intransigence of South Africa's white minority government and its system of apartheid, which deprived the black majority of basic civil rights and economic opportunity. State and city governments managed the investment of large sums of money that were held in their employee retirement funds. Using those funds to pressure the South African government did more than a resolution stating a position on a foreign policy issue. As Phyllis and I argued, "U.S. investments in South Africa have helped the South African regime, not hindered it . . . [and] are not insignificant in the South African economy. . . . We believe that U.S. corporations have a responsibility to ensure that their operations and employment practices are carried out in an atmosphere in which fundamental human rights are paramount."

I spent the next seven years working on this issue. With gay rights beyond reach for the time being, South African divestiture became my major human rights cause in the legislature. I brought in speakers, attended conferences, and met a fascinating array of people. Many South African exiles were working in the United States during this period, trying to increase international support for the anti-apartheid movement, and several came to Minnesota at my invitation to testify before legislative committees. We heard from Donald Woods, a white journalist who had played a leading role in publicizing the case of Steve Biko, the leader of the Black Consciousness movement who had died of "head injuries" while being interrogated by South African authorities. On another occasion, our guest was Dennis Brutus, a distinguished poet who was classified as "colored" by South African law, a separate category for people of mixed race; his refusal to accept this arbitrary division led to imprisonment and exile. And I collaborated regularly with Dumisani Kumalo, a black South African who was working on divestiture issues with the American Committee on Africa and the Africa Fund. He made several visits to Minnesota and invited me to attend a conference for legislators interested in South Africa at the United Nations in 1981. There I met, among others, Julian Bond, then a state senator in Georgia. I never fully realized how quickly the world can change until I read in 1999 that Nelson Mandela had appointed Dumisani Kumalo to be South Africa's ambassador to the United Nations. A young man expelled from his homeland, shuttling from state to state in a foreign country seeking support for his cause, had returned home to become a leading diplomat of a newly liberated nation.

Initially, the divestiture bill was not received with enthusiasm in the Minnesota legislature. There was strong opposition from several quarters: the boards of the various state pension funds and the portfolio managers who advised them; corporations doing business in South Africa, including Minnesota-based firms such as 3M, Honeywell, and Control Data; and, most important, the State Board of Investment, which actually made investment policy and which consisted of the governor, the attorney general, the secretary of state, the state auditor, and the state treasurer. The opponents mounted several arguments, all of which I thought I could answer. First, they maintained that the state held the funds in trust and that it was bound by the principle of fiduciary responsibility to consider only the long-term financial interests of the employees and retirees to whom the money actually belonged. I brought in an investment manager from Shearson/American Express who held that "there is no reason to imagine that creating an investment portfolio excluding companies in Southern Africa is a financially unsound idea." In fact, we argued, the volatility of the situation in South Africa could create additional risk. Second, the opponents pointed out that withdrawing foreign investments and weakening the South African economy would hurt blacks as well as whites. My answer to that was that we were being asked to divest by the African National Congress, which represented the vast majority of black South Africans. Finally, our local companies insisted that their South African facilities adhered to the Global Sullivan Principles, a set of guidelines designed to foster racial equality in the workplace, and that their presence was hence ameliorating the rigors of the apartheid system. But, we countered, the situation for black South Africans was worsening, not improving, and the Sullivan Principles did nothing for those employees when they left work and faced the cruelties of the passbook system, rigid racial segregation, police brutality, and suppression of dissent.

I was persuaded, however, that immediate total divestiture might have a destabilizing effect on the portfolio (and, in any case, couldn't pass). So in 1981, together with Randy Staten, the only African American member of the House, I introduced a bill that would not require divestiture of existing investments but would prohibit future investments in companies with a presence in South Africa. This approach seemed more palatable to our colleagues, and we put together an impressive list of labor, religious, and civic groups that supported it. By early 1982, it had passed out of committee in both houses and I managed to win final passage in the Senate. The next day, the State Board of Investment, which had been quiet up to this point, voted unanimously to oppose the bill. Knowing that he no longer had the necessary votes in the house, Representative Staten amended the bill so that it would apply only to deposits in banks that had investments in South Africa. In this drastically watered-down version, it passed both houses, only to be vetoed by Governor Quie.

We came back again with a future investments bill in 1983 and, by this time, the solid opposition of the investment board had begun to break down. Secretary of State Joan Growe, now a candidate for the DFL endorsement for U.S. Senate, supported the bill. But it still didn't pass. We did not succeed until 1985, and then our victory came not in the legislature but through the action of the investment board. State treasurer Robert Mattson reversed his position, arguing that "revolution and civil war now seem inevitable" in South Africa and that it was therefore no longer a safe place for investments. Rudy Perpich, who had replaced Quie as governor, and Attorney General Skip Humphrey, joined Mattson and Growe in a four to one vote in favor of a plan to gradually phase out all investments in South Africa over the next four years. Only the state auditor, Arne Carlson, the sole Republican on the board, voted no, arguing that "we are playing with someone else's money."

The 1979 session ended in a profound sadness in the Senate that overshadowed our conflicts with the governor and the House. On the morning of April 25, I was awakened very early by a phone call from

Milt Goldstein with the news that Bob Lewis, my closest friend in the Senate, had died in his sleep. He had not been sick and his death was totally unexpected. He was forty-seven years old. He had been one of the few colleagues whom I absolutely trusted. We agreed on most issues, but when we didn't I never doubted that he had good reasons for his position; he was a man of total integrity. I had a hard time realizing that suddenly and without warning he was gone. His death left a gap not only in my life but in the life of the Senate. Nick Coleman liked him immensely and recognized his talent. After the 1976 election, he had made Bob the chair of the Finance Subcommittee on Health, Welfare and Corrections, jumping him ahead of his colleagues of equal seniority—including me. When Bob died, Roger Moe, the chairman of the Finance Committee, took over the subcommittee for the remainder of the 1979 session. Nick left it up to Roger to make the permanent replacement.

Most Capitol veterans considered the Senate Finance Committee and the House Appropriations Committee to be the heart of state government. All of the major funding decisions were made there and in the joint conference committees that grew out of them each session. Members coveted seats on the money committees, as they were called, and their chairs were regarded as the most important legislative leaders other than the majority leader of the Senate and the speaker of the House. In my second term, I was appointed to Finance and was given seats on both the Health, Welfare and Corrections Subcommittee and a catchall subcommittee known simply as State Departments. I knew the work was important, but it was often a slog. We spent hours listening to departmental bureaucrats presenting their budgets, and we were expected to ask them detailed and probing questions. And in the end, the decisions were made by a handful of legislative leaders who chaired the conference committees. The subcommittees themselves had a unique status. To chair one was regarded as a step above chairing the subcommittee of a policy committee, yet not quite fully equivalent to chairing a full committee. That would change over the years: by the 1990s, senators rejected policy committee chairmanships in order to chair finance subcommittees (by then called divisions). After all, there was little significant policy that could be made in areas like education, human services, and transportation unless you had the money to implement it.

I never begrudged Bob Lewis his appointment to chair the Health, Welfare and Corrections Subcommittee. But when he died, I wanted to replace him. Fortunately, I had developed a good relationship with Roger Moe. Roger was seven years younger than me but had been elected while still in his twenties and had two years more seniority. He had been a small-town high school teacher and represented a mostly rural, heavily Norwegian district in the far northwestern part of the state. I was always impressed, given the conservative makeup of his constituency, how consistently liberal his voting record was. He had, for example, supported gay rights without hesitation and without complaining about how much it was going to hurt him politically. Roger was well respected within the Senate, and when the chairmanship of Finance opened in 1977, he defeated several more senior colleagues for the position. After the 1979 session ended, he told me and two colleagues that he would decide on Bob's replacement before the 1980 session. I worked hard in the interim to impress him. I was in constant motion, visiting every correctional institution and mental hospital in the state, writing memos, holding hearings, and trying to master the arcane intricacies of state budget making. In the fall, Roger told me that the chairmanship was mine.

I also found time in the interim to travel to somewhere a little more exotic than state prisons. Always fascinated by the prospect of visiting places where travel had long been forbidden or discouraged—such as the Soviet Union in 1967 and China in 1975—I signed up in the summer of 1979 for a trip to Cuba. For a brief period, during the Carter administration, the ban on travel to Cuba had been lifted, and although there were still no direct flights or individual tourism, some travel agencies were offering group tours via Montreal. I contacted a travel agency in New York that had long specialized in tours to Communist countries and arranged to go to Cuba in June for two weeks. The group was an eclectic one, ranging from officers of the Communist Party USA to older, apolitical couples who had been everywhere else and wanted to add Cuba to their travel dossier. We spent several days in Havana, then traveled the length of the island, ending up in Santiago de Cuba.

As with the China tour, we visited a lot of social institutions, particularly schools and clinics, as education and health care were the two major achievements of the Cuban revolution. Other than a cigar factory, we were shown little in the way of industry, probably because there wasn't much to show. There was, of course, a lot less to see in terms of scenery or cultural monuments than there had been in China, but it was interesting nonetheless. There was still a sense of faded glory in Havana, and some of the smaller towns displayed well-preserved buildings from the colonial period. And the people were wonderfully welcoming, delighted to have American visitors despite all they had been told about the evils of the American government. Everywhere there was interest in American pop culture. One morning, our guide greeted us with what she was sure would be heartbreaking news to all of us; she told us sadly that John Wayne had died—news that was clearly more important to her than to anyone in our group. But much of what we saw looked badly run down, with dilapidated buildings and rutted roads and streets. We stayed in the old Havana Hilton, now the Havana Libre, a sad shell of what it must have once been. And everywhere, even in the best hotels, the food was terrible. On an island, surrounded by a bountiful sea, we were never served fresh seafood. Our hosts blamed everything bad on the American boycott, and it was hard to judge how much of that was true. It was also hard to know how much to trust the Cubans who eagerly told us how the revolution had improved their lives.

As always, I plunged full throttle into politics in the summer and fall of 1979 with the usual endless round of meetings, door knocks, and fund-raisers. Just days before the city convention in May, Al Hofstede had announced that he would not be a candidate for reelection as mayor. Hofstede had run against Stenvig three times, winning twice and losing once, and with Stenvig no longer a significant factor, he could have won easily in 1979. But the DFL had an exceptionally attractive candidate ready to replace Hofstede. Don Fraser, after sixteen years representing Minneapolis in the U.S. House, had given up his seat the previous year in his unsuccessful run for the Senate. He was still in Washington, but when he heard of the vacancy, he immediately returned home, was easily endorsed, and went on to win in November and serve fourteen years as mayor. An unusually thoughtful and farsighted politician, Fraser was an outstanding mayor, and my only regret was the he presided over a system that did not give him enough power over a fractious and parochial city council.

Before the end of the year, two highly contentious races for the 1980 elections were emerging, one on the national and one on the local level, and I was immediately drawn into both. By August, I was already attending meetings to prepare for Senator Ted Kennedy's presidential campaign against Jimmy Carter. Carter had been a big disappointment. The first Democratic president in the twentieth century without a real reform program, he had failed to accomplish even the modest agenda that he had set for himself. Moreover, the polls suggested that he could not be reelected and that Kennedy was favored by a margin of almost two to one. Yet in Minnesota, few Democratic politicians wanted to take on their own president, especially with the still-popular Walter Mondale as vice president. Only Secretary of State Joan Growe and Lee Greenfield and I signed up early for the Kennedy campaign. Enthusiasm was high when he visited Minnesota for a well-attended rally in November, and it looked for a while that we were supporting a likely winner. But the Iran hostage crisis led many Americans to rally behind the incumbent president. And in a disastrous television interview with Roger Mudd, Kennedy had difficulty explaining his lapse of judgment in the famous incident at Chappaquiddick and, perhaps even more important, justifying his decision to challenge the president. We entered the new year still backing Kennedy but with diminished hopes.

If I made the bold decision in supporting Kennedy over Carter, I took a more cautious approach in a challenge to one of my Senate colleagues. Karen Clark had come to see me in July to tell me that she was planning to run against Steve Keefe in the Senate district adjoining mine. Karen was an open lesbian who had been active for a number of years in gay rights and feminist organizations. I had known her, although not well, respected her abilities, and realized that she would have enthusiastic support in the gay and, particularly, the lesbian communities. Her quarrel with Steve, however, was not over gay rights, which he fully supported. It focused on two other highly emotional issues: Steve Keefe voted consistently against freedom of choice on abortion and had been the chief author of the stadium bill. These were unpopular positions in his district, as they were in mine, and left Steve politically vulnerable. Political activists had tried to persuade Representative Linda Berglin to run for the Senate, but she had refused to risk a safe House seat to challenge an incumbent senator. Karen was ready to take on the fight. Both Karen and Steve, of course, wanted my support.

No decision ever gave me more sleepless nights than this one. On the one hand, there was nothing I wanted more than an openly gay colleague in the legislature. I had two Senate colleagues whom I knew were gay. One was more or less out within the gay community and led an openly gay social life. We would often sit together on the Senate floor and evaluate the good-looking male staff members as they walked by. The other was a married man, more deeply closeted, who did not come out to me until after he left the Senate and his marriage broke up. But neither of them publicly acknowledged their sexuality and were of little use to me in planning strategy and sharing the workload on gay issues. I knew that if Karen Clark were elected I would have an active partner in the Senate and would no longer be the only one who could speak personally on gay issues. On the other hand, Steve Keefe had been a strong ally and good friend. We disagreed on abortion and the stadium but agreed on almost everything else, and he had been very supportive of me when I had come out. It was difficult for me to turn on him. I also believed there needed to be a very strong reason to dump an incumbent of one's own party and while I believed that the criterion had been met with Jimmy Carter, it had not with Steve Keefe. I could have tried to stay neutral, but that would have been difficult given my prominence in the gay community and in Minneapolis politics. So I decided to support Steve Keefe. Karen told me that she understood but many of her supporters did not. I had given my critics in the gay community another reason to believe that I was a waffler and a compromiser, insufficiently committed to the gay cause.

The 1980 session was short and much of my time was taken up with my new responsibility as chair of the Health, Welfare and Corrections Subcommittee of Finance. Because we were working only on a supplementary budget that year we combined all of the Finance subcommittee bills into a single bill that we called, rather unfortunately, the "garbage bill" because it contained a little bit of everything. The press had a field day with that label and said that it was a perfect name for sloppy and slightly smelly lawmaking. The conference committee on the "garbage bill" was the first major conference committee on which I ever served, and while I was excited by being in the center of the action, I had to agree that some of the procedure was sloppy and perhaps a bit smelly. The major problem with conference committees was that they delegated some of the most important decisions of the legislative session to just ten legislators and then left the full body with the option only of voting the conference committee report up or down with no amendments allowed. Conference committee members often abused their power by inserting items that had never even been considered in either house. The meetings ran long into the night and crucial decisions were made when everyone was dead tired. And even members of the conference committees were frequently shut out of the final decisions as the two chairmen—one from each house—would go off into a private room and work out a deal. I was only beginning to see these problems in 1980. But after serving on dozens of conference committees in subsequent years, I became a strong critic of the system and eventually a supporter of a unicameral legislature as the only viable alternative.

Toward the end of the session, I received an unexpected telephone call from my old graduate school friend Don Smith. I had not seen much of Don since we had left Yale. He had stayed on to teach at Yale for a few years after I came to Minnesota and then took a job at Grinnell College in Iowa. He, Al Jones, and I had a brief reunion in Iowa in 1973, and I had dinner with Don at a history convention a few years later. But we had not maintained our friendship on a regular basis and I was surprised when he asked if he could come to Minnesota to see me. I told him that, of course, he would be welcome and he came to visit in early April. Before he arrived, I suspected why he wanted to see me. Don had never married and I could never remember his having had a girlfriend. We had never discussed our sexuality but he surely knew about my public coming out. That indeed was what he wanted to talk to me about. Don had been deeply in the closet, scarcely even acknowledging his homosexuality to himself. As is so often the case, a closeted life exacted a high price. Don's career was going well. He had chosen to go to a college that put a premium on teaching over research, and he had developed into a popular and highly effective teacher whose students often kept in touch with him for years after they left Grinnell. But he had little social life outside of the college and no romantic attachments, and his personal frustrations had been quite unsettling. He needed to talk about his sexuality and I was one of the few people he knew with whom he could do that.

Don and I talked a lot that weekend and we continued to talk a lot over the years to come. Once our friendship was renewed, we began to see each other on a regular basis. In additional to our both being gay, we shared two strong common interests—classical music and politics. Don would come to Minnesota five or six times a year to attend a concert and we would spend the weekend together analyzing the current political situation. A few years later, we began to travel together and took some memorable trips to France and Italy. Although Don never ran for public office, he became deeply involved in Democratic Party politics in Iowa and, in presidential election years, always had a lot to say about the famous Iowa caucuses. He never found a romantic partner, as I did a few years later, but I think Don began to feel more comfortable about his sexuality as the years went on. I would like to think that his ability to talk openly and frankly to me helped him as he sorted out his emotions.

Despite my failure to pass a gay rights bill, I was still much in demand as a speaker on gay rights issues, and shortly after the end of the 1980 legislative session I went to Sioux Falls to talk to the local group. Upon my return, on April 19, I discovered that my father and my brother had been frantically trying to reach me. My mother was in the hospital and was not expected to survive the night. I had last seen my parents in January. My mother had suffered from scleroderma for twenty-five years and it now affected her digestive system. She was having ever more frequent intestinal blockages, which needed, of course, immediate attention. Although just sixty-nine, she was becoming increasingly frail. I was concerned that she was not getting proper medical care in Mexico, but both of my parents insisted that nothing could be done beyond what the doctors there did. And my mother saw her doctor in Chicago every summer when the two of them came north to visit. But this time the blockage could not be opened, sepsis set in, and she was too weak for a colostomy. When I talked to my father the next morning, he told me that she had died during the night.

I had long assumed that my mother would want to be buried in

Michigan City, in the little Jewish section of the municipal cemetery near her parents and her brother. My father, I knew, was totally un-sentimental about such things and told us on many occasions that he didn't care what happened to his body after he died. But my mother was more traditional and still felt strong ties to her Jewish heritage. I was surprised, therefore, just a year or two before she died, when she told me that she no longer felt any connection to Michigan City and that there was no one left there that she really cared about. She would prefer, she said, to be buried in Minneapolis, where, she assumed, I would live for the rest of my life. She would still want a Jewish funeral, but she insisted that it should be very simple. In keeping with these wishes, my brother and I decided that he would go to Guadalajara to help my father with the arrangements there and I would organize the funeral in Minneapolis. My mother died on a Saturday night; we hoped that we could bury her by Thursday.

The international transfer of a dead body is not a simple procedure and my brother had his hands full arranging for the transport of my mother's body to the United States. In addition, he had to console my father and begin the difficult task of sorting through our mother's personal belongings. My job was less difficult. I did not then belong to a synagogue, but Rabbi Max Shapiro of Temple Israel readily agreed to officiate at the funeral and I purchased a plot at the Temple Israel cemetery. I also found a local funeral home that would receive the body when it arrived from Mexico. There was one hitch. I received a telephone call from the funeral director telling me that the body had arrived but that the casket came with a crucifix attached. What should he do? Take it off, I replied. Fortunately, I was the only one at the funeral who noticed the tell-tale pattern of screw holes on the side of the casket. We had just a small graveside ceremony. My aunt and uncle, Roz and Lester, came in from Michigan City and my mother's sister, Cele, whom I had not seen since I had called her a racist eighteen years earlier, flew in from California. A few nephews and nieces also attended, and of course a number of my friends came. Rabbi Shapiro conducted a brief, dignified service that was, I think, exactly what my mother would have wanted.

My mother's death affected me more than I realized at the time. I showed no outward sign of emotion and told myself that it was better for me just to keep busy. I even met my classes at the university while

I was waiting for my father and brother to arrive from Mexico. But my mother's death left an enormous void in my life. We had been very close, and with one notable exception I had loved sharing with her all the details of my life. For many years after, when something interesting happened, my first thought would be how much my mother will enjoy hearing about it—and then I would realize that she was no longer around. I had recurrent dreams, too, in which she appeared and when I reminded her that she was dead she would assure me that she wasn't. Then I would wake up to the sure knowledge that she was. Perhaps my greatest regret was that she never met Jun, whom I started living with two years after she died. I think she would have been enormously pleased that I found a partner as down-to-earth and thoughtful as Jun. Her assumption, I believe, was that if I ever paired up with someone it would be a self-absorbed intellectual to whom she would never be able to relate.

The most immediate issue for my brother and me was what my father would do now. We suggested that he come back from Mexico and live somewhere near, although not with, one of us. He would have none of that. He insisted that he wanted to stay in Mexico and that he could live alone. He stayed with me for about three weeks before returning. I had a conference in Houston in June, so I piggybacked on that and went to Guadalajara to see how he was doing. I was not encouraged. My father came from the generation that lived at home until marriage. His mother took care of him until it was time to turn him over to his wife. He had never cooked or kept house for himself. He complained to me, for instance, that when he took chicken from the freezer and cooked it, it was always too dry. When I opened the freezer, I immediately saw why: the chicken was just lying there—totally unwrapped. Still, he insisted that he was learning and that he would do just fine and that we shouldn't worry about him.

About four months later, I was talking to my father on the phone when he indicated that he wanted to tell me something that I might not like to hear. "You might think it's too soon," he said. It turned out that he had a girlfriend, a Mexican woman just a few years younger than he, who was spending a lot of time at his house. Both my brother and I were enormously relieved and did not think this at all disrespectful of our mother. Later on we met Marina and found her to be a kind and caring woman who loved our father deeply. They eventually married and she saved him from what would otherwise have been a lonely and frustrating widowhood.

I was attending too many funerals during these years. Just before the end of the 1980 legislative session, Nick Coleman announced that he would not run for reelection and was retiring from political life. Nick had tried twice for higher office—for governor in 1970 and for the U.S. Senate in 1978—and found his path blocked. He believed that he had accomplished all that he could as Senate majority leader. And he had a new, younger wife with whom he wanted to spend more time. He was looking forward to a more leisurely future. Then in June, just days after a testimonial dinner celebrating his career, he went to the doctor with what he thought was a bad case of the flu. He was diagnosed with a severe form of leukemia that his doctor told him was untreatable. Nick did not give up easily. He found a doctor at the University of Minnesota who was willing to try an experimental treatment on him—and for a while the leukemia went into remission. But in March 1981, Nick Coleman died. He was only fifty-five. In just two years, I had lost my mother and two of my best friends in the Senate. And this was before the AIDS epidemic had begun to cut its path through the gay community.

The 1980 elections brought mixed results. The most dramatic outcome emerged from Karen Clark's challenge to Steve Keefe. In late February, just a month before the endorsing convention, Steve had decided to drop out and retire from the Senate. I was surprised as I had always seen him as a highly ambitious person who would do anything to preserve his political career. But he told me that he could not get endorsed and that, while he might be able to eke out a victory in a DFL primary, it just wasn't worth it. Linda Berglin, who had initially refused to challenge Steve, now jumped in. The contest between Linda and Karen had a wholly different complexion from the race between Steve and Karen. There were no major policy differences; Karen's supporters simply thought that Linda was behaving opportunistically while Linda's people thought she was far better qualified than Karen and would be a more effective senator. I now supported Karen Clark, which many people had trouble understanding. Why would I support Karen against the liberal Linda Berglin when I failed to support her against a candidate who opposed freedom of choice on abortion and supported the stadium? My support for Steve Keefe had to do with personal loyalty and my views about incumbency. With Steve out of the race, I had no reason not to support a woman who would join me as an openly gay colleague in the legislature.

The endorsing convention was a classic that is still frequently spoken of in awe by Minneapolis politicos. It went countless ballots and lasted until the wee hours of the morning, and on several occasions Karen Clark was close to getting the 60 percent vote that she needed. But Linda's floor leaders were Jeff Spartz and his allies, and they had become highly skillful in managing conventions. In the end there was no endorsement, which made the better-known Linda Berglin a likely winner in an open DFL primary. Karen, however, had an alternative; she could run for the House seat that Linda was vacating. She didn't live in the district, but she could move just a few blocks and be easily elected to the House instead of waging an uphill race for the Senate. Unfortunately, Karen and her partner had just remodeled their house and her partner did not take kindly to this idea. But Karen wanted to be a legislator and she did it. Her relationship with her partner was strained and lasted just a couple of more years. But Karen was elected to the House and began what would become the longest career in elective office of any openly gay or lesbian person in the country. She also became my valued ally, my partner in the effort to pass gay and lesbian rights legislation over the next two decades.

My own race was overshadowed by all of this. After Steve Carter's weak showing in 1976, the Republicans essentially gave up on the district and, unlike Steve Keefe, I remained highly popular among the DFL activists. I was unanimously endorsed, had no primary opposition, and faced, literally, a magician in the general election. The Republicans apparently thought it would take a bag of tricks to beat me as they endorsed a man who owned a magic store and did magic acts for parties and events. He ran a barely visible campaign that netted him less than 30 percent of the vote. Statewide, the Senate continued to hold a strong DFL majority and the House also returned to solid DFL control after the tie vote of 1978.

The major disappointment was the national election. Teddy Kennedy's campaign showed some signs of life in the spring, but it was too late to prevent Jimmy Carter from winning the nomination. Even though I had disappointed in his presidency, I supported Carter against Ronald Reagan. Despite the weakened economy, high inflation and interest rates, and the Iran hostage crisis, it seemed hard for me to believe that Reagan could win. I thought that he was far too conservative to win a national election and saw him as a simpleton, a movie actor who had learned to play the part of a presidential candidate. Of course I was wrong and watched in disbelief as Reagan won with a substantial majority. On election night, a Democrat whom I did not know accosted me and accused those of us who had supported Kennedy of causing this debacle. We had weakened Carter, he said, and given the Republicans all the talking points they needed to defeat him. I rejected this argument at the time but have wondered in retrospect if there is anything to it. I suspect that Reagan would have defeated Carter even had there not been a Kennedy challenge. At the same time, there is no doubt that internal party rifts usually end up helping the opposition.

At the first meeting of the DFL caucus after the election, we chose Roger Moe to succeed Nick Coleman as majority leader. Roger was still in his midthirties, but he had been in the Senate for ten years and had been widely respected for his leadership on the Finance Committee. His style was totally different from Nick's—the cool, detached Norwegian as opposed to the fiery, passionate Irishman. Roger made it clear that he would be far more low key, carry few bills himself, and lead by consensus. He did exactly that. In fact, my one criticism of Roger Moe, whom I greatly admired and who led the Senate for the remainder of my career, was that he sometimes waited too long for a consensus to develop. Many caucus meetings would end indecisively and, while Nick would tell us what we were going to do before we left the room, Roger would simply leave it up in the air. There were many occasions when I wanted to say to him, "OK, Roger, everyone has had a say. Now let's decide what we're going to do."

I now had enough seniority to become a committee chair and I weighed my options carefully. Both the Health and Human Services Committee and the Commerce Committee had vacancies and either, I thought, would be a good fit. I knew that Roger Moe thought well of me, and his aide, Mark Andrew, even dropped hints that Roger would be happy to see me as chair of Finance. I never expected Finance but I did anticipate a good position. But Roger Moe did not make the decisions unilaterally. The caucus elected an organizing committee, and, since the committee met during the hours when I was teaching, I didn't run for it. Nor did I hang around when it did meet to press my case. It was a foolish mistake. Too late I learned that the chairmanships I wanted were going to other senators. I was made the chairman of a newly created committee on public employees and pensions. I had little interest in this subject. Moreover, two joint legislative commissions, one on pensions, the other on employee relations, made most of the final decisions in this area, leaving relatively little for a committee to do. I had learned a hard lesson. If I didn't look out for my own interests, no one else was going to do it for me.

I complained to Roger Moe about my assignment, and he agreed that I had not come out well. He explained that there were just too many people to take care of and several of them were aggressively pursuing their cases. But he pointed out that it would only be for two years as the Senate would have to run again after reapportionment in 1982 and there would be another reorganization. He also told me that if the committee was wholly distasteful to me, I could keep my present assignment as chair of the Finance Subcommittee on Health, Welfare and Corrections. A few years later, as those subcommittees grew in importance and prestige, I would have done that. But in 1981 a full committee chairmanship gave me a second staff member while a subcommittee chairmanship did not. So I swallowed hard and accepted the chairmanship of the Public Employees and Pensions Committee, which we soon began calling PEAP (pronounced like the sound of a chicken). Don Jorovsky stayed on as my secretary and I hired Marcia Greenfield, who had been working in the Senate for eight years, to be my administrative assistant. At least, I would be surrounded by friends.

I never developed any strong interest in pensions. I soon learned that this was a complicated and contentious area, and I had all I could do to gain a basic understanding of the issues involved. The various pensions funds and the public employee unions were constantly asking for increases in benefits, many of which would have placed excessive obligations on the state. At least this experience taught me the importance of being able to say no. The vice-chair of my committee was Don Moe, Roger's brother, who had just moved over to the Senate from the House, where he had been the resident expert on pension issues. He knew a lot more than I did and was deeply committed to fiscal responsibility; the pension fund leaders viewed him as an intransigent adversary. I found myself often mediating between the funds and Don Moe.

My chairmanship did give me jurisdiction over one issue that I genuinely cared about: South African divestiture. But given the opposition of the State Board of Investment, I never got very far with my bills. I decided to try a new tactic that would go beyond the South African issue itself. I had read Jeremy Rifkin's book *The North Shall Rise Again,* which argued that the billions of dollars invested by states and municipalities should be used to build local economies rather than simply placed in corporate stocks and bonds. At the same time, a local left-leaning foundation, the Minnesota Project, funded largely by department store heir and DFL political activist Mark Dayton, had issued a report urging the State Board of Investment to include a Minnesota preference in its investment policy. This would help provide much-needed funds for small business development, energy systems, housing, and family farming here at home. Karen Clark and I introduced a strategic investment bill that would give preference to Minnesota companies and at the same time prohibit investments in corporations that violated laws on human rights, the environment, and labor relations as well as prohibit doing substantial business in countries that condone violations in these areas. Once again, the investment board and the pension funds accused me and my allies of trying to do good with other people's money and skirting time-honored principles of fiduciary responsibility. The bill passed both houses on very close votes, but in the House of Representatives the prohibition section was removed. The session ended with the bill in conference committee, and neither Karen nor I was able to envision a compromise that we could support that would muster enough votes to pass the legislature.

This bill began my long working relationship with Karen Clark. In addition to the strategic investment bill, we introduced a gay and lesbian human rights bill in 1981 and continued to work together on this issue throughout the 1980s, even though we knew there was no realistic chance for passage. We thought it was important to keep the issue before the legislature and to mobilize the gay and lesbian community each year so that it was clear the issue was not going away. When Wisconsin became the first state in the country to pass this kind of legislation in 1982, we had many conversations with the legislative and community leaders there, attempting to understand how they did it. But it took a decade before we were able to emulate our neighboring state.

As Karen and I took on these issues, we learned that we could work well together despite real differences in our personalities and our approaches to politics. I had become more of a pragmatist by this time in my career and had lost the political purity that I had had in the 1960s. Karen remained an idealist, able to compromise when absolutely necessary, but still willing to take on issues that I considered quixotic. Moreover, I did not have the patience I once had and hated sitting through endless meetings so that everyone's ideas, no matter how foolish, could be heard. Karen was continually calling "community meetings" and insisted on establishing the broadest possible consensus before moving ahead on an issue. Karen was also far more a product of the counterculture than I was; we particularly disagreed on issues involving alternative medicine—herbal remedies, naturopathy, faith healing. Some years later, when Karen was seriously ill with ovarian cancer, she told me she was comforted to know that several of her Indian constituents were beating drums on her behalf. I told her that I hoped she had a good surgeon, too; fortunately, she did. Karen's openness and total lack of cynicism made her far more beloved in the local gay and lesbian community than I was. It was very hard to accuse her of being an elitist or a sellout, charges that were often leveled against me. But I never begrudged her this and we remained good friends and trusted allies. My time in the legislature would have been far more difficult had she not been elected to the House.

One other bill that I authored in 1981 had perhaps the most unusual constituency I ever worked with. The extended debate over sentencing, which had lasted throughout most of the 1970s, had ended with the adoption of a sentencing guidelines system that had taken effect on May 1, 1980. The specific guidelines were set by a commission, not by the legislature, and they tended to set shorter terms for property crimes and longer terms for crimes against persons. But they applied only to offenders sentenced after May 1, 1980, which resulted in more than one thousand preguidelines inmates who were serving longer terms than later inmates who committed similar offenses. These inmates felt cheated and raised fifteen thousand dollars to hire a lobbyist to work to make the guidelines retroactive. I told their lobbyist, a highly respected young lawyer (and future judge) named Kevin Burke, that across-the-board retroactivity could never pass. But we worked out a plan that would allow preguidelines inmates to petition their sentencing judges for reduced terms. Each judge would have full discretion to grant or reject a petition on a case-by-case basis and there could be no appeal. Even this modified plan was highly controversial as legislators feared that it could be construed as being "soft on criminals." And our constituency did not always help, as when they predicted prison riots if the bill did not pass. But ultimately we got the bill through and the inmates presented me with a beautiful plaque for my efforts—which I was never sure whether I wanted to display publicly in my office. Later, when some of the petitions were denied, I was asked to try to achieve full retroactivity. I had a quick response to that: "Forget about it."

In June 1981, my father would turn seventy-five and my brother and I discussed for several months what we should do for him. With our mother gone, a party seemed senseless. So we decided that we would take him on a trip and Greece seemed the logical destination. Richard and Athena were building a summerhouse there. It was located less than an hour from Athens, on an undeveloped site on the slope of a mountain with spectacular views of the sea stretching almost to the famous temple at Cape Sounion. They could stay there, but the house was not yet ready for guests. My father and I would stay down on the seashore in a resort motel, just a few miles away. Our father was pleased with our proposal, although it meant that he would need to leave Marina for a few weeks; they were not yet married, so we did not include her in our plans, even though they were seeing each other regularly.

I went to Europe for almost a month. I first went to England and met a gay couple from Minneapolis in London, where we shared an apartment for a few days. Then we went out to Cornwall, a part of England I had not seen when I had been there before. We had a particularly memorable stay at a B and B in an old farmhouse, where we were hosted by an elderly couple who gave us wonderful breakfasts and then planned our days for us. From England, I flew to Athens and met my family. We spent the first week near Richard and Athena's house, had plenty of time for the beach, and took side trips into Athens and to the spectacular ruins at Delphi. The second week we were joined by Athena's mother and went to the island of Spetses, where we stayed in an old turn-of-the-century resort hotel that catered to British tourists. Spetses was delightful and my stay there was enhanced by reading John Fowles's strange novel *The Magus,* which is set on the island and, in part, at the hotel where we stayed.

When I returned I found myself once again embroiled in Minneapolis politics. Our city council member, Judy Corrao, whom I had never particularly admired, had by now proved herself a disappointment even to some of those who had strongly supported her. She had become far too close to the high-powered lobbyists who were a constant presence at city hall. In particular, on the most contentious issue confronting the council at the time, choosing a cable television provider, she had supported the company with the slickest lobbying operation rather than the one that most of her constituents thought would offer the best service. A number of DFL Party activists decided it was time to replace her and we had an excellent candidate. I first met Kathy O'Brien when she was a graduate student in history at the university. She married a fellow graduate student, Jeff Loesch, and the two of them soon became involved in politics, first on the West Bank and then in the Seward neighborhood where I lived. Kathy was smart and capable and, most important, had the kind of internal compass that was necessary to maintain her integrity amidst the pressures of city government.

Once again, the split in the south Minneapolis DFL became a factor in the race. Kathy had supported Jeff Spartz in his challenge to Dick Hanson in 1976. Nevertheless, Spartz and his allies remained loyal to Corrao, while the Spear-Greenfield group formed the core of the O'Brien campaign. Neither candidate could win the 60 percent needed for party endorsement, and we spent the summer working on a hard-fought primary. This time we prevailed. Corrao had alienated a large segment of her constituency while Kathy O'Brien proved to be as good a candidate as I thought she would be. The primary, however, did not end it. Despite the heavily Democratic makeup of the ward, the Republicans sensed that the DFL split gave them an unexpected opportunity and they ran a strong candidate. It was one of their last serious efforts to win an election in Minneapolis and we became worried when the Republican garnered a strong endorsement from the

Minneapolis Star. In the end, Kathy won handily and went on to a distinguished career on the city council and eventually as city coordinator and a vice president of the University of Minnesota.

Meanwhile, Al Quie was having difficulty governing the state. When he was elected in 1978, there had been high hopes for his administration. He had been a successful member of Congress who had demonstrated an ability to work well with colleagues of both parties. While Democrats were disappointed to lose the governorship, few thought it would be the end of the world. Personally, I liked Al Quie. He is sometimes characterized as the first of the Christian conservative politicians, but while he was open about the role that his faith played in his political life, I never found in him the hard edge and the fanaticism that was so apparent in much of the Christian right. His problems as governor stemmed not from his positions on social issues but from his inability to manage the budget. His congressional experience did not prepare him for the administrative and policy-making tasks of the governorship. He saw his mandate as turning back the agenda of the "tax and spend" DFL liberals, and in his first two years he pushed the legislature to cut taxes, particularly through his indexing proposal which tied tax brackets to the rate of inflation.

Then, in late 1980, when the economy weakened, the state quickly went from surpluses, which we had enjoyed throughout the previous decade, to serious deficits. Quie did not seem to know how to fix the problem. If he backed off of his tax cuts, he would have alienated his own party. He instead proposed a series of "shifts," which simply deferred spending to the next biennium, and raids on dedicated funds, which again just took money from one pocket and put it in another. Nothing seemed to work. Each time we supposedly balanced the budget, we were back in deficit again within a few months. We had three special sessions in 1981 and three more in 1982. The first two in 1981 were brief; one of them I missed completely as I was off in Europe when it was called. But the third, which began on December 1, lasted the entire month and was grueling. We were forced to make cuts in programs that few of us thought were wise and, perhaps most inexcusably, took money from a pension fund that actually belonged to public employees. The session was also difficult for me personally. I had arranged my teaching schedule to conform to the legislative schedule, but I had not counted on lengthy special sessions. The December session came just as I was finishing the fall quarter at the university and giving final exams, so I found myself constantly shuttling between campus and Capitol. After a brief adjournment for Christmas, the legislature came back and met until the afternoon of New Year's Eve, before finally patching together a budget plan. By that time, we were just a few days away from beginning the new session.

The 1982 session was dominated by redistricting, a subject that arouses little interest in most Americans. They are told who their representatives are and they realize that occasionally the district lines shift, but they have little awareness of how it all comes about. For politicians, however, redistricting is a matter of survival. Every ten years, after the census, we are required to redistrict, and since the Supreme Court decisions of the 1960s, if the legislature can't do it itself the courts will do it for us. Redistricting raises concerns at several levels. For the parties, the major goal is a redistricting plan that will lead to legislative majorities. The DFL had done well with the court-drawn plan of 1972, and some DFL leaders thought it would not be a bad idea to leave it to the courts again. On the individual level, however, each legislator wants to save his or her own hide. And if the legislature draws the map, each incumbent can have input, studying the maps as they develop, pushing for a safe district, sometimes even trying to get the strongest potential opponent drawn out of the district. From the time the census tract numbers became available in late 1980 until early 1982, this process went on as we tried to formulate a plan that could pass both houses and be approved by the governor.

It was, of course, an uphill struggle. With a Republican governor and a DFL-dominated legislature, agreement was unlikely. It was hard even to get the Senate and the House to agree on plans. For those of us in the inner city, the lack of agreement was particularly worrisome. In 1972, eight Senate districts had been created that were either entirely or mostly within the city of Minneapolis. But during the 1970s, the population of Minneapolis had not kept pace with growth in the suburbs. We were sure to lose at least one, possibly two districts. There would have to be consolidation. As we worked on the issue in the legislature, we came up with ways to do this while still protecting most of the incumbents, although a couple of the more junior members, including perhaps Karen Clark, would probably have to run against each other. But if it were left to the courts, all bets were off, and even the most senior members would not be safe. By the start of 1982, with the election just months away and no sign of progress in the legislature, the federal appeals court for the Eighth Circuit appointed a panel of three judges to come up with a redistricting plan. They would finish their job, they said, by early March.

When I came into the Senate chamber for session on March 4, I was immediately told the news: I had been put into the same district as my senior colleague and mentor, Jack Davies. Jack soon came up and shook my hand and guaranteed me that it would be a fair fight. I then went into the retiring room to study the maps. Minneapolis had been reduced to six and a half Senate districts. My district had been totally dismembered—divided roughly into thirds and combined with neighboring districts, all of which had DFL incumbents. Even if I moved into another part of the district to escape a showdown with Jack, I would have to run against another colleague. Lee Greenfield was in no better shape. His half of my Senate district had been combined with the House district of Donna Peterson, a protégée of Jeff Spartz's who had won a special election just a few years earlier. That night I was on the phone with all my political allies. I hated the idea of running against Jack. I knew that he was vulnerable in the district, that he had ignored constituent services for a number of years, and that I might be able to beat him. But it would simply be no fun to run against someone who had been a friend and ally in the Senate. The alternative was to quit. But I loved the legislature and was just beginning to move into a position of influence. Moreover, going back to the university full time had little appeal.

I tried to gauge how much support I would have if I did take on Jack Davies. Two conversations in particular stick in my mind. One was with Martin Sabo. I asked Martin not if he would support me but if he thought I could win. "You might," he said, "but you'll need a strong stomach." The redrawn district, he pointed out, included some of the most conservative working-class areas in the city. "You will be gay-baited there like you never have before." The other was with Jeff Spartz, whose support I thought I would need in order to win. Jeff told me that he had no trouble supporting me against Jack. The problem, he said, involved Lee Greenfield and Donna Peterson. He knew how close Lee and I were, and he was loyal to Donna. "If you and Lee run as a team," he said, "that would make it very difficult for me to support you." I also watched Jack's behavior in the Senate. On controversial bills, he was watching carefully to see how I voted. I knew that, despite our friendship, he was going to do everything he could to win. It would be a nasty campaign.

And then a third option opened. Senator Robert Tennessen had for twelve years represented a district centering on the chain of lakes that stretched along the western edge of Minneapolis, where many of the city's most affluent residents lived. As the court had redrawn it, the district came east to include some poorer neighborhoods, dominated by apartment buildings, where many young people found affordable space as they were beginning their careers. The district also included the Loring Park neighborhood, which had long been a center of gay community life. Bob suggested to me immediately after the new district lines came out that he might not run again. He had been an active and productive senator, but his sharp tongue and quick temper had created enemies and reduced his effectiveness. Moreover, he thought it might be time to devote more attention to his career as a lawyer. "Give me a week or two to decide," he told me. "If I don't run, my district might be a good fit for you."

Like the other options, moving to another district had both pros and cons. Tennessen's district would in many ways be a good fit. The less affluent precincts were heavily Democratic and the young people who dominated them were not likely to be troubled by my sexual orientation. The lakes area had once been a Republican stronghold, but it was rapidly changing. Some of the people who lived there were still conservative on economic issues, particularly taxation, but they were social liberals, alienated by the increasing influence of the religious right in the Republican Party. These were the rich folk who chose to stay in the city rather than move to the suburbs, a decision that in itself reflected a liberal sensibility. Many were professional people— lawyers, doctors, architects—who wanted to be close to their offices and to the cultural attractions of the city. They were people whom I could relate to far better than the blue-collar Democrats whose support I would need to beat Jack Davies. And finally, there were the gays and lesbians. Minneapolis did not have the kind of concentrated community that could be found in cities like San Francisco and Chicago; there were not enough gay people to elect me. But they would form a base to recruit volunteers for the campaign I would need to wage.

On the other hand, there were drawbacks, both political and personal. Tennessen's district included only a few blocks of my old district; I would be running in almost entirely new territory. And I would be open to charges of carpetbagging, of moving into a district to which I had no loyalty, merely to run for office. Beyond that, I would have to quickly sell my house and reestablish myself in the new district. I loved my comfortable, Craftsman-style house close to the Mississippi River and hated the thought of leaving it. And 1982 was not a good time to sell a house as interest rates were in double digits and few people could afford financing. Then I would have to buy a house or rent an apartment in the new district by May 2, less than two months away, as state law required a candidate to have lived in a district six months before the election. Renting would be easier, but I feared that it would simply contribute to the notion that I was a carpetbagger with no interest in establishing permanent roots in the district.

As he promised, Bob Tennessen made his decision promptly. He told me that he had decided not to run. Now, if I were willing to move, there was an open seat in a district that I could probably win. But I needed to determine how the DFL activists there would receive me. There were two DFL House members; did either one want to move to the Senate? Would I be regarded as an interloper? The following Sunday, I was shopping in Lund's grocery store in Uptown, the very heart of the district. Even though it was a bit of a trek from my house, I had been going there for years as it was the best market in town. It was also a great place to meet people. In the course of buying my groceries, I first ran into Representative Dee Long, one of the House members from the district. No, she told me, she was happy in the House and was not running for the Senate. She would be glad to support me. Then I met Gary Cohen, a longtime activist in the district who had been a city council candidate the year before. "If you move in," he told me, "I'll be your campaign treasurer and start raising money for you right away." When I returned home, I started calling other key Democrats in the district and I continued to get a positive response. Todd Otis, the other House member, asked for a few days to think about it. When he called on Tuesday to tell me that he was not running for the Senate, my mind was made up. I would move and run in the new district.

When I told Lee Greenfield about my decision, he told me to wait briefly before publicly announcing it. "We may be able to parlay this into something that solves my dilemma, too," he said. He called Jeff Spartz and Donna Peterson and invited them to lunch. The four of us met at Kim Long, one of the first of the many Vietnamese restaurants to locate along University Avenue in St. Paul following the influx of refugees from Southeast Asia. By the time we had gone from the spring roll to the chicken stir-fry, we had made a deal. I would leave the district and try my luck across town. Donna would run for the Senate seat, challenging Jack Davies, whom she and Jeff thought was vulnerable. This left Lee with a clear shot at the House seat; he would not have to run against Donna. And we would all support each other. Not only did this give each of us what we wanted, it also effectively ended the split in south Minneapolis DFL politics that had begun six years earlier with the Spartz-Hanson race. We referred to this agreement for years to come as the Treaty of Kim Long. The odd man out, of course, was Jack Davies. I felt bad about that, but at least I would not be the one running against him. Donna did not share the admiration that I had for Jack and had no hesitation in opposing him. When I told Jack that I was moving and would not be his opponent, he breathed a huge sigh of relief. But, I added, "Donna is going to run against you." "I'm not worried about Donna," he said. "I was worried about you." He turned out to be wrong as Donna beat him handily in November.

The endorsing convention for the new Fifty-ninth District was scheduled for May 15. By that time, I had to sell and buy a house and establish my credentials in the district. It was going to be a busy year, one that would bring many changes in my life. I still didn't know how far-reaching those changes would be.

11

A NEW DISTRICT, A NEW PARTNERSHIP, AND NEW RESPONSIBILITIES, 1982–1988

Nancy Keefe was a seasoned real estate agent who over the years must have heard just about every strange whim a client might have. But even so, she had a bit of trouble understanding my requirements. Immediately after engaging her as my agent, I sent her a map of the Fifty-ninth District and told her that was where I needed to live. She soon called with a list of houses to show me. One was on Forty-second Street.

"Which side of the street?" I asked.

"The south side," she replied.

"I'm not interested in that one," I said. "It's outside the district."

There was a moment of silence on the other end of the line as she tried to absorb that her client could live on one side of the street but not the other. Soon she understood the rules and kept me busy looking at appropriate houses. The nicest parts of the district, around the lakes, were out of my price range. The precincts just south of downtown were dominated by apartment buildings and offered few single-family homes. There were affordable houses in the district and within a few weeks I had discovered the one I wanted: a Victorian, built in 1895 by Theron Healy, a designer of local renown, with dark woodwork, parquet floors, stained glass, and elaborate built-in cabinets in the dining room. Unlike many houses of its vintage, it had never been broken up into smaller units, and most of the original features were intact. It had been owned for the past seventeen years by a gay couple who had given it the loving attention it deserved.

In terms of its size and amenities, the house was a step up from the house I had lived in for the past nine years, but I could buy it for a reasonable price primarily because of its location. The neighborhood would be a step down for me. Loring Hill East, or "The Wedge" as it was commonly known because of its distinctive shape, had for the past two decades been a "neighborhood in transition"; it was not yet clear in 1982 what it was transitioning into. Developed for upper-middle-class professionals at the turn of the twentieth century, it had gone into decline after World War II, and many of its lovely old homes had become multiunit dwellings and rooming houses. Even more damaging, in the 1950s and 1960s houses were torn down and replaced with ugly, poorly constructed, walk-up apartment buildings. By the time I moved in, there were signs of a comeback. New construction had been halted, and young people (both gay and straight) were buying and restoring old houses. Still, I would be leaving a quiet, tree-lined street overlooking the Mississippi River for a crowded block in the heart of the city that included what were euphemistically called "problem properties." I loved the house and was willing to take my chances, so the realtors began negotiating on the price and terms of sale.

The real problem was not finding a new house but selling my old one. The high interest rates made it difficult to secure financing, and I did not have a large mortgage on the house that a potential buyer could assume. Fortunately, several of my friends had long admired the house and expressed interest in buying it. First, Mark Snyder told me that he would buy my house if he could sell the one he currently owned. That was easier said than done and, after a month, he gave up. Then Kathy O'Brien, whom I had helped elect to the city council the year before, told me that she and her husband, Jeff Loesch, were ready to move up from their much smaller house just a few blocks away. Within a couple of weeks they had raised the money and we completed the deal. Kathy and Jeff genuinely wanted the house and lived there happily for the next decade, but I also believe they were trying to help me solve a difficult dilemma and for that I will always be grateful. I got the price I needed for the house without having to put it on the market and was able to proceed with the purchase of my new house in the Wedge. I didn't quite get it all done by May 2, but by early June the move was complete.

Now the question was how I would be accepted in the new district. I did not consider myself a carpetbagger, as I was in the same city and had moved just a few miles. Several of my new neighbors were suspicious of my motives and considered me an opportunist. But the fact that I had sold my old house and bought a new one convinced most of them that I was committed to the neighborhood. Within the DFL Party, I was welcomed warmly. At the endorsing convention in May, I lined up a group of nominators that included some of the best-known Democrats in the district. It turned out to be overkill: my liberal record and my unique status as an openly gay elected official were perfectly in tune with the views of the party activists, and I was nominated by acclamation. In the September primary, I also ran unopposed.

I knew that the general election would not be as easy. While the district was clearly trending toward the DFL, it had elected Republican legislators until just a few years earlier and was still represented by Republicans on the Minneapolis city council. An open seat, with a DFL candidate who had moved in from the outside, would certainly be seen by the Republicans as an opportunity to reverse the trend. I was worried in particular by three potential candidates—all elected officials, all women, and all moderate to liberal Republicans. Barbara Carlson and Sally Howard served on the city council and Patti Baker on the park board. Barbara was perhaps too flamboyant and Patti too prim, but Sally, an intelligent and thoughtful woman, would have been a formidable opponent.

Fortunately, all of them decided against making the race. The Republicans then settled on another, less well-known woman, Nancy Gimmestad, who served as the aide to the Republican members of the city council. Gimmestad worked hard and ran a serious campaign. She too was a moderate Republican who combined conservative positions on taxes and labor relations with more liberal views on social issues. She did, I think, make one serious tactical error—trying to compromise on the abortion issue in a way that pleased neither side. She supported a woman's right to choose but opposed state-funded abortions for women on medical assistance. I characterized this as "abortions for the rich but not for the poor." Her position caused several prominent Republican women in the district to endorse me.

Although she was not the strongest opponent I could have faced, Nancy Gimmestad made me work harder than I had in any campaign since 1972. I was well known among political activists, but most people in the Fifty-ninth District didn't know who I was. I needed to get my name before the voters. Bert Black, an enthusiastic young Democrat whom I had met in the old district while he was in law school, agreed to manage my campaign, and we put together a cadre of volunteers to work with us. Our literature emphasized my experience and my record of achievement at the legislature. We touted my liberalism on social and human rights issues, but we soft-pedaled any hint of economic radicalism, which was less attractive in the more affluent Fifty-ninth than it had been in the old district. A gay couple, who had done some of the best-known commercial graphic designs in the city, created a clever and attractive logo to use on lawn signs and literature; we could not legally use the word "reelect" since I was running in a new district, but the logo incorporated an image of the state Capitol, implying incumbency. We organized the usual lineup of door knocks and fund-raisers that started in the summer and went on up to election eve. I did not go out to campaign personally every night as I had earlier in my career, but I was out three or four times a week knocking on doors or attending neighborhood meetings and tried to hit every section of the district. The silk stocking area around the lakes presented me with some completely new questions. What do you do when a uniformed maid answers the door? Do you assume she lives there and make your pitch to her? Or do you ask for her boss? That was not a dilemma I had faced in my old district.

I also faced another opponent in the November election. My critics in the gay community, who thought I was too close to the establishment, saw another chance to embarrass me now that I was running in a district with a large gay population. Robert Halfhill filed against me as the candidate of what he called the Gay Survival Fund (this group seemed to regularly come up with new organizations although they generally involved the same people). Halfhill had been active in gay and left-wing politics for years. Unlike Jack Baker and Tim Campbell, he was a political radical across the board, not just a gay militant. He had been a Trotskyite in the 1960s and although he had by now broken with the Socialist Workers Party, he still held the view that the Democrats and Republicans were two peas in the same pod. He attacked me for not having introduced gay rights legislation after the defeat in St. Paul in 1978 and came down particularly hard on me for accepting the endorsement of the Minneapolis Police Federation. I used his candidacy to portray myself as a sensible independent thinker, rejecting the Republican economic solutions offered by Gimmestad as well as the radical ideology of Halfhill. But, although I knew Halfhill couldn't win, he worried me as a potential spoiler in a close race. He had run for city council in the Seventh Ward the year before and received enough votes to tip the race to the Republican. I could not simply take the gay and lesbian vote for granted.

I did not, of course, need a gay challenger to remain sensitive to gay issues, and under any circumstances I would have responded to the case of Judge Crane Winton. In February, one of the local television stations had run a weeklong investigative series on the sexual abuse of children in Minnesota. While this was a subject of genuine importance, the series coincided with what the television industry calls "sweeps week," when survey companies evaluate the audience of each station for purposes of setting advertising rates. This usually encourages sensationalism, and the series on child abuse was no exception. The final program was particularly disturbing. It purported to uncover the abusive activities of Judge Winton, a Hennepin County district court judge, who had been allegedly picking up underage boys in Loring Park and taking them to his nearby home for sex. One boy in particular, a hustler nicknamed "John-John," was interviewed at length and fingered the judge. I had trouble with this story on several grounds. First, it seemed totally disconnected to the rest of the series, which had focused on much younger children. Second, while picking up young male hustlers might be unsavory to many people, including many gay people, it is a stretch to call it "child abuse" when it involves a sixteen- or seventeen-year-old boy who openly solicits sex in a park known for its gay sexual activity. Finally, there was no empathy at all for a well-respected judge, obviously a closeted gay man, who had been denied normal outlets for sexual expression by the social mores of his generation.

Criminal charges were soon brought against Judge Winton and he pleaded guilty to a misdemeanor, paid a fine, and avoided jail time. The state chief justice decided that he would be able to stay on as a district court judge. But this still left him open to action before the Board on Judicial Standards, which could recommend his removal from the bench. I didn't personally know the judge, but my experience in these kinds of cases led me to expect a statement from him apologizing for his behavior and characterizing it as an aberration caused by stress or alcoholism and not part of his basic character. I was surprised when he told the court, at the time it accepted the plea bargain, that he was a gay man who, throughout his life, had carefully hidden his sexuality. "My resolution to keep my sexual orientation a secret was made on the assumption that one can separate and compartmentalize the various aspects of one's self. That assumption, I have come to conclude, is incorrect." His decision to conceal his sexual orientation, he continued, "led to years of loneliness and a sense of isolation"

and "precluded an open and honest relationship with another man."
So, he concluded, "when my sense of loneliness became more than I
could bear, I sought a form of companionship that I otherwise would
not seek." I admired his candor and wrote to him in early July offering
my support. "I know personally," I told him,

> how difficult it is for a public official to speak openly and
> forthrightly about his homosexuality and I truly admire your
> honesty and courage. Your experiences as an adolescent and
> young man—far from being isolated as we all thought they
> were—are shared by most gay people of our generation. I,
> too, tried to hide until I came to realize, as you have, that it is
> impossible to deny an important part of one's self—and that
> society has no right to expect us to do so. I can only hope that
> your "coming out"—despite the painful circumstances that
> brought it about—will ultimately prove as personally liberat-
> ing as mine has been.

He told me that he had followed my career and would certainly
like to meet me. We had dinner together in late July and I offered to do
whatever I could to help. He told me that he might like me to testify
on his behalf in the upcoming hearings to determine his fitness to remain a judge. I told him I would gladly do that and we agreed to keep
in touch with each other. Later in the summer, he called and invited
me to his house for dinner.

When I arrived at Crane Winton's house on October 5, I expected
that we would be discussing his case, so I was surprised to see that he
had invited another guest, a good-looking Asian man whom he introduced to me as Jun. "Jun burns hair in Stillwater," Crane said. That, in
the judge's somewhat dated slang, meant that Jun operated a beauty
salon, which, in fact, was not actually in Stillwater, but in nearby Bayport, about thirty miles east of the Twin Cities. Jun also told me that
his full name was Junjiro Tsuji, that he was Japanese, that he had lived
in Minnesota since 1969, and that he had recently become an American citizen. During dinner, Jun was particularly attentive toward me
and was interested to hear that I was a state senator and had come
to dinner directly from a round of door knocking. When Crane went

into the kitchen to prepare the food, Jun put his hand on my knee and began running it up my thigh. I was totally unprepared for that. In the ten years since I first began leading a gay life, I had only once been pursued by another man—and he was much older than I. Jun, on the other hand, was young and I found him sexually attractive. Crane soon noticed what was going on and, when we left his house at the end of the evening, he said that he assumed we were going home together. He was right. Jun came to my house and we quickly had sex. He told me that he could not stay the night as he had to be at his shop at six the next morning, but assured me that he wanted to see me again. I hoped that he really meant it.

At the time I met Jun, I had virtually given up hope that I would find a life partner. As astute as I was in managing the political aspects of my gay life, I was incredibly awkward in my attempts to establish personal relationships. I had totally given up on the bars. Although I had at first found them liberating, it didn't take long before I realized that most men went to arrange one-night stands and I was not the type they wanted. I had no talent for the kind of small talk, laden with sexual innuendo, that was expected at the bars. After a while, the smoke and the noise and the constant rejections convinced me that I had better things to do with my time. I had met a number of gay men through politics and, in a couple of cases, this led to brief affairs. But I was not much good at handling these kinds of relationships either. Often they ended with some variation on the line: "I really like and respect you and want you to be my friend, but I am not interested in you sexually." I wanted to say, but never did, "I have enough friends— I need something more." Therefore I found myself in an anomalous situation. I was one of the best-known gay people in the state. I was in continual demand as a speaker on gay issues. I was a hero to at least part of the gay community. But I went home alone almost every night and often reached out in frustration in my bed just wishing that I could touch someone on the other side. I had totally lost confidence in my ability to forge a successful relationship. Had Jun not made the first move, I almost certainly would have remained alone.

Jun called the next day and invited me to dinner at a Japanese restaurant on Saturday night. I began to learn more about him. Despite his youthful appearance, he was only three years younger than I. He came from a large family in Kyoto, still had a mother and nine sisters and brothers in Japan, and went back once a year to visit. He had come to the United States not, like the classic immigrant, for economic opportunity, but because he was attracted to Western men, particularly older ones. He had studied some English in Japan and spent a year in St. Louis in an ESL program, but when he arrived in Minnesota to live with a man he had met in Japan, he still could not handle the business courses he enrolled in at the university. So he went to beauty school, where he could learn by watching rather than by listening and reading in an unfamiliar language. Jun met another man, John, and went to live with him in suburban Washington County, where he eventually bought the house from him. John helped Jun borrow money to establish his own business in Bayport, and he had worked hard and made a success of it. He still lived with John, but, he quickly informed me, the relationship was near its end. As for Crane Winton, Jun told me that they were friends and occasional sex partners, but there was no more to it than that. He really liked me, he said, and hoped that we could develop a relationship.

I had no illusions that a relationship would be easy at this point in my life. I was set in my ways and would have trouble adjusting to life with another person. And Jun and I were very different. He had not graduated from college, was by no definition an intellectual, and had little interest in the things that excited me—politics, classical music, French food. At our first dinner date, I realized that we also disagreed on some basic issues. Jun had come to a strange country alone, barely speaking the language, and through hard work and determination had done well. He couldn't understand why other people needed handouts from the government and sharply questioned my support for social programs. He admitted that on the one occasion he had voted since becoming a citizen, he voted Republican.

Temperamentally, too, we had little in common. I came from a highly verbal culture where little was left unsaid and people related to each other by arguing and, often, yelling. In Japanese culture, this kind of behavior was considered rude and boorish. People were expected to restrain themselves and treat others politely and agreeably while keeping their emotions to themselves. That would probably be the greatest barrier that Jun and I would have to overcome. And yet there was much about Jun that was immediately appealing. From the beginning, I trusted him. He was sweet and caring, and I knew that if we became partners I could always count on him. It took me awhile to get used to his Japanese accent and limited English vocabulary, but when I did I found him refreshingly direct and often endearingly funny. He regaled me with stories of how he was seduced by American men in Japan, and, when I pointed out that he didn't seem to have resisted, he would shrug and say with a smile, "What could I do? We lost the war."

I was determined not to mishandle what might be my last chance for a long-term relationship. I called Crane Winton and told him that Jun and I were seeing each other and hoped that he had no objection. He confirmed what Jun had told me, that they were casual friends, and he wished me the best. Jun and I got together every weekend throughout much of the fall. He went to Japan for two weeks in November, but when he returned the relationship resumed. For the first time since my affair with Sally, I felt that I was with someone who really cared about me. And for the first time in my life, I had gay sex that was fulfilling and satisfying. By the end of the year, Jun was spending most nights at my house, even though this meant that he needed to get up at 5:30 a.m. for the long drive to his shop. I knew that we were both serious when he asked for his own garage door opener! He still had his house in Washington County, where John continued to live. We agreed that he should wait to see how our relationship progressed before he decided to sell it. But we did make plans for a trip to Mexico in January where he would meet my father and his wife and we could spend some uninterrupted time together.

In the meantime, I was elected by a surprisingly large margin. Given my move into the district, the strength of Gimmestad's campaign, and Bob Halfhill's role as a spoiler, I expected a close race. Gimmestad had attacked me vigorously at the end as a carpetbagger who was too liberal for the district on issues such as taxes, small-business incentives, and crime control. But she won only the three most affluent precincts around the lakes and I ran up large margins everywhere else, winning by a margin of 60 percent to 35 percent. Halfhill's challenge totally fizzled; he received only 2 percent of the vote. Nancy Gimmestad graciously called me and congratulated me (one of the few opponents I have ever had to do so), and I sensed that with her loss, the Republicans would never again seriously contest the district. I was right.

The real interest on election night was in the governor's race. With

Quie out of the picture, it was an open seat and most DFLers thought there was an excellent chance of retaking it. The Republicans had endorsed Quie's lackluster lieutenant governor, but he was easily beaten in the primary by a prominent businessman, Wheelock Whitney, who identified with the moderate wing of the party. It was one of the early indications of what would become a pattern in both parties in the 1980s and 1990s—ideological activists, the right wing in the Republican Party, liberals in the DFL—endorsing candidates who were out of step with the electorate as a whole. The DFL had its own endorsement problem in 1982. It chose the well-liked attorney general, Warren Spannaus, certainly not a left-winger and a man who should have been a strong candidate. But former governor Rudy Perpich, out of sight and out of the country for much of the past four years, returned and mounted a strong primary challenge. While I had been an admirer of Perpich early in his career, I was appalled by the crassness of the deal he made in 1982. Although I knew him to be personally pro-choice on abortion—and his brothers had been outspoken on the issue—he promised the powerful antiabortion group, Minnesota Citizens Concerned for Life, that he would support their issues if they would endorse him for governor. I worked for Spannaus in the primary, but with MCCL backing and greater name recognition, Perpich won. He went on in November to beat Whitney and reclaim the governorship for the DFL.

The DFL also did well in legislative races and captured solid majorities in both houses. One race of particular interest to me was in the district I abandoned. Although Jack Davies had initially expressed little concern about running against Donna Peterson, he was taken aback by the ease with which she won the DFL endorsement. He then concluded that, as the endorsed candidate, she would probably win the DFL primary, so he made the highly risky decision of filing instead as an independent in the general election. Independents have had some success in Minnesota, most famously with the election of Jesse Ventura as governor in 1998. But since we returned to party designation in 1973, they have rarely won seats in the legislature, which is organized along party lines. Donna trounced Jack and ended his political career. I had stayed as far away from the race as possible. I had been present at the meeting at Kim Long, which in a way committed me to Donna.

But Jack was a friend and mentor and I saw no reason to go out of my way to oppose him. Besides, I had my hands full in my new district. His defeat did, however, provide an opportunity for me. Now there was an open committee chairmanship that I really wanted—Judiciary. No nonlawyer had ever before chaired that committee, but I saw no reason why I could not be the first. And I had learned two years before that I needed to fight for what I wanted in the Senate.

As it turned out, I secured the chairmanship of the Judiciary Committee without opposition. While Judiciary was a powerful committee with a wide jurisdiction, many legislators were wary of it. For non-lawyers, some of the issues it debated were impossibly arcane. Even after I became chair, I had trouble staying awake during discussions of the Torrens system of property registration or the intricacies of privacy law. Moreover, the legislature's most controversial "hot button" topics—abortion, gay rights, gun control—all came before the Judiciary Committee. I loved being involved in the debates on those issues, but many legislators preferred to avoid them. So when I expressed interest in chairing the committee, my colleagues were glad to let me have it. And no one seemed troubled by my lack of a law degree. I was told more than once that after eight years of service on the committee, I was already talking like a lawyer anyway.

I chaired Judiciary for the next ten years. During that time, it became the busiest and most active policy committee in the Senate. Initially, I was assisted by the same two staff members who had worked with me before—Marcia Greenfield and Don Jorovsky—even though our workload was far greater than it had been with the Public Employees and Pensions Committee. Each session, we were assigned a committee page, which gave us some additional temporary help. Don moved to another position with the Senate in 1984 and I replaced him with Eric Stults, a young gay activist who turned out to be an excellent secretary and, later, legislative assistant. A few years later, I was able to persuade Roger Moe that the Judiciary Committee required a third permanent staff member and I hired Mark Wallem, a politically involved gay man who was also a lawyer. I never had any doubts about either the personal loyalty or the competence of my staff, which allowed me to delegate considerable responsibility to them. Eric and Mark stayed with me for ten years and Marcia for the rest of my career—even though the work schedule was often brutal and the pay barely competitive. I think they shared with me the excitement of being at the center of the political action.

I divided the Judiciary Committee into five subcommittees—Criminal Law, Civil Law, Judicial Administration, Privacy, and Revisor's Bills—and I sent complicated bills that required detailed work to subcommittee so that they could be shaped and polished before coming to the full committee. With the highly controversial issues that involved contentious testimony, I skipped the subcommittee step as I saw no reason to go through highly polemical debates more than once. I often scheduled hearings on subjects of this kind—abortion, gay rights, capital punishment—in the evening when we would not be under time restraints. While I had strong views on many of the issues that came before the committee, I tried to run the committee in as even-handed a manner as possible. I let everyone have his or her say and did not advocate positions from the chair. When I wanted to become involved in the debate, I turned the chair over to another member of the committee. Sometimes, the public testimony was so ignorant or bigoted that it was hard for me to contain myself. But I felt strongly that I had the most to gain by developing a reputation as a fair and impartial committee chair, and it was indeed that reputation that enabled me win the Senate presidency in the next decade.

Several issues dominated the committee during the years that I chaired it. Preeminent was the debate surrounding crime and sentencing. On the one hand, the adoption of the sentencing guidelines system, which had become effective in 1980, provided us with the framework to deal with this issue. Yet, as the decade wore on, and as crime became an ever more visible issue in Minnesota and the nation, the guidelines came under constant attack. We were the first state to develop sentencing guidelines and I believe they served us well. Individual guidelines for each offense were established by a commission made up of criminal justice system professionals appointed by the governor. The commission established the severity level of each crime and the judge then consulted a grid to combine the severity level with the offender's prior criminal record in order to determine the presumptive sentence. A judge could depart upward or downward from the presumptive sentence on the basis of the particular circumstances of the offense, but the judge was required to give written reasons for the departure. This system, it seemed to me, provided a degree of uniformity without depriving the judiciary of all discretion. Most judges adapted well to it. It also ended the often capricious system of parole, which had been the dominant feature of the old indeterminate sentencing system.

When we adopted the guidelines in 1978, most legislators thought they represented a toughening of the sentencing system. Parole was particularly unpopular among many citizens who saw it as a springboard to dangerous early releases. The idea that an offender would serve the actual time to which he was sentenced (minus credit for good behavior) was appealing to many people across the political spectrum. But when the guidelines resulted in reduced average sentences for some crimes, especially property crimes, a backlash set in. As crime rates rose during the 1980s, legislators responded with bills to impose mandatory minimum sentences for various crimes, in effect overruling the guidelines. And there were periodic attempts to repeal the guidelines altogether. I did everything I could to thwart these efforts although there were times when the best I could do was make a bad idea just a little less bad. No one has ever fully understood why crime rates went up in the 1980s and then back down in the 1990s. Demography seems to have had a lot to do with it. But there is little evidence that people made their decisions about whether to commit a particular crime on the basis of the sentence for that crime. This argument ascribes far too much rationality to criminals. Yet I constantly heard how criminals were flocking to Minnesota to kill and rob and deal drugs because of our too-lenient laws. And whenever there was high-profile crime in the state—a rape or a kidnapping or a murder—legislators fell all over each other to be the first to introduce legislation to increase the sentence for that particular crime. I called it the "crime of the year" syndrome.

Minnesota was, of course, not alone in its response to crime during these years. Many states spent rapidly increasing portions of their budgets to build and support new prisons, often at the expense of schools and universities and health-care facilities. I saw some sense in incapacitating murderers and rapists for long periods of time, and our guidelines system was tough on violent criminals. But many of the new prison beds throughout the country were accommodating low-level drug dealers and users who could be better handled in community-based facilities and treatment programs. And some states were rushing to enact an idea called "three strikes and you're out," which required a mandatory life sentence for anyone who had been convicted of three felonies, regardless of their severity level. I was not successful in stopping a draconian drug law in Minnesota, but I did stop "three strikes"—which I thought was a singularly stupid idea. And while Minnesota significantly expanded its prison system during the 1980s and 1990s, it never engaged in the prison-building mania of states such as California and Texas.

The Judiciary Committee was often viewed as the most important of the policy committees because many of the decisions it made did not require rereferral to the Finance Committee. The Education and Health and Human Services policy committees, for example, could do very little that did not require funding, and hence all their decisions were second-guessed after they were rereferred. But I soon came to see that it was a mistake to separate bills that increased criminal sentences from prison funding. I insisted that every sentencing bill that was introduced be accompanied by a "bed impact" statement, prepared by the staff of the Minnesota Sentencing Guidelines Commission, that would estimate the number of new prison beds the bill would require. If the impact was significant, the bill would be rereferred to the appropriate division of the Finance Committee. This opened the eyes of many legislators to the cost of what they were proposing when they introduced drastic sentencing bills. I also insisted that we pay more attention to the "front end" of the system, that if we were going to spend money on prisons, we should also spend money on prevention. It made no sense, I argued, to spend twenty-five thousand dollars a year to house and feed an inmate while we were doing nothing for the "at risk" children who were likely to be the criminals of the future.

AFTERWORD

John Milton

Allan Spear began work on his autobiography in late 2005 and had completed five chapters by September 2007, when he, Lee and Marcia Greenfield, Kathy O'Brien and her husband, Jeff Loesch, and Allan's partner, Junjiro Tsuji, traveled to Ireland. He had the manuscript on that trip and invited them to read it. According to Marcia Greenfield, his friend and former staff aide in the Senate, he gave her chapters 6–9 in February 2008, just prior to undergoing heart surgery. From March of that year until his condition worsened in late summer, he finished chapter 10 and wrote seventeen pages of chapter 11.

Since he'd been retired for eight years, one might wonder why this history professor with an encyclopedic mind and fine storytelling skills did not finish his life story. His partner of twenty-six years, Junjiro Tsuji, recalls urging him to work on the book, with Allan replying, "Maybe I should, but who would want to read it? My story isn't that interesting."

At the point where Allan's narrative left off, the 1983 session of the legislature was under way. The previous year, he'd moved into a new, open Senate district, where the incumbent had retired. He'd won his fourth term and been appointed chair of the prestigious Judiciary committee. Senator Jack Davies, who, along with Senator Nick Coleman, was described by Allan as his most important mentors, had chaired Judiciary for a decade, but after the 1982 reapportionment, Davies lost his Senate seat and the chair was vacant.[1] Allan, with eight years' service on Judiciary and having chaired three of its subcommittees, was now so respected by his DFL colleagues that the appointment was well

---

1. Senators Davies and Spear had been in the same district after reapportionment in 1972, and Davies moved so as to retain most of the district he'd represented for several years. The reapportionment of 1982 put them together again, and Allan moved to the nearby south Minneapolis district being vacated by retiring Senator Bob Tennessen. Donna Peterson ran against Davies in the general election and sent him into retirement.

deserved. Davies's departure opened up the important committee chair that Allan was most qualified to fill.

"By 1983, everybody knew how capable and bright he was, and how gifted he was as an orator," former majority leader Roger Moe says. "He had learned the internal politics of the legislative process, and he'd learned that to get anything meaningful done, you have to have patience. And he'd learned the value of timing—when something would go and when it wouldn't. It all came together for Allan as chair of Judiciary." Larry Pogemiller, another long-term Minneapolis DFL senator and now majority leader, adds, "Of all the people I've served with, he was one of the finest committee chairs." And former Senate secretary Pat Flahaven recalls, "While chairing Judiciary, Allan was fair, balanced, and knowledgeable. He'd done his homework as a member of the committee, so when the chair opened up, there was considerable respect for Allan's work, and the fact that he was not a lawyer wasn't a big issue." Allan was, in fact, the first nonlawyer to chair Judiciary, an ironic sequel to his one-year stint at Harvard Law School, which he has described as "the most frustrating of my life."

Crime Prevention and the AIDS Epidemic

As chair of Judiciary, Allan was able to exert a major influence on the allocation of Minnesota's criminal justice resources. His philosophy, which he describes at the end of chapter 11, moved Minnesota toward a more balanced approach to crime—one that invested in "front end" prevention as well as incarceration. As a result of his leadership on this issue, Minnesota was able to avoid the enormous public expenditures incurred by many other states, such as California, which built a series of expensive and dysfunctional fortress prisons that had little effect on public safety but a devastating impact on state services.

The 1980s, after every major office seemed swept away by a politically conservative tsunami, was not an auspicious time for plowing new ground in human rights. As Allan noted later, the 1978 repeal of the GLBT rights ordinance in St. Paul—one of the state's most liberal cities—by a referendum vote of almost two to one, "meant effectively that passage of a statewide gay and lesbian rights bill was years away . . . legislators were not likely to risk a vote for gay rights on a statewide basis."[2] And just as clearly, the legislature was not ready to decriminal-ize the "sodomy laws," even when, in yet another attempt, Allan had argued quite logically to his Senate colleagues that decriminalizing con-sensual sodomy, fornication, and adultery by consenting adults was not only "one of the shortest bills to be introduced this year," it also was "not a gay rights bill. In fact, it affects the behavior of heterosexual men and women more than it does gay men and lesbians. Adultery and for-nication are, after all, heterosexual pastimes." The bill failed once again, as it did in one final attempt the year before Allan retired.[3]

Growing conservatism across the country didn't mean there wasn't work to be done. Allan's approach was to push on, with groundbreaking work in protection for and services to vulnerable adults, especially those with disabilities and elderly persons in nursing homes and resi-dential centers. And from his position as chair of the mostly ignored Public Employees and Pensions Committee, he challenged Minnesota's corporate and state investments in companies doing business in South Africa, where the apartheid system deprived the black majority of its human rights. Responding to his efforts and those of others, the State Board of Investment voted in 1985 to phase out pension fund hold-ings in certain firms doing business in South Africa, putting pressure on its white minority government.

For the gay and lesbian community the most devastating wave in the mid-1980s was the coming of the AIDS epidemic. There was wide-spread confusion and conflicting data about how big the threat would be, whether a cure would be found, and how best to care for the eco-nomic, social, and medical needs of those diagnosed HIV positive. Not only did it threaten to bring grave illness and, at first, almost certain death, initially it also stifled much of the resolve to fight on for human rights. Allan noted in the outline for chapter 11 (which he didn't live to complete) that he was personally touched by the loss of friends

---

2. From Allan's "Remembrance" in Steve Endean, *Bringing Lesbian and Gay Rights into the Mainstream,* ed. Vicki L. Eaklor (Binghamton, N.Y.: Haworth Press, 2006).

3. From Allan's speech asking colleagues to pass Senate File 271 in 1981. The so-called sodomy laws across the country were virtually unassailable until 2003, when the U.S. Supreme Court struck down all state laws that criminalized these forms of consensual adult behavior.

Steve Endean, with whom he'd worked closely on gay rights since the early 1970s, and Brian Coyle, a Minneapolis activist elected to the city council three times. Coyle was an early participant, along with Allan and Representative Karen Clark, in the International Network of Gay and Lesbian Officials (INGLO), formed in 1985 to encourage public officials who were gay, lesbian, bisexual, or transgender to come out, and to support them.

Perhaps the most important response to the AIDS crisis in this state was the Minnesota AIDS Project (MAP), formed in late 1982 to prevent the HIV virus from speading and to support those living with the disease. According to its long-term lobbyist, Bob Tracy, Allan, Senator Linda Berglin, and Representative Lee Greenfield guided the legislative effort. Berglin and Greenfield chaired the committees to which bills were referred, and Allan was well positioned as chair of Judiciary. These three, Tracy recalls, not only directed what did get passed—funding of programs for prevention and support—they also stopped punitive bills that would exacerbate the impact of AIDS on the gay community. "It was a big legislative agenda," Tracy says, "and they did the heavy lifting, with support from leaders like Moe in the Senate and a series of liberal Speakers of the House. Allan's position on Judiciary helped us deal with the quarantine issue, which threatened to punish victims of HIV. His office was the center of operations for the effort to stop attempts by conservatives to criminalize those who suffered from the disease." As a result, Minnesota took a more enlightened response to AIDS.

In 2005, for a MAP lecture series named after him, Allan described how the gay rights movement and response to HIV converged in Minnesota:

> By all odds, [AIDS] should have stopped the movement for gay civil rights, but it did not . . . instead it had the opposite effect . . . it established homosexuality as a legitimate topic because of the disease. The plague provided a unifying cultural focus—it's remarkable that this disastrous disease served to unify the movement.

He recalled that with all the AIDS-related issues being raised at the Capitol, there was concern over who would keep the GLBT rights agenda alive. "It turned out that lesbians filled the gap," he said. "In the

mid-'80s the women stepped forward and provided leadership . . . Ann
DeGroot emerged in what would become OutFront Minnesota."

> I was in the center of efforts to sensitize members of Minneso-
> ta's legislature about the AIDS issue. At first, most politicians
> ignored it, then they overreacted. For most of them, victims
> were complicit—if only they'd not chosen to lead their lives
> that way . . . Then there emerged a fear that the heterosexual
> community would next be getting the disease, so there was
> pressure to require testing. We got invaluable assistance from
> legislators who specialized in health-care issues—most nota-
> bly Senator Linda Berglin and Representative Lee Greenfield,
> so if a bad idea got into the conference committee, we could
> make sure it wouldn't see the light of day. We got a lot of
> help from the Minnesota Department of Health (Mike Moen
> virtually camped out in my office), but the real catalyst was
> Bob Tracy . . . he belongs in my pantheon of heroes with Steve
> Endean and Brian Coyle.
>
> I believe that progress comes from working within the
> system, patience, dedication, accepting that change comes
> incrementally . . . when I retired five years ago, I thought
> about what had changed the most, what was least expected.
> For me, it was how the GLBT community reacted to the threat
> from AIDS, how new leaders emerged to continue the fight . . .
> these have been and still are our guiding lights.[4]

Passing Gay Rights in Minnesota

On May 23, 1973, shortly after that year's legislative session was
adjourned, Allan wrote a letter on his Senate stationery to Majority Leader Nick Coleman, expressing his appreciation for Coleman's
effort to include gay and lesbian people in the state's Human Rights
Act.[5] The Minnesota Senate had indeed been the first state legislative

---

4. From Allan's lecture at the Allan Spear Forum of the Minnesota AIDS Project
on December 1, 2005.

5. From a copy of the letter, sent by Allan to this writer after our conversation
about Nick Coleman on June 29, 2007.

body in the country to pass a gay rights bill, but the House didn't follow suit and the bill died. Thereafter, session after session, the legislature never came closer. Any satisfaction over that success in 1973 would have to wait another twenty years for fulfillment.

Despite the distraction of the AIDS threat, public opinion was gradually changing on gay rights. Wisconsin passed the first statewide rights law in 1982, and several other states, mostly in New England and on the West Coast, had followed.[6] Openly gay public officials such as Coyle, Congressmen Gerry Stubbs and Barney Frank of Massachusetts, and lesbians such as Minnesota's representative Karen Clark and Dane County (Wisconsin) supervisor Tammy Baldwin, later a state representative and member of Congress, had been active with Allan in forming INGLO. So it seemed to be time for what Allan called "regrouping in Minnesota" (in his notes for chapter 12). This time, there would be a well-planned strategy, not—as in the 1970s—reliance on the common sense and goodwill of legislative colleagues to vote for the elusive "right thing to do." There would be more planning, broadening the effort statewide, especially beyond the Twin Cities where there were less visible clusters of support, as well as building a coalition of human rights groups, women's and minority organizations, major religious denominations, labor unions, and student groups.

Moreover, the Senate had been changing and, on GLBT rights, for the better. Whereas in the 1970s there were piranha—led by Senators Charlie Berg, Bob Brown, Florian Chmielewski, Mike Menning, and Wayne Olhoft—swimming in both DFL and Republican streams, now only Berg and Chmielewski remained. In the late 1970s, there were only four women in the body; the elections of 1990 and 1992 raised the number to nineteen female senators, twelve of whom voted for gay rights. The Judiciary committee in 1993 was now chaired by Ember Reichgott, an attorney from the Minneapolis suburbs, with a number of liberal nonlawyers on the committee to smooth passage of a human rights bill. And progressive Senate newcomers like Ellen Anderson, Don Betzold, Carol Flynn, Jane Krentz, Ted Mondale, Steve Murphy, Sandy Pappas, Jane Ranum, and Deanna Wiener brought

---

6. Although it followed Wisconsin by eleven years, Minnesota became the first of twelve states and the District of Columbia to ban discrimination based on both sexual orientation and gender identity.

fresh energy to the historically sedate chamber. There were even moderate Republicans who could be counted on to give any proposal a fair hearing: Bill Belanger of Bloomington; Dean Johnson, the minority leader; Sheila Kiscaden from Rochester; and a former corporate executive from Minnetonka, Martha Robertson. It was time to strike, clearly, though with little support from rural senators, it would still be an uphill climb. As Allan himself once revealed to a gushing audience at the 1978 Conference on Alternative State and Local Policies at St. Paul's Concordia College, Minnesota had a grand tradition of progressive politics, yes indeed, but it was "only a little better" than other states on the tough issues.

Fortuitously, there was a movement in St. Paul to reinstate the city gay rights ordinance that was repealed ten years earlier. In 1988, the city council passed a new ordinance. When the opposition tried to overturn it again, the voters of St. Paul strongly refused to accept that. Scott Dibble, a future senator who by then had come out, was active in GLBT politics, and was considering a run for public office, says, "It was hoped this success in St. Paul would provide momentum for the push at the legislature." Apparently, it did.

A statewide push was implemented by the task force appointed in April 1990 by Governor Rudy Perpich, then finishing his third term. Allan and Perpich had been kindred spirits on many liberal issues since 1968, when both supported Senator Gene McCarthy's presidential campaign. They worked closely after Perpich's return to the governor's office in 1983; with Rudy in the corner office, Allan could be sure that liberal bills passed by the legislature, except those relating to abortion, would not be vetoed.[7]

Perpich, despite having spent four years in exile as a vice president of computer-maker Control Data Corporation in Europe, had not forgotten his roots. His Iron Ranger sympathy with lower-income families and people who'd suffered ethnic or religious discrimination—

---

7. One of the several factors in Perpich's 1978 defeat by Republican congressman Al Quie was the ambivalence of Perpich's stand on abortion. When he decided to try for another term in 1982, Perpich—a traditional Catholic—vowed to make sure every voter knew he was staunchly "pro-life." With a huge turnout in his home region, northern Minnesota, Perpich won in 1982 and again in 1986, becoming the longest-serving governor in Minnesota history.

for that matter, anyone who'd been forgotten in Minnesota—was as strong as ever, and Allan worked with Perpich after his return on issues relating to civil and human rights. He convinced the governor to appoint a task force to visit every corner of the state and come back with findings about the closeted life of GLBT Minnesotans.

With Allan's suggestions, Perpich appointed a task force of sixteen Minnesotans in April 1990, and Allan arranged for Geraldine Sell, a Minneapolis reader for the blind and community activist, to chair the group. Roughly half the members were gay, lesbian, bisexual, or transgender. Allan was a member and attended when his teaching schedule at the university and legislative meetings permitted. "Allan asked me if I'd be chair of the task force," Sell says, "and he was clearly involved in the effort. He kept on top of things throughout the year." Over the next eleven months, task force members visited nine communities in different regions of the state. In some places, they held up to four meetings to better assess the situation and afford privacy to GLBT residents still in the closet. In addition to several places in the Twin Cities area, they visited Bemidji, Duluth, Mankato, Morris, Northfield, Red Wing, St. Peter, Virginia, and Winona.

From its findings, the task force agreed on four principal recommendations, the first and most important of which was amending the state Human Rights Act to protect gays and lesbians from discrimination. When the final report was submitted in January 1991, Perpich was gone, defeated for reelection in November by former representative and state auditor Arne Carlson, a Republican. Fortunately, Carlson was a moderate who'd supported gay rights as a member of the House. He accepted and approved the report, and appointed a second task force that included several of the original members. In its initial meetings, the second task force took a big step forward, concluding that "the findings from the first task force report justified the inclusion of issues of concern to bisexual and transgender persons in its mission." To address this issue, "language was needed to collectively identify persons covered by the sexual orientation amendment."[8]

Inclusion of bisexual and transgender people was easier said than done. Karen Clark—the first openly gay or lesbian person to run and

---

8. From the introduction to a draft of the second task force report.

be elected to the Minnesota Legislature, and the longest-serving openly lesbian member to serve in a legislature anywhere in the country—recalls how Minnesota became the first state to include transgender people. "Allan went through a learning process on that issue," she says, "and it happened because we went to the legislature only after we'd spent a lot of time and effort in a 'bottom-up' approach." Clark relates how the GLBT community, under the banner of "It's Time, Minnesota," first got itself organized by "finding people all over the state who were living their lives privately, not really daring to come out except in small, local support groups. Then, after organizing, we shifted the emphasis to lobbying."

Language that became "all-inclusionary" evolved, bringing transgender leaders into the discussion. "We were fortunate that the transgender community had gotten itself organized, so we had an emerging community working with us. Allan grew to have great respect for them, and when he 'got it,' he became one of the strongest supporters of the inclusionary language." The resulting language in the law—"actual or perceived sexual orientation"—includes everyone, Clark says.

Dibble, who later became Allan's successor in the Senate, recalls that inclusion of transgender in the 1991 version of the bill had become a major reason for its failure that year; it drew the heaviest attack from cultural conservatives. "We knew its inclusion in 1993 would draw fire," he says, "but if we left it out, there would be fire from the other side. By carefully crafting a description of those who'd be covered in the definitions section of the bill, we were able to include everyone."

So the stage was set. Allan by then had been elected president of the Senate, Moe was still a strong and supportive majority leader, and Reichgott was chair of Judiciary, which included Allan and liberal senators Berglin, Don Betzold, Dick Cohen, Skip Finn, Kiscaden, Krentz, Gene Merriam, Ranum, and Robertson. That lineup ensured the bill would emerge from Judiciary without crippling amendments, and it did, with only one dissenting vote (Republican David Knutson). Meanwhile, the companion bill with Clark as chief author was moving through the House.

Throughout February and March, lobbying for and against the bill continued unabated. Religious fundamentalists led the charge to dismember or kill the bill, and as it reached the floor of the Senate, the vote count was positive but tight. Two or three votes swinging to the other side would make the difference. In the rough-and-tumble of "wedge issue" politics, it was still too close to call.

Earlier in the session, Allan had called Endean, his old friend and ally in the gay rights battles of the 1970s, who was in Washington, D.C., and dying of AIDS. He wanted to alert him about the push for passage. "I told him he should come to Minnesota if he possibly could," Allan wrote in his Remembrance for Endean's memoir. "I thought that we could finally pass the bill and I wanted him to see it. The climate had changed since the late 1970s and it looked like we had the votes in both Houses to finally win the struggle that Steve had begun twenty years earlier. On the day of the vote he was deathly sick, but he sat in the gallery, first in the Senate, then in the House, to watch the bill pass."

The fate of this bill would not be decided by a party-line vote. Allan knew there'd be fierce opposition from his old nemesis, Chmielewski, the polka band leader from Sturgeon Lake who was serving his eighth term in the Senate. He'd be joined by DFLers Berg, Joe Bertram, Carl Kroening, Keith Langseth, Bob Lessard, Don Samuelson, and Leroy Stumpf—all except Kroening from conservative rural districts. And the opposition could count on Republicans Dick Day, Knutson, Gary Laidig, Pat McGowan, Tom Neuville, Pat Pariseau, and Linda Runbeck. The wild card, as it turned out, would be from Republican ranks.

On March 18, the debate on Senate File 444 began. Allan handed the president's gavel to Reichgott and went down to his desk on the floor to speak. "Madame Chair, and members of the Senate, Senate File 444 is a bill that you've already heard more about than you want to hear and I will simply try, I hope in fairly brief fashion, to tell you this morning what is in the bill, and what is not in the bill." Holding the microphone from his desk and rocking back and forth as was his custom, Allan outlined how the bill would prohibit discrimination based on sexual orientation in housing, employment, public accommodations, public service, access to education, and access to credit. He countered the argument that it would offer special privileges to gays and lesbians:

> Human rights laws do not give special privileges to anyone; human rights laws merely recognize that in an imperfect

society some groups have faced discrimination and some
categories have been the basis for unfair discrimination, so
we include in our human rights laws those categories around
which there have been historic patterns of discrimination—
race, religion, gender, nationality. We don't include things like
eye color, for example, because we haven't experienced in our
society discrimination based on eye color. The question, then,
of whether or not a group should be included in our human
rights law is whether that group or that category forms the
basis of discrimination, and I would argue that historically
and still today there is in our society—has been and is—a
pattern of discrimination based on sexual orientation.

He recounted the findings of the governor's task force, saying they
"listened to those who told stories of loss of jobs, of lack of promotion, of inability to find housing," and that members of the task force
"were convinced beyond a shadow of a doubt that discrimination is
still a persistent factor in many parts of Minnesota." So, Allan said,
"this bill does not ask for special privileges for anyone, it only asks
that discrimination end, it only asks that we have a level playing field."
In support of the legislation, he pointed to polls showing that most
Americans opposed discrimination on the basis of sexual orientation,
and while not approving the gay lifestyle, "they think that discrimination is wrong." He listed the wide variety of organizations that had
endorsed the bill, and then, in a dramatic conclusion, he said:

Finally, I'd like to say something on the personal side about
this bill and this is not something that comes easily for me—I
think those of you who have known me for a while know that
I don't talk a lot about my personal life, but I refuse to let
other people question the validity of my own life experiences.
I've been told by many people that oppose this bill that sexual
orientation should not be included in the human rights law
because it is a choice, because it is a choice that people make,
and if they make a choice, they can change that choice . . .
well, let me tell you, I'm a fifty-five-year old gay man and I'm
not just going through a phase!
    I can also assure you that my sexual orientation is not

something I chose like I would choose to wear a blue shirt and a red tie today . . . why in the world would I have chosen this? I grew up in the 1950s—everyone I knew was presumably straight, all of my models . . . homosexuality was only something people whispered about . . . my first awareness of what I was filled me with absolute panic.

I did everything I could to change: I dated girls, I denied my inner feelings, I sought psychiatric care—I didn't make a choice about that . . . I could do nothing about what I was . . . I did make a choice, my choice had to do with how I would deal with who I was . . . I chose, after many years of hiding who I was, to be open, to be who I am, and to live my life without shame or apology, and that's a choice I've never regretted . . . But I was fortunate—when I came out I was already a tenured college professor, I lived in a tolerant urban community and had supportive friends and family. Not all gay and lesbian people are that fortunate . . . many today continue to live in fear in hostile communities, in jobs they easily could lose if their sexual orientation was discovered . . . they're forced to live lives based on lies and deception . . .

Much has been made in the debate that's been waged over this bill about how sexual orientation is determined . . . most experts agree that it is determined at birth or very early in life—it's not something that is chosen . . . we are what we are and we are asking only that we have the same rights that others take for granted, nothing special, just the right to a job commensurate with our ability, the right to decent housing, the right to a good education, and that's all this bill does . . .

I've been working on this bill for twenty years—the first time it came before the Minnesota Senate was exactly twenty years ago, when the late senator Nick Coleman asked the Minnesota Senate to pass it, and I think the Senate has considered this bill about eight times over the last twenty years, so it's not exactly a new issue . . . it's going to be resolved, and the time to resolve it is now . . . it's time, Minnesota.

Late in the debate, the Republican minority leader, Dean Johnson, rose to speak. His résumé, in addition to election twice to the House

and four times to the Senate, included many years of service as pastor of Calvary Lutheran Church in the western Minnesota town of
Willmar, and as a general in the Minnesota National Guard. He was
widely respected by members of both caucuses.

Johnson conceded that this was a tough vote, but that men and
women throughout American history have been elected "because they
have good judgment," and he argued that even while he didn't fully
understand the gay and lesbian lifestyle, he thought it prudent to vote
as a majority to give rights to the minority. He argued that "in political history and American history, the arguments are the same . . .
from Abraham Lincoln, when he was chastised in his arguments about
slavery, the arguments that Hubert Humphrey used about civil rights,
the arguments that were used against the Jews, they are in fact the
same." Johnson accepted that this issue created "a great element of
fear" among the people of Minnesota, within the Senate, and "within
Dean Johnson," but, he added, "if we pass this and the House passes
it and the Governor signs it, it is the right thing to do." It would be
easy to vote against it, he admitted, more popular with the folks back
home, but he believed "we were elected to lead, to do what is right and
to do what is just, and to seek justice."

Johnson paused, then told the senators about a colleague of his in
the National Guard, Captain Pamela Mindt. For twelve years, he'd
referred men and women to her for mental health counseling, though
she was now one of those that the Department of Defense wanted to
dismiss as an officer because of her sexual orientation:

> During those twelve years of association with Captain Mindt
> it never once occurred to me, never once occurred to me
> to even ask myself quietly, are you gay or homosexual or
> heterosexual—it didn't matter, because she did the job, she
> performed her duties as a commissioned officer in the Min-
> nesota Army National Guard. She's an excellent employee . . .
> now, should the Pam Mindts of Minnesota have to live with
> fear of reprisal? job loss? loss of a place to live?
> So, Madame President, members of the Senate, if you feel
> stress, if you feel scared, I'm no different than you, but today
> I'm going to vote—green—yes—in favor of Senate File 444,
> and extend to a group of people in the State of Minnesota

what I consider their civil rights, their human rights, that they too can live with dignity.[9]

Johnson's speech, just before the roll was called, was credited with shifting a few undecided votes to support the bill. When the roll was called, there were thirty-seven ayes and thirty nays, and the bill was passed. Five Republicans, including Johnson, voted for it; thirteen DFL senators voted against, all but one from non-metro Minnesota. When the presiding senator, Reichgott, announced the vote, a loud cheer cascaded down from the galleries, and Allan received congratulations from those who'd supported this long-awaited victory.[10] Then he walked over to the House chamber to give Karen Clark a congratulatory hug. "We jumped for joy," recalled Clark in an article by Doug Grow on MinnPost.com shortly after Allan's death. "It was one of those watershed moments."

President of the Senate

On the first day of the 1993 session of the legislature, Allan left his desk on the floor of the chamber, walked down the center aisle, and mounted the carpeted steps to the highest perch in the chamber: the desk and high-backed leather chair of the president of the Senate. He would preside over the body during the final eight of his twenty-eight years as a senator.

---

9. Dean Johnson was elected three more times to the Senate. He switched to the DFL caucus in January 2000 and was elected twice after that. He was elected DFL majority leader in 2004, thus becoming the first senator to lead both minority and majority caucuses. In 2006, Johnson was defeated for reelection after a campaign that used Johnson's support for GLBT rights against him.

10. Since there was different language in the House and Senate bills, a conference committee was appointed. Final passage of the conference committee report occurred on April 1 by a vote of thirty-eight to twenty-nine, and the bill went to Governor Arne Carlson, who signed it at 10:27 a.m. the following day. One of the eleven House Republicans to vote for the bill was first-termer Tim Pawlenty, who'd expressed concerns but agreed, after conversations with Scott Dibble and Karen Clark, to vote for it. Nine years later, while running for governor, Pawlenty renounced his vote, saying it was the only one he regretted as a legislator. Pawlenty was endorsed by the Republican Party and won two terms as governor of Minnesota.

His predecessor at that lofty height, Jerry Hughes of Maplewood, had decided, after twenty-six years in the Senate, not to run for another term, and this created an opportunity for another senator to move up. After the elections of 1992, Allan was among the top four senators in seniority, with only two elected before him.

There had been talk in the DFL caucus, which handily retained control after the November elections, about who'd be the next president, and one or two of the most senior members of the caucus had put their names forth. But Roger Moe, having the most influence in this choice, was concerned that a senator might politick his way to the position, while the person he wanted at the president's desk was one who knew the rules of the Senate, and more important, one whom members of both caucuses would trust to make fair rulings. So Moe approached Allan to see if he'd be interested in the position. "Allan wasn't sure," Marcia Greenfield recalls. "He asked me, would the caucus really do this? He didn't want to run and lose. Equally important, would the job be more than a figurehead?" Both questions were answered to Allan's satisfaction, and through the organizing committee of a dozen senators, Moe guided the recommendation of Allan to the full caucus. There was one other candidate, Chmielewski, but he was not able to offset Allan's immense credibility with his colleagues. Allan, who'd entered the Senate with a reputation as a community activist, a liberal firebrand, an egghead, a history professor from arguably the most liberal district in the state, was ready for this new challenge, and his election was decisive.

Moe, whose Senate career lasted for thirty-two years, and who served as majority leader from 1981 to his retirement in 2002, recalls Allan in the president's chair:

> He'd become a senior member of the caucus and well
> respected . . . even as he was regarded as a liberal, he was
> always fair. When I needed a ruling from the president, Allan
> would rule fairly . . . and even if I wanted him to rule in a cer-
> tain way, he'd say, or send a note down from the desk, "sorry,
> can't get there with my understanding of the rules."
>   Allan got to be president because everyone knew he'd
> become a true student of the legislative process . . . he was
> one of the top legislators I worked with in all my years in the
> Senate . . . Allan will go down in the history of this state as
> one of the great senators—extremely fair-minded and decent—

solid convictions and principles, but yet was able to work things out, get things done.

Pogemiller, currently Senate majority leader, adds this tribute:

> Allan's reputation for being a very fair chair of Judiciary overcame any concerns that he was too liberal, too pro-choice, and gay . . . there must have been lobbying of the pro-life senators by pro-life organizations and pro-life constituents, but not enough to stop him . . . the senators who backed him believed they'd be treated fairly by him . . . and this sense of comfort continued throughout his eight years as president.[11]

Flahaven, who as secretary of the Senate, a position from which he recently retired after thirty-six years, was able to observe President Spear from close range:

> Allan was always stable and friendly, didn't make enemies of people who opposed him on issues . . . he didn't personalize his opponents . . . even in the heat of debate on issues he really cared about, he'd never get angry or vindictive . . . he had been learning all through the years he was moving up . . . he was a quick study, and worked very hard . . . so when he became president, he stepped in with a great knowledge of the process, and of the rules . . . I loved working with him.
>
> Allan will probably will go down as one of the most significant state senators in Minnesota history . . . he knew the rules, he knew how to handle people . . . I don't recall one instance when the floor spun out of control when he was president . . . he just gave a sense of stature and calmness to the proceedings, and he was extremely fair.[12]

---

11. Until Allan was elected, except for two years under Jack Davies, all Senate presidents had been "pro-life" on the issue of a woman's right to choose.

12. These comments by Senate leaders are from the Allan Spear Memorial DVD produced in late 2008 by Senate Media Services.

Growing Recognition

During Allan's last years, his achievements were increasingly recognized, in Minnesota and across the country. The Minnesota AIDS Project gave him its first Paul and Sheila Wellstone Lifetime Leadership Award and named its annual Allan Spear Forum Series in honor of him. His college alma mater, Oberlin, awarded him an honorary degree in May 1997. In the commencement address, Allan urged graduating seniors "to be political":

> While my life has been profoundly influenced by the identity politics that emerged from the ferment of the 1960s, I make no apologies for traditional politics either. I am an avowed political junkie. I love the give-and-take of political campaigns. I'm fascinated by political oratory; I pore over election returns. The compromises and adjustments that I've been forced to make in my twenty-five years in public office have perhaps tempered my idealism, but haven't destroyed it. Practical politics is a necessary counterpoint to the politics of commitment. It is as important to understand what can be done as it is to know what should be done.

Allan challenged the notion that "all the big causes seem to be settled":

> We thought that in the fifties, too . . . but let me suggest that perhaps we need to reconsider what we mean when we speak of "Big Causes." Shouldn't it be enough to know that there are children throughout the world that don't have a full rice bowl every day, that racial prejudice and distrust still haunt our land a generation after Martin Luther King marched at Birmingham, that despite medical breakthroughs in the AIDS epidemic thousands cannot afford the drugs they need to stay alive, that air pollution and contaminated groundwater and too many automobiles threaten our most precious natural treasures? Let me urge you, then, whatever the future may bring, to be political. Not necessarily in the traditional sense . . . what ought to be for everyone, however, is politics in the broader sense of that word—an engagement with the

world in which we live, a reaching-out from our own lives to
that place where our lives intersect with those of others . . .
there is still much to do in the world.

In May 2008, the Minnesota Historical Society, to celebrate the
state's sesquicentennial, named Allan one of the 150 people and
groups that shaped the state. He was the only state legislator who did
not become a governor or member of Congress to be so recognized.

While Allan worked on his autobiography, the stature he'd earned
in the national GLBT community led to his being asked to write the
foreword to Ricardo Brown's *The Evening Crowd at Kirmser's* and
a Remembrance in Steve Endean's *Bringing Lesbian and Gay Rights
into the Mainstream.*

In Brown's book, he wrote:

Gay people in Western society had long suffered from a special
kind of oppression. Unlike members of racial or ethnic minorities, most gay men and lesbians were able to hide their identity. So long as their sexual orientation was secret, they could
participate fully in all aspects of society . . . They spun elaborate webs of lies and subterfuges to hide their sexual orientation from family, friends, and coworkers. Above all, they lived
in constant fear of exposure . . .

[This book] provides an unusual glimpse of gay life in a
middle-sized, provincial city among ordinary working-class
people . . .

Much maligned by gay liberationists as an exploitative
institution, the gay bar needs to be seen historically—much
like the Irish saloon, or the Jewish coffeehouses, or the African
American barber shop—as a building block of community, a
free space where the sense of camaraderie that led to liberation was first formed.

And in Endean's memoir of the struggle for gay rights, Allan credited him with embodying gay political activity in Minnesota in the
1970s, and being almost single-handedly responsible for the ordinances passed in Minneapolis and St. Paul. He recalled that in the Minnesota legislature (in 1977), "we came close, but we underestimated

the strength of the religious right which was then just emerging as a force in American politics":

> Steve was one of the pioneers who shifted the focus of the gay rights movement from radical protest to patient and painstaking efforts to achieve incremental change. He carefully learned how to lobby legislators and worked ceaselessly to gain their trust and respect . . . if we want be effective at the legislature, he insisted, we had to play by its ground rules . . . he was one of the giants of the gay and lesbian rights movement.

Allan's Passions

From his notes for chapter 13 of his autobiography, it's clear that Allan planned to describe his personal life and his passions: good food and wine, classical music, and ambitious global travel. And he planned to write an epilogue titled "Life after Politics" that would include his retirement years. His life away from the abrasive encounters of politics was shared for many years with Milt and Rosalie Goldstein, Lee and Marcia Greenfield, Don Jorovsky and Jo Matson, Phyllis and Don Kahn, Kathy O'Brien and Jeff Loesch, Don Smith, Mark Snyder, and, for the last twenty-six years of his life, his partner, Jun Tsuji.

The Goldsteins, family friends from Michigan City, Indiana, invited Allan for dinner soon after his arrival in Minnesota and remained close friends the rest of his life. "We were his folks' generation, so we were like his uncle and aunt. Like family," Rosalie Goldstein recalls. On Mondays, the day Allan's cleaning lady came, they would meet for breakfast at the Good Day Café, a popular place with a convivial atmosphere near their home in Golden Valley. The Goldsteins did not go with Allan to the "fancy restaurants," nor did they travel with him, but they were perennial guests to celebrate Jewish holy days.

"The key features of Allan's life," says Snyder, his colleague at the university, "were his multiple identities, personal and professional, which he balanced with apparent ease, allowing them to complement and enhance each other, weaving them together into an almost seamless whole."

"He had a full life—music, food and wine, travel, and he relished sharing his passions with his friends," O'Brien says. According to his traveling companions, Allan would not only research the restaurants completely, he'd also check the menus and make reservations. Before eating, he'd photograph the food, and after returning home, he'd put together a slide show of the trip. "Many of his travel photos were of food," O'Brien recalls. "He'd invite friends over for a slide show and dinner. He was very serious about it."

Marcia Greenfield says, "Cooking was a creative outlet for Allan. It was also a way that he nurtured his friends." One of her favorite stories is from the mid-1980s, when Allan, then chair of Judiciary, took committee members and staff on a fact-finding trip to the northern part of the state. Allan brought all the ingredients for Julia Child's famous recipe for Salade Niçoise aboard the state airplane, and while others sipped wine and sliced a baguette, Allan assembled the dish in the Greenfields' punch bowl, placed in the center aisle of the plane (Child's recipe calls for Boston head lettuce, green beans, shallots, red tomatoes, cooked "boiling" potatoes, chunk tuna, hard-boiled eggs, anchovy fillets, black Niçoise olives, capers, and parsley), and dressed it with Julia's basic vinaigrette.

Smith, Allan's friend from grad school who taught history at Grinnell College in Iowa, was his frequent travel companion. On the road, he recalls, "the daily pattern would be to have what Americans call a 'continental breakfast,' in our hotel if it came with the rooms, in a nearby café if not. After seeing some sights in the morning, we would shop at some point before one o'clock in a local market for the makings of a picnic lunch. Allan always enjoyed this kind of shopping: I've seen him in markets in country after country, and even when we weren't picnicking he couldn't resist an opportunity to check a market out. It was rarely difficult to find a good place to picnic; we'd just pull our rental car off the road and spread it out.

"Once we went to Sicily," Smith says, "and this trip was particularly memorable in that it demonstrated Allan's persistence and resourcefulness in finding good food. We arrived in Siracusa in the midst of a winter gale; the power seemed to be out everywhere and we had to maneuver around the water that had blown into our hotel room. The restaurant where we had booked a table was closed, but with Allan's nose for a good restaurant we found one that was open and apparently cooking on gas, for we ate by candlelight." And, Smith says, they ate well.

Jun Tsuji was the beneficiary of his partner's prowess in the kitchen. "He always liked to try something new . . . he'd find new recipes in books and magazines, and he was so happy trying to do something for me and his friends. He tried many different recipes," says Jun, "but his favorite foods were French and Italian—the pasta, how he loved fresh pasta!" Jun remembers their celebrating twenty-six years of being together on October 6, 2008, and Allan—scheduled for surgery three days later—insisted on dinner at Chambers Kitchen in downtown Minneapolis, an "Asian fusion" restaurant founded by Jean-Georges Vongerichten, the wunderkind chef from Alsace, who'd won three Michelin stars for his New York restaurant. Two days later, Allan was admitted to the hospital for surgery, and finding the food undesirable, he asked his partner to "bring some good food" from D'Amico and Sons, the take-out service of one of his favorite Italian restaurants.

Allan's taste in music led him to the Minnesota Orchestra, the St. Paul Chamber Orchestra, and the Schubert Club. Smith and Snyder shared season tickets for the orchestral seasons, and the Kahns joined him at the Schubert Club, where for several years Allan served on the board of directors. According to Smith, Schubert and Dvořák were among Allan's favorites; he esteemed Bartók as perhaps the greatest of twentieth-century composers.

Allan's Political Legacy

Allan Spear generously shared with less-established politicians the benefits of what he'd learned and earned during his long career in politics. He provided guidance and support to Mark Andrew, who became chairman of the state DFL Party and chair of the Hennepin County Board; Sharon Sayles Belton, the first African American and first female mayor of Minneapolis; Joan Campbell, a member of the Metropolitan Council and later of the city council; O'Brien, elected to the city council and now a vice president of the university; Dibble, the first openly gay man to run for and be elected to the House, and later Allan's successor in the Senate; Carol Flynn, who, while Allan was president, served in the Senate from Minneapolis; Margaret Anderson Kelliher, current Speaker of the House; and Keith Ellison, the first African American from Minnesota and first Muslim to be elected to the U.S. Congress. All were beneficiaries of Allan's wisdom and judgment.

Campbell recalls Allan's saying that since O'Brien wasn't going to run for a fourth term on the Minneapolis City Council, he was urging Campbell to run for the seat. "Allan made me feel like I was someone who could blossom . . . he encouraged me to use my political instincts." Dibble recalls how at the national INGLO conference in West Hollywood in late 1996, after the elections of that year, "Allan confided in me that he'd run for the last time, that he planned to serve the next four years in the Senate and not run again in 2000, and I should think about it." Dibble was elected to the House in 2000 and moved up to the Senate in 2002.

Reflecting on Allan's mentorship, O'Brien says, "his life was what we'd want of our leaders . . . once he'd reached a leadership role as Senator, he helped me and several others stay centered, and taught us how to deal with the pressures. A recurring theme in his life had been about being on the outside politically, working to make change, and finding a way to get inside to make a difference. Once inside, he used that position to help others get in—all with the end of helping people in the community. Allan influenced, you might say he 'created leadership' as he guided the careers of several of us. We looked to him as a kind of political father. Right to the end of his life, he supported other emerging leaders. Right to the end, Allan was always thinking about how he could help others become leaders and improve the quality of their leadership."

Allan Spear died on October 11, 2008. "He had heart surgery in March 2008," Marcia Greenfield recalls. "In late summer, Allan began to tire more easily, which was one of the original signs of the heart valve problem, and it was discovered that he had an infection in the new valve. His cardiologist tried to knock out the infection so that he could then replace the damaged valve, but was not completely successful in doing this and scheduled surgery for October 9."

Don Jorovsky, a longtime staff aide in the Senate and Allan's close friend, shared his memories of that last year at Allan's memorial service. They went to a rally for Barack Obama; it was just prior to his first heart surgery, "but Allan really wanted to go. It was difficult but worth it. We talked about the campaign constantly, often optimistically. But in September the polls looked bad and he said to me, 'Being a Democrat is a lot like being a [Chicago] Cubs fan. First you get up hope, then something happens and you start to wonder, oh why did I even hope, it's going to be another loss.' As the Jewish High Holidays approached and he faced a second heart surgery, Allan reminded me several times, this was when the Lord decides for the next year who will live and who will not—and he said, 'I think He already has me on the second list.' The surgery took place on Yom Kippur, and two days later we sat in his hospital room and discussed every aspect of the presidential campaign for hours. The polls were up and he was optimistic again about Obama winning. Things seemed fine. Yet a few hours later he was gone."

Allan's surgery on October 9 was long and arduous, yet when he woke up the following day, he called O'Brien's office and left this message: "Tell her I'm awake and I'm here, and to come see me." Allan was looking forward to a full agenda after he got discharged: getting back to the book, helping Obama get elected, backing a DFL candidate for governor in 2010, more travel, and more of the best food and wine.

On the day he died, the Goldsteins arrived with fresh strawberries and raspberries, and someone had brought a chunk of Camembert. Rosalie says, "He enjoyed the treat, and was finishing that day's puzzle in the *New York Times*. He seemed as alive as ever, and then later he had the blood clot and suddenly he was gone." Allan's partner, Jun, recalls several visitors that last day with whom Allan was engaged in political discussions. "I brought some food from D'Amico, we watched the evening news, and he was happy that Obama was looking good. Soon after, I stepped out of the room to let the doctors see him. When I went back in, he was gone." Jun later learned that Allan had paid all his current bills and had contributed a hundred dollars one more time to Obama with a credit card.

News of Allan's death traveled fast in political circles and in the GLBT community, and tributes came from many parts of the country.

Dibble wrote: "Allan was a cherished friend, a mentor and a hero. Minneapolis lost one of its greatest elected representatives. Minnesota lost one of our exemplary great statesmen, and our nation lost one of the leading figures in the movement for civil rights and greater equality for all."

Clark added her tribute: "Allan was a good friend and also a trusted legislative ally. I could always go to him for thoughtful advice . . . time and time again we teamed up, especially for those who lacked a voice at the Minnesota Capitol."

U.S. Representative Tammy Baldwin of Wisconsin also mourned his death: "In Senator Allan Spear's passing, I have lost a mentor. Allan encouraged countless individuals to enter the political arena and use their talents to confront the challenges of the day . . . while Allan made history as one of the pioneers of the GLBT civil rights movement, his legacy is that of principled public service . . . I will miss my dear friend and role model Allan Spear. But, as with all great mentors, I will keep the lessons he shared forever."

On October 14, Senator Barack Obama, soon to be the president-elect of the United States, wrote to Jun: "I join with all Minnesotans who mourn the loss of Allan Spear. His evenhandedness, command of the issues, and ability to reach across the aisle and work with colleagues of both parties were legendary and should inspire us all. He was a man of great courage who served as one of the nation's first openly gay legislators."

In addition to those mentioned or cited in this afterword, the author thanks the following interviewees: former Minnesota Speaker of the House and congressman Martin Sabo, and Peter Wattson, Senate counsel and secretary of the Senate. Thanks also to Jun Tsuji for permission to access the Allan Spear Papers at the Minnesota Historical Society.

The author made frequent use of the Legislators Past and Present archive of the Minnesota Legislative Reference Library.

In addition to a review of newspaper files of the Minneapolis and St. Paul dailies, and publications received from the interviewees, a useful reference was Dudley Clendinen and Adam Nagourney, *Out for Good: The Struggle to Build a Gay Rights Movement in America* (New York: Simon and Schuster, 1999).

INDEX

abortion: as legislative issue, 262–63, 264, 271–73, 376, 377, 399; position on, 236, 237, 252, 253, 262, 344, 382, 426n11

academic career, 125–26, 140–42; activism balanced with, 87, 116–17, 201; politics balanced with, 154–55, 169, 175, 259, 302, 364. *See also* teacher(s): experience as

activism. *See* antiwar movement; civil rights movement; gay rights movement; politics; student protest movement

ADA. *See* Americans for Democratic Action

Adams, Jim, 152, 190, 235; Spear's 1968 campaign against, 153–55, 156–59, 165, 246

adoptions: by gay people, 312; as legislative issue, 342–43

Advocate articles, 245, 258

affirmative action: in academics, 111, 170, 200, 301; in politics, 213, 215–16, 228, 229, 230, 231, 383

African American community: in Chicago, 55, 90, 92; development of, 81–82, 93, 125, 228; first Minnesota legislator from, 257, 262, 264; Great Migration of, 82, 90, 92, 95; in Michigan City, 93–94; in Minneapolis and St. Paul, 173–74; tensions between white community and, 80, 92, 94, 144–47, 171–75, 177, 188, 189–90. *See also Black Chicago: The Making of a Negro Ghetto, 1890–1920;* civil rights movement; racial violence

African American history: as academic field, 61–62, 65, 125, 126, 185; courses on, 107, 108–9, 125, 144, 170–72, 204, 283; black–white

tensions over teaching, 144–46, 172, 185; Jewish people's interest in, 16; scholarship in, 80–85, 88–89, 90–91, 92–100, 169, 195

Afro-American Studies Department (University of Minnesota), 173, 183–85, 204

age discrimination legislation, 343–44

AIDS epidemic, 413–15, 416

Alice B. Toklas Memorial Democratic Club, 324, 334

Altholz, Joe, 245

American Indian Language and Culture Act of 1977, 291, 315–16, 318, 342

American Indian Movement (AIM), 290

Americans for Democratic Action (ADA): endorsement, 253

Amicus, 270

Anderson, Ellen, 416

Anderson, Jim, 217, 219

Anderson, Wendell: as governor, 234, 260, 270, 302, 327; handling of student protests, 227; in 1970 gubernatorial race, 181, 190, 192; in 1978 U.S. Senate race, 360, 361; self-appointment to U.S. Senate, 334–35, 349; support for Spear's coming out, 306

Andrew, Mark, 431

Angwin, Richard, 351, 354

Anthony, Don, 63, 64

anti-Semitism, 14–15, 16, 103–4

antiwar Democrats: in Minneapolis, 176, 179, 180–82, 232, 243, 329–30; in Minnesota, 147–51, 155–56, 163, 191, 213, 217, 228, 237; in 1968 presidential election, 155, 163–66, 167, 170

antiwar movement: Amsterdam

Currier, Theodore, 54, 55
Curtis, Lewis, 74–75

Daley, Richard, 165
dating, 32–33, 38, 64, 71, 78. *See also* relationships
Davies, Jack, 149, 151–52, 316, 318; effects of redistricting on, 235, 392, 393, 395, 406–7, 411–12; as mentor to Spear, 263–64, 392, 407, 411; as president of Senate, 426n11; on stadium legislation, 344, 345, 366, 367
Davis, Madeline, 242
Day, Dick, 420
Dayton, Mark, 386
death, 432–33
Degler, Carl, 315
DeGroot, Ann, 415
De Maio, Tony, 161, 162
Demars, Lou, 321
Democratic-Farmer-Labor Party (DFL): changes in, 349–50, 360–62; control of Minnesota Legislature by, 233–34, 235, 246–47, 257, 260, 364, 383, 406; endorsement process, 151, 154, 156–58, 240, 255, 383, 406; feminist caucus, 273; formation of, 162, 359; gay caucus, 187, 209, 215–18, 217–18, 237; goo-goo (good government) faction, 176, 190, 333, 345; Humphrey faction, 153–54, 156, 191, 213, 232, 237, 238, 239, 245, 263; involvement in, 115, 190–95, 211; labor faction, 176, 345; left wing of, 162–63, 241; liberals in, 115, 361, 406; McCarthy faction, 153, 154, 156, 162, 165–66, 176, 177, 180, 182, 190, 191–92; in Minneapolis, 176, 190, 282, 345–47; Mondale supported by, 327; Rochester platform of 1972, 238–39, 257; Spartz-Hanson division, 329–30, 345, 351, 389, 395; Spear-Greenfield group, 345, 346, 389. *See also* antiwar Democrats
Democratic Party, national: affiliation with, 7, 28, 47, 51, 106, 432–33; disillusionment with, 123, 129, 146, 148; divisions in, 212, 384. *See also* antiwar Democrats
Derus, John, 321
Deutsch, Harold, 99, 100, 110, 111
Dewey, Thomas E., 7, 19–20
Dibble, Scott, 417, 419, 424n10, 431, 432, 433
Dickman, Scott, 351
Dignity, 341
Dinkytown (Minneapolis neighborhood): protest of commercial development in, 188–89, 224, 253
disabilities, people with, 13, 19. *See also* vulnerable adults bill
dissertation, 89, 99; choice of topic, 90–91; completion of, 104–5, 106; final acceptance of, 107; research for, 92–93, 95; writing of, 97. *See also Black Chicago: The Making of a Negro Ghetto, 1890–1920*
divorce. *See* no-fault divorce bill
Dotterman, Gary, 250
Douglas, Aaron, 53
Doves. *See* antiwar Democrats, in Minnesota
draft resistance, 118, 187, 226. *See also* antiwar movement
Duberman, Martin, 186, 310
Du Bois, W. E. B., 53, 62, 93
Dump Johnson campaign, 147, 148, 150–51, 155, 167, 212, 250
Dump Nixon campaign, 250
Durenberger, David, 361
Duster, Alfreda Barnett, 92

education: college, 33–34, 40, 41, 42–49, 51–52, 61–64; elementary school, 17; graduate, 72–100, 107,

Wright, Arthur and Mary, 74, 98
Wright, John, 184

yachna: definition, 16n1
Yale University: graduate study at,
72, 73–85, 88–89, 90–91, 97–100,
107, 108, 119; junior faculty at,
98, 101; lack of diversity at, 73, 74

Young, Marilyn, 322
Youngdale, Jim, 162
Young Democrats: involvement in,
47, 51
Young Presidents Organization
(YPO): presentation to, 214–15

Zimmerman, Norman, 114, 279

ALLAN H. SPEAR was elected to the Minnesota Senate in 1972 and served for twenty-eight years, retiring in 2000. He was president of the Senate from 1993 to 2000. He was one of the first openly gay state legislators in the country, and he fought to amend Minnesota's Human Rights Act to prohibit discrimination based on sexual orientation. He was associate professor of history at the University of Minnesota from 1964 to 2000 and author of *Black Chicago: The Making of a Negro Ghetto*, published in 1967. The Minnesota Historical Society named him one of 150 Minnesotans who shaped the state.

BARNEY FRANK is the United States House Representative for Massachusetts's Fourth Congressional District and chairman of the Committee on Financial Services. In 1987 he became the second openly gay Congressman in U.S. history.

JOHN MILTON was elected to the Minnesota Senate in 1972 and 1976, where he was a colleague of Allan Spear. He has been a contributing writer for several state and national publications and is author of the historical novel *The Fallen Nightingale* and the political novel *Time to Choose*.